BOOKS BY HIS DIVINE GRACE
A. C. BHAKTIVEDANTA SWAMI PRABHUPĀDA

Bhagavad-gītā As It Is
Śrīmad-Bhāgavatam (completed by disciples)
Śrī Caitanya-caritāmṛta
Kṛṣṇa, the Supreme Personality of Godhead
Teachings of Lord Caitanya
The Nectar of Devotion
The Nectar of Instruction
Śrī Īśopaniṣad
Light of the Bhāgavata
Easy Journey to Other Planets
Teachings of Lord Kapila, the Son of Devahūti
Teachings of Queen Kuntī
Message of Godhead
The Science of Self-Realization
The Perfection of Yoga
Beyond Birth and Death
On the Way to Kṛṣṇa
Rāja-vidyā: The King of Knowledge
Elevation to Kṛṣṇa Consciousness
Kṛṣṇa Consciousness: The Matchless Gift
Kṛṣṇa Consciousness: The Topmost Yoga System
Perfect Questions, Perfect Answers
Life Comes from Life
The Nārada-bhakti-sūtra (completed by disciples)
The Mukunda-mālā-stotra (completed by disciples)
Geetār-gān (Bengali)
Vairāgya-vidyā (Bengali)
Buddhi-yoga (Bengali)
Bhakti-ratna-boli (Bengali)
Back to Godhead magazine (founder)

BOOKS COMPILED FROM THE TEACHINGS
OF ŚRĪLA PRABHUPĀDA AFTER HIS LIFETIME

The Journey of Self-Discovery
Veda: Secrets from the East
Civilization and Transcendence
The Laws of Nature
Renunciation Through Wisdom
Beyond Illusion and Doubt

Available from www.krishna.com & www.blservices.com

VEDA

SECRETS *from the* EAST

VEDA

SECRETS *from the* EAST

An anthology

His Divine Grace A.C. Bhaktivedanta Swami Prabhupāda
Founder-*Ācārya* of the International Society for Krishna Consciousness
and his disciples

THE BHAKTIVEDANTA BOOK TRUST

Readers interested in the subject matter of this book are invited to contact ISKCON Reader Services or the International Society for Krishna Consciousness (see address list in back of book).

ISKCON Reader Services
P.O. Box 730, Watford
WD25 8ZE, United Kingdom
Tel: +44 (0) 1923 857244
readersservices@pamho.net
www.iskcon.org.uk
www.krishnawisdom.com

Veda: Secrets from the East is an anthology of articles drawn from *Back to Godhead* magazine, *Beyond Illusion and Doubt*, *Consciousness: The Missing Link*, *Journey of Self-Discovery*, *The Nectar of Devotion*, *Path of Perfection*, *The Science of Self-Realization*, *Śrī Īśopaniṣad*, and *The Quest for Enlightenment* – all published by the Bhaktivedanta Book Trust. The article, "Reverence for All Life," by Girirāja Swami, is from *Watering the Seed*, 2nd edition, Torchlight Publishing, 2009. The articles were edited by Rāyrāma Dāsa, Hayagrīva Dāsa, Jayādvaita Swami, and Draviḍa Dāsa, and the material was assembled by Sutapa Dāsa and Kaiśorī Devī Dāsī.

Cover artwork and design by Matthew Whitlock (Madhusūdana Dāsa)
www.ashram-arts.com

www.krishna.com
www.bbt.info

ISBN 978-1-84599-071-8

Printed in Germany, 2009

Contents

2 Karma & Reincarnation

3 Science and the Vedas

4 The "Love Vacuum"

5 Ancient Wisdom, Modern Times

6 Spiritual Traditions & Teachers

Appendixes

Foreword

The first time I met His Divine Grace A.C. Bhaktivedanta Swami Prabhupāda was on a spring evening in 1975. I'd come to spend a few weeks in the country house given to him by George Harrison of the Beatles, and I'd been reading his books with interest for some months. His followers had been filling the gaps in my understanding, but I wanted to meet the spiritual master for myself. So when I heard he was coming to England I extended my visit.

He was shorter in stature than I had imagined, yet his presence in a room was uncannily powerful. Dressed in light orange robes, with yellow clay markings on his forehead, and carrying the cloth-wrapped bamboo rods of a monk, he looked as if he'd been transported from an ancient world into the present day. He was 79 years old, yet he walked with the energy and alertness of one much younger. Although sensitive to every detail of his environment, he appeared to have his anchor set in an internal world, a spiritual dimension he described as "Kṛṣṇa consciousness."

After taking his seat, he put on his spectacles and read aloud a Sanskrit verse from the 5,000-year-old *Bhagavad-gītā*. Some thoughtful moments passed, then he looked up and scanned the young faces of those who sat before him – including my own – and began to speak. Years of study and a lifetime of spiritual practice allowed him to articulate the Vedic knowledge with scholarly authority and a deep personal wisdom. He knew his subject because he lived it, and realized it, and he passionately wanted others to understand and share in it.

Śrīla Prabhupāda's sober demeanor and the urgency of his delivery were tempered by his natural humility and a childlike innocence. He had a genuine warmth and affection for his students, and a remarkable wit. Listeners could be suspended in pin-drop silence at one moment, then dissolve in laughter the next. He explained the deepest complex philosophical ideas through colorful analogies or stories or by using vivid examples from nature. During early-morning walks, in conversations in his room with visitors and friends, and in his daily classes, he instructed and illuminated us, gently helping us to comprehend what was, for us Westerners, quite an unusual way of thinking. At the same time, it was strangely familiar.

As he spoke, Śrīla Prabhupāda seemed to be talking about something we already knew deep down, but of which we needed reminding. The effect was not of being converted to a set of beliefs, but of being gently woken up. At the end of his brief visit, I personally felt freed from any doubts about his own personal authenticity, and I knew I would be continuing with the daily practices of Kṛṣṇa consciousness for some time.

Yet Śrīla Prabhupāda was not always comfortable to listen to. He was a compassionate, saintly teacher, with a warm, generous, and friendly heart. As such, he seldom criticized individuals, but he did speak strongly when particular beliefs of political and intellectual leaders threatened the welfare of others. His justification for this was clear and uncompromising. Every action taken by human beings, he explained, is the cumulative result of choices informed by their particular view of reality. This understanding of reality might be a relatively rudimentary one, confined to the seeking of immediate gratification of biological urges and defense from competitors. Or it could be a sophisticated sociopolitical framework, conceived with the intentions of affording the greatest happiness for the greatest number of people. But if it had already failed, or if people were being hurt, repressed, or degraded by it, or if problems were imminent, then Śrīla Prabhupāda spoke out against it. He felt completely justified in pointing out the inadequacies of prevailing worldviews when people were suffering.

He could not tolerate constant changes in political theory. He had lived through great upheavals – two world wars, the horrors of partition in India – and had witnessed the wholesale destruction that splits along artificial lines of race and religion had produced. He therefore condemned the whimsical social experimentation of politicians and their vain, empty rhetoric, calling it "cheating the innocent." He was unreservedly critical of fashionable scientific theories which proposed to explain the mysteries of consciousness and life itself – but which failed to practically demonstrate evidence for the claims. He charged that scientific reasoning without a clear philosophical understanding would result only in the exploitation of the natural world, followed by scarcity. So he termed such unbalanced research "bluffing" and "theft." And when he learned that some leading thinkers denied the existence of God he called them "fools and rascals."

Yet he regarded much of what passed as religion to be social conventions with "watered down" versions of the religions' original teachings. He was a critic of modern, overly mechanized urban living divorced from food production and called it a way of life in which "the blind lead the blind." He called educational institutions devoid of morality and knowledge of the soul "slaughterhouses," and human life lived without ultimate purpose "a life wasted."

But he spoke positively, at great length and in detail, on all subjects from the *Vedas,* the ancient wisdom preserved in the beautiful Sanskrit language. The teachings came from a time before all the diverse religions we now know made their appearance, yet they presented the essential truths that all the later prophets and teachers would speak. Śrīla Prabhupāda presented a radical departure from a shortsighted way of life – a lifestyle based on quick fixes – and inspired countless thousands of people to take up daily practices of spirituality and meditation. He started farms, vegetarian restaurants, schools, temples, communities, and numerous other artistic and cultural projects. In the West he came to be regarded as an authentic voice from the East, and in India as a reformer, invigorating a tired tradition with fresh enthusiasm.

He had met his own spiritual master in Calcutta in 1922 at the age of 26, and it was from him that he had received the sacred commission to teach in the English language. As a lineage-holder of the Vedic teachings, Śrīla Prabhupāda was the latest in a long chain of preceptors dating back to Kṛṣṇa. In addition, he was doing what no other had done before him – making the teachings accessible to those who spoke the most common language on earth. To do this he traveled constantly, delivering the knowledge personally and guiding the lives of those who decided to follow it.

The effects of Śrīla Prabhupāda's teachings and the rapid worldwide expansion of his movement prompted the noted British historian Dr. A. L. Basham to remark, "Not since the time of the Roman Empire has someone brought an entire religion from east to west ..."

Dr. Harvey Cox, Professor of Divinity at Harvard University, said something similar: "There aren't many people you can think of who successfully implant a whole religion in a completely alien culture. That's a rare achievement in the history of religion. The fact that we now have in the West a vigorous, disciplined, and seemingly well-organized movement – not merely a philosophical movement or a yoga or meditation movement – introducing the devotion to God that he taught is a stunning accomplishment. Perhaps he was one in a hundred million."

We live at a turning point in history, a time when many cultures of the world have set aside their traditional ways in favor of a more global culture. This means, in practice, a Western-originated postmodern consumerist capitalism. The problems with having this as an operating norm can already be seen everywhere. Material progress has come at a great price, and it's a price our small, delicately balanced planet can no longer afford. Short-term happiness – pursued at the expense of others around us – is not happiness at all.

To restore ourselves to balance with nature and the universe, we need to behave once again as if our spiritual aspirations were important – because they are. They are in fact the most important needs we have. There is a subtle, but very real, link between unrecognized spiritual hunger, rampant consumption, and social and economic imbalance. By addressing individual and collective spiritual needs, we can achieve a healthy balance.

Through the pages of this book, you'll be introduced to a new way of looking at life and the possibilities open to every one of us. You'll discover teachings on spirituality that have proven successful for centuries but remain relatively unknown. Some sections you read may be challenging. They don't readily match up with conventional wisdom. But as you read the entire book with an open mind you may be very pleasantly surprised at the results.

As a teenager, I was curious enough about Eastern philosophy to spend a few days in the personal company of a remarkable spiritual teacher. Nearly forty years later, I can happily testify that putting the ideas in this very good book into practice can bring you what Śrīla Prabhupāda described as "a blissful, happy life – a life of Kṛṣṇa consciousness."

Hare Kṛṣṇa,
Kripamoya Dāsa

Chapter One

An Introduction to Kṛṣṇa Consciousness

What Is Kṛṣṇa Consciousness, or Bhakti-yoga?

His Divine Grace A.C. Bhaktivedanta Swami Prabhupāda

The basic principle of the living condition is that we have a general propensity to love someone. No one can live without loving someone else. This propensity is present in every living being. Even an animal like a tiger has this loving propensity at least in a dormant stage, and it is certainly present in the human beings. The missing point, however, is where to repose our love so that everyone can become happy.

~

Bhakti means "devotional service." Every service has some attractive feature that drives the servitor progressively on and on. Every one of us in this world is perpetually engaged in some sort of service, and the impetus for such service is the pleasure we derive from it. Driven by affection for his wife and children, a family man works day and night. A philanthropist works in the same way for love of the greater family, and a nationalist for the cause of his country and countrymen. That force that drives the philanthropist, the householder, and the nationalist is called *rasa,* or a kind of mellow (relationship) whose taste is very sweet.

Bhakti-rasa is a mellow different from the ordinary *rasa* enjoyed by mundane workers. Mundane workers labor very hard day and night in order to relish a certain kind of *rasa,* which is understood as sense gratification. The relish or taste of the mundane *rasa* does not long endure, and therefore mundane workers are always apt to change their position of enjoyment. A businessman is not satisfied by working the whole week; therefore, wanting a change for the weekend, he goes to a place where he tries to forget his business activities. Then, after the weekend is spent in forgetfulness, he again changes his position and resumes his actual business activities.

Material engagement means accepting a particular status for some time and then changing it. This position of changing back and forth is technically known as *bhoga-tyāga,* which means a position of alternating sense enjoyment and renunciation. A living entity cannot steadily remain either in sense enjoyment or in renunciation. Change is going on perpetually, and we cannot be happy in either state, because of our eternal constitutional position. Sense gratification does not endure for long, and it is therefore called *capala-sukha,* or flickering happiness.

For example, an ordinary family man who works very hard day and night and is successful in giving comforts to the members of his family thereby relishes a kind of mellow, but his whole advancement of material happiness immediately terminates along with his body as soon as his life is over. Death is therefore taken as the representative of God for the atheistic class of men. The devotee realizes the presence of God by devotional service, whereas the atheist realizes the presence of God in the shape of death. At death everything is finished, and one has to begin a new chapter of life in a new situation, perhaps higher or lower than the last one. In any field of activity – political, social, national, or international – the result of our actions will be finished with the end of life. That is sure.

Bhakti-rasa, however, the mellow relished in the transcendental loving service of the Lord, does not finish with the end of life. It continues perpetually and is therefore called *amṛta,* that which does not die but exists eternally. This is confirmed in all Vedic literatures. *Bhagavad-gītā* says that a little advancement in *bhakti-rasa* can save the devotee from the greatest danger – that of missing the opportunity for human life. The *rasas* derived from our feelings in social life, in family life, or in the greater family life of altruism, philanthropy, nationalism, socialism, communism, etc., do not guarantee that one's next life will be as a human being. We prepare our next life by our actual activities in the present life. A living entity is offered a particular type of body as a result of his action in the present body. These activities are taken into account by a superior authority known as *daiva,* or the authority of God. This *daiva* is explained in *Bhagavad-gītā* as the prime cause of everything, and in *Śrīmad-Bhāgavatam* it is stated that a man takes his next body by *daiva-netreṇa,* which means by the supervision of the authority of the Supreme.

In an ordinary sense, *daiva* is explained as destiny. *Daiva* supervision gives us a body selected from 8,400,000 forms; the choice does not depend on our selection but is awarded to each of us according to our destiny. If our body at present is engaged in the activities of Kṛṣṇa consciousness, then it is guaranteed that we will have at least a human body in our next life. A human being engaged in Kṛṣṇa consciousness, even if unable to complete the course of *bhakti-yoga,* takes birth in the higher divisions of human society so that he can automatically further his advancement in Kṛṣṇa consciousness. Therefore, all bona fide activities in Kṛṣṇa consciousness are *amṛta,* or permanent.

This eternal engagement in *bhakti-rasa* can be understood by a serious student. Adoption of *bhakti-rasa,* or Kṛṣṇa consciousness, will immediately bring one to an auspicious life free from anxieties and will bless one with transcendental existence, thus minimizing the value of liberation. *Bhakti-rasa* itself is sufficient to produce a feeling of liberation, because it attracts the attention of the Supreme Lord, Kṛṣṇa. Generally, neophyte devotees are anxious to see Kṛṣṇa, or God, but God cannot be seen or known by our present materially blunt senses. The process of devotional service as it is recommended in the Vedic literatures will gradually elevate one from the material condition of life to the spiritual status, wherein the devotee becomes purified of all designations. The senses can then become uncontaminated, being constantly in touch with *bhakti-rasa.* When the purified senses are employed in the service of the Lord, one becomes situated in *bhakti-rasa* life, and any action performed for the satisfaction of Kṛṣṇa in this transcendental *bhakti-rasa* stage of life can be relished perpetually. When one is thus engaged in devotional service, all varieties of *rasas,* or mellows, turn into eternity. In the beginning one is trained according to the principles of regulation under the guidance of the *ācārya,* or spiritual master, and gradually, when one is elevated, devotional service becomes automatic and spontaneous eagerness to serve Kṛṣṇa. There are twelve kinds of *rasas,* as will be explained in this book, and by renovating our relationship with Kṛṣṇa in five primary *rasas* we can live eternally in full knowledge and bliss.

The basic principle of the living condition is that we have a general propensity to love someone. No one can live without loving someone else. This propensity is present in every living being. Even an animal like a tiger has this loving propensity at least in a dormant stage, and it is certainly present in the human beings. The missing point, however, is where to repose our love so that everyone can become happy. At the present moment the human society teaches one to love his country or family, or his personal self, but there is no information where to repose the loving propensity so that everyone can become happy. That missing point is Kṛṣṇa, and we can learn how to stimulate our original love for Kṛṣṇa and how to be situated in that position where we can enjoy our blissful life.

In the primary stage a child loves his parents, then his brothers and sisters, and as he daily grows up he begins to love his family, society, community, country, nation, or even the whole human society. But the loving propensity is not satisfied even by loving all human society; that loving propensity remains imperfectly fulfilled until we know who is the supreme beloved. Our love can be fully satisfied only when it is reposed in Kṛṣṇa.

Our loving propensity expands just as a vibration of light or air expands, but we do not know where it ends. Practicing *bhakti-yoga* teaches us the science of loving every one of the living entities perfectly by the easy method of loving Kṛṣṇa. We have failed to create peace and harmony in human society, even by such great attempts as the United Nations, because we do not know the right method. The method is very simple, but one has to understand it with a cool head. Loving Kṛṣṇa, the Supreme Personality of Godhead, is simple and natural. If we learn how to love Kṛṣṇa, then it is very easy to immediately and simultaneously love every living being. It is like pouring water on the root of a tree or supplying food to one's stomach. The method of pouring water on the root of a tree or supplying foodstuffs to the stomach is universally scientific and practical, as every one of us has experienced. Everyone knows well that when we eat something, or in other words, when we put foodstuffs in the stomach, the energy created by such action is immediately distributed throughout the whole body. Similarly, when we pour water on the root, the energy thus created is immediately distributed throughout the entirety of even the largest tree. It is not possible to water the tree part by part, nor is it possible to feed the different parts of the body separately. *Bhakti-yoga* will teach us how to turn the one switch that will immediately brighten everything, everywhere. One who does not know this method is missing the point of life.

As far as material necessities are concerned, the human civilization at the present moment is very much advanced in living comfortably, but still we are not happy, because we are missing the point. The material comforts of life alone are not sufficient to make us happy. The vivid example is America: the richest nation of the world, having all facilities for material comfort, is producing a class of men completely confused and frustrated in life. I am appealing herewith to such confused men to learn the art of devotional service, and I am sure that the fire of material existence burning within their hearts will be immediately extinguished. The root cause of our dissatisfaction is that our dormant loving propensity has not been fulfilled despite our great advancement in the materialistic way of life. *Bhakti-yoga* does not condemn any way of materialistic life, but the attempt is to give information to religionists, philosophers, and people in general how to love Kṛṣṇa. One may live without material discomfiture, but at the same time he should learn the art of loving Kṛṣṇa. At the present moment we are inventing so many ways to utilize our propensity to love, but factually we are missing the real point: Kṛṣṇa. We are watering all parts of the tree, but missing the tree's root. We are trying to keep our body fit by all means, but we are neglecting to supply foodstuffs to the stomach. Missing Kṛṣṇa means missing one's self also. Real self-realization and realization of Kṛṣṇa go together simultaneously. For example, seeing oneself in the morning means seeing the sunrise also; without seeing the sunshine no one can see himself. Similarly, unless one has realized Kṛṣṇa there is no question of self-realization.

Who Is Kṛṣṇa?

His Divine Grace A. C. Bhaktivedanta Swami Prabhupāda

Kṛṣṇa, the Supreme Personality of Godhead, is a historical person who appeared on this earth 5,000 years ago. He stayed on this earth for 125 years and played exactly like a human being, but His activities were unparalleled. From the very moment of His appearance to the moment of His disappearance, every one of His activities is unparalleled in the history of the world, and therefore anyone who knows what we mean by Godhead will accept Kṛṣṇa as the Supreme Personality of Godhead.

~

In the Western countries, whenever someone sees a picture of Kṛṣṇa he immediately asks, "Who is Kṛṣṇa?" The immediate answer is that Kṛṣṇa is the Supreme Personality of Godhead. How is that? Because He conforms in exact detail to descriptions of the Supreme Being, the Godhead. In other words, Kṛṣṇa is the Godhead because He is all-attractive. Outside the principle of all-attraction, there is no meaning to the word "Godhead." How is it one can be all-attractive? First of all, if one is very wealthy, if he has great riches, he becomes attractive to the people in general. Similarly, if someone is very powerful, he also becomes attractive, and if someone is very famous, he also becomes attractive, and if someone is very beautiful or wise or unattached to all kinds of possessions, he also becomes attractive. So from practical experience we can observe that one is attractive due to (1) wealth, (2) power, (3) fame, (4) beauty, (5) wisdom, and (6) renunciation. One who is in possession of all six of these opulences at the same time, who possesses them to an unlimited degree, is understood to be the Supreme Personality of Godhead. These opulences of the Godhead are delineated by Parāśara Muni, a great Vedic authority.

We have seen many rich persons, many powerful persons, many famous persons, many beautiful persons, many learned and scholarly persons, and persons in the renounced order of life unattached to material possessions. But we have never seen any one person who is unlimitedly and simultaneously wealthy, powerful, famous, beautiful, wise, and unattached, like Kṛṣṇa, in the history of humanity. Kṛṣṇa, the Supreme Personality of Godhead, is a historical person who appeared on this earth 5,000 years ago. He stayed on this earth for 125 years and played exactly like a human being, but His activities were unparalleled. From the very moment of His appearance to the moment of His disappearance, every one of His activities is unparalleled in the history of the world, and therefore anyone who knows what we mean by Godhead will accept Kṛṣṇa as the Supreme Personality of Godhead. No one is equal to the Godhead, and no one is greater than Him. That is the import of the familiar saying "God is great."

There are various classes of men in the world who speak of God in different ways, but according to the Vedic literature and according to the great *ācāryas,* the authorized persons versed in the knowledge of God in all ages, like *ācāryas* Śaṅkara, Rāmānuja, Madhva, Viṣṇu Svāmī, Lord Caitanya, and all their followers by disciplic succession, all unanimously agree that Kṛṣṇa is the Supreme Personality of Godhead. As far as we, the followers of Vedic civilization, are concerned, we accept the Vedic history of the whole universe, which consists of different planetary systems, called Svargaloka, or the higher planetary system, Martyaloka, or the intermediary planetary system, and Pātāla-loka, or the lower planetary system. The modern historians of this earth cannot supply historical evidences of events that occurred before 5,000 years ago, and the anthropologists say that 40,000 years ago *Homo sapiens* had not appeared on this planet because evolution had not reached that point. But the Vedic histories, such as the *Purāṇas* and *Mahābhārata*, relate human histories that extend millions and billions of years into the past.

For example, from these literatures we are given the histories of Kṛṣṇa's appearances and disappearances millions and billions of years ago. In the fourth chapter of the *Bhagavad-gītā* Kṛṣṇa tells Arjuna that both He and Arjuna had had many births before and that He (Kṛṣṇa) could remember all of them but Arjuna could not. This illustrates the difference between the knowledge of Kṛṣṇa and that of Arjuna. Arjuna might have been a very great warrior, a well-cultured member of the Kuru dynasty, but after all, he was an ordinary human being, whereas Kṛṣṇa, the Supreme Personality of Godhead, is the possessor of unlimited knowledge. Because He possesses unlimited knowledge, Kṛṣṇa has a memory that is boundless.

The knowledge Kṛṣṇa possesses is so perfect that He remembers all the incidents of His appearances some millions and billions of years in the past, but Arjuna's memory and knowledge are limited by time and space, for he is an ordinary human being. In the fourth chapter Kṛṣṇa states that He can remember instructing the lessons of the *Bhagavad-gītā* some millions of years ago to the sun god, Vivasvān.

Nowadays it is the fashion of the atheistic class of men to try to become God by following some mystic process. Generally the atheists claim to be God by dint of their imagination or their meditational prowess. Kṛṣṇa is not that kind of God. He does not become God by manufacturing some mystic process of meditation, nor does He become God by undergoing the severe austerities of the mystic yogic exercises. Properly speaking, He never becomes God because He is the Godhead in all circumstances.

Within the prison of His maternal uncle Kaṁsa, where His father and mother were confined, Kṛṣṇa appeared outside His mother's body as the four-handed Viṣṇu-Nārāyaṇa. Then He turned Himself into a baby and told His father to carry Him to the house of Nanda Mahārāja and his wife Yaśodā. When Kṛṣṇa was just a small baby the gigantic demoness Pūtanā attempted to kill Him, but when He sucked her breast He pulled out her life. That is the difference between the real Godhead and a God manufactured in the mystic factory. Kṛṣṇa had no chance to practice the mystic yoga process, yet He manifested Himself as the Supreme Personality of Godhead at every step, from infancy to childhood, from childhood to boyhood, and from boyhood to young manhood.... Although Kṛṣṇa plays like a human being, He always maintains His identity as the Supreme Personality of Godhead.

Since Kṛṣṇa is all-attractive, one should know that all his desires should be focused on Kṛṣṇa. In the *Bhagavad-gītā* it is said that the individual person is the proprietor or master of his own body but that Kṛṣṇa, who is the Supersoul present in everyone's heart, is the supreme proprietor and supreme master of each and every individual body. As such, if we concentrate our loving propensities upon Kṛṣṇa only, then immediately universal love, unity and tranquility will be automatically realized. When one waters the root of a tree, he automatically waters the branches, twigs, leaves, and flowers; when one supplies food to the stomach through the mouth, he satisfies all the various parts of the body.

The art of focusing one's attention on the Supreme and giving one's love to Him is called Kṛṣṇa consciousness. We have inaugurated the Kṛṣṇa consciousness movement so that everyone can satisfy his propensity for loving others simply by directing his love toward Kṛṣṇa. The whole world is very eager to satisfy the dormant propensity of love for others, but the various invented methods like socialism, communism, altruism, humanitarianism, and nationalism, along with whatever else may be manufactured for the peace and prosperity of the world, are all useless and frustrating because of our gross ignorance of the art of loving Kṛṣṇa. Generally people think that by advancing the cause of moral principles and religious rites they will be happy. Others may think that happiness can be achieved by economic development, and yet others think that simply by sense gratification they will be happy. But the real fact is that people can be happy only by loving Kṛṣṇa.

Kṛṣṇa can perfectly reciprocate one's loving propensities in different relationships called mellows, or *rasas.* Basically there are twelve loving relationships. One can love Kṛṣṇa as the supreme unknown, as the supreme master, the supreme friend, the supreme child, the supreme lover. These are the five basic love *rasas.* One can also love Kṛṣṇa indirectly in seven different relationships, which are apparently different from the five primary relationships. All in all, however, if one simply reposes his dormant loving propensity in Kṛṣṇa, then his life becomes successful. This is not a fiction but is a fact that can be realized by practical application. One can directly perceive the effects that love for Kṛṣṇa has on his life.

In the ninth chapter of the *Bhagavad-gītā* this science of Kṛṣṇa consciousness is called the king of all knowledge, the king of all confidential things, and the supreme science of transcendental realization. Yet we can directly experience the results of this science of Kṛṣṇa consciousness because it is very easy to practice and is very pleasurable. Whatever percentage of Kṛṣṇa consciousness we can perform will become an eternal asset to our life, for it is imperishable in all circumstances. It has now been actually proved that today's confused and frustrated younger generation in the Western countries can directly perceive the results of channeling the loving propensity toward Kṛṣṇa alone.

It is said that although one executes severe austerities, penances, and sacrifices in his life, if he fails to awaken his dormant love for Kṛṣṇa, then all his penances are to be considered useless. On the other hand, if one has awakened his dormant love for Kṛṣṇa, then what is the use in executing austerities and penances unnecessarily?

The Kṛṣṇa consciousness movement is the unique gift of Lord Caitanya to the fallen souls of this age. It is a very simple method that has actually been carried out during the last so many years in the Western countries, and there is no doubt that this movement can satisfy the dormant loving propensities of humanity. It is said in the *Bhagavad-gītā* that even a little effort expended on the path of Kṛṣṇa consciousness can save one from the greatest danger. Hundreds of thousands of examples can be cited of people who have escaped the greatest dangers of life due to a slight advancement in Kṛṣṇa consciousness. We therefore request everyone to take advantage of this great movement and its literature, which offers an immense treasure of knowledge in art, science, literature, philosophy, and religion.

Teachings of the Vedas

His Divine Grace A.C. Bhaktivedanta Swami Prabhupāda

This lecture was given by Śrīla Prabhupāda on October 6, 1969, at Conway Hall, London, England. In his talk he explains the meaning of the Vedas *and the dangers of living a life without recourse to transcendental perspective such as the* Vedas *provide.*

~

Ladies and gentlemen, today's subject matter is the teachings of the *Vedas*. What are the *Vedas*? The Sanskrit verbal root of *veda* can be interpreted variously, but the purport is finally one. *Veda* means knowledge. Any knowledge you accept is *veda,* for the teachings of the *Vedas* are the original knowledge. In the conditioned state, our knowledge is subjected to many deficiencies. The difference between a conditioned soul and a liberated soul is that the conditioned soul has four kinds of defects. The first defect is that he must commit mistakes. For example, in our country, Mahatma Gandhi was considered to be a very great personality, but he committed many mistakes. Even at the last stage of his life, his assistant warned, "Mahatma Gandhi, don't go to the New Delhi meeting. I have some friends, and I have heard there is danger." But he did not hear. He persisted in going and was killed. Even great personalities like Mahatma Gandhi, President

Kennedy – there are so many of them – make mistakes. To err is human. This is one defect of the conditioned soul.

Another defect: to be illusioned. Illusion means to accept something that is not: *māyā. Māyā* means "what is not." Everyone is accepting the body as the self. If I ask you what you are, you will say, "I am Mr. John; I am a rich man; I am this; I am that." All these are bodily identifications. But you are not this body. This is illusion.

The third defect is the cheating propensity.Everyone has the propensity to cheat others. Although a person is fool number one, he poses himself as very intelligent. Although it is already pointed out that he is in illusion and makes mistakes, he will theorize: "I think this is this, this is this." But he does not even know his own position. He writes books of philosophy, although he is defective. That is his disease. That is cheating.

Lastly, our senses are imperfect. We are very proud of our eyes. Often, someone will challenge, "Can you show me God?" But do you have the eyes to see God? You will never see if you haven't the eyes. If immediately the room becomes dark, you cannot even see your hands. So what power do you have to see? We cannot, therefore, expect knowledge (*veda*) with these imperfect senses. With all these deficiencies, in conditioned life we cannot give perfect knowledge to anyone. Nor are we ourselves perfect. Therefore we accept the *Vedas* as they are.

You may call the *Vedas* Hindu, but "Hindu" is a foreign name. We are not Hindus. Our real identification is *varṇāśrama. Varṇāśrama* denotes the followers of the *Vedas,* those who accept the human society in eight divisions of *varṇa* and *āśrama.* There are four divisions of society and four divisions of spiritual life. This is called *varṇāśrama.* It is stated in the *Bhagavad-gītā* (4.13), "These divisions are everywhere because they are created by God." The divisions of society are *brāhmaṇa, kṣatriya, vaiśya, śūdra. Brāhmaṇa* refers to the very intelligent class of men, those who know what is Brahman. Similarly, the *kṣatriyas,* the administrator group, are the next intelligent class of men. Then the *vaiśyas,* the mercantile group. These natural classifications are found everywhere. This is the Vedic principle, and we accept it. Vedic principles are accepted as axiomatic truth, for there cannot be any mistake. That is acceptance. For instance, in India cow dung is accepted as pure, and yet cow dung is the stool of an animal. In one place you'll find the Vedic injunction that if you touch stool, you have to take a bath immediately. But in another place it is said that the stool of a cow is pure. If you smear cow dung in an impure place, that place becomes pure. With our ordinary sense we can argue, "This is contradictory." Actually, it is contradictory from the ordinary point of view, but it is not false. It is fact. In Calcutta, a very prominent scientist and doctor analyzed cow dung and found that it contains all antiseptic properties.

In India if one person tells another, "You must do this," the other party may say, "What do you mean? Is this a Vedic injunction, that I have to follow you without any argument?" Vedic injunctions cannot be interpreted. But ultimately, if you carefully study why these injunctions are there, you will find that they are all correct.

The *Vedas* are not compilations of human knowledge. Vedic knowledge comes from the spiritual world, from Lord Kṛṣṇa. Another name for the *Vedas* is *śruti*. *Śruti* refers to that knowledge which is acquired by hearing. It is not experimental knowledge. *Śruti* is considered to be like a mother. We take so much knowledge from our mother. For example, if you want to know who your father is, who can answer you? Your mother. If the mother says, "Here is your father," you have to accept it. It is not possible to experiment to find out whether he is your father. Similarly, if you want to know something beyond your experience, beyond your experimental knowledge, beyond the activities of the senses, then you have to accept the *Vedas*. There is no question of experimenting. It has already been experimented. It is already settled. The version of the mother, for instance, has to be accepted as truth. There is no other way.

The *Vedas* are considered to be the mother, and Brahmā is

called the grandfather, the forefather, because he was the first to be instructed in the Vedic knowledge. In the beginning the first living creature was Brahmā. He received this Vedic knowledge and imparted it to Nārada and other disciples and sons, and they also distributed it to their disciples. In this way, the Vedic knowledge comes down by disciplic succession. It is also confirmed in the *Bhagavad-gītā* that Vedic knowledge is understood in this way. If you make experimental endeavor, you come to the same conclusion, but just to save time you should accept. If you want to know who your father is and if you accept your mother as the authority, then whatever she says can be accepted without argument. There are three kinds of evidence: *pratyakṣa, anumāna,* and *śabda. Pratyakṣa* means "direct evidence." Direct evidence is not very good because our senses are not perfect. We are seeing the sun daily, and it appears to us just like a small disc, but it is actually far, far larger than many planets. Of what value is this seeing? Therefore we have to read books; then we can understand about the sun. So direct experience is not perfect. Then there is *anumāna,* inductive knowledge: "It may be like this" – hypothesis. For instance, Darwin's theory says it may be like this, it may be like that. But that is not science. That is a suggestion, and it is also not perfect. But if you receive the knowledge from the authoritative sources, that is perfect. If you receive a program guide from the radio station authorities, you accept it. You don't deny it; you don't have to make an experiment, because it is received from the authoritative sources.

Vedic knowledge is called *śabda-pramāṇa.* Another name is *śruti. Śruti* means that this knowledge has to be received simply by aural reception. The *Vedas* instruct that in order to understand transcendental knowledge, we have to hear from the authority. Transcendental knowledge is knowledge from beyond this universe. Within this universe is material knowledge, and beyond this universe is transcendental knowledge. We cannot even go to the end of the universe, so how can we go to the spiritual world? Thus to acquire full knowledge is impossible.

There is a spiritual sky. There is another nature, which is beyond manifestation and nonmanifestation. But how will you know that there is a sky where the planets and inhabitants are eternal? All this knowledge is there, but how will you make experiments? It is not possible. Therefore you have to take the assistance of the *Vedas.* This is called Vedic knowledge. In our Kṛṣṇa consciousness movement we are accepting knowledge from the highest authority, Kṛṣṇa. Kṛṣṇa is accepted as the highest authority by all classes of men. I am speaking first of the two classes of transcendentalists. One class of transcendentalists is called impersonalistic, Māyāvādī. They are generally known as Vedāntists, led by Śaṅkarācārya. And there is another class of transcendentalists, called Vaiṣṇavas, like Rāmānujācārya, Madhvācārya, Viṣṇu Svāmī. Both the Śaṅkara-sampradāya and the Vaiṣṇava-sampradāya have accepted Kṛṣṇa as the Supreme Personality of Godhead. Śaṅkarācārya is supposed to be an impersonalist who preached impersonalism, impersonal Brahman, but it is a fact that he is a covered personalist. In his commentary on the *Bhagavad-gītā* he wrote, "Nārāyaṇa, the Supreme Personality of Godhead, is beyond this cosmic manifestation." And then again he confirmed, "That Supreme Personality of Godhead, Nārāyaṇa, is Kṛṣṇa. He has come as the son of Devakī and Vasudeva." He particularly mentioned the names of His father and mother. So Kṛṣṇa is accepted as the Supreme Personality of Godhead by all transcendentalists. There is no doubt about it. Our source of knowledge in Kṛṣṇa consciousness is the *Bhagavad-gītā,* which comes directly from Kṛṣṇa. We have published *Bhagavad-gītā As It Is* because we accept Kṛṣṇa as He is speaking, without any interpretation. That is Vedic knowledge. Since the Vedic knowledge is pure, we accept it. Whatever Kṛṣṇa says, we accept. This is Kṛṣṇa consciousness. That saves much time. If you accept the right authority, or source of knowledge, then you save much time. For example, there are two systems of knowledge in the material world: inductive and deductive. From deductive, you accept that man is mortal.

Your father says man is mortal, your sister says man is mortal, everyone says man is mortal – but you do not experiment. You accept it as a fact that man is mortal. If you want to research to find out whether man is mortal, you have to study each and every man, and you may come to think that there may be some man who is not dying but you have not seen him yet. So in this way your research will never be finished. In Sanskrit this process is called *āroha,* the ascending process. If you want to attain knowledge by any personal endeavor, by exercising your imperfect senses, you will never come to the right conclusions. That is not possible.

There is a statement in the *Brahma-saṁhitā:* Just ride on the airplane which runs at the speed of mind. Our material airplanes can run two thousand miles per hour, but what is the speed of mind? You are sitting at home, you immediately think of India – say, ten thousand miles away – and at once it is in your home. Your mind has gone there. The mind-speed is so swift. Therefore it is stated, "If you travel at this speed for millions of years, you'll find that the spiritual sky is unlimited." It is not possible even to approach it. Therefore, the Vedic injunction is that one must approach – the word "compulsory" is used – a bona fide spiritual master, a guru. And what is the qualification of a spiritual master? He is one who has rightly heard the Vedic message from the right source. And he must practically be firmly established in Brahman. These are the two qualities he must have. Otherwise he is not bona fide.

This Kṛṣṇa consciousness movement is completely authorized from Vedic principles. In the *Bhagavad-gītā* Kṛṣṇa says, "The actual aim of Vedic research is to find out Kṛṣṇa." In the *Brahma-saṁhitā* it is also stated, "Kṛṣṇa, Govinda, has innumerable forms, but they are all one." They are not like our forms, which are fallible. His form is infallible. My form has a beginning, but His form has no beginning. It is *ananta.* And His form – so many multiforms – has no end. My form is sitting here and not in my apartment. You are sitting there and not in your apartment. But Kṛṣṇa can be everywhere at one time. He can sit down in Goloka Vṛndāvana, and at the same time He is everywhere, all-pervading. He is original, the oldest, but whenever you look at a picture of Kṛṣṇa you'll find a young boy fifteen or twenty years old. You will never find an old man. You have seen pictures of Kṛṣṇa as a charioteer from the *Bhagavad-gītā*. At that time He was not less than one hundred years old. He had great-grandchildren, but He looked just like a boy. Kṛṣṇa, God, never becomes old. That is His supreme power. And if you want to search out Kṛṣṇa by studying the Vedic literature, then you will be baffled. It may be possible, but it is very difficult. But you can very easily learn about Him from His devotee. His devotee can deliver Him to you: "Here He is, take Him." That is the potency of Kṛṣṇa's devotees.

Originally there was only one *Veda*, and there was no necessity of reading it. People were so intelligent and had such sharp memories that by once hearing from the lips of the spiritual master they would understand. They would immediately grasp the whole purport. But five thousand years ago Vyāsadeva put the *Vedas* in writing for the people in this age, Kali-yuga. He knew that eventually the people would be short-lived, their memories would be very poor, and their intelligence would not be very sharp. "Therefore, let me teach this Vedic knowledge in writing." He divided the *Vedas* into four: *Ṛg*, *Sāma*, *Atharva*, and *Yajur*. Then he gave the charge of these *Vedas* to his different disciples. He then thought of the less intelligent class of men – *strī*, *śūdra*, and *dvija-bandhu*. He considered the woman class and *śūdra* class (worker class) and *dvija-bandhu*. *Dvija-bandhu* refers to those who are born in a high family but who are not properly qualified. A man who is born in the family of a *brāhmaṇa* but is not qualified as a *brāhmaṇa* is called *dvija-bandhu*. For these persons he compiled the *Mahābhārata*, called the history of India, and the eighteen *Purāṇas*. These are all part of the Vedic literature: the *Purāṇas*, the *Mahābhārata*, the four *Vedas* and the *Upaniṣads*. The *Upaniṣads* are part of the *Vedas*. Then Vyāsadeva summarized all Vedic knowledge for scholars and philosophers in what is called the *Vedānta-sūtra*. This is the last word of the *Vedas*.

Vyāsadeva personally wrote the *Vedānta-sūtra* under the instructions of Nārada, his Guru Mahārāja (spiritual master), but still he was not satisfied. That is a long story, described in *Śrīmad-Bhāgavatam.* Vedavyāsa was not very satisfied even after compiling many *Purāṇas* and *Upaniṣads,* and even after writing the *Vedānta-sūtra.* Then his spiritual master, Nārada, instructed him, "You explain the *Vedānta-sūtra.*" *Vedānta* means "ultimate knowledge," and the ultimate knowledge is Kṛṣṇa. Kṛṣṇa says that throughout all the *Vedas* one has to understand Him: *vedaiś ca sarvair aham eva vedyaḥ.* Kṛṣṇa also says, *vedānta-kṛd veda-vid eva cāham:* "I am the compiler of the *Vedānta-sūtra,* and I am the knower of the *Vedas.*" Therefore the ultimate objective is Kṛṣṇa. That is explained in all the Vaiṣṇava commentaries on Vedānta philosophy. We Gauḍīya Vaiṣṇavas have our commentary on Vedānta philosophy, called *Govinda-bhāṣya,* by Baladeva Vidyābhūṣaṇa. Similarly, Rāmānujācārya has a commentary, and Madhvācārya has one. The version of Śaṅkarācārya is not the only commentary. There are many Vedānta commentaries, but because the Vaiṣṇavas did not present the first Vedānta commentary, people are under the wrong impression that Śaṅkarācārya's is the only Vedānta commentary. Besides that, Vyāsadeva himself wrote the perfect Vedānta commentary, *Śrīmad-Bhāgavatam. Śrīmad-Bhāgavatam* begins with the first words of the *Vedānta-sūtra: janmādy asya yataḥ.* And that *janmādy asya yataḥ* is fully explained in *Śrīmad-Bhāgavatam.* The *Vedānta-sūtra* simply hints at what is Brahman, the Absolute Truth: "The Absolute Truth is that from whom everything emanates." This is a summary, but it is explained in detail in *Śrīmad-Bhāgavatam.* If everything is emanating from the Absolute Truth, then what is the nature of the Absolute Truth? That is explained in *Śrīmad-Bhāgavatam.* The Absolute Truth must be consciousness. He is self-effulgent (*sva-rāṭ*). We develop our consciousness and knowledge by receiving knowledge from others, but for Him it is said that He is self-effulgent. The whole summary of Vedic knowledge is the *Vedānta-sūtra,* and the *Vedānta-sūtra* is explained by the writer himself in *Śrīmad-Bhāgavatam.* We finally request those who are actually after Vedic knowledge to try to understand the explanation of all Vedic knowledge from *Śrīmad-Bhāgavatam* and the *Bhagavad-gītā*.

The Six Benefits of Practicing Bhakti-yoga

His Divine Grace A.C. Bhaktivedanta Swami Prabhupāda

Happiness derived from pure devotional service is the highest because it is eternal, whereas happiness derived from material perfection is temporary. There is no way to prevent oneself from falling from material happiness. But practicing pure devotional service offers transcendental pleasure.

~

There are six positive benefits when one takes to Kṛṣṇa consciousness. The first is that one feels immediate relief from all kinds of material distress. The great *ācārya* Bhaktivinoda Ṭhākura has written a song stating that when we surrender to Kṛṣṇa we are relieved from all kinds of anxiety. This is very simple to understand. Everyone in the material world is full of anxiety. That is the nature of material existence: problems, one after another. So if someone assures us that "You just depend on me and I will take charge of your problems," just imagine how much relief we will feel. Still, if it is an ordinary human being offering us his protection, we may doubt his ability to help us because we know the capacity of an ordinary human being. But when God, Kṛṣṇa, says He will take charge of us, then we can feel full relief. Kṛṣṇa is not an ordinary man; He is the all-powerful Supreme Personality of Godhead, the master of all yogic powers, and the Absolute Truth. So when He assures us that "I take charge of you, and I shall deliver you from the reactions to your sinful activities," we can believe Him.

Suffering is caused by our sinful activities. We enjoy the results of our pious activities and suffer the results of the impious. But whether we enjoy or suffer in this material world, suffering is the common factor. The karmic reactions for performing pious activities are birth in a good family, wealth, good education, and beauty. So suppose I perform pious activities and get myself these results. But even if I take birth in the family of a king or a very rich man, the suffering of taking birth is the same. As a poor man suffers in his mother's womb, so a rich man suffers. Suffering is the same whether one is rich or poor. Similarly, disease is not less painful for the rich than for the poor. So as long as we live in the material world our suffering and enjoyment are actually on the same level. There is no real difference between them.

But if we take to Kṛṣṇa consciousness, devotional service to Kṛṣṇa, Kṛṣṇa assures us that "I shall get you released from all kinds of karmic reactions." And when Kṛṣṇa takes charge of us He gradually educates us in *bhakti-yoga,* devotional service, so that we may go back to Him. That is real auspiciousness. The so-called auspiciousness of this world – the attainment of wealth, education, beauty, and high parentage – is too adulterated with suffering to actually be considered auspicious.

And as our lives become auspicious when we practice devotional service, so do the lives of other living beings. Therefore devotional service is the best welfare work; it creates good for everyone in all parts of the world without discrimination. Political, sociological, and humanitarian acts tend to be partial. That is, they are aimed at a certain section of human beings or animals. But chanting the Hare Kṛṣṇa mantra, which is the primary means to awaken the soul's dormant Kṛṣṇa consciousness, can benefit all beings. Even birds, beasts, and insects can awaken to their soul's purpose and become liberated from material suffering simply by hearing the mantra.

At the present moment groups of people are engaged in welfare activities to help their society, community, or nation. The United Nations is an attempt to help the world. Their representatives have been tackling various problems for years, but they have not been able to create world harmony. The nations have not united. This is because of the limits of national interest. But Kṛṣṇa consciousness can benefit everyone. Everyone can become attracted by Kṛṣṇa and derive the result.

People want peace, but to get peace they must accept God as the supreme enjoyer. We are not the enjoyers. At the present moment all our activities are self-centered. We think everything in the world is meant for our pleasure. This is wrong. Kṛṣṇa is the enjoyer, the supreme leader, and our best friend. He is the proprietor of everything. That is Kṛṣṇa consciousness. This idea should be spread all over the world. Then automatically and very easily the nations will unite.

The next benefit is that one feels great happiness in Kṛṣṇa consciousness. Happiness derived from pure devotional service is the highest because it is eternal, whereas happiness derived from material perfection is temporary. There is no way to prevent oneself from falling from material happiness. But practicing pure devotional service offers transcendental pleasure. There is a difference between transcendental pleasure and material pleasure. Material pleasure means sense gratification, and transcendental pleasure means satisfying God. Devotees are satisfied when they see that Kṛṣṇa is pleased. Material pleasure means enjoying directly through the senses, and spiritual pleasure is experienced through Kṛṣṇa. If Kṛṣṇa is satisfied, the devotee is satisfied. The leaves and twigs of a tree are satisfied when they serve the tree's root. Kṛṣṇa is the root; He is the origin of everything. Transcendental pleasure means gaining pleasure by serving the root, Kṛṣṇa.

Transcendental pleasure is also free from envy. If I am interested in selfish pleasure, when I see you happy I tend to become unhappy, and if I see you unhappy I become pleased. It is human nature that if someone is put into difficulty others become happy, and when others are happy, someone is envious of their happiness.

Spiritual pleasure is free of this envy. When devotees see that Kṛṣṇa or others are happy they become happier. That is the nature of those who are experiencing spiritual pleasure. In the spiritual world there is even a competition to please Kṛṣṇa, but that competition is based on giving Kṛṣṇa pleasure and is not caused by envy. Therefore there is no distress in the spiritual world.

But pure devotional service is rarely achieved because it requires the help of someone fully devoted to Kṛṣṇa. Such persons are free of both material desire and material obligation. They have completely taken shelter of Kṛṣṇa, giving up all other duties. And this is the next advantage of practicing *bhakti-yoga:* one can become free of material obligation.

We all have duties and obligations. We must satisfy our family, our country, the animals in our care, other living entities, the demigods, and the saints. We read the scripture, but we must acknowledge that we have received the scripture from he who has revealed it. We are indebted to him. We enjoy and use the sunshine so are indebted to the sun god. We use the moon's rays, the air, the water – so many beings help us live in this world, and we cannot live without their gifts. Who is supplying all our necessities? Of course, they are supplied by God, but He supplies them through His universal administrators, the demigods. Therefore the *Vedas* recommend that one perform sacrifices to show gratitude to the demigods. Those sacrifices are ultimately meant to please the master of the demigods, Kṛṣṇa, so when we take to Kṛṣṇa consciousness we become free of the obligation to express gratitude to each being who has helped us. Fulfilling material obligations is like watering the leaves and twigs of a tree, and worshiping Kṛṣṇa is like watering the root. If we don't water the root of the tree we are bound to water each leaf and twig.

The next benefit of practicing devotional service is that we become liberated from material consciousness. As a matter of fact, those who have achieved pure devotional service deride even the concept of liberation. Why doesn't a devotee care about liberation? Because as soon as someone has come to practice pure devotion, liberation is already achieved. There is no need to make a separate endeavor to attain it.

Another name for liberation, *mukti*, is *kaivalya* – the idea that the soul can merge into the undifferentiated form of God and lose its identity. But for one who has realized Kṛṣṇa and His transcendental nature, pastimes, and love for His devotees, the idea that "I have become one with the Supreme" reminds one of hell. Rather, the devotee prefers to remain immersed in the happiness of serving Kṛṣṇa and exchanging with Him in love.

The next effect of practicing pure devotional service is that Kṛṣṇa consciousness has the power to attract Kṛṣṇa. Actually, practicing devotional service is the *only* means to attract Him. Kṛṣṇa is the Supreme Personality of Godhead with full opulence. We cannot draw Him to us with our wealth, reputation, education, beauty, strength, or power of renunciation because He is already self-satisfied and full in Himself. He is the reservoir of all these things. What do we have to offer Him? But we offer what we have in Kṛṣṇa's service and we benefit. The *Vedas* give an example: When a person decorates himself and then looks in the mirror, the person in the reflection is also decorated. Similarly, if we please Kṛṣṇa, we too feel pleasure. It is therefore in our interest to practice *bhakti-yoga*.

But even though Kṛṣṇa doesn't require anything from us, He is always ready to engage in loving pastimes with us. Kṛṣṇa will be happy that we are doing so much for Him. Although He has everything, He is attracted by our sincerity of purpose. My guru used to say, "Don't try to see Kṛṣṇa. Serve in such a nice way that Kṛṣṇa will want to see you." When Kṛṣṇa sees us, our mission is perfect. We cannot perceive Kṛṣṇa by our senses, but when we engage those same senses in satisfying Kṛṣṇa, then Kṛṣṇa will see us. And when Kṛṣṇa sees us, our life will be successful.

The sixth benefit is that a person engaged in Kṛṣṇa consciousness can immediately develop all good qualities. This is because chanting the Hare Kṛṣṇa mantra cleanses the heart of material conceptions. The soul is naturally pure, uncontaminated by the material nature. Although we think we are connected to matter, this is simply an illusion or misidentification. Just as oil and water do not mix, but oil may appear to have fallen into water, so the soul does not mix with matter even though it may appear to be situated in the material world. Rather, the soul is cent percent spiritual.

That we misidentify ourselves with our present body and mind is like seeing a dream. Dreams are false. We are separate from the self we see in the dream. Still, while we are dreaming we may believe we are enjoying or suffering. Similarly, when the soul seems to be situated in material consciousness we think we are enjoying or suffering the things in this world. But it is not true. If we change our consciousness we can immediately transfer ourselves to the spiritual platform.

And because the spiritual platform relates to the soul's true nature, the more advanced we become in Kṛṣṇa consciousness the more the soul's original characteristics, which are very pure, become manifest. The factual example is before us. My European and American disciples were addicted to so many nonsense habits, but since they have taken to Kṛṣṇa consciousness they gave them up immediately and without any great endeavor. So pure character and pure qualities manifest when one practices devotional service.

And the opposite is also true: Those who do not practice devotional service cannot have any good qualities no matter how well educated they are. We often see that even university-educated people live like animals. Without God consciousness people cannot rise beyond the sphere of the body and mind and are forced to perform only material activities. They are unable to do any actual good in this world.

We also see that those who are practicing other forms of yoga remain restless. Many yoga systems teach that if you become silent, you will realize that you are God. This system may be all right for materialistic persons, but how long will they be able to keep silent? Artificially they may sit down to meditate, but immediately after their yogic performance they engage again in illicit sex, gambling, meat-eating, and other nonsensical things.

Actually, yoga practice means *yoga indriya-saṁyamaḥ*. The whole *aṣṭāṅga-yoga* process is meant to control the senses. The senses are like serpents. Even by a touch of its tongue a serpent can cause harm. As it is difficult to enchant a snake, so it is difficult to control the senses. But the yoga system is especially meant to control them – and to control the mind. When the mind and senses are controlled, one is then meant to concentrate on Viṣṇu. This is yoga. But practically we see so many students attending yoga classes who are habituated to nonsense habits – illicit sex, intoxication, and meat-eating. That kind of yoga cannot help themselves or anyone else.

Rather, one must develop good character through mind and sense control. Those who are engaged in Kṛṣṇa consciousness automatically give up all nonsense habits and develop high character, and one can develop the highest character by becoming a pure devotee of Kṛṣṇa. The conclusion is that no one can truly have any good qualities if he is lacking Kṛṣṇa consciousness.

To experience these six benefits we have to take to devotional service. Then we shall understand Kṛṣṇa because Kṛṣṇa will reveal Himself to us. If we are engaged in Kṛṣṇa's service constantly – *teṣāṁ satata-yuktānāṁ bhajataṁ prīti-pūrvakam* – then Kṛṣṇa says *dadāmi buddhi-yogaṁ taṁ yena mām upayānti te:* "I give the understanding by which they can come to Me." (*Gītā* 10.10) If you have devoted your heart and soul to serving God, Kṛṣṇa, then Kṛṣṇa is within yourself. He'll give you intelligence and purify your heart.

Understanding Ourselves: Who Am I?

Viśākhā Devī Dāsī

Because we belong to the superior, spiritual energy, we cannot understand our true identity or achieve eternal happiness in full knowledge if we continue to act on the false platform of the inferior, material energy.

~

A Simple Test for Thoughtful People

Am I my head or my face? No, it is *my* face. Am I my chest? No, it is *my* chest. Am I my arm or my hand? No, they are *my* arm and hand. Am I my leg? No, it is *my* leg. All the parts of my body – indeed, my entire body – is mine. But who am *I*, the owner of the body?

If we perform the experiment as above, we can immediately come to the very first understanding in spiritual life: we are not our bodies; rather we are conscious of them. Under the influence of illusion, however, we falsely identify ourselves with our bodies and think we belong to a certain family, nation, race, religion, political party, and so on. The goal of human life is to awaken from this illusion and become reinstated in our real identities as fully conscious spiritual beings.

Our daily lives can be compared to acting in a play. We have become so absorbed with our temporary roles in this play that we have completely forgotten our true offstage identities. Someone is taking the part of our parent, another person is acting as our lover, another as our friend or foe, but actually it is all simply a performance; our real identities are something else. Our very bodies are nothing more than costumes, but out of illusion we identify ourselves with them and try to relate to others on the basis of these costumes. The resulting relationships are not false; they are real, but they are temporary and therefore illusory. When the curtain falls on our play – when death comes – all the different relationships we have cultivated during our lives will be finished, and our real self, an individually conscious spirit soul, will be transferred to a new situation.

The Nature of Consciousness

Modern scientists have touched on the properties of the spirit soul in their research into antimaterial particles. A fundamental assumption of their theory is that there may exist another world, an antimaterial world, composed of antiparticles. They conjecture that this antimaterial world might consist of atomic and subatomic particles spinning in reverse orbits to those of the world we know.

But if we really want to find out about the nature of consciousness and its source, the antimaterial spirit soul, we must go beyond the tentative gropings of mundane scientists. We must search out the revealed knowledge contained in the *Vedas,* the most ancient and widely recognized source of transcendental science in the world. Since the soul is imperceptible by our gross senses, the authoritative Vedic wisdom is the only means for understanding it. We must accept many things solely on the basis of superior authority. For example, if I want to know who my father is I must accept the authority of my mother. I cannot find his identity experimentally; I must simply use intelligent discrimination to find the right source of knowledge. Similarly, to understand the science of the soul we must turn to the Vedic literature, and specifically to the *Bhagavad-gītā*. *Bhagavad-gītā* contains the essence of the *Vedas*, for it is spoken by Lord Śrī Kṛṣṇa, the supreme, all-knowing Personality of Godhead.

In the *Bhagavad-gītā* (13.34), Lord Kṛṣṇa says, "As the sun, situated in one place, illuminates the entire universe, so a small particle of spirit [the soul situated in the heart] illuminates the entire body with consciousness." Just as sunshine proves the sun is present in the sky, consciousness proves the soul is present in the body. When the soul leaves the body, consciousness disappears and the body dies. Thus consciousness is the symptom of the soul's presence in the body.

The Antimaterial World

The material scientists misconceive the soul, a particle of antimatter, to be only another variety of material energy. But real antimatter must be antimaterial, or spiritual. If matter is subject to annihilation, then antimatter must be indestructible. Lord Kṛṣṇa explains this quality of the soul in the following excerpts from the *Bhagavad-gītā* (2.18, 2.16, 2.20):

"An immeasurable particle of antimaterial energy is engaged within the material body (which includes the mind and intelligence). The material body is destructible, and as such it is changeable and temporary, as is the material world. But the antimaterial force is indestructible and therefore permanent. For the antimaterial particle, which is the vital force, there is never birth nor death, nor, having once been does it ever cease to be. It is unborn, eternal, ever-existing, undying, and primeval. When the material body is annihilated, the antimaterial particle is never affected." The Lord further explains how the soul transmigrates from one body to another. "The material body progressively changes from childhood to boyhood, from boyhood to youth, and from youth to old age, after which the antimaterial particle leaves the old, unworkable body and enters another material body." (*Gītā* 2.13)

Thus with some reflection we can understand a few of the

characteristics of the material and the antimaterial energies. The material energy is unconscious, lifeless, and temporary, being subject to the influence of time. Referred to in the *Bhagavad-gītā* as the inferior or external energy, the material energy has eight divisions: earth, water, fire, air, ether, mind, intelligence, and false ego. All mundane knowledge is limited to these eight material principles. On the other hand, the antimaterial energy stands in opposition to all the material qualities. The antimaterial particle of energy is the living force, described in the *Bhagavad-gītā* as the superior or internal energy. The material body is animated by this living force, and when it is separated from the body, the body becomes useless and dies. The nature of the antimaterial particle (the soul) is *sat-cid-ānanda* – eternal, full of knowledge, and blissful – and as such it is undoubtedly superior to the material energy.

Uncovering Our Real Identity

Because we belong to the superior, spiritual energy, we cannot understand our true identity or achieve eternal happiness in full knowledge if we continue to act on the false platform of the inferior, material energy. But if all our relationships in this material world are temporary and illusory, then with whom can we establish a meaningful and lasting relationship? Lord Kṛṣṇa answers this question in the *Bhagavad-gītā* (9.17–18): "I am the father of this universe, the mother ... and the most dear friend." Thus we do not have to give up personal relationships, but rather reestablish our real, eternal relationship with our most dear friend, Lord Śrī Kṛṣṇa, the Supreme Personality of Godhead.

The Lord explains elsewhere in the *Bhagavad-gītā* how this material world is actually a perverted reflection of the spiritual world: everything in this material world is there in Lord Kṛṣṇa's abode, but in its ideal, perfect form, for that is the world of antimatter or spirit. In the eternal kingdom of God there are trees, animals, flowers, people, and so on, but unlike in the material world they all exist in intimate loving relationships with Kṛṣṇa.

Each of us has a place in the spiritual world for that is our eternal home. As spiritual beings we are not meant for this temporary world of matter. We are like a fish out of water: Just as a fish can never be happy with any number of comforts outside of the water, we can never be truly happy outside of the spiritual atmosphere of Kṛṣṇa's abode. If we persist in trying to find pleasure in this material world, only repeated frustration and suffering await us. But if we make it our only business to cultivate our eternal relationship with Kṛṣṇa, we can gain reentry into that transcendental realm of Vaikuṇṭha, the world without anxiety, and attain a life of complete knowledge and endless bliss.

You Are Beyond This Body

A conversation between His Divine Grace
A. C. Bhaktivedanta Swami Prabhupāda and his disciples

In a conversation dated May 1, 1976, Śrīla Prabhupāda discusses how the soul makes use of the mind and intelligence to manipulate the body, just as a pilot manipulates an airplane's instrument panel to fly wherever he wants. Real knowledge begins when we learn we are beyond this body.

~

Śrīla Prabhupāda: The Lord says, *mamaivāṁśo jīva-loke jīva-bhūtaḥ sanātanaḥ*. Find this verse.
Disciple: That's *Bhagavad-gītā*, fifteenth chapter, text seven: "The living entities in this conditioned world," Kṛṣṇa says, "are My eternal, fragmental parts." He adds, *manaḥ-ṣaṣṭhānīndriyāṇi prakṛti-sthāni karṣati:* "Due to conditioned life, they are struggling very hard with the six senses, which include the mind."
Śrīla Prabhupāda: So the soul uses his mind and intelligence – his subtle senses, his subtle instruments – to manipulate his gross machine, his material body. In this way, he is just like an airplane pilot who uses his subtle electronic instruments to manipulate his gross machine, causing it to fly this way or that. Where is the difficulty in understanding this? This material body in which we are now living is simply a machine.

And *bhrāmayan sarva-bhūtāni:* "All living beings in this material world are simply wandering." *Bhrāmayan* – "wandering." Just as the pilot uses his airplane to wander here or there, so the soul uses his material body to wander here or there. This is going on. *Ūrdhvaṁ gacchanti sattva-sthā – adho gacchanti tāmasāḥ:* Sometimes the soul goes up, sometimes down. Just as a pilot uses his airplane's wings and other features for going up or down, so the soul uses his body's arms and other features for going up or down.

Bhagavad-gītā says, "Those situated in the mode of goodness gradually go upward to the higher planets; those in the mode of passion live on the earthly planets; and those in the abominable mode of ignorance go down to the hellish worlds." So whether we look at the soul in the body or the pilot in the plane we see the same thing: If the pilot is not expert, then at an untimely moment he goes down to the lowest place. Finished. *Adho gacchanti tāmasāḥ.* If the pilot is third class, then instead of flying high he plummets from the sky and everything is spoiled.

Everything depends on the pilot. The machine is not so important. The machine can go up if the pilot knows how to make it. Similarly, the machine can go down. And this is happening. If the pilot cannot handle his machine nicely, immediately it will be smashed. That is due to the pilot's mismanagement. At times I have seen that as soon as a flight is over the passengers and crew applaud. [*Laughter as Śrīla Prabhupāda claps.*] "The danger is over."

Anyway, *ūrdhvam* and *adhaḥ:* Depending on how you use this bodily machine you can go up or down. And *madhye tiṣṭhanti rājasāḥ:* If you become passionately attached to these middle planets, then you can stay here for still another lifetime.

In this way we must present this subject matter of self-realization. The living entity, the soul, is the important thing in this body, and just see how the soul is struggling. Due to ignorance of our real identity apart from the body, we struggle. *Manaḥ-ṣaṣṭhānīndriyāṇi prakṛti-sthāni karṣati:* "On account of being entangled in this material world, the soul is struggling very hard with the six senses of the material body, which include the mind." This is his position.

Disciple: Śrīla Prabhupāda, you often say that transmission of the knowledge of self-realization requires both a proper speaker – Lord Kṛṣṇa or His pure devotee – and a proper hearer.

Śrīla Prabhupāda: Yes. Only if someone is interested in knowing the truly important thing in life can he understand this knowledge, this science of self-realization. But if he's an animal – simply eating, sleeping, and mating – what will he understand? An animal is not interested in knowing how the world works. He gets his food and sex – his animal propensities – that's all.

But when the soul receives a human body, he must come to the human platform and become inquisitive. Like Sanātana Gosvāmī he must ask, *'ke āmi,' 'kene āmāya jāre tāpa-traya'*: "Who am I? Why must I endure all these miseries, culminating in death?" Of course, the modern animalistic human is not interested in these essential questions. Instead he inquires, "How shall I develop my economic position?" But Sanātana Gosvāmī already had a high-grade economic position and had left it behind. He was not interested in such temporary affairs. He was interested in knowing "Who, actually, am I? What is my position? Why am I suffering in this material atmosphere?" That is human life.

Disciple: Returning to *Bhagavad-gītā,* isn't it also true that Arjuna asks these same questions?

Śrīla Prabhupāda: Oh, yes. *Karpaṇya-doṣopahata. Karpaṇya-doṣa:* "Due to miserly weakness, my dear Kṛṣṇa, I have neglected my real duty, which is to understand my actual, spiritual self and then to serve You. Rather, I have been thinking about the bodily welfare of my nonsensical relatives and teachers, even though they are waging a war to usurp my kingdom. What is this foolishness on my part? After all, no matter how tender my sentiments, what benefit will these rascals get? It may be that they are going to die in this war. But sooner or later, in this way or that, they will die. What can I do? Therefore why am I perplexed about their bodily fate? I know this perplexity is my defect. I cannot cause these living entities' deaths or births, nor can I prolong their lives. All this is beyond my tiny jurisdiction. Still, I am anxious: If I kill them, what will happen? What will happen?"

Kṛṣṇa says, "You may kill them or not kill them, Arjuna, but rest assured, they'll be killed today or tomorrow. *Gatāsūn agatāsūṁś ca nānuśocanti paṇḍitāḥ:* A learned man knows that this material body will be finished today or tomorrow – so why should he be concerned about the body?" Rather, he should show concern for the person within the body – whether that person is going to heaven or to hell, up or down, *ūrdhvaṁ gacchanti* or *tāmo gacchanti.* This is the real concern. The material body will be finished today, tomorrow, or after a hundred years. Who can protect his body? But one should be concerned about the owner of the body. Where is *he* going and what will his next position be?

In *Bhagavad-gītā* Lord Kṛṣṇa clearly delineates this issue: According to the modes of nature in which you live your present life, you are deciding whether, in your next life, you will go up or down or remain in the same status. Three outcomes are possible: up, down, or the same status.

Disciple: These days, though, Śrīla Prabhupāda, people may say, "I have a soul," but they live in a pretty degraded way, as if they think, "I am this material body – that's all there is." They live as if they'll have no next life, or that they think in the next life they're automatically going upward because (as many say) they've accepted God or Jesus or Muhammad into their hearts. Meanwhile, they go on breaking God's laws all over the place and generally catering to their own bodily whims.

Śrīla Prabhupāda: Therefore they're rascals, and for the rascals *Bhagavad-gītā's* teachings are given. *Learn.* People are giving far too much emphasis on the material body: "When this current body is finished, everything is finished." They do not know anything beyond the body. But real knowledge begins when we learn, "No, you are beyond this body." This is real knowledge. This is the beginning of knowledge. Any other knowledge except this is ignorance. Unfortunately, people accept ignorance as knowledge.

On Seeking the Right Thing in the Wrong Place

A conversation between His Divine Grace
A. C. Bhaktivedanta Swami Prabhupāda and disciples

Suppose a child is crying. If some woman other than his mother takes him on her lap, he will continue to cry. But as soon as he's on the lap of his mother he immediately stops. Why? He can understand, "Now I have the real thing."

~

Devotee: Śrīla Prabhupāda, people often think that devotees are inhibited or repressed – that they never get any pleasure.

Śrīla Prabhupāda: Everyone is looking for pleasure, because we're meant for that. But because people have forgotten Kṛṣṇa, the reservoir of pleasure, they're trying to find pleasure in things other than Kṛṣṇa. Therefore they are becoming frustrated. They do not know that unless they come to Kṛṣṇa consciousness, they will find no real pleasure.

Suppose a child is crying. If some woman other than his mother takes him on her lap, he will continue to cry. But as soon as he's on the lap of his mother he immediately stops. Why? He can understand, "Now I have the real thing." He sucks his mother's breast and is satisfied. Similarly, when we finally come to Kṛṣṇa we'll be fully satisfied. We won't want anything further.

Devotee: Earlier you were speaking about the importance of being inquisitive.

Śrīla Prabhupāda: Being inquisitive about the ultimate source of happiness is the standard of human life. That inquisitiveness cannot be found in the cats and dogs. And unless a person becomes inquisitive about the ultimate source of happiness he's an animal, not a human being. Ninety-nine point nine percent of all people are not inquisitive in this way. They're searching after happiness, but they are not inquisitive about the ultimate source of happiness. So they are being baffled.

Devotee: It seems as if the very things that they think will make them happy turn out to be the causes of misery.

Śrīla Prabhupāda: Yes. For example, in the name of happiness they have invented the motorcar. But when two motorcars crash head on, life is lost. Yet people aren't inquisitive enough to ask, "We have invented this machine for happiness, so why has this disaster happened?" They don't have the intelligence to ask this question. They simply go on searching after happiness in the material world. And when we say, "No, not in that way; come *this*way, to Kṛṣṇa consciousness, and you'll find real happiness," they laugh.

Devotee: What about the scientists, Śrīla Prabhupāda? They're very inquisitive; they're trying to find the cause of the material world.

Śrīla Prabhupāda: Yes, we give them credit for that. But they are looking for the cause of this world in the wrong place. And when they're given correct information they do not take it. We say to the scientists, "You are searching for the cause of the world? Here is Kṛṣṇa, the original source of everything." But they will not accept Him. That is their foolishness.

Devotee: You were just saying that everyone is looking for happiness. But shouldn't that desire be purified? Shouldn't we give up all desire for happiness?

Śrīla Prabhupāda: No, no, happiness is life. How can you give it up?

Devotee: But if we desire happiness, we're being selfish –

Śrīla Prabhupāda: The problem is, you do not know that the ultimate goal of your selfishness is to realize Kṛṣṇa (*na te viduḥ svārtha-gatiṁ hi viṣṇum*). Everyone is self-interested, but no one knows how to fulfill his real self-interest.

Devotee: But isn't it better to give up ego altogether?

Śrīla Prabhupāda: Why? That is Māyāvāda [impersonalistic] philosophy. We want to make our ego purified. We want to understand, "I am a servant of Kṛṣṇa." That egoism is wanted – not that I make my egoism zero.

Devotee: Why do the impersonalists want to eradicate the ego?

Śrīla Prabhupāda: They are disappointed in life, so they think, "Let me finish my ego. Let me become zero." But egoism cannot be finished. Because you are an individual soul you will always have a sense of "I am." Now I am thinking I am Indian, you are thinking you are American, someone else is thinking he is Russian, and so on. But I am not Indian and you are not American: we are all part and parcel of Kṛṣṇa. We have to come to *this* egoism, the real egoism – that I am an eternal servant of Kṛṣṇa.

Devotee: Śrīla Prabhupāda, the materialistic scientists are so inquisitive. Why aren't they able to come to the point of understanding that Kṛṣṇa is the source of everything?

Śrīla Prabhupāda: Because they are envious of Him. They are unwilling to accept His instructions. You have to take direction from Kṛṣṇa. He says, "I am the goal of all knowledge. I am the destination. Come to Me." If you don't take this instruction you are unfortunate. You will be baffled in your attempt to acquire knowledge.

Devotee: Śrīla Prabhupāda, I saw a report that said atheism is much greater among scientists than among the people in general. And the scientists are very influential in the universities and high schools, in government, in industry –

Śrīla Prabhupāda: Therefore we say, "You blind leaders, you rascals, don't try to lead unless you are willing to take Kṛṣṇa's instructions." We must make our inquiries to Kṛṣṇa and take His direction. Then we'll be happy.

People Must Know the Aim of Life

A conversation between His Divine Grace
A. C. Bhaktivedanta Swami Prabhupāda and Allen Ginsberg

Instead of taking people to the highest, topmost stage – to the platform of inquiring about the Absolute – today's educators and leaders are merely giving facilities for how one can satisfy his or her senses.

~

Allen Ginsberg: Your Divine Grace, I'm trying to imagine ways by which this spiritual movement of yours can become more and more widespread and more and more acceptable to people. I don't know how. It's difficult for me to conceive that everybody in America will –

Śrīla Prabhupāda: Nothing is accepted by everybody.

Allen Ginsberg: I mean, it's hard to imagine a vast number of modern Americans living a life based on ancient Sanskrit yoga scriptures, totally vegetarian food offered to the Lord, and celibacy except for procreation. And many of us have been thinking, What form of religious practice, what form of simple meditation exercises, could be set forth in America that could be adopted by a great, great, great, great many people on a large scale? We haven't solved the problem.

One thing I've noticed is that your Kṛṣṇa temples have spread quite a bit and are firmly rooted and solidly based. There are a number of them now. So that really is a very solid root. And I think that will continue.

Śrīla Prabhupāda: Yes.

Allen Ginsberg: But I'm wondering, What future is there? What's the future of such a technical religious observance where you require so much sophistication in terms of diet – no flesh-eating, fasting from grains and beans twice a month, and sophistication in the daily ritual, like *ārati* and all the other things you've been teaching. How far can your movement spread by its very complexity?

Śrīla Prabhupāda: Yes, these practices are a little complex. The whole idea is to keep the devotees always engaged in Kṛṣṇa consciousness. That is the program. Gradually we shall introduce more and more of this Kṛṣṇa culture so that the devotees feel the richness and have no need to go outside Kṛṣṇa consciousness.

First you have to understand that we are trying to make people Kṛṣṇa conscious. So how can a person remain Kṛṣṇa conscious twenty-four hours a day? That is the program.

Allen Ginsberg: Well, the orthodox Jews have a heavy, complicated, moment-by-moment ritual daily existence for that same purpose. It is to keep them conscious of their religious nature. It has maintained a small group of Jews over the centuries as an integral unit, but has tended to disappear in the later generations now because modern life does not allow that much Kṛṣṇa consciousness or Jewish consciousness or religious consciousness and attention, act by act, throughout the day. So my question is, How far can total Kṛṣṇa devotion – act by act, all day – spread? How many people can that encompass in a place like America? Or are you intending only to get a few devotees, like several hundred or a thousand who will be solid and permanent?

Śrīla Prabhupāda: Yes, yes, that is my program because Kṛṣṇa consciousness is not possible for everyone. In the *Bhagavad-gītā* we learn *bahūnāṁ janmanām ante:* Only after many, many births can a person come to this full understanding. So at any one point in time it is not possible that a mass of people, a large number of people, will be able to fully grasp it. You see? *Bahūnāṁ janmanām ante jñānavān māṁ prapadyate:* "After many births, one who is at last in knowledge surrenders unto Me." Elsewhere in *Bhagavad-gītā* we find *manuṣyāṇāṁ sahasreṣu:* Out of millions of men, just one may inquire how to liberate himself from this material world. And out of millions of such liberated persons, just one may actually understand Kṛṣṇa.

So ordinarily, understanding Kṛṣṇa is not a very easy thing. That is why, when Kṛṣṇa came as Lord Caitanya five hundred years ago that He was so munificent that He gave us an easy process, the chanting of His holy names. Otherwise, Kṛṣṇa consciousness is not easy, because insofar as the Absolute Truth is concerned, Kṛṣṇa is the last word, and generally people are just like animals, absorbed in this temporary material world.

Out of many such materially illusioned persons one becomes interested in the scriptures. Now most persons – if they're at all attracted to the scriptures – are attracted to the ritualistic ceremonies recommended there for improving their economic condition. You see? People take up religion, or *dharma,* with the motive of *artha* – improving their economic position. *Artha* means money.

Why *artha*? Why do you want money? For *kāma,* your futile attempt to satisfy these temporary, illusory senses. And when you become frustrated by sense gratification you seek *mokṣa,* liberation, and supposedly merge with the Absolute. These four are going on. *Dharma, artha, kāma, mokṣa.*

But scriptures like *Śrīmad-Bhāgavatam* say that *dharma* is not meant for acquiring money, and that money is not meant for satisfying the senses, and that sense gratification should be accepted simply to maintain the body. That's all.

The real business of human life is *tattva-jijñāsā,* understanding the Absolute Truth. *Jīvasya tattva-jijñāsā na artho yaś ceha karmabhiḥ. Kāmasya nendriya-prītir lābho jīveta yāvatā. Kāmasya,* sense gratification, does not mean you have to increase the volume of sense gratification. No. *Jīveta yāvatā:* You have to accept sense gratification only insofar as you need it for living nicely. The real business of human life is *jīvasya tattva-jijñāsā.* Every human being should be inquisitive about the Absolute Truth. But you won't find the mass of people trying to come to this point. It is not possible. Don't expect it.

Allen Ginsberg: Your plan in America, then, is to set up centers so that those who are that concerned can pursue their studies and practice a ritual?

Śrīla Prabhupāda: Personally I have no ambition, but it is the mission of human life to come to this point. So there must at least be some center or institution that gives people this idea.

Of course, it is not that everyone will come. For instance, during my studies, at the University of Calcutta a professor's salary was thirteen or fourteen hundred dollars a month. Yet there were comparatively few students, and the fees collected from each student were at most thirty-six dollars per month. You see? But still, the classes had to be maintained because the ideal must be there.

So our mission is, the intelligent persons of the world must know that the aim of human life is not simply seeking after sense gratification. As the *Śrīmad-Bhāgavatam* says, *jīvasya tattva-jijñāsa:* Human life is meant for inquiring about the ultimate truth. That is the same thing that the *Vedānta* had said before, because the *Śrīmad-Bhāgavatam* is nothing but the explanation of *Vedānta.* So *Vedānta* says, *athāto brahma-jijñāsā:* This human form of life is meant for inquiring about Brahman, the Supreme Spirit. *Atha* means "now," and *athaḥ* means "after," signifying that now, after passing through untold lower species of life, when the soul at last rises to the level of civilized human life, at that time his business is to inquire about the Absolute Truth. What is the Absolute Truth? That is the whole Vedānta philosophy: What is the Absolute Truth? And as I have said, this same thing is explained in the *Bhāgavatam. Jīvasya tattva-jijñāsā. Jīvasya* means that for all living entities the main business is to inquire about the Absolute Truth.

Yet nowadays, thanks to so-called educators and leaders,

people are being misled. Instead of taking people to the highest, topmost stage – to the platform of inquiring about the Absolute – these misleaders are merely giving facilities for how you can satisfy your senses nicely.

Allen Ginsberg: OK. But now in America there is a feeling of spiritual bankruptcy due to our overemphasis on sense satisfaction. Everyone agrees.

Śrīla Prabhupāda: That feeling must be there. *Must* be there.

Allen Ginsberg: Everyone agrees that our civilization has come to the end of its possibilities materially. So everyone understands that. It's in the *New York Times* editorials as well as in the editorials of ISKCON journals. Everyone, then, is looking for an alternative to material extension.

Śrīla Prabhupāda: They should inquire about the Absolute Truth.

Hatha-yoga and the Bhagavad-gītā

Satyarāja Dāsa

Hatha-yoga, a practice that is now sweeping the West in its many forms and alterations, is an ancient practice. Few people realize that the traditional text on all forms of yoga is the Bhagavad-gītā, and for those interested in hatha-yoga, its sixth chapter is worth studying.

~

According to a 2003 survey by the Sporting Goods Manufacturers Association, an estimated 13.4 million Americans practice yoga,* and many more experiment with it every year. Yoga is everywhere – from Mumbai to Moscow to Monte Carlo. But while yoga is meant to bring one closer to God, many of today's *yogīs* have a different agenda, the most common being to keep their bodies in shape.

"They're not necessarily deeply spiritual, but looking more to do yoga as another form of exercise," says Jennifer McKinley, co-founder and general manager of Plank, a Charlestown, Massachusetts, maker of chic, high-end yoga mats, totes, and

* In 2009, this number has increased to 15 million.

other accessories. Launched in 2005, the company projects sales in the upcoming year that will rival that of Western exercise equipment.

In an increasingly secular world, we naturally want to adapt valuable ancient techniques for contemporary purposes, but yoga is losing its essence in the process.

Yoga is a science left to us by the sages of India. The word *yoga* literally means "to link up," and its implication, originally, was similar to the Latin root of the word *religion*, which means "to bind fast." Thus, yoga and religion are both meant to bring us to the same end: linking up and binding with God.

The Inner Message of the Yoga-sūtras

Today's *yogīs* might find it interesting that traditionally the preeminent text on yoga is *Bhagavad-gītā* – not Patañjali's famous *Yoga-sūtras*. But the *Gītā* is not your usual yoga text, full of difficult bodily poses and strenuous meditation techniques. Rather, it offers a practical outline for achieving the goal of yoga – linking with God – by encouraging the chanting of Kṛṣṇa's names, by teaching how to act under Kṛṣṇa's order, and by explaining the importance of doing one's duty in spiritual consciousness. These activities, properly performed under the guidance of an adept, allow one to bypass much of what is considered essential in conventional yoga.

And yet there is harmony between the *Gītā* and the *Yoga-sūtras*. For example, both Lord Kṛṣṇa and Patañjali indicate that we must transcend all false conceptions of "I" and develop love for God, which Patañjali calls *iśvara-praṇidhāna* ("dedication to God").

Patañjali wrote in the third century CE, but little is known about his life. His only surviving text, the *Yoga-sūtra*, would indicate that toned physical and mental tabernacles are helpful in the pursuit of spiritual truth. In fact, his major accomplishment is that he took age-old practices meant for improving the body and the mind and codified them for the benefit of spiritual practitioners.

But Patañjali's *Yoga-sūtras* merely hint at the truths illuminated in the *Bhagavad-gītā,* which might be considered the post-graduate study of Patañjali's work. Even so, Patañjali intended his method to be used for ultimate spiritual benefit, as some of his verses, especially later ones, clarify. Still, many yoga practitioners today use his method solely for physical and mental health because in the beginning of his work Patañjali mainly focuses on basic methods related to the body and the mind, without much spiritual commentary.

In *sūtra* 3.2, for example, we learn that *dhyāna,* or meditation, is the one-pointed continuous movement of the mind toward a single object. But Patañjali's technique can be used for concentration on any object, not just on God. And even though he tells his readers the point of his *sūtras* – to get closer to God – one may be tempted to use his methods for selfish ends, as he says later in the text. Ultimately, one-pointed concentration is for focusing on God, though it's not until one graduates to the *Bhagavad-gītā* that one clearly learns how to do this.

As Professor Edwin Bryant points out in his excellent article"Patañjali's Theistic Preference, Or, Was the Author of the Yoga-sutras a Vaishnava?"* Patañjali was trying to gear his diverse audience toward the worship of the Supreme Personality of Godhead, even if he was doing so in a roundabout way. Much like today, many forms of religion beleaguered the India of his time; practitioners worshiped numerous aspects of the Supreme. Consequently, he opted for a stepwise approach in his *Yoga-sūtras* that he believed would accommodate his varied audience.

Still, he asserts that the ultimate object of meditation is Īśvara, which means "controller" and generally refers to God. Although there are many controllers and many forms of the Godhead,

* Edwin F. Bryant, "Patañjali's Theistic Preference, Or, Was the Author of the Yoga-sutras a Vaishnava," in *The Journal of Vaishnava Studies,* volume 14, number 1 (Fall 2005).

Bhagavad-gītā (18.61) says that the ultimate *īśvara* is Kṛṣṇa. Other texts tell us this as well. Consider the ancient *Brahma-saṁhitā* (5.1):

īśvaraḥ-paramaḥ kṛṣṇaḥ
sac-cid-ānanda vigrahaḥ
anādir ādir govindaḥ
sarva-kāraṇa-kāraṇam

"Kṛṣṇa, who is known as Govinda, is the Supreme Godhead [*īśvaraḥ-paramaḥ*]. He has an eternal blissful spiritual body. He is the origin of all. He has no other origin, and He is the prime cause of all causes."

Patañjali advises his audience to choose an *iṣṭa-devatā*, a deity of their choice. His reasoning is transparent: He is trying to teach a method of meditation, and learning this method is easiest if one practices on a subject close to one's heart.

Did Patañjali have Kṛṣṇa in mind when he outlined the yoga process and its goal of love of God? For one learned in the Vedic literature, it is obvious that the answer is yes. In the words of Edwin Bryant,

> Kṛṣṇa is promoted by the *Gītā* as possessing all the qualities listed by Patañjali as pertaining to *īśvara*, namely, being transcendental to karma, of unsurpassed omniscience, teacher of the ancients, untouched by time, represented by *om*, and awarding enlightenment. Kṛṣṇa is not touched or bound by karma (*Gītā* 4.14, 9.9), and, in terms of omniscience, he is the beginning, middle, and end of all (10.20 & 32), who pervades the entire universe with but a single fragment of himself (10.42). Kṛṣṇa taught the ancients (here specified as Vivasvān, the sun god, who in turn imparted knowledge to Manu, the progenitor of mankind [4.1]) and is himself time (10.30 & 33; 11.32). He is also the syllable *om* (9.17). And, of course, Kṛṣṇa assures his devotees that he will free them from the snares of this world such that they attain the supreme goal (9.30–32; 10.10; 8.58). There is thus perfect compatibility

between Patañjali's unnamed *īśvara* and Kṛṣṇa as depicted in the *Gītā*.*

The commentarial tradition of the *Yoga-sūtras* bears this out. Patañjali's major commentators were Vyāsa (fifth century CE, not to be confused with the compiler of the Vedic literature), Vacaśpati Miśra (ninth century CE), Bhoja Rāja (eleventh century CE), and Vijñānabhikṣu (sixteenth century CE). All identify the *īśvara* of the *Yoga-sūtras* with Viṣṇu or Kṛṣṇa and show how the *Bhagavad-gītā* expresses the culmination of all Vedic wisdom relating to yoga.

The Gītā's Eight Limbs

The *Bhagavad-gītā* addresses all eight limbs of *rāja-yoga,* the form of yoga popular today as *aṣṭaṅga-yoga* or hatha-yoga.** For example, *yama,* the first limb, consists of five ethical principles: truthfulness, continence, nonviolence, noncovetousness, and abstention from stealing. These fundamental disciplines of yoga are mentioned in the *Gītā,* as is *niyama,* the second limb, which consists of things like worship, cleanliness, contentment, austerity, and self-reflection.

Now, the third limb of Patañjali's method, *asana,* is less obvious in the *Gītā.* The term *asana* appears infrequently on Lord Kṛṣṇa's lips. But when it does, it refers to "the place where one sits for spiritual practice." The *Gītā* does not give tips on sitting postures. Its sixth chapter, though, comes close. Verses 11 and 12 state: "To practice yoga, one should go to a secluded place and should lay *kuśa* grass on the ground and then cover it with a deerskin and a soft cloth. The seat [*āsana*] should be neither too high nor too low and should be situated in a sacred place. The yogi should then sit

* Ibid.

** This has been pointed out by my friend Graham Schweig, professor of religion at Christopher Newport University, Virginia. Much of the material in this article on the eight limbs of yoga comes from his interviews and lectures.

on it very firmly and practice yoga to purify the heart by controlling his mind, senses, and activities and fixing the mind on one point."

Here Kṛṣṇa uses the word *asana* in a general rather than technical sense. He is talking about sitting to focus the mind.

It's easy to lose focus, and that's basically Arjuna's argument against hatha-yoga. In fact, Patañjali himself identifies nine obstacles on the path: doubt, disease, lethargy, mental laziness, false perception, lack of enthusiasm, clinging to sense enjoyment, lack of concentration, and losing concentration. His commentators list several others as well, including inordinate attraction to yogic powers, a misconceived view of meditation, oversimplification of yoga's eight limbs, and irregularity of practice. All of these problems are traceable to the difficult nature of Patañjali's method and are why Arjuna views hatha-yoga as virtually impossible. By the end of the sixth chapter he denounces it as too difficult. Kṛṣṇa agrees, telling Arjuna that the ultimate yogi always thinks of God. He further tells him that such meditation is real yoga, implying that using one's body and mind in Kṛṣṇa's service is the perfect *asana*.

The *Gītā* also discusses *prāṇāyāma*, or breath control, the fourth limb. Kṛṣṇa says that *yogīs* can use the incoming and outgoing breath as offerings to Him. He speaks about dedicating one's life breath to God. He tells Arjuna that His devotees' *praṇa*, or air of life, is meant for God and that Arjuna should use it "to come to Me." In fact, if one follows Arjuna's example and offers every breath to Kṛṣṇa – by speaking about Him, chanting His glories, and living for Him – there is little need for breath control as delineated in Patañjali's *sūtras*. Breathing for God is the essence of *prāṇāyāma*. Srila Prabhupada writes, "Chanting of the holy name of the Lord and dancing in ecstasy are also considered *prāṇāyāma*." (*Śrīmad-Bhāgavatam* 4.23.8, purport)

The fifth limb of yoga, *pratyāhāra*, deals with the withdrawal of the senses, a major subject in the *Bhagavad-gītā*. In the second chapter Kṛṣṇa tells Arjuna that the yogi withdraws his senses from sense objects, "as the tortoise draws its limbs within the shell." Taken superficially, this might seem to suggest full renunciation of the world. But that's not what Kṛṣṇa is getting at. Rather, as other verses make clear, He's teaching how to renounce the fruits of work, not work itself, and how to be in the world but not of it. In other words, His teaching centers on how to withdraw one's attachment to sense objects for personal enjoyment. He instructs us to use these same objects in the service of God. That is true *pratyāhāra*.

The Upper Limbs

And then we have the culmination of yoga practice – the last three limbs of *rāja-yoga: dhāraṇa, dhyāna,* and *samādhi,* or concentration, meditation, and complete absorption.

While *yama* and *niyama* are preliminary steps, these three are called *saṁyama,* "the perfect discipline" or "perfect practice." *Bhagavad-Gītā* speaks extensively of these upper limbs. For example, Lord Kṛṣṇa states, "Just fix your mind upon Me, the Supreme Personality of Godhead, and engage all your intelligence in Me. Thus you will live in Me always, without a doubt. My dear Arjuna, O winner of wealth, if you cannot fix your mind upon Me without deviation, then follow the regulative principles of *bhakti-yoga* [*abhyāsa-yogena*]. In this way develop a desire to attain Me." (*Gītā* 12.8–9)

The process of Kṛṣṇa consciousness is practical *dhāraṇa,* or spiritual concentration. By seeing paintings of Kṛṣṇa, we use our sense of sight for God; by chanting and hearing we engage the tongue and the ear; by offering incense to Kṛṣṇa we engage our sense of smell. All the senses can help us engage in *dhāraṇa,* leading to advanced states of meditation and absorption.

The holy name is particularly effective in this regard. That's why Kṛṣṇa says that of austerities He is the austerity of *japa,* private chanting, especially while counting on beads. Chanting is the king of austerities because by chanting we can easily reach the goal of yoga. It all comes together in the practice of *japa* because by chanting God's names we focus on Him with our voice, ears, and sense of touch. And *kirtana,* congregational chanting, not only takes us to deep levels of absorption but engages the senses of onlookers as well. In *sūtra* 1.28, Patañjali, too, promotes "constant chanting."

Overall, Patañjali's ambivalence might appear confusing. When he first mentions *īśvara-praṇidhāna,* dedication to God, he presents it as optional, while later he gives it far more attention, with six verses elaborating on the nature of *īśvara.* In the beginning he seems to allow variance in the object of meditation (1.34–38), but ultimately he advises the yogi to focus on *īśvara,* who in Patañjali's words is the "special supreme soul" who alone can bestow *samādhi,* yogic perfection.

Patañjali says in *sūtra* 3.3 that *samādhi* occurs when the object of your meditation appears in your heart of hearts without any competitors or distractions. You have no other interest, as if your intrinsic nature loses meaning.

The *Bhagavad-gītā* makes it clearer. In *samādhi* your intrinsic nature doesn't lose meaning. Rather, it takes on new meaning: You see yourself in relation to Kṛṣṇa. You are now His devotee; He's the focus of your life. That state of perfect and total absorption is called Kṛṣṇa consciousness.

Chapter Two

Karma & Reincarnation

Reincarnation Explained

His Divine Grace A. C. Bhaktivedanta Swami Prabhupāda

Remembrances of past lives can be fascinating, but the real goal of understanding reincarnation is to become free from the painful cycle of birth and death. In a lecture delivered in London in August of 1973, Śrīla Prabhupāda warns, "This is not a very good business – to die and take birth again. We know that when we die we'll have to enter again into the womb of a mother – and nowadays mothers are killing the children in the womb."

~

The *Bhagavad-gītā* states,

dehino 'smin yathā dehe
kaumāraṁ yauvanaṁ jarā
tathā dehāntara-prāptir
dhīras tatra na muhyati

"As the embodied soul continuously passes, in this body, from boyhood to youth, and then to old age, the soul similarly passes into another body at death. A sober person is not bewildered by such a change."

Usually people cannot understand this simple verse. Therefore Kṛṣṇa says, *dhīras tatra na muhyati:* "Only a sober person can understand." But what is the difficulty? How plainly Kṛṣṇa has explained things!

There are three stages of life. The first, *kaumāram*, lasts until one is fifteen years old. Then, from the sixteenth year, one begins youthful life, *yauvanam*. Then, after the fortieth or fiftieth year, one becomes an old man, *jarā*. So those who are *dhīra* – sober-headed, cool-headed – can understand: "I have changed my body. I remember how I was playing and jumping when I was a boy. Then I became a young man and I enjoyed my life with friends and family. Now I am an old man. When this body dies I shall enter a new body."

In the previous verse Kṛṣṇa said to Arjuna, "All of us – you, Me, and all the soldiers and kings who are present here – we existed in the past, we are existing now, and we shall continue to exist in the future." This is Kṛṣṇa's statement. But rascals will say, "How was I existing in the past? I was born only in such-and-such a year. Before that I was not existing. At the present time I am existing. That's all right. But as soon as I die I'll not exist." But Kṛṣṇa says, "You, Me, all of us – we were existing, we are still existing, and we shall continue to exist." Is that wrong? No, it is a fact. Before our birth we existed in a different body, and after death we shall continue to exist in a different body. This is to be understood.

For example, seventy years ago I was a boy, then I became a young man, and now I have become an old man. My body has changed, but I, the proprietor of the body, exist unchanged. Is this difficult to understand? *Dehino 'smin yathā dehe. Dehinaḥ* means "the proprietor of the body," and dehe means "in the body." The body is changing, but the soul, the proprietor of the body, remains unchanged.

Anyone can understand that his body has changed. In the next life the body will also change. But we may not remember; that is another thing. In my last life, what was my body? I do not remember. Forgetfulness is our nature, but our forgetting something does not mean it did not take place. No. In my childhood I did so many things I no longer remember, but my father and mother remember them. So forgetting does not mean that things did not take place.

Similarly, death simply means I have forgotten what I was in my past life. Otherwise I, as spirit soul, have no death. Suppose I change my clothes. In my boyhood I wore certain clothes, in my youth I wore different clothes. Now, in my old age, as a *sannyāsī* [renunciant], I wear different clothes again. The clothes may change, but that does not mean that the owner of the clothes is dead and gone. No. This is a simple explanation of transmigration of the soul.

Also, all of us are individuals. There is no question of merging together. Every one of us is an individual. God is an individual, and we are also individuals. *Nityo nityānāṁ cetanaś cetanānām* (*Kaṭha Upaniṣad* 2.2.13): "Of all the eternal, conscious, individual persons, one is supreme." The difference is that God never changes His body, but we change our bodies in the material world. When we go to the spiritual world, there is no more change of body. Just as Kṛṣṇa has His *sac-cid-ānanda-vigraha,* eternal form of bliss and knowledge, so when we go back to Godhead we will also get such a body. The difference is that even when Kṛṣṇa comes to the material world He does not change His body. Therefore one of His names is Acyuta, "He who never falls."

Kṛṣṇa never changes. He never falls down because He is the controller of *māyā,* the material energy. We are controlled by the material energy, and Kṛṣṇa is the controller of the material energy. That is the difference between Kṛṣṇa and us. And not only does He control the material energy, but He controls the spiritual energy also – He controls *all* energies. Everything we see, everything manifested, is Kṛṣṇa's energy. Just as heat and light are the energies of the sun, so everything manifested is made of the energies of Kṛṣṇa.

There are many energies, but they have been divided into three principal ones: the external energy, the internal energy, and the marginal energy. We living entities are the marginal energy. Marginal means that we may remain under the influence of the external energy or we may remain under the influence of the internal energy – as we like. We have that independence. After speaking the *Bhagavad-gītā* Kṛṣṇa says to Arjuna, *yathecchasi tathā kuru:* "Whatever you like you can do." Kṛṣṇa gives Arjuna his independence. He does not force one to surrender. That is not good. Something forced will not stand. For example, we advise our students, "Rise early in the morning." This is our advice. We do not force anyone. Of course, we may force someone once or twice, but if he does not practice it, force will be useless.

Similarly, Kṛṣṇa does not force anyone to leave this material world. All conditioned souls are under the influence of the external, or material, energy. Kṛṣṇa comes here to deliver us from the clutches of the material energy. Because we are part and parcel of Kṛṣṇa we are all directly Kṛṣṇa's sons. And if a son is in difficulty the father also suffers, although indirectly. Suppose the son has become a madman – or, like nowadays, a hippy. The father is sorry: "Oh, my son is living like a wretch." So the father is not happy. Similarly, the conditioned souls in this material world are suffering so much, living like wretches and rascals. Kṛṣṇa is not happy. Therefore He personally comes to teach us how to return to Him (*yadā yadā hi dharmasya glānir bhavati ... tad-ātmānaṁ sṛjāmy aham*).

When Kṛṣṇa comes He comes in His original form, but unfortunately we misunderstand Kṛṣṇa and consider Him one of us. In one sense He *is* one of us because He is the father and we are His sons. But He's the chief: *nityo nityānāṁ cetanaś cetanānām.* He's more powerful than us. He's the most powerful, the supreme powerful. We have a little power, but Kṛṣṇa has infinite power. That is the difference between Kṛṣṇa and us. We cannot be equal to God. Nobody can be equal to Kṛṣṇa or greater than Him. Everyone is under Kṛṣṇa. *Ekale īśvara kṛṣṇa, āra saba bhṛtya:* Everyone is Kṛṣṇa's servant; Kṛṣṇa is the only master. *Bhoktāraṁ yajña-tapasāṁ sarva-loka-maheśvaram:* "I am the only enjoyer; I am the proprietor," Kṛṣṇa says. And that is a fact.

So although we change bodies Kṛṣṇa does not change His. We

should understand this. The proof is that Kṛṣṇa remembers past, present, and future. In the fourth chapter of *Bhagavad-gītā* you'll find that Kṛṣṇa says He spoke the philosophy of *Bhagavad-gītā* to the sun god some 120,000,000 years ago. How does Kṛṣṇa remember? Because He does not change His body. We forget things because we change our body at every moment. That is a medical fact. The corpuscles of our blood change at every second and the body changes imperceptibly. That is why the father and mother of a growing child do not notice how his body is changing. A third person, if he comes after some time and sees that the child has grown, says, "Oh, the child has grown so big." But the father and mother have not noticed that he has grown so big because they are always seeing him and the changes are taking place imperceptibly, at every moment. So our body is always changing, but I, the soul, the proprietor of the body, do not change. This is to be understood.

We are all individual, eternal souls, but because our body changes we suffer birth, death, old age, and disease. The Kṛṣṇa consciousness movement is meant to get us out of this changing condition. "Since I am eternal, how can I come to the permanent position?" That should be our question. Everyone wants to live eternally; nobody wants to die. If I come before you with a revolver and say, "I am going to kill you," you will immediately cry out because you do not want to die. This is not a very good business – to die and take birth again. It is very troublesome. This we all know subconsciously. We know that when we die we'll have to enter again into the womb of a mother – and nowadays mothers are killing the children in the womb. Then again another mother ... The process of accepting another body again and again is long and very troublesome. In our subconscious we remember all this trouble, and therefore we do not want to die.

So our question should be this: "If I am eternal, why have I been put into this temporary life?" This is an intelligent question and this is our real problem. But rascals set aside this problem. They think about how to eat, sleep, have sex, and defend. Even if you eat and sleep nicely, ultimately you have to die. The problem of death remains, but they don't care about this real problem. They are very alert to solve their temporary problems, which are not actually problems at all. The birds and beasts also eat, sleep, have sexual intercourse, and defend themselves. They know how to do all these things, even without the human beings' education and so-called civilization. So these things are not our real problems. The real problem is that we do not want to die but death takes place. This is our real problem.

But the rascals do not know it. They are always busy with temporary problems. For example, suppose there is severe cold. This is a problem. We have to search out a nice coat or a fireplace, and if these are not available we are in distress. Severe cold is a problem. But it is a temporary problem. Severe cold, winter, has come, and it will go. It is not a permanent problem. My permanent problem is that because of ignorance I am taking birth, I am accepting disease, I am accepting old age, and I am accepting death. These are my real problems. Therefore Kṛṣṇa says *janma-mṛtyu-jarā-vyādhi-duḥkha-doṣānudarśanam:* Those who are actually in knowledge see these four problems – birth, death, old age, and disease.

Now, Kṛṣṇa says, *dhīras tatra na muhyati:* "A sober person is not perplexed at the time of death." If you prepare yourself for death, why should you be perplexed? For example, if in your childhood and boyhood you prepare yourself nicely, if you become educated, then you will get a nice job, a nice situation, and be happy. Similarly, if you prepare yourself in this life for going back home, back to Godhead, then where is your perplexity at the time of death? There is no perplexity. You'll know, "I am going to Kṛṣṇa. I am going back home, back to Godhead. Now I'll not have to change material bodies; I'll have my spiritual body. Now I shall play with Kṛṣṇa and dance with Kṛṣṇa and eat with Kṛṣṇa." This is Kṛṣṇa consciousness: to prepare yourself for the next life.

Sometimes a dying man cries out, because according to karma those who are very, very sinful see horrible scenes at the time of death. The sinful man knows he is going to accept some abominable type of body. But those who are pious, the devotees, die without anxiety. Foolish people say, "You devotees are dying and the nondevotees are also dying. What is the difference?" There is a difference. A cat catches her kitten in her mouth, and she also catches a mouse with her mouth. Superficially we may see that the cat has caught both the mouse and the kitten in the same way, but there are differences in the method of catching. The kitten is feeling pleasure: "Oh, my mother is carrying me," and the mouse is feeling death: "Oh, now I'm going to die." This is the difference. So although both devotees and nondevotees die, there is a difference of feeling at the time of death – just like the kitten and the mouse. Don't think that both of them are dying in the same way. The bodily process may be the same, but the mental situation is different.

In *Bhagavad-gītā* Kṛṣṇa says,

janma karma ca me divyam
evaṁ yo vetti tattvataḥ
tyaktvā dehaṁ punar janma
naiti mām eti so 'rjuna

If you simply try to understand Kṛṣṇa you can go to Him at the time of death. Everything about Kṛṣṇa is divine, transcendental. Kṛṣṇa's activities, Kṛṣṇa's appearance, Kṛṣṇa's worship, Kṛṣṇa's temple, Kṛṣṇa's glories – everything is transcendental. If one understands these things, or even *tries* to understand, then one becomes liberated from the process of birth and death. This is what Kṛṣṇa says. So become very serious to understand Kṛṣṇa, and remain in Kṛṣṇa consciousness. Then these problems – birth, death, old age, and disease – will be solved automatically and very easily.

A *dhīra,* a sober person, will think, "I want to live eternally. Why does death take place? I want to live a healthy life. Why does disease come? I don't want to become an old man. Why does old age come?" *Janma-mṛtyu-jarā-vyādhi.* These are real problems. One can solve these problems simply by taking to Kṛṣṇa consciousness, simply by understanding Kṛṣṇa. And to help one understand Kṛṣṇa the *Bhagavad-gītā* is there, very nicely explained. So make your life successful. Understand that you are not the body. You are embodied, but you are not the body. A bird may live in a cage, but the cage is not the bird. Foolish persons take care of the cage and not the bird, and the bird suffers starvation. We are suffering from spiritual starvation. Therefore nobody is happy in the material world. Spiritual starvation. That is why you see that in an opulent country like America – where there is enough food, enough homes, enough material enjoyment – still the young people are not satisfied. They are suffering from spiritual starvation. Materially you may be opulent, but if you starve spiritually you cannot be happy.

A spiritual rejuvenation is required. You must realize *ahaṁ brahmāsmi:* "I am not this body; I am *brahman,* spirit soul." Then you'll be happy. *Brahma-bhūtaḥ prasannātmā na śocati na kāṅkṣati samaḥ sarveṣu bhūteṣu*. Then there will be equality, fraternity, brotherhood. Otherwise it is all bogus – simply high-sounding words. There cannot be equality, fraternity, and so on without Kṛṣṇa consciousness. Come to the spiritual platform; then you will see everyone equally. Otherwise you will think, "I am a human being with hands and legs, and the cow has no hands and legs, so let me kill the cow and eat it." Why? What right do you have to kill an animal? You have no vision of equality for want of Kṛṣṇa consciousness. Therefore in this material world, so-called education, culture, fraternity – all these are bogus. Kṛṣṇa consciousness is the right subject matter to be studied. Then society will be happy. Otherwise not. Thank you very much.

Do We Live More Than Once?

Jayādvaita Swami

The case history of a little girl from West Bengal suggests she remembered a life she had lived before.

~

When Sukla Gupta was a year and a half old and barely able to talk, she used to cradle a pillow or a block of wood in her arms and address it as "Minu." Minu, she said, was her daughter.

And if you believe the story Sukla gradually told over the next three years, Minu actually was her daughter – but in a previous life.

Sukla, the daughter of a railway worker in Kampa, a village in West Bengal, India, was one of those rare children whose testimony and behavior give evidence for the theory that your personality survives the death of your body and travels on to live in another body. This is the theory of reincarnation.

For some five hundred million of the world's people, reincarnation is more than a theory – it is a fact, a given, a part of their everyday understanding. It's what they've learned from their scriptures, and what generations of their forefathers have believed for thousands of years.

Aside from people in the East, Western philosophers at least as far back as Plato have found it reasonable to believe that our souls have lived before, in other bodies, other lives, and will live again in new ones.

If we have lived other lives, you might ask, why don't we remember them? But memory is a tricky thing. We're lucky if we can remember where we've put our car keys. So even if past lives are a fact, it's not surprising we can't remember them.

But at least a few of us apparently can.

Sukla talked not only about her daughter, Minu, but also about her husband, "the father of Minu" (a good Hindu wife avoids speaking of her husband by name). She also talked about his younger brothers Khetu and Karuna. They all lived, she said, at Rathtala in Bhatpara.

Sukla's family, the Guptas, knew Bhatpara slightly – it was a city about eleven miles south – but they had never heard of a place called Rathtala, nor of the people Sukla had named. Yet Sukla developed a desire to go there, and she insisted that if her parents didn't take her she would go alone.

What do you do when your daughter starts speaking that way? Sri K. N. Sen Gupta, Sukla's father, talked about the matter with some friends. He also mentioned it to one of his railway co-workers, Sri S. C. Pal, an assistant station master. Sri Pal lived near Bhatpara and had two cousins there. Through these cousins he learned that Bhatpara indeed had a district called Rathtala. He also learned of a man there named Khetu. Khetu had had a sister-in-law named Mana who had died several years before, in 1948, leaving behind an infant daughter named Minu.

Sri Sen Gupta decided to investigate further.

The story of Sukla is one of nearly two thousand in the files of Dr. Ian Stevenson, Carlson Professor of Psychiatry at the University of Virginia. Over the past two decades, Dr. Stevenson has gathered reports of people in various parts of the world who showed evidence suggesting that they had remembered past lives. About one thousand three hundred of these cases Dr. Stevenson has investigated personally, including the case of Sukla. [Among

Dr. Stevenson's books are *Twenty Cases Suggestive of Reincarnation* (in which the case of Sukla appears) and the multivolume *Cases of the Reincarnation Type.* Both are published by the University of Virginia.]

When someone seems to have truthful memories of a former life, Dr. Stevenson interviews him, the people around him, and if possible the people of the life apparently remembered, looking for a more ordinary, normal way to explain things. He looks for fraud. He looks for stories with holes in them and conflicting, unreliable reports. But sometimes, as in the case of Sukla, normal explanations just don't seem to fit.

After Sri Sen Gupta learned of the family in Rathtala, he decided to yield to Sukla's desire to go there. With the consent of that family, he arranged for a visit. Sukla said that she could show the way to the house.

So in 1959, when Sukla was a little more than five, Sri Sen Gupta and five other members of his family journeyed with her to Bhatpara. When they arrived, Sukla took the lead. Avoiding various possible wrong turns, she brought them straight to the house of Sri Amritalal Chakravarty, allegedly her father-in-law in her past life.

As the party approached, Śrī Chakravarty happened to be out on the street. When Sukla saw him, she looked down shyly, following the usual custom for a young woman in the presence of an older male relative.

But when Sukla went to enter the house she was confused. She didn't seem to know the right entrance. Her confusion, however, made sense: after the death of Mana, the woman whose life Sukla seemed to remember, the entrance had been moved from the main street to an alley on the side.

And the party soon found that Sukla recognized not only the house but also the people in it, including those she said were her mother-in-law, her brothers-in-law, her husband, and her daughter.

Fraud? When some Hollywood movie actress claims she

remembers a past life as the Queen of Persia, that's likely the right explanation. But here we're dealing with a little village girl. She starts talking about a past life as soon as she's old enough to speak. She knows all sorts of things about people neither she nor her family has ever met. Careful investigators find no evidence of fraud and no normal way the girl could have learned what she knows. And her behavior actually fits the story of her previous life.

Inside Amritalal Chakravarty's house, Sukla found herself in a room with some twenty or thirty people. But when she was asked, "Can you point out your husband?" she correctly indicated Sri Haridhana Chakravarty. Following the proper Hindu etiquette, she identified him as "Minu's father."

Sukla and Haridhana Chakravarty were to meet again several times, and Sukla always longed for these meetings. When he was to visit her house, Sukla told her family to make him a meal with prawns and *buli.* She said that this was his favorite food. Her family did what she said and later found that she had chosen correctly.

Sukla behaved toward Haridhana Chakravarty like a perfect Hindu wife. After he ate his meal, she would eat whatever food was left on his plate, as a devoted Hindu wife would do. But she never ate food from the plate of anyone else.

To try to account normally for this kind of behavior, another explanation sometimes put forward is what is technically known as cryptomnesia, "hidden memory."

Psychologists know that our minds record more than we consciously remember. Under hypnosis, an old man may vividly describe his fifth birthday party, an event for which his normal consciousness has lost all the details. Or he may recall exactly what he read in a long-forgotten book some thirty years before.

So the hypothesis of cryptomnesia supposes that what appear to be memories of a past life are merely memories of something one has heard or read and consciously forgotten.

This may in fact be the best explanation for many of the "past-life regressions" now becoming popular in journeys through hypnosis. Asked by a hypnotist to go back to a past life, a subject obediently searches his forgotten memories and uses them to dramatize an entirely fictitious "former existence."

In one notable case, back in 1906, a clergyman's daughter under hypnosis told vividly of a past life in the court of King Richard II. She poured out a wealth of details, nearly all of which proved to be true, even though many of them were so obscure that they sent researchers hunting through scholarly English histories the girl was most unlikely to have read. Finally, however, it came out that all these detailed facts appeared in a novel, *Countess Maud,* that the girl had read when twelve years old and had entirely forgotten.

But the case of Sukla, remember, is that of a girl less than five years old. And her recollections of a past life took place not under hypnosis but as part of her usual waking consciousness.

We may suppose that she gathered these memories normally, but this is only a supposition – there's no evidence of any normal channel through which these memories could have come.

Moreover, Sukla didn't just recall information – she actually recognized people, people who in this life were complete strangers.

She recognized Mana's mother-in-law from a group of thirty people. She pointed out Mana's brother-in-law Kshetranath, and she knew his nickname, "Khetu." She also recognized another brother-in-law, whose nickname was "Kuti." But she identified him correctly by his given name, Karuna, which even his neighbors didn't know.

She also said that her first child, a son, had died while still an infant. This was true for the life of Mana. And Sukla tearfully recognized Mana's daughter, Minu, and showered her with affection.

If there isn't a normal way to explain this, maybe there is some other less-than-normal explanation. Perhaps Sukla learned about Mana and her family through extrasensory perception.

Research has clearly shown that there is such a thing as ESP.

In rigidly controlled experiments, the late Dr. J. B. Rhine and other parapsychologists have shown persuasive evidence for telepathy (the ability to read another person's thoughts) and clairvoyance (the ability to perceive objects and events without using your senses). And experiments have shown that both telepathy and clairvoyance can work over long distances.

But although ESP may seem hard to believe, to use it to explain a case like Sukla's you'd have to believe in super-ESP. Not only would this five-year-old girl have to have incredible psychic powers, but she would have to use them to zero in on a specific family in an unfamiliar city and learn intimate details of their lives. She'd also have to be selective about what her psychic radar picked out, so that she'd "remember," for example, the location of her father-in-law's house but be unaware that the entrance had changed, since that took place after Mana's death.

And then, for purposes yet unknown, Sukla would have to mold what she'd learned into a drama in which she immersed herself in the role of the departed Mana.

Most dramatic in Sukla's case were her strong maternal emotions towards Minu. From babyhood Sukla had played at cradling Minu in her arms, and after she learned to talk she spoke of her longing to be with Minu. Sukla's meeting with Minu had all the appearances of a tearful reunion between mother and daughter.

Once Mana's cousin tested Sukla by falsely telling her that Minu, away in Rathtala, was ill with a high fever. Sukla began to weep, and it took a long time for her family to reassure her that Minu was actually well.

Minu was twelve and Sukla only five. And Minu had grown taller, so Sukla said, "I am small." "But within this limitation," Dr. Stevenson says, "Sukla exactly acted the role of a mother towards a beloved daughter."

And after taking other possibilities into account, Dr. Stevenson cautiously submits that perhaps we can understand this case most suitably by accepting that Sukla *was* Minu's mother, just as she thought herself to be.

This brings us back to the idea of reincarnation. Of course, science can never "prove" that reincarnation is a fact. For that matter, science can never actually "prove" anything. Through science, all we can do is gather data as carefully as possible and then try to explain them in the most consistent and reasonable way. And when the body of data grows, our explanations have to grow with it.

Because of the work of Dr. Stevenson and other researchers, we now find ourselves facing a considerable body of data suggesting that reincarnation is a fact.

Yet science doesn't go far in making clear to us what that fact is.

How does it work? Why does it happen? Who or what is reincarnated? How long do you have to wait between births? Does it happen to all of us, or only a few?

Perhaps one day scientific investigation will come up with answers to these questions. For now, investigators can do little more than gather data and speculate.

So if reincarnation happens to everyone, you can figure on going through it yourself – perhaps countless times – before science even begins to figure out what's going on.

The members of the Hare Kṛṣṇa movement, however, have a different way of getting understanding.

Faced with an unfamiliar but complex machine, you can observe it and try to figure out how it works. You can monkey with the thing and see what happens. You can call in friends and get their ideas of what the pulleys, gears, and wires are supposed to do. And maybe you'll figure it out. Maybe.

But the sure way to understand the machine is to learn about it from the person who built it.

So the direct way to understand the machinery of the universe – including the subtle machinery of reincarnation – is to learn about it from the person behind it.

That there's a person behind this machine comes near to being self-evident. It's axiomatic. Of course, you're free to reject the axiom. But then you're faced with the task of explaining how things "just happen" to work, how everything in the universe "just happens" to fit together, without any intelligence behind it.

You can say that everything happens "by chance" (which is no explanation at all). You can ascribe everything to some ultimate impersonal force that, without intelligence or volition, gets everything to work. Or you can sidestep the problem by saying that everything we see is merely an illusion: "The machine doesn't even exist." But then you have to explain where the illusion comes from. And that puts you right back where you started.

It's easier and more reasonable, therefore, to assume that behind the workings of the cosmic machine is the supreme intelligence, or the Supreme Person. This is the entity to whom we refer when we use the name Kṛṣṇa.

For various excellent reasons, we accept that the book known as *Bhagavad-gītā* conveys the words of Kṛṣṇa Himself. So the members of the Hare Kṛṣṇa movement, like devotees of Kṛṣṇa for thousands of years, learn about reincarnation from the words of *Bhagavad-gītā*.

In *Bhagavad-gītā* Kṛṣṇa tells us that reincarnation happens to everyone. "For one who is born," Kṛṣṇa says, "death is certain. And after death one is sure to be born again."

Kṛṣṇa compares this journey through a succession of lives to the changing of clothing. Your true self – your "soul" – is eternal, but it goes through temporary bodies, one after another.

So it's not that you "become a different person" when you change from one body to the next, any more than you become somebody else when you change your clothes or when you grow from a child to an adult. You're always the same you, but you watch your body and mind transform from those of a child to those of a youth and then those of an old man or woman. Similarly, Kṛṣṇa says, death is but a transformation from one body to the next.

Still, death is like nothing else under the sun. It's the biggest jolt there is. And when we get to the other side, we forget all about what we were doing in the life before, just as a person who falls asleep forgets what he was doing during the day and then wakes up and forgets about his dreams.

In rare cases, though, memories may persist, as they apparently did with Sukla Gupta. Sukla remembered her home, her family, and her clothing from the previous life. She talked about the three *saris* she used to wear, especially the two made of fine Benares silk. And when she visited what she said was her former home, she found the *saris* stored in a trunk, jumbled in with clothing that belonged to others. She picked out the three saris she said were hers, and in fact they had been Mana's.

Sukla talked about a brass pitcher in a particular room of the house. When she visited, the pitcher was still there. The room had been Mana's bedroom, and Sukla correctly showed where Mana's cot had previously been. And tears came to Sukla's eyes when she saw her old sewing machine, the one that Mana had previously used.

But even if we forget our previous lives, they influence our present one nonetheless. The *Bhagavad-gītā* says that it's what we've done and thought in our past lives that determines what kind of body we start out with in this one. And by what we do in this life, we're paving our way to the next.

According to the *Bhagavad-gītā,* we've already been through many millions of lifetimes, and it's possible we'll have to go through many millions more. Some of them may be in human bodies and some in the bodies of lower forms like animals and trees.

But by spiritual realization, the *Gītā* says, we can free ourselves from spinning through this endless cycle of incarnations. We can transcend material existence altogether and return to our eternal home, in the spiritual world with Kṛṣṇa.

The *Gītā* points out that each of us is eternal and Kṛṣṇa is also eternal. And our real existence is our eternal life with Kṛṣṇa.

As we travel from lifetime to lifetime, we can't hold on to anything, for everything in the material world is temporary. Everything material fades away and ultimately loses meaning.

The *Bhagavad-gītā* therefore advises that now, in this present human life, we should fully use our energy and time for spiritual realization.

By the time Sukla was seven, her memories of her former life had begun to fade. Yet even before the memories left her, that life was already gone. Sukla had mentioned that in her former life, as Mana, she'd had two cows and a parrot. But after Mana's death the cows had died, and the parrot had flown away.

Do Bad Things Happen to Good People?

Ravīndra Svarūpa Dāsa

A rabbi's best-selling book proposes a radical solution to the problem of evil. Does it work? This article was written when the book, When Bad Things Happen to Good People, *first appeared, in 2004.*

~

About five years ago, when we were having an altar installed in our new temple, the overseer from the marble company would regularly bring his seven-year-old son along to watch. The boy was very handsome, with jet-black hair and pale skin and long, dark eyelashes. He was well-behaved and always seemed in a good humor even though he could hardly walk at all. I never saw him take more than a few steps, leaning on a wall and straining his torso with an awkward twisting motion and then swinging forward a leg clamped into a large, clumsy brace.

The boy had been born crippled. While he was cheerful despite that, his father was not. His father was an angry man. "When that boy was born I stopped going to church," he told me once, as he knelt on our altar putting grout between the marble slabs. "I never did anything bad enough to deserve this. Sure, I'm not a saint, but I don't deserve this. And even if I did, what could *he* have done?"

The aggrieved father, an unsophisticated marble contractor, was raising a problem that has long preoccupied Western religious thinkers, so much so that it has created a special discipline called *theodicy*, a branch of theology concerned with justifying the ways of God to man. Theodicy deals with what is usually called "the problem of evil." St. Augustine cast it into the form of a dilemma: "Either God cannot or God will not eliminate evil from the world. If He cannot, He is not all-powerful; if He will not. He is not all-good." This formulation makes the logic of the problem clear: to show that the existence of a world with evil in it is compatible with the existence of a God who is *both* all-powerful *and* all-good. To deny either one of these attributes would easily explain evil, but orthodox theologians have always considered that unacceptable.

Those who find the problem of evil intractable usually deny the existence of God outright rather than settle for a God limited either in power or goodness. Would such a finite being really qualify to be called "God"? Would he be worthy of our worship?

Although philosophers and theologians have left us a huge body of technical literature on the problem of evil it is far from a theoretical concern. It is everybody's problem, sooner or later. Suffering is universal. But oddly enough, practically as widespread is the sufferer's feeling that he has been unfairly singled out. From millions come the outraged cry: "Why *me*! What did *I* do to deserve this?"

It is for such people that Harold S. Kushner, a Massachusetts rabbi, has written his book *When Bad Things Happen to Good People.* It is a painfully honest treatment of what the author claims is the one theological issue that reaches folks "where they really care."

Kushner's book grew out of his personal pain; his testimony commands respect. He tells how his son was afflicted from infancy with progeria, a disease that brings on rapid aging, so that Kushner saw him grow bald and wrinkled, stooped and frail, until he died of old age in his fourteenth year. Kushner presents the victim's point of view, and he lets us hear the real voices of people in pain. In that stark light, the standard religious justifications for our misfortunes, which Kushner lays out one by one, do indeed seem like facile verbal shuffles that don't take people's suffering seriously but simply try, however lamely, to get God off the hook.

Kushner effectively criticizes the standard answers handed out by priests, ministers, and rabbis, and he offers instead his own radically unorthodox solution. His book has been a best-seller for months, and he has attracted a large and grateful following among Jews, Catholics, and Protestants. Indeed, the popularity of his view among members of America's mainstream churches and synagogues suggests something of a grassroots theological rebellion.

The most reprehensible device of theodicy, in Kushner's view, is to remove the blame from God by putting it onto the sufferer, to explain suffering "by assuming that we deserve what we get, that somehow our misfortunes come as punishment for our sins." To accept that bad things happen to us as God's punishment, Kushner says, may help us make sense of the world, give us a compelling reason to be good, and sustain our belief in an all-powerful and just deity – yet it is not "religiously adequate."

By "religiously adequate" Kushner means "comforting." Seeing suffering as a punishment for sin is not comforting because it teaches people to blame themselves for their misfortunes, and so creates guilt, and it also "makes people hate God, even as it makes them hate themselves."

Kushner tells us of a couple who blamed their teenage daughter's sudden death on their own failure to observe the prescribed fast on a Jewish holy day: "They sat there feeling that their daughter's death had been their fault; had they been less selfish and less lazy about the Yom Kippur fast some six months earlier, she might still be alive. They sat there angry at God for having exacted his pound of flesh so strictly, but afraid to admit their anger for fear that He would punish them again. Life had hurt them and religion could not comfort them. Religion was making them feel worse."

It is a virtue of Kushner's work to bring this anger at God up front, to talk at length about what few believers have had the courage to admit, even to themselves. Many people must be grateful that someone has recognized their real feelings and has dealt with them openly.

But the worst thing about the belief that our misdeeds cause our misfortunes, says Kushner, is that it doesn't even fit the facts. People do suffer ills they don't deserve; bad things happen to good people all the time. Kushner adamantly maintains this. To the thousands who resent life's unfair treatment, who proclaim in outrage and indignation, "I didn't do anything to deserve this!" Kushner answers, comfortingly, "That's right, you didn't."

And Kushner is not talking about saints, about people who never do wrong. Rather, he wants to know "why ordinary people, nice friendly neighbors, neither extraordinarily good nor extraordinarily bad, should suddenly have to face the agony of pain and tragedy." They are neither much better nor very much worse than most people we know; why should their lives be so much harder?

Here, tapping into a great psychic underground of resentment, Kushner has found his following. He has been willing to openly acknowledge a vast repressed sense of betrayal, a great silenced accusation that leaks unwillingly from the hearts of believers and wends its way up to the divine ear as the universal unvoiced anti-prayer: "You didn't hold up your end of the bargain!"

Kushner insists that the innocent suffer, and as conclusive proof he advances that grievance which has been the bane of Judeo-Christian theodicy and which occasioned his own harrowing foray into the problem of evil: the suffering and death of children.

This is what drove the marble contractor to take up atheism, the usual response of those who feel God has failed them. But atheism is the response Kushner wants to prevent with his book. To restore the faith of those who have been spiritually devastated by misfortune, Kushner offers his own story of how he and his wife "managed to go on believing in God and in the world after we had been hurt."

Kushner is indeed convinced that the existence of a God both all-good and all-powerful is incompatible with the evils of our world; yet he wants us to go on believing in God. His conclusion, then, is simple: we *can* go on believing in God – but not in a God who is all-powerful. God is good, but there are limits to what He can do. God does not want us to suffer; He is as angry and upset at our misfortunes as we are. But He is also helpless.

This is Kushner's credo: "I believe in God," he says, but – "I recognize His limitations." As a result, Kushner tells us in relief, "I no longer hold God responsible for illnesses, accidents, and natural disasters, because I realize that I gain little and I lose much when I blame God for these things. I can worship a God who hates suffering but cannot eliminate it more easily than I can worship a God who chooses to make children suffer and die, for whatever exalted reason."

It is not hard for me to put myself in the place of Kushner or the marble contractor: I have children of my own. I can even understand why, given the kind of religion they know, Kushner can worship only a finite deity, and the marble contractor can't bear to enter a church. Nevertheless, I don't have the problem with God that they do. When bad things happen, I don't find myself calling into question either His power or His goodness.

Of course, I am a devotee of Kṛṣṇa; my religious convictions are founded on the Vedic theism revealed in the *Bhagavad-gītā* and the *Śrīmad-Bhāgavatam*. To espouse those convictions has been viewed by most normal Americans as a radical thing to do. But now we find that many normal Americans are willing to do something that, in its way, is more radical than what I've done. They are abandoning one of the most basic and universal theistic tenets: they are becoming worshipers of God-the-not-almighty.

I want to tell you how we handle the problem of evil. If you, like so many others, are unsatisfied with the standard Judeo-Christian theodicy, perhaps you will consider our Kṛṣṇa conscious view before following Rabbi Kushner.

In the *Bhagavad-gītā* Kṛṣṇa explains that you and I, like all living beings, are spiritual entities, souls. We now animate bodies made of matter, but we are not these bodies. Our involvement with matter is unfortunate, for it is the cause of all our suffering. We rightly belong in the spiritual kingdom, where life is eternal, full of knowledge and bliss. There everyone is joyously surrendered to the control of God as they directly serve Him in love. Every action is motivated exclusively by the desire to satisfy God.

But some of us perversely wished God's position for ourselves. We wanted independence so that we could try to enjoy and control others like God does. Yet we cannot, of course, take God's place; He alone has no master. But to grant our desires, God sends us to the material world, where He now controls us indirectly, through His material nature and its laws. Here we can forget God, strive to fulfill *our* desires, and have the illusion of independence.

Yet we are controlled by the laws of nature, and these force us to perpetually inhabit a succession of temporary material bodies. In ignorance, we identify ourselves with each body we enter, and we suffer again and again the pains of birth, old age, disease, and death. Life after life we transmigrate through plant, animal, and human bodies, sometimes on this planet, sometimes on far better ones, sometimes on far worse.

Once we take a human birth, our destiny is shaped by karma. In the *Bhagavad-gītā* (8.3) Kṛṣṇa succinctly defines karma as "actions pertaining to the development of material bodies." This means that there are actions we do now that determine our future material births. What kind of actions? Those motivated by material desire. We may do them directly for ourselves or indirectly for our extended self – our family, friends, community, nation, and the like. Such acts sentence us to future births in the material world, there to reap what we have sown.

Karma is of two kinds: good and bad.

Every civilized society recognizes a set of commandments that have divine authority and that regulate material enjoyment. Such commandments, for example, restrict the enjoyment of sex to marital relations and oblige the wealthy to be philanthropic. They also encourage religious and charitable acts, which earn the performer merit. And they prescribe atonements for transgressors. Thus people are allowed to pursue material enjoyment, but they must observe moral and religious codes. And those who follow these codes, who live pious lives of restricted sensual pleasure, are assured of even greater enjoyment in the life to come.

If we act according to scriptural regulations, the *Vedas* tell us, we will produce good karma and in future births enjoy the benefits of our piety. For example, if a person is born in an aristocratic family, is beautiful, well-educated, or wealthy, he is reaping the benefits of good karma. The *Vedas* also tell us that if a person is extraordinarily pious he may be reborn on one of the higher planets in this universe, where the standard of sensual pleasure is far greater than anything we have on earth.

Conversely, there is bad karma. We create bad karma when we disregard scriptural injunctions and restrictions in our pursuit of sense pleasure – that is, when we act sinfully. Bad karma brings us suffering and misfortune, such as birth in a degraded family, poverty, chronic disease, legal problems, or physical ugliness. Exceptionally bad karma will take us into animal bodies or down to lower planets of hellish torment.

The law of karma is as strict, relentless, and impartial as the grosser natural laws of motion and gravity. And, like them, it applies to us whether we know about it or not. For example, if I eat the flesh of animals even though I can live as well without it, my bad karma will force me to be born as an animal and to be slaughtered myself. Or if I arrange to have a child killed in the womb, I simultaneously arrange for myself to be killed in the same way, again and again, without ever seeing the light of day.

So when you and I were born we inherited, along with our blue eyes or our black hair, the consequences of our past good and bad deeds. We have a long history, and the happiness and distress our lives will bring is set. We are indeed children of destiny, hostages to fortune, but it is a destiny we created for ourselves, a fortune self-made. And in this life we are continuing to create our future.

But of all this Kushner is unaware, and he can make no sense of his suffering. He has the unshakable conviction that God owes him an agreeable and happy life, that God is obliged to arrange matters for his satisfaction. But God fails, bringing on Kushner's crisis of faith. It can only be that God is either bad or weak, Kushner reasons, and then settles for weakness.

Yet in spite of Kushner, God is both all-good and all-powerful. But He does not engineer our suffering – we do. We are the authors of our karma. And it is our decision, not His, that brings us down into the material world, into the realm of suffering.

So the answer to the question "Why do bad things happen to good people?" is "They don't." All of us here in the material world are – how shall I put it? – *not of the best sort.* Reprobates and scapegraces – each of us persona non grata in the kingdom of God. We are sent here because we seek a life independent of God, and He grants our desire as far as possible. But since His position is already taken, we can only play at being God while deceiving ourselves that we are independent of Him.

At the same time, the material world reforms us, teaches us through reward and punishment to acknowledge God's supreme position. For by natural law we are rationed out the pleasures we desire according to our observance of the divine regulations, following the ways of good karma. The practice of good karma, then, amounts to a materially motivated religion, an observance of God's orders on the inducement of material reward. By this practice, spanning many lifetimes, I may, it is hoped, become habituated to following God's commands and reconciled to His supremacy. Thereupon I become eligible at last to take up the pure and eternal religion, in which, completely free of all material desires, I serve God in loving devotion, asking nothing in return. This religion, called *bhakti* in the *Vedas,* causes my return to the kingdom of God. The acts of *bhakti* are karmaless: they produce no future material births, good or bad.

From the *Vedas,* then, we learn of two clearly distinct religions, one pure and the other impure. Practicing good karma can elevate us in the material world, secure for us a vast life span on heavenly planets, and so on. In other words, it can make us first-class inmates of the material world. But *bhakti* alone can release us from the prison altogether. Even the best karma cannot free us from suffering, as Kṛṣṇa warns in the *Bhagavad-gītā* (8.16): "From the highest planet in the material world down to the lowest, all are places of misery where repeated birth and death take place." But *bhakti* destroys all karmic reaction, extirpates all material desires, revives our pure love for God, and delivers us beyond birth and death to His abode. There we never taste temporary, material pleasure but rather relish eternal, spiritual bliss by serving Kṛṣṇa and thus joining in *His* bliss.

It is a signal virtue of the Vedic tradition that it distinguishes so clearly between the religion of good karma and the religion of *bhakti* and offers *bhakti* purely, without compromise. Most of us, whether Catholic, Protestant, or Jew, have been taught a kind of common karmic religion: God has put us on this earth to enjoy ourselves, and if we do so within the ordained limits, not forgetting to show God gratitude and proper respect, He will see to our success. We should ask God to meet our needs and fulfill our lawful desires, for He is the greatest order supplier. If we are observant and good, He will reward us well in this life and even better in the next.

This is the religion Kushner professed: "Like most people, my wife and I had grown up with an image of God as an all-wise, all-powerful parent figure who would treat us as our earthly parents did, or even better. If we were obedient and deserving, He would reward us. If we got out of line, He would discipline us, reluctantly but firmly. He would protect us from being hurt or from hurting ourselves, and would see to it that we got what we deserved in life."

Of course, Kushner begins to reconsider his religion when he discovers that it doesn't work. At this point, most people (like the marble contractor) become atheists. The idea of God as order supplier is thus responsible for a great deal of unbelief. But Kushner wants to preserve his faith in God, or at least in God's goodness, by denying His power.

Kushner's chief defense of his position is that it is "religiously adequate," that is, comforting. You will recall that he accused conventional theodicy of making people feel worse – causing them to feel guilty and to hate God. The explanation of suffering I have presented shouldn't make anyone feel worse. True, it says that we cause our own suffering, yet the point is not to make us feel guilty. The point is to let us know we've made some mistakes and should correct them. And why should we resent God for our suffering? Suffering comes by the law of karma. But karma is the impartial working of causal law. Hostility toward God is what has put us under that law; it certainly won't help us get out. For His part, God is making every effort to get us out: He comes to this world from time to time to teach the path of *bhakti*, which will destroy all our karma. He sends His representatives throughout the world on the same mission, and He even stays with us as the indwelling Supersoul during our sojourn in the material world, ready to give us the intelligence to approach Him when we put aside our ancient enmity.

Kushner has the right instincts: he too would like people to cease their enmity toward God, and he even recognizes the ignobility of worshiping Him on the condition that He satisfy our demands. But if only we recognize God's limitations, he says, we won't be angry at Him when things go wrong in our life, nor will we worship Him for the satisfaction of our desires. Kushner thus urges the religious adequacy of his own theodicy.

But it is far from adequate. Kushner's problem is that he cannot overcome the conditioning of karmic religion. He needs something more spiritually powerful than good instincts to free him from the implicit hostility toward God, the unconscious, deep-seated unwillingness to serve Him unconditionally, that binds the conditioned soul to karma.

Kushner is still hostile. Because God did not satisfy his demands, Kushner must think of Him as ineffectual and weak.

Kushner once thought of God as a parent who always gratifies our desires. But now Kushner views Him as needing our forgiveness – for having failed as a parent: "Are you capable of forgiving and loving God even when you have found out that He is not perfect, even when He has let you down and disappointed you by permitting bad luck and sickness and cruelty in His world, and permitting some of those things to happen to you? Can you learn to love and forgive Him despite His limitations ... as you once learned to forgive and love your parents even though they were not as wise, as strong, or as perfect as you needed them to be?"

Kushner asserts that his hostility toward God is no more, but what he has really done is simply change the form in which it is expressed – from rage to condescension. And this idea of God will only support our unwillingness to acknowledge His supremacy, and thus it will help keep us in the material world, where we will continue to suffer. Thus Kushner's theodicy will not make us feel better; it will only make us feel worse.

Furthermore, if we think God weak and ineffectual, it is certain that we will not be able to surrender to Him fully and serve Him without any personal consideration. The condition that makes such service and surrender possible is His promise of complete protection. "Declare it boldly," Kṛṣṇa tells His disciple Arjuna, "My devotee never perishes" (*Gītā* 9.31). Because we can depend on God completely, we can surrender to Him completely: "Abandon all varieties of religion and just surrender unto Me. I shall deliver you from all sinful reactions. Therefore you have nothing to fear" (*Gītā* 18.66).

If we accept Kushner, we will always have to look out for ourselves; we will have to act for our own sake, and so we will remain involved with karma. Our service to God will never be total and unconditional. Indeed, as long as we insist on taking care of ourselves, God will leave us to our own devices.

But if we accept Kṛṣṇa, if we give up independent action and depend completely on God, devoting all our effort to His service, He will take complete care of us. We shouldn't expect God to remove all inconvenience, but if difficulty comes we should simply tolerate it, recognizing that our residual bad karma is playing itself out, and continue to expect God's mercy.

God will minimize the karmic reaction due us, but the ultimate way He protects us is by bestowing spiritual consciousness upon us and destroying the ignorance by which we identify ourselves with matter. Kṛṣṇa describes that consciousness in the *Bhagavad-gītā* (6.22–23): "In that joyous state, one is situated in boundless transcendental happiness and enjoys himself through transcendental senses." Being situated in such a position, one is never shaken even in the midst of the greatest difficulty. This, indeed, is actual freedom from all miseries arising from material contact. God frees us not so that we can goof off, not so we can get some "reward," but so that we can serve Him wholeheartedly, without any other concern.

So if we accept Kṛṣṇa, we can solve the problem of evil. That solution doesn't lie in rejecting either the goodness or the power of God but rather in taking advantage of that goodness and power to perform pure devotional service – and in that way end all our suffering forever.

Fatalism and Real Free Will

A conversation between His Divine Grace
A.C. Bhaktivedanta Swami Prabhupāda and his disciples

The following conversation, dated June 28, 1976, was in response to the questionnaire sent out to international religious leaders by Bhavan Journal *in their search for answers to the spiritual questions perplexing the Indian public.*

~

Puṣṭa Kṛṣṇa: The traditional charge against Hinduism is that it is fatalistic, that it inhibits progress by making people slaves to the belief in the inevitability of what is to happen. How far is this charge true?

Śrīla Prabhupāda: The charge is false. Those who have made that charge do not know what Hinduism is. First of all, the Vedic scriptures make no mention of such a thing as Hinduism, but they do mention *sanātana-dharma,* the eternal and universal religion, and also *varṇāśrama-dharma,* the natural organization of human society. That we can find in the Vedic scriptures.

So it is a false charge that the Vedic system inhibits the progress of mankind. What is that "progress"? A dog's jumping is progress? [*Laughter.*] A dog is running here and there on four legs, and you are running on four wheels. Is that progress?

The Vedic system is this: The human being has a certain amount of energy – better energy than the animals', better consciousness – and that energy should be utilized for spiritual advancement. So the whole Vedic system is meant for spiritual advancement. Human energy is employed in a more exalted direction than to compete with the dog.

Consequently, sometimes those who have no idea of religion notice that the Indian saintly persons are not working hard like dogs. Spiritually uncultured people think the dog race is life. But actual life is spiritual progress. Therefore *Śrīmad-Bhāgavatam* says that the human being should exert his energy for that thing which he did not get in many, many lives. Through many, many lives the soul has been in the forms of dogs or demigods or cats or birds or insects. There are 8,400,000 material forms. So this transmigration is going on. But in every one of these millions of forms the business is sense gratification. The dog is busy for sense gratification: "Where is food? Where is shelter? Where is a mate? How to defend?" And the man is doing the same business in different ways. This struggle for existence goes on life after life. Even a small insect engages in the same struggle – *āhāra-nidrā-bhaya-maithunam* – eating, sleeping, defending, and mating. Bird, beast, insect, fish – everywhere the same struggle: "Where is food? Where is sex? Where is shelter? How to defend?"

So the *śāstra* [scripture] says we have done these things in many, many past lives, and if we don't get out of this struggle for existence, we'll have to do them again in many, many future lives. So these things should be stopped. Therefore Prahlāda Mahārāja advises his friends, "My dear friends, material pleasure – which is due simply to this material body – is essentially the same in any body. And just as misery comes without our trying for it, so the happiness we deserve will also come, by higher arrangement." A dog has a material body and I have a material body. So my sex pleasure and the dog's sex pleasure is the same. Of course, a dog is not afraid of having sex on the street in front of everyone; we hide it in a nice apartment. That's all. But the activity is the same. There is no difference.

Still, people are taking this sex pleasure between a man and woman in a nice decorated apartment as very advanced. But this is not advanced. And yet they are making a dog's race for this "advancement." Prahlāda Mahārāja says we are imagining that there are different types of pleasure on account of different types of body, but the pleasure is fundamentally the same.

Naturally, according to the different types of body, there are some external differences in the pleasure, but the basic amount and quality of this pleasure has very well defined limitations. That is called destiny. A pig has a certain type of body, and his eatable is stool. This is destined. You cannot change it – "Let the pig eat *halavā*." That is not possible. Because the soul has a particular type of body, he must eat a particular type of food. Can anyone, any scientist, improve the standard of living of a pig? Is it possible? [*Laughter.*]

Therefore Prahlāda Mahārāja says that everything about material pleasure is already fixed. The uncivilized men in the jungle are having the same sex pleasure as the so-called civilized men who boast, "Instead of living in that hut made of leaves, we are living in a skyscraper building. This is advancement."

But Vedic civilization says, "No, this is not advancement. Real advancement is self-realization – how much you have realized your relationship with God."

Sometimes people misunderstand, thinking that sages who try for self-realization are lazy. In a high court a judge is sitting soberly, apparently doing nothing, and he is getting the highest salary. And another man in the same court – he's working hard all day long, rubber-stamping, and he is getting not even one-tenth of the judge's salary. He's thinking, "I am so busy and working so hard, yet I am not getting a good salary. And this man is just sitting on the bench, and he's getting such a fat salary." The criticism of Hinduism as "inhibiting progress" is like that: it comes out of ignorance. The Vedic civilization is for self-realization. It is meant for the intelligent person, the person who will not just work like an ass but who will try for that thing which he did not achieve in so many other lives – namely, self-realization.

For example, we are sometimes labeled "escapists." What is the charge?

Disciple: They say we are escaping from reality.

Śrīla Prabhupāda: Yes, we are escaping their reality. But their reality is a dog's race, and our reality is to advance in self-realization, Kṛṣṇa consciousness. That is the difference. Therefore the mundane, materialistic workers have been described as *mūḍhas,* asses. Why? Because the ass works very hard for no tangible gain. He carries on his back tons of cloth for the washerman, and the washerman in return gives him a little morsel of grass. Then the ass stands at the washerman's door, eating the grass, while the washerman loads him up again. The ass has no sense to think, "If I get out of the clutches of this washerman, I can get grass anywhere. Why am I carrying so much?"

The mundane workers are like that. They're busy at the office, very busy. If you want to see the fellow, "I am very busy now." [*Laughter.*] So what is the result of your being so busy? "Well, I take two pieces of toast and one cup of tea. That's all." [*Laughter.*] And for this purpose you are so busy?

Or, he is busy all day simply so that in the evening he can look at his account books and say, "Oh, the balance had been one thousand dollars – now it has become two thousand." That is his satisfaction. But still he will have the same two pieces of bread and one cup of tea, even though he has increased his balance from one thousand to two thousand. And still he'll work hard. This is why *karmīs* are called *mūḍhas.* They work like asses, without any real aim of life.

But Vedic civilization is different. The accusation implied in the question is not correct. In the Vedic system, people are not lazy. They are very busy working for a higher purpose. And that busyness is so important that Prahlāda Mahārāja says, *kaumāra ācaret prājño:* "Beginning from childhood, one should work for self-realization." One should not lose a second's time. So that is Vedic civilization.

Of course, the materialistic workers – they see, "These men are not working like us, like dogs and asses. So they are escaping."

Yes, escaping your fruitless endeavor.

The Vedic civilization of self-realization begins from the *varṇāśrama* system of social organization. *Varnāśramācāravatā puruṣeṇa paraḥ pumān viṣṇur ārādhyate:* "Everyone should offer up the fruits of his occupational duty to the lotus feet of the Lord Viṣṇu, or Kṛṣṇa." That is why the Vedic system is called *varṇāśrama* – literally, "social organization with a spiritual perspective."

The *varṇāśrama* system has four social and four spiritual divisions. The social divisions are the *brāhmaṇas* [teachers and priests], *kṣatriyas* [administrators and military men], *vaiśyas* [farmers and merchants], and *śūdras* [laborers and craftsmen], while the spiritual divisions are the *brahmacārīs* [students], *gṛhasthas* [householders], *vānaprasthas* [retirees], and *sannyāsīs* [renunciants]. But the ultimate goal is *viṣṇur ārādhyate* – the worship of the Supreme Lord, Viṣṇu, by all. That is the idea.

But the members of the modern so-called civilization do not know of *varṇāśrama*. Therefore they have created a society that is simply a dog's race. The dog is running on four legs, and they are running on four wheels. That's all. And they think the four-wheel race is advancement of civilization.

Vedic civilization is different. As Nārada Muni says, the learned, astute person will use this life to gain what he has missed in countless prior lives – namely, realization of self and realization of God. Someone may ask, "Then shall we do nothing?" Yes, do nothing simply to improve your material position. Whatever material happiness is allotted for you by destiny, you'll get it wherever you are. Take to Kṛṣṇa consciousness. You'll get these other things besides.

"How shall I get them?"

How? *Kālena sarvatra gabhīra-raṁhasā:* by the arrangement of eternal time, everything will come about in due course. The example is given that even though you do not want distress, still distress comes upon you. Similarly, even if you do not work hard for the happiness that is destined to be yours, still it will come.

Similarly, Prahlāda Mahārāja says, *na tat-prayāsaḥ kartavyam:* you should not waste your energy for material happiness, because you cannot get more than what you are destined to have. That is not possible. "How can I believe it – that by working harder I will not get more material happiness than I would otherwise have had?"

Because you are undergoing so many distressing conditions even though you do not want them. Who wants distress? For example, in our country Mahātma Gandhi was killed by his own countrymen. He was a great man who was protected by so many followers. He was loved by all. Yet still he was killed. This is destiny. Who can protect you from all these distressing conditions?

"So," you should conclude, "if these distressing conditions come upon me by force, the other kind of condition, the opposite number, will also come. Therefore why shall I waste my time trying to avoid distress and gain so-called happiness? Let me utilize my energy for Kṛṣṇa consciousness." That is intelligence. You cannot check your destiny.

Puṣṭa Kṛṣṇa: Yes, the usual charge is that this Vedic system of civilization is fatalistic, and that as a result people are not making as much material progress as they otherwise would.

Śrīla Prabhupāda: No, no, the Vedic system is not fatalistic. It is fatalistic only in the sense that one's material destiny cannot be changed. But your spiritual life is in your hands. Our point is that the whole Vedic civilization is based on the understanding that destiny allows only a certain amount of material happiness in this world, and that our efforts should therefore be directed toward self-realization. Nobody is enjoying uninterrupted material happiness. That is not possible. A certain amount of material happiness and a certain amount of material distress – these both must be present always. So just as you cannot check your distressing condition of life, similarly you cannot check your happy condition of life. It will come automatically. Therefore don't waste your time with these things. Better you utilize your energy for advancing in Kṛṣṇa consciousness.

Puṣṭa Kṛṣṇa: So, then, Śrīla Prabhupāda, would it be accurate, after all, to say that people who have this Vedic conception would not try for progress?

Śrīla Prabhupāda: No, no. Progress – first you must understand what actual progress is. The thing is that if you try to progress vainly, what is the use of trying? If it is a fact you cannot change your material destiny, why should you try for that? Rather, whatever energy you have, utilize it for understanding Kṛṣṇa consciousness. That is real progress. Make your spiritual understanding – your understanding of God and self – perfectly clear.

For instance, in our International Society for Krishna Consciousness our main business is how to make advancement in Kṛṣṇa consciousness. We are not enthusiastic about opening big, big factories with big, big money-earning machines. No. We are satisfied with whatever material happiness and distress we are destined. But we are very eager to utilize our energy for progressing in Kṛṣṇa consciousness. This is the point.

The Vedic system of civilization is meant for realizing God: *viṣṇur ārādhyate*. In the Vedic system, people try for that. Actually, the followers of *varṇāśrama-dharma* – they never tried for economic development. You'll still find in India millions of people taking bath in the Ganges during Kumbha-melā. Have you been to the Kumbha-melā festival?

Disciple: No.

Śrīla Prabhupāda: At the Kumbha-melā millions of people come to take bath in the Ganges because they are interested in how to become spiritually liberated from this material world. They're not lazy. They travel thousands of miles to take bath in the Ganges at the holy place of Prayāg. Although they are not busy in the dog's race, these people are not lazy. *Yā niśā sarva-bhūtānāṁ tasyāṁ jāgarti saṁyamī:* "What is night for ordinary beings is the time of wakefulness for the self-controlled." The self-controlled man wakes up very early – practically in the middle of the night – and works for spiritual realization while others are sleeping. Similarly, during the daytime the dogs and asses think, "We are working, but these spiritualists, they are not working."

So there are two different platforms, the material and the spiritual. Followers of the Vedic civilization, which is practiced in India – although nowadays it is distorted – actually, these people are not lazy. They are very, very busy. Not only very, very busy, but also *kaumāra ācaret prājño dharmān bhāgavatān iha* – trying to become self-realized from the very beginning of life. They are so busy that they want to begin the busy-ness from their very childhood. Therefore it is wrong to think they are lazy.

People who accuse followers of Vedic civilization of laziness or of inhibiting progress do not know what real progress is. The Vedic civilization is not interested in the false progress of economic development. For instance, sometimes people boast, "We have gone from the hut to the skyscraper." They think this is progress. But in the Vedic system of civilization, one thinks about how much he is advanced in self-realization. He may live in a hut and become very advanced in self-realization, but if he wastes his time turning his hut into a skyscraper, then his whole life is wasted, finished. And in his next life he is going to be a dog, although he does not know it. That's all.

Puṣṭa Kṛṣṇa: If destiny cannot be checked, then why not, when a child is born, simply let him run around like an animal? And then whatever happens to him …

Śrīla Prabhupāda: No, the advantage of this human form of life is that you can train the child spiritually. That is possible. Therefore it is said that one should use this priceless human form to attain what you could not attain in so many millions of lower forms. For that spiritual purpose you should engage your energy. That advantage is open to you now in the human form. *Ahai-*

tuky apratihatā: pure devotional service to the Lord, or Kṛṣṇa consciousness, is open to you now, and it cannot be checked. Just as your advancement in so-called material happiness is already destined and cannot be checked, so your advancement in spiritual life cannot be checked if you endeavor for it. No one can check your spiritual advancement. Try to understand this.

Puṣṭa Kṛṣṇa: So, we can't say that the Vedic system, or *sanātana-dharma,* is fatalistic. There actually *is* endeavor for progress.

Śrīla Prabhupāda: Certainly – for spiritual progress. As for "fatalistic," I have often given an example. Let us say a man is condemned by a court of law to be hanged. Nobody can check it. Even the judge who gave the verdict cannot check it. But if the man begs for the mercy of the king, the king can check the execution. He can go totally above the law. Therefore the *Brahma-saṁhitā* says, *karmāṇi nirdahati kintu ca bhakti-bhājām:* destiny can be changed by Kṛṣṇa for His devotees. Otherwise it is not possible.

Therefore our only business should be to surrender to Kṛṣṇa. And if artificially you want to be happier by economic development, that is not possible.

Puṣṭa Kṛṣṇa: Another question?

Śrīla Prabhupāda: Hm? No, first of all make sure that everything is clear. Why are you so eager to progress? [*Laughter.*] Try to understand what is what. The first thing is that your destiny cannot be changed. That's a fact. But in spite of your destiny, if you try for Kṛṣṇa consciousness, you can achieve spiritual success. Otherwise, why did Prahlāda Mahārāja urge his friends, "Take Kṛṣṇa consciousness up from your very childhood"? If destiny cannot be changed, then why was Prahlāda Mahārāja urging this? Generally destiny means your material future. That you cannot change. But even that can be changed when you are in spiritual life.

Puṣṭa Kṛṣṇa: What is the meaning of *apratihatā*? You said that spiritual development cannot be checked.

Śrīla Prabhupāda: Suppose you are destined to suffer. *Apratihatā* means that in spite of your so-called destiny to suffer, if you take to Kṛṣṇa consciousness your suffering will be reduced, or there will be no suffering – and in spite of any suffering you can make progress in spiritual life. Just like Prahlāda Mahārāja himself. His father put him into so many suffering conditions, but he was not impeded. Rather, he made spiritual progress. He didn't care about his father's attempts to make him suffer. That state of existence is called *apratihatā*. If you want to execute Kṛṣṇa consciousness, your material condition of life cannot check it. That is the real platform of progress.

Of course, insofar as your material condition is concerned, generally that cannot be checked. You have to suffer. But in the case of a devotee, that suffering can be stopped or minimized. Otherwise, Kṛṣṇa's statement would be false when He said, *ahaṁ tvāṁ sarva-pāpebhyo mokṣayiṣyāmi*, "I will deliver you from all the reactions to your sinful activities." Suffering must befall me on account of my sinful activities, but Kṛṣṇa says, "I will deliver you from all the reactions to your sinful activities." This should be clear. Ordinarily, destiny cannot be checked. So instead of wasting your time trying to change your economic condition or your material destiny apart from Kṛṣṇa consciousness, you should employ your priceless human energy for attaining Kṛṣṇa consciousness, which cannot be checked.

We see so many men working so hard. Does this mean that every one of them will become a Ford? A Rockefeller? Why not? Everyone is trying his best. But Mr. Ford was destined to become a rich man. His destiny was there, and so he became a rich man. Another man may work just as hard as Ford, but this does not mean he will become as rich as Ford. This is practical. You cannot change your destiny simply by working hard like asses and dogs. But you *can* utilize your special human energy for improving your Kṛṣṇa consciousness. That's a fact.

Disciple: Śrīla Prabhupāda, if destiny cannot be changed, what does Kṛṣṇa mean when He says in the *Gītā*, "Be thou happy by this sacrifice"?

Śrīla Prabhupāda: Do you know what is meant by sacrifice?

Disciple: Sacrifice to Viṣṇu, to Kṛṣṇa.

Śrīla Prabhupāda: Yes. That means pleasing Kṛṣṇa. If Kṛṣṇa is pleased, He can change destiny. *Karmāṇi nirdahati kintu ca bhakti-bhājām:* for those who serve Him with love and devotion, Kṛṣṇa can change their destiny. So sacrifice, *yajña,* means pleasing Kṛṣṇa. Our whole Kṛṣṇa consciousness movement means pleasing Kṛṣṇa. That is the whole program. In all other business there is no question of pleasing Kṛṣṇa. When one nation declares war upon another, there is no question of pleasing Kṛṣṇa or serving Kṛṣṇa. They're pleasing their own senses – serving their own whims. When the First and Second World Wars began, it was not for pleasing Kṛṣṇa. The Germans wanted that their sense gratification not be hampered by the Britishers. That means it was a war of sense gratification. "The Britishers are achieving their sense gratification; we cannot. All right, fight." So there was no question of pleasing Kṛṣṇa.

Chapter Three

Science and the Vedas

Do We Have to Believe Darwin?

A conversation between His Divine Grace
A. C. Bhaktivedanta Swami Prabhupāda and his disciples

"Man came from the monkey, they say. So why is he not coming now?" During a morning walk conversation in Durban, South Africa, in 1975, Śrīla Prabhupāda looks at the question of the missing link and the power of scientific speculation.

~

Śrīla Prabhupāda: Man came from the ape. So why is man not coming from the ape now?
Devotee: It only happened once, and that was enough to start the whole thing.
Śrīla Prabhupāda: Only once? Another rascaldom! We see the flowers and fruits are coming every season. Why once? This is dogmatic. Do we have to accept it? Our experience is that, by nature's way, the same flower is coming again in the same field.
Devotee: Well, actually Darwin said that there is a missing link.
Śrīla Prabhupāda: What is that missing link? Simply bluffing, and it is going on in the name of science. Just see the fun. Simply misleading, and people are such rascals – civilized man, so-called – they are accepting it as a great theory: "Darwin's theory is a very big discovery." Simply childish rascaldom. There is no reasoning.

There is no sense. Man came from the monkey, they say. So why is he not coming now?
Devotee: Well, sometimes there's a freak of nature.
Śrīla Prabhupāda: "Sometimes" – it is simply for Darwin. To support his rascaldom, nature has to serve him: "sometimes." Just see. Why should we believe all this? "Sometimes" is not nature's law. Nature's law is the same, symmetrical. Nature is not obliged to serve Mr. Darwin. "Sometimes," he said, and only he knew. The rest of us are simply supposed to believe him. "Sometimes" it was done, and it was revealed to Darwin. How did he come to know? How is it that no one but Darwin could understand?
Devotee: They use the same argument against us: that so few people can understand God.
Śrīla Prabhupāda: No. We don't say that. We say that God first spoke to the sun god, and the sun god spoke to his son, Manu, and Manu spoke to Ikṣvāku, who spoke to his son, and in this way, the knowledge came down. *Evaṁ paramparā-prāptam*. That is quite reasonable. We don't say, "God spoke to me."

God spoke to Brahmā, and Brahmā spoke to Nārada. Nārada spoke to Vyāsadeva. Vyāsadeva spoke to others. If my forefather said to my grandfather, and my grandfather said to my father, and the same information is passed down through my family, then what is wrong? *Evaṁ paramparā-prāptam*. Kṛṣṇa spoke to Arjuna, and what Arjuna understood we are understanding in the same way. How Arjuna understood it is written in the *Bhagavad-gītā*.

We don't accept knowledge like that: "Darwin simply knew it." No. They are number-one rascals, all these so-called scientists. "There is a missing link. Only once from a monkey, man came." What is this nonsense? Do we have to believe this? Does it make any sense? But because Mr. Darwin is speaking we are expected to accept it.
Devotee: Certain changes take place. Just like if you're in a hot climate all the time, your blood thins. If you take that further, all of these changes can mount up to some big physical change.
Śrīla Prabhupāda: No change is taking place. Nature is working

symmetrically, always. The sun is rising in the morning. That has been going on for millions, millions, millions, millions of years.
Devotee: *Gradually* the change is taking place.
Śrīla Prabhupāda: No. What change is taking place? In the morning the sun rises on the eastern side. That is going on. The seasonal flower changes according to the season – winter, spring, summer. Everything is going on symmetrically; because it is going on symmetrically we can say that next February it will be a nice season here. Why? Because you have your own experience of last February. We are certain that the same thing will happen next February. Therefore we can say, "There is no such change." This is nature's way: *prakṛteḥ kriyamāṇāni guṇaiḥ karmāṇi sarvaśaḥ*. It is very symmetrical. Everything is going on nicely. Nature's way.
Devotee: One of the strong points of Darwin's theory –
Śrīla Prabhupāda: I don't find any. Simply foolishness. [*Laughter.*] A foolish rascal like you will believe it.
Devotee: They argue that five thousand years ago they had no history. So they think that before that time, there was no civilization. Therefore man was like the monkey.
Śrīla Prabhupāda: We don't speculate. We have got millions of years of history. A child may think something, but an elderly man will not think like that. Because the rascals are thinking in some way, do we have to believe it? Why should I take their word?

We are taking the word of Lord Kṛṣṇa. We accept Him as Supreme. All the great sages accept Him. Why should I accept this rascal Darwin? We are not so foolish. We cannot accept.
Devotee: The scientists always say, "Last year we made a mistake, and now it's all right."
Śrīla Prabhupāda: Hmm. "Now we are advanced." And what is the guarantee that your present theories are correct? You will advance again. That means you are always incorrect.

You say that by chance man came from nature. But you don't find nature working by chance. Therefore your theory is disproved. If your calculations have even one error, then your whole statement must be accepted as nonsense.

Devotee: People think that life is always getting better.
Śrīla Prabhupāda: Therefore, they are rascals. This is called *māyā* [illusion]. They remain rascals, and still they think they are advanced.

Evolution in Fact and Fantasy

A conversation between His Divine Grace
A.C. Bhaktivedanta Swami Prabhupāda and his disciples

Los Angeles, June 1972: Śrīla Prabhupāda asserts that Darwin's theory of evolution is inconclusive and illogical. But Darwin's is not the only theory of evolution. The Vedas *explain that an evolutionary process governs the progress of the soul. "We accept evolution," Śrīla Prabhupāda says, "but not that the forms of the species are changing. The bodies are all already there, but the soul is evolving by changing bodies and by transmigrating from one body to another.... The defect of the evolutionists is that they have no information of the soul."*

~

Devotee: Darwin tried to show how the origin of living species could be fully explained by the purely mechanical, unplanned action of natural forces. By the process he called "natural selection," all the higher, complex forms of life gradually evolved from more primitive and rudimentary ones. In a given animal population, for example, some individuals will have traits that make them adapt better to their environment; these more fit individuals will survive to pass on their favorable traits to their offspring. The unfit will gradually be weeded out naturally. Thus a cold climate will favor those who have, say, long hair or fatty tissue, and the species will then gradually evolve in that direction.

Śrīla Prabhupāda: The question is that in the development of the body, is there any plan that a particular kind of body – with, as you say, long hair or fatty tissue – should exist under certain natural conditions? Who has made these arrangements? That is the question.

Devotee: No one. Modern evolutionists ultimately base their theory on the existence of chance variations.

Śrīla Prabhupāda: That is nonsense. There is no such thing as chance. If they say "chance," then they are nonsense. Our question remains: Who has created the different circumstances for the existence of different kinds of animals?

Devotee: For example, a frog may lay thousands of eggs, but out of all of them only a few may survive to adulthood. Those who do are more fit than the others. If the environment did not favorably select the fittest, then too many frogs –

Śrīla Prabhupāda: Yes, frogs and many other animals lay eggs by the hundreds. A snake gives birth to scores of snakes at a time, and if all were allowed to exist there would be a great disturbance. Therefore big snakes devour the small snakes. That is nature's law. But behind nature's law is a brain. That is our proposition. Nature's law is not blind, for behind it there is a brain, and that brain is God. We learn this from the *Bhagavad-gītā: mayādhyakṣeṇa prakṛtiḥ sūyate sa-carācaram.* Whatever is taking place in material nature is being directed by the Supreme Lord, who maintains everything in order. The snake lays eggs by the score, and if many were not killed the world would be overwhelmed by snakes. Similarly, male tigers kill the cubs. The economic theory of Malthus states that whenever there is overpopulation there must be an outbreak of war, epidemic, famine, or the like to curb it. These natural activities do not take place by chance but are planned. Anyone who says they are a matter of chance has insufficient knowledge.

Devotee: But Darwin has a huge amount of evidence –

Śrīla Prabhupāda: Evidence? That is all right. We also have got evidence. Evidence must be there. But as soon as there is evidence, there should be no talk of "chance."

Devotee: For example, out of millions of frogs, one may happen to be better adapted to living in the water.

Śrīla Prabhupāda: But that is not by chance! That is by plan! He doesn't know that. As soon as one says "chance" it means his knowledge is imperfect. A man says "chance" when he cannot explain. It is evasive. So the conclusion is that he is without perfect knowledge and therefore unfit for giving any knowledge. He is cheating, that's all.

Devotee: Well, Darwin sees a "plan" or "design" in a sense, but –

Śrīla Prabhupāda: If he sees a plan or design, then whose design? As soon as you recognize a design you must acknowledge a designer. If you see a plan, then you must accept a planner. That he does not know.

Devotee: But the "plan" is only the involuntary working of nature.

Śrīla Prabhupāda: Nonsense. There is a plan. The sun rises daily according to exact calculation. It does not follow our calculation; rather, we calculate according to the sun. Experiencing that in such-and-such season the sun rises at such-and-such time, we learn that according to the season the sun rises exactly on the minute, the second. It is not by whimsy or chance but by minute plan.

Devotee: But can't you say it's just mechanical?

Śrīla Prabhupāda: Then who made it mechanical? If something is mechanical, then there must be a mechanic, a brain, who made the machine. Here is something mechanical [*Śrīla Prabhupāda points to a Telex machine*]: Who made it? This machine has not come out by itself. It is made of iron, and the iron did not mold itself into a machine; there is a brain who made the machine possible. So everything in nature has a plan or design, and behind that plan or design is a brain, a very big brain.

Devotee: Darwin tried to make the appearance and disappearance of living forms seem so natural and involuntary that God is removed from the picture. Evolutionary theory makes it appear as if combinations of material ingredients created life, and then various species evolved one from another naturally.

Śrīla Prabhupāda: That is foolishness. Combination means God. God is combining. Combination does not take place automatically. Suppose I am cooking. There are many ingredients gathered for cooking, but they do not combine together by themselves. I am the cooker, and in cooking I combine together ghee, spices, rice, *dāl,* and so on; and in this way, nice dishes are produced. Similarly, the combination of ingredients in nature requires God. Otherwise how does the moment arise in which the combination takes place? Do you place all the ingredients in the kitchen and in an hour come back and say, "Oh, where is my meal?" Nonsense! Who will cook your meal? You'll starve. But take the help of a living being and then we'll cook and we can eat. This is our experience. So if there is combination, then who is combining? They are fools not to know how combination takes place.

Devotee: Scientists now say life arose out of four basic elements: carbon, hydrogen, nitrogen, and oxygen.

Śrīla Prabhupāda: If the basic principle is chemicals, who made the chemicals? That question should be asked.

Devotee: Isn't it possible that one day science will discover the source of these chemicals?

Śrīla Prabhupāda: There is no question of discovering: the answer is already known, although it may not be known to you. We know. The *Vedānta* says *janmādy asya yataḥ:* the original source of everything is Brahman, Kṛṣṇa. Kṛṣṇa says *ahaṁ sarvasya prabhavo mattaḥ sarvaṁ pravartate:* "I am the origin of everything." So we know that there is a big brain who is doing everything. We know. The scientists may not know. That is their foolishness.

Devotee: They might say the same thing about us.

Śrīla Prabhupāda: No, they cannot say the same thing about us. We accept Kṛṣṇa, but not blindly. Our predecessors, the great *ācāryas* and learned scholars, have accepted Kṛṣṇa as the origin of everything, so we are not following blindly. We claim that Kṛṣṇa is the origin, but what claim can the scientist make? As soon as he says "chance," it means that he has no knowledge. We don't say "chance." We have an original cause, but he says chance. Therefore he has no knowledge.

Devotee: They try to trace back the origin by means of excavation. And they have found that gradually through the years the animal forms are evolving toward increasingly more complex and specialized forms, from invertebrates to fishes, then to amphibians, then to reptiles and insects, to mammals and birds, and finally to humans. In that process many species, like the dinosaurs, appeared, flourished, and then disappeared forever – became extinct. Eventually, primitive apelike creatures appeared, and from them man gradually developed.

Śrīla Prabhupāda: Is the theory that the human body comes from the monkeys?

Devotee: Humans and monkeys are related. They come from the same –

Śrīla Prabhupāda: Related? Everything is related; that is another thing. But if the monkey body is developing into a human body, then why, after the human body is developed, doesn't the monkey species cease to exist?

Devotee: The humans and the monkeys are branches of the same tree.

Śrīla Prabhupāda: Yes, and both are now existing. Similarly, we say that at the time the evolutionists say life began, there were human beings existing.

Devotee: They find no evidence for that.

Śrīla Prabhupāda: Why no evidence?

Devotee: In the ground. By excavation. They find no evidence in the ground.

Śrīla Prabhupāda: Is the ground the only evidence? Is there no other evidence?

Devotee: The only evidence they accept is the testimony of their senses.

Śrīla Prabhupāda: But they still cannot prove that there was no human being at the time they say life originated. They cannot prove that.

Devotee: It appears that in certain layers of earth there are remains of apelike men –

Śrīla Prabhupāda: Apelike men or manlike apes are still existing now alongside human beings. If one thing has been developed by the transformation of another thing, then that original thing should no longer be in existence. When in this way a cause has produced its effect, the cause ceases to exist. But in this case we see that the cause is still present, that there are still monkeys and apes.

Devotee: But monkeys did not cause men; both came from the same common ancestor. That is their account.

Śrīla Prabhupāda: We say that we all come from God, the same ancestor, the same father. The original father is Kṛṣṇa. As Kṛṣṇa says in the *Bhagavad-gītā, sarva-yoniṣu kaunteya:* "Of as many forms as there are …" *ahaṁ bīja-pradaḥ pitā:* "I am the seed-giving father." So what is your objection to this?

Devotee: Well, if I examine the layers of earth, I find in the deepest layers no evidence –

Śrīla Prabhupāda: You are packed up with layers of earth, that's all. That is the boundary of your knowledge. But that is not knowledge; there are many other evidences.

Devotee: But surely if men were living millions of years ago they would have left evidence, tangible evidence, behind them. I could see their remains.

Śrīla Prabhupāda: So I say that in human society bodies are burned after death, cremated. So where does your excavator get his bones?

Devotee: Well, that's possible, but –

Śrīla Prabhupāda: According to our Vedic system, the body is burned to ashes after death. Where, therefore, would the rascal get the bones? Animals are not burned; their bones remain. But human beings are burned, and therefore they cannot find their bones.

Devotee: I'm just saying that it appears, through layer after layer of deposits in the earth, that biological forms tend to progress from simple and primitive forms to more and more complex and specialized ones, until finally civilized man appears.

Śrīla Prabhupāda: But at the present moment both simple and complex forms are existing. One did not develop into the other. For example, my childhood body has developed into my adult body, and the child's body is no longer there. So if the higher, complex species developed from the simpler, lower species then we should see no simple species. But all species now exist simultaneously.

When I see all 8,400,000 species of life existing, what is the question of development? Each species exists now, and it existed long ago. You might not have seen it, but you have no proper source of knowledge. You might have missed it. That is another thing.

Devotee: But all the evidence shows otherwise. Five hundred million years ago there were no land animals; there were only aquatics.

Śrīla Prabhupāda: That is nonsense. You cannot give a history of five hundred million years! Where is the history of five hundred million years? You are simply imagining. You say "historical evidence," but where is your evidence? You cannot give a history for more than three thousand years, and you are speaking about five hundred million. This is all nonsense.

Devotee: If I dig far into the ground, layer by layer –

Śrīla Prabhupāda: By dirt you are calculating five hundred million years? It could be ten years. You cannot give the history of human society past three thousand years, so how can you speak of four hundred or five hundred million years ago? Where were you then? Were you there so you can say that all these species were not there? This is imagination. In this way everyone can imagine and say some nonsense.

We accept evolution, but not that the forms of the species are changing. The bodies are all already there, but the soul is evolving by changing bodies and by transmigrating from one body to another. I have evolved from my childhood body to my adult body, and now my childhood body is extinct. But there are many other children. Similarly, all the species are now existing simultaneously, and they were all there in the past.

For example, if you are traveling in a train you find first class, second class, third class; they are all existing. If you pay a higher fare and enter the first-class carriage, you cannot say, "Now the first class is created." It was always existing. So the defect of the evolutionists is that they have no information of the soul. The soul is evolving, transmigrating, from one compartment to another compartment, simply changing place. The *Padma Purāṇa* says that there are 8,400,000 species of life and the soul evolves through them. This evolutionary process we accept: the soul evolves from aquatics to plants, to insects, to birds, to animals, and then to the human forms. But all these forms are already there. They do not change. One does not become extinct and another survive. All of them are existing simultaneously.

Devotee: But Darwin says there are many species, like dinosaurs, that are seen to be extinct.

Śrīla Prabhupāda: What has he seen? He is not so powerful that he can see everywhere or everything. His power to see is limited, and by that limited power he cannot conclude that one species is extinct. That is not possible. No scientist will accept that. After all, all the senses by which you gather knowledge are limited, so how can you say this is finished or that is extinct? You cannot see. You cannot search out. The earth's circumference is twenty-five thousand miles; have you searched through all the layers of rock and soil over the whole earth? Have you excavated all those places?

Devotee: No.

Śrīla Prabhupāda: Therefore our first charge against Darwin is this: He says there were no human beings millions of years ago. That is not a fact. We now see human beings existing along with all other species, and it should be concluded that this situation always existed. Human life has always been there. Darwin cannot say there was no human life.

Devotee: We don't see any dinosaurs existing.
Śrīla Prabhupāda: You do not see because you have no power to see. Your senses are very limited, so what you see or don't see cannot be authoritative. So many people – the majority of people – say, "I don't see God." Shall we accept, then, that there is no God? Are we crazy for being devotees of God?
Devotee: No, but dinosaurs –
Śrīla Prabhupāda: But simply by dinosaurs being missing you cannot make your case. What about all the other species?
Devotee: Many, many others are also extinct.
Śrīla Prabhupāda: Say I accept that many are extinct – because the evolutionary process means that as an earlier species gradually changes into a later species, the earlier vanishes, becomes extinct. But we see that many monkeys are still here. Man evolved from the simians, but simians have not disappeared. Monkeys are here and men are here.
Devotee: But still I'm not convinced. If we make geological investigations all over the world, not just here and there, but in many parts of the world, and in every case we find the same thing –
Śrīla Prabhupāda: But I say you have not studied all over the world. Has Darwin studied all the continents on this planet? Has he gone down into the depths of the seas and there excavated all the layers of the earth? No. So his knowledge is imperfect. This is the relative world, and here everyone speaks with relative knowledge. Therefore we should accept knowledge from a person who is not within this relativity.
Devotee: Actually, Darwin hit upon his theory because of what he observed on his voyage in 1835 to the Galapagos Islands, off the coast of South America. He found there species that exist nowhere else.
Śrīla Prabhupāda: That means he has not seen all the species. He has not traveled all over the universe. He has seen one island, but he has not seen the whole creation. So how can he determine what species exist and don't exist? He has studied one part of this earth, but there are many millions of planets. He has not seen all of them;

he has not excavated the depths of all the planets. So how can he conclude, "This is nature"? He has not seen everything, nor is it possible for any human being to see everything.

Devotee: Let's just confine ourselves to this planet.

Śrīla Prabhupāda: No, why should we? Nature is not only on this planet.

Devotee: Because you said that on this planet there were complex forms of living beings millions and millions of years ago.

Śrīla Prabhupāda: We are not talking about this planet, but about anywhere. You are referring to nature. Nature is not limited or confined to this planet. You cannot say that. Nature, material nature, includes millions of universes, and in each and every universe there are millions of planets. If you have studied only this planet, your knowledge is insufficient.

Devotee: But you said before that millions of years ago on this planet there were horses, elephants, civilized men –

Śrīla Prabhupāda: Yes, yes.

Devotee: But from hundreds of different sources there is no evidence.

Śrīla Prabhupāda: I say they are existing now – men, horses, snakes, insects, trees, so why not millions of years ago?

Devotee: Because there is no evidence.

Śrīla Prabhupāda: That doesn't mean ... ! You limit your study to one planet. That is not full knowledge.

Devotee: I just want to find out for the time being about –

Śrīla Prabhupāda: Why the time being? If you are not perfect in your knowledge, then why should I accept your theory? That is my point.

Devotee: Well, if you claim that millions of years ago there were complex forms of life on this planet –

Śrīla Prabhupāda: Whether on this planet or on another planet that is not the point. The point is that all species exist and keep on existing by the arrangement of nature. We learn from the Vedic texts that there are 8,400,000 species established. They may be in your neighborhood or they may be in my neighborhood – the number and types are fixed. But if you simply study your neighborhood it is not perfect knowledge. Evolution we admit. But your evolutionary theory is not perfect. Our theory of evolution is perfect. From the *Vedas* we know that there are 8,400,000 forms of bodies provided by nature, but the soul is the same in all, in spite of the different types of body. There is no change in the soul, and therefore the *Bhagavad-gītā* says that one who is wise, a *paṇḍita,* does not see the species or the class; he sees oneness, equality. *Paṇḍitāḥ sama-darśinaḥ.* One who sees to the bottom sees the soul, and he does not find there any difference between all these species.

Devotee: So Darwin and other material scientists who have no information about the soul –

Śrīla Prabhupāda: They're missing the whole point.

Devotee: They say that all living things tend to evolve from lower to higher. In the history of the earth –

Śrīla Prabhupāda: That may be accepted. For example, in an apartment building there are different kinds of apartments: first-class apartments, second-class apartments, third-class apartments. According to your desire and qualification, as you are fit to pay the rent, you are allowed to move up to the better apartments. But the different apartments are already there. They are not evolving. The residents are evolving by moving to new apartments as they desire.

Devotee: As they desire.

Śrīla Prabhupāda: Yes. According to our mentality at the time of death, we get another "apartment," another body. But the "apartment" is already there, not that I'm creating the "apartment."

And the classes of "apartments" are fixed at 8,400,000. Just like the hotelkeeper: he has experience of his customers coming and wanting different kinds of facilities. So he has made all sorts of accommodations to oblige all kinds of customers. Similarly, this is God's creation. He knows how far a living entity can think, so He has made all these different species accordingly. When God thinks, "Come on, come here," nature obliges. *Prakṛteḥ kriyamāṇāni guṇaiḥ karmāṇi:* Nature is offering facility. God, Kṛṣṇa, is sitting in the heart of the living entity as Paramātmā, and He knows, "He wants this." So the Lord orders nature, "Give him this apartment," and nature obliges: "Yes, come on; here is your apartment." This is the real explanation.

Devotee: I understand and accept that. But I'm still puzzled as to why there is no geological evidence that in former times on this planet there were more complex forms.

Śrīla Prabhupāda: Why are you taking geological evidence as final? Is it final? Science is progressing. You cannot say it is final.

Devotee: I have excavated all parts of the world, and every time –

Śrīla Prabhupāda: You have not excavated all parts of the world.

Devotee: Well, on seven continents.

Śrīla Prabhupāda: Seven continents is not the whole world. You say you have excavated the whole world, but we say no, not even an insignificant portion. So your knowledge is limited. Dr. Frog has examined his three-foot-wide well, and now he claims to know the ocean.

Experimental knowledge is always imperfect, because one experiments with imperfect senses. Therefore, scientific knowledge must be imperfect. Our source of knowledge is different. We do not depend on experimental knowledge.

Now you see no dinosaurs, nor have I seen all the 8,400,000 different forms of life. But my source of knowledge is different. You are an experimenter with imperfect senses. I have taken knowledge from the perfect person, who has seen everything, who knows everything. Therefore, my knowledge is perfect.

Say, for example, that I receive knowledge from my mother: "Here is your father." But you are trying to search out your father on your own. You don't go to your mother and ask; you just search and search. Therefore, no matter how much you search, your knowledge will always remain imperfect.

Devotee: And your knowledge says that millions of years ago there were higher forms of life on this planet.

Śrīla Prabhupāda: Oh, yes, because our Vedic information is that the first created being is the most intelligent, the most intellectual person within the universe. That is Lord Brahmā, the cosmic engineer. So how can we accept your theory that intellect develops by evolution? We have received our Vedic knowledge from Brahmā, who is so perfect.

Dr. Frog has studied his three-foot well, his little reservoir of water. The Atlantic Ocean is also a reservoir of water, but there is a vast difference. Dr. Frog cannot inform us about the Atlantic Ocean. But we take knowledge from the one who has made the Atlantic Ocean. So our knowledge is perfect.

Devotee: Wouldn't there be evidence in the earth, some remains?

Śrīla Prabhupāda: Our evidence is intelligence, not stones and bones. Our evidence is intelligence. We get Vedic information by disciplic succession from the most intelligent. It is coming down by *śruti,* hearing. Vyāsadeva heard from Nārada, Nārada heard from Brahmā – millions and millions of years ago. Millions and millions of our years pass, and it is not even one day for Brahmā. So millions and billions and trillions of years are not very astonishing to us, for that is not even one day of Brahmā. But Brahmā was born of Kṛṣṇa, and intelligent philosophy has been existing in our universe from the date of Brahmā's birth. Brahmā was first educated by God, and His knowledge has been passed down to us in the Vedic literature. So we get such intelligent information in the *Vedas.*

But those so-called scientists and philosophers who do not follow this system of descending knowledge, who do not accept knowledge thus received from higher authorities – they can't have any perfect knowledge, no matter what research work they carry out with their blunt senses. So whatever they say, we take it as imperfect.

Our method is different from theirs. They are searching after dead bones and we are searching after living brains. This point should be stressed. They are dealing with dead bones and we are dealing with living brains. Which should be considered better?

Modern Science: Simply Bluffing

A conversation between His Divine Grace A. C. Bhaktivedanta Swami Prabhupāda and Dr. Thoudam Singh, PhD

At the present moment, the scientists are stressing the gross situation. But of the subtle situation they have no knowledge.

~

Dr. Singh: Many of my scientific colleagues say that intelligence is simply a molecular interaction within the brain.
Śrīla Prabhupāda: Some molecular interaction may be occurring, but the interaction is not simply molecular. Intelligence has to do with the soul, not simply with the brain.
Dr. Singh: They say the brain is the source of intelligence.
Śrīla Prabhupāda: No. Take electricity, for example. Electricity moves between gross elements and through a gross wire. But the electricity itself – it is not those elements, not that wire. It is subtle.
Dr. Singh: Yes, it is subtle, but –
Śrīla Prabhupāda: You cannot see this subtle thing directly; you can see it only when it interacts with something gross. But the subtle thing is independent and distinct from the gross things.

Dr. Singh: That is actually true. That's a fact. For example, when we speak of Newton's law of gravitation, we can establish a mathematical formula, but we do not know how gravitation acts.
Śrīla Prabhupāda: Not directly seen.
Dr. Singh: Yes. Even though gravitation does exist, we can't really see it. Modern science admits that. Newton himself admitted that.
Śrīla Prabhupāda: So although we cannot see the soul directly, why not admit that it exists? The soul is the most subtle, but we can see it through its effects. So why not admit it exists?
Dr. Singh: Yes. Far too many scientists have left the soul out of their discussion of reality. Instead, they try to reduce reality to matter. And yet we see the existence of the soul. It is beyond our comprehension, but it exists. We should not ignore the soul simply because it is inconceivable.
Śrīla Prabhupāda: Actually the soul is conceivable because we can understand much about it by observing the way it interacts with matter. Yet largely, the soul is outside our experience.
Dr. Singh: Yes.
Śrīla Prabhupāda: The soul is not inconceivable. It is conceivable.
Dr. Singh: Oh, yes. Again, if we take the example of physical phenomena and laws, we can perceive that they exist, but precisely how they exist we do not know.
Śrīla Prabhupāda: That is another thing. But you have to admit they exist. And we have to accept that the soul exists.
Dr. Singh: Yes. That is the missing point in modern science.
Śrīla Prabhupāda: The mind exists, the intelligence exists, the sense of ego exists, the soul exists – although they are not entirely perceivable by our gross senses.
Dr. Singh: So consciousness, the soul, exists – independent and distinct from matter.
Śrīla Prabhupāda: Yes. This you have to bring into the scientists' discussion. Now they should begin to inquire, How does the soul enter the subtle material situation? How does the soul create and enter a subtle or mental body? And how does this subtle body create the gross situation, the gross body?

At the present moment, the scientists are stressing the gross situation. But of the subtle situation they have no knowledge. And yet the subtle situation can be perceived.

Dr. Singh: Yes, that is true.

Śrīla Prabhupāda: So you have to convince other scientists. This subtle mental, intellectual, and psychological situation is so very important. It can carry the soul to the spiritual world. But one has to make himself fully spiritualized, fully devoted to the Lord. At the time you pass from your gross body, if you have made your subtle body fully spiritualized, then it will carry you to the spiritual world.

So just consider how critically important is this Kṛṣṇa conscious culture, this spiritual culture. Just consider. And yet these so-called scientists who are setting society's cultural tone – they know nothing of this true culture. Nothing.

We can perceive two energies – *para* and *apara,* the higher and lower – spirit and matter. And *we* get confirmation from Lord Kṛṣṇa. In *Bhagavad-gītā* He discusses His two energies in these very terms, *para* and *apara:* higher and lower – spirit and matter. So the soul in the material world is situated between this *apara,* or inferior, material energy and the *para,* or superior, spiritual energy. This subtle situation, his subtle body, is his medium back to the spiritual world. If the soul makes his subtle body – his mind, intelligence, and self-identification, or ego – spiritualized, then he goes to the spiritual world.

You see? If the soul spiritualizes his mind and intelligence and ego – if he focuses them on his actual, spiritual identity and his loving relationship with Kṛṣṇa the Supreme Spirit – then he will be transferred to the spiritual world. This you have to prove or demonstrate in scientific terms. These pseudoscientists are seeing simply the gross situation, the gross body. That's all.

They see the gross body functioning for some time and then ceasing to function, and they think, "This person was living, but now he is living no more." No, the soul is always living. But now he is being carried to another situation, another life, by the subtle situation *he* created in this life.

These pseudoscientists are thinking, "This gross situation, this gross body, is finished – everything is finished." That's not the fact. Kṛṣṇa confirms, *tathā dehāntara-prāptir dhīras tatra na muhyati:* "As the soul passes, in this lifetime, from a childhood body to a teen-age body to an old-age body, so at the time of death he passes into still another body."

Dr. Singh: That is a drawback in modern science.

Śrīla Prabhupāda: Without this spiritual perspective, everything they say is a drawback. Simply bluffing. *Harāv abhaktasya kuto mahad-guṇāḥ:* anyone who does not use his human intelligence to spiritualize himself, to become a devotee of the Lord – his whole life is a drawback.

The Principle of Reincarnation

Bhaktisvarūpa Dāmodara Swami

The scientific study of reincarnation may shed new light on many subtle phenomena inexplicable by currently accepted theories – phenomena such as the wide variety of living forms, innate abilities clearly not acquired from the environment, and near-death experiences. In recent years scholars in various disciplines have shown great interest in studying reincarnation, but to study it meaningfully we must first know whether life is an eternal entity that transcends the temporary, physical body or merely a combination of molecules moving according to the laws of physics and chemistry.

~

The Reductionist Approach: Atoms and the Void

Modern science deals primarily with the objective aspects of nature. Relying on an experimental approach based on limited sensory data, it has pursued the goal of unfolding the hidden laws of nature, and ultimately of finding the original cause of the world we perceive. Most modern scientists now believe that blind physical laws and the laws of chance govern the cosmos. They say there is no designer, no creator, no God – no intelligence behind the whole cosmic phenomenon. Following this hypothesis, they attempt to reduce everything, including life, to the interactions of atoms and molecules, the familiar objects of study of physics and chemistry.

What Is Life?

Basing itself on a mountain of laboratory data, the currently predominant scientific theory holds that life is a coordinated chemical reaction. This theory involves the basic assumption that the various life forms we see today originated by chance in an ancient chemical environment, the "primordial soup," and that they have developed by the influence of chance and blind mechanical laws acting over a long time period. In the words of Jacques Monod, "Chance alone is at the source of every innovation, of all creation in the biosphere. Pure chance, absolutely free but blind, is at the very root of the stupendous edifice of evolution: this central concept of modern biology is no longer one among other possible or even conceivable hypotheses. It is today the sole conceivable hypothesis, the only one that squares with observed and tested fact."* This is the neo-Darwinian concept. According to this idea, as time passed, the action of various forms of energy (ultraviolet rays from the sun, lightning, ionizing radiation, and heat) caused the small and simple molecules to combine together to form the biomonomers (amino acids, for example), and these biomonomers in turn gave rise to biopolymers (such as proteins and nucleic acids). It has been assumed that by the proper interactions, the self-organization of these molecules took place, and life eventually arose.

Unfortunately, this theory, however attractive it may be, will remain only a theoretical model until its propounders can actually produce some form of life in the laboratory by chemical reactions. But just how likely is this? Assuming that the primitive atmos-

* Jacques Monod, *Chance and Necessity,* translated by Austryn Wainhouse (New York: Alfred A. Knopf, 1971), 112–13.

phere was of a reducing kind, Stanley Miller passed an electric discharge through a gaseous mixture of ammonia, water vapor, carbon dioxide, and hydrogen.* The reaction product was found to contain aldehydes, carboxylic acid, and some amino acids. Since amino acids are the basic building blocks of protein molecules, which in turn are the fundamental components of living cells, Miller's experiment has been regarded as a landmark in the case for chemicals' being the origin of life. Subsequent experiments in the study of the origin of life involved some changes in the components of the reactants. When the simple molecules of hydrogen cyanide (HCN) were subjected to ultraviolet radiation, the basic building blocks of nucleic acids (the purines adenine and guanine) were synthesized. In experiments simulating the earth's presumed primitive atmosphere, the simple molecules of formaldehyde (CH_2O) were generated, and these simple formaldehyde molecules in turn underwent various base-catalyzed condensation reactions to produce innumerable sugars. These are regarded as the progenitors of biological sugars. The action of ultraviolet light and ionizing radiation on solutions of formaldehyde produced the sugar molecules ribose and deoxyribose, which are the components of nucleic acids.

Practically speaking, then, at this stage of scientific knowledge most of the important chemicals found in the living cell (including the gene) can be synthesized in the chemical laboratory. And those in the forefront of microbiology and biochemistry have made a vigorous effort to put all the necessary chemicals together and prepare the first synthetic life in the test tube. Unfortunately, there are no life symptoms visible when all these chemicals are combined. Even without taking so much trouble to synthesize all these chemicals, scientists can actually isolate the necessary chemicals from an already living body and then recombine them. If life were a chemical combination, scientists could actually make life in the test tube by assem-

* Stanley Miller, *Science*, vol. 117, number 528 (1953).

bling all these important chemicals. They cannot do this, however. Thus there are abundant reasons for doubting that life is a chemical process.

Undoubtedly, in the last few decades great advancements have been made in the fields of cell biology, molecular biology, and biochemistry. Indeed, the discovery of the genetic code and many metabolic pathways of the living systems are products of brilliant and dedicated researchers. Because of the great successes of science and technology in many areas of human endeavor (medicine, agriculture, space science, and so on), inquisitive and enthusiastic scientific minds are tempted to believe that the brilliant ambition to synthesize life in the test tube will one day be fulfilled. Scientific and popular journals have thus reported many claims that certain molecular arrangements might give rise to life. They present, for example, the coacervate droplets of Oparin and the protenoid microspheres of Fox as forerunners of a living cell. But a close look at these entities reveals them to be purely physico-chemical phenomena. Coacervate droplets are wholly explicable in the realm of micellar chemistry, and Fox's microspheres are explicable in terms of the chemistry of peptides and polypeptides.

Therefore, despite great scientific discoveries and achievements, the bright hope and enthusiasm for understanding life in molecular terms seem to be losing ground, and many prominent scientists in various fields are beginning to doubt the validity of this concept. In a book called *Biology Today,* Nobel Prize–winning chemist Albert Szent-Györgyi remarked, "In my search for the secret of life, I ended up with atoms and electrons, which have no life at all. Somewhere along the line, life ran out through my fingers. So, in my old age, I am now retracing my steps."*

Not only do molecules, atoms, and electrons lack life symptoms, but also the chemical view of life fails to correspond with life's observed subtleties – human beings' unique feeling, willing, and thinking capacities, for example. If life were an interplay of

* Albert Szent-Györgyi, *Biology Today* (California: CRM Books, 1972).

molecules, we should be able to explain these subtle aspects of life in terms of molecules only. What will be the genetic component or molecule that induces the friendly feeling of love and respect among people? Which molecule or genetic code will be responsible for the subtle artistic nuances in *Hamlet* or Bach's Mass in B Minor? Can a mechanistic view of life account for life's value- and goal-oriented nature, especially among human beings? That there are no plausible molecular mechanisms to explain these subtle aspects of life makes it reasonable to propose that life transcends physics and chemistry.

A New Paradigm for Life and the Absolute Truth

If life were accepted as a totally temporary, material phenomenon, then the idea of a previous or future life of a living being would be eliminated, and with it the question of reincarnation. Of course, as we have seen, there is every reason to believe that life is transcendental to matter and thus independent of the physico-chemical laws that govern matter. What we need now, to study reincarnation scientifically, is a new scientific paradigm that will explain the origin of life, its characteristics, and how it behaves in the world of matter.

Before discussing this new scientific paradigm, we will find it useful to briefly discuss the nature of the Absolute Truth. As mentioned earlier, according to modern science the Absolute Truth (defined as "the ultimate cause of all phenomena") seems to be vaguely incorporated into the physical laws called the laws of nature. In other words, modern science posits the Absolute Truth as blind, impersonal, and wholly within the framework of the push-pull mechanisms of atoms and molecules. Now, if nature were simply an array of particles moving according to mathematical equations, it would be possible to predict events such as birth, death, accidents, and wars with the help of these equations. Indeed, it should be possible to understand all the intricacies of life – past, present, and future – in terms of mathematical equations. However, all careful thinkers, especially the scientists, know that this is impossible – that a purely mathematical approach to the understanding of life is too restrictive and very unsatisfying. Therefore we need a new paradigm for the origin and nature of life.

The new scientific paradigm we are proposing, which accounts for both the subtle complexities of life and the apparently nonphysical character of the Absolute Truth, comes basically from the scientific and theological background of the *Vedas*. According to the ancient wisdom outlined in the *Bhagavad-gītā* (a basic Vedic text), the Absolute Truth is the supreme person, possessing supreme consciousness and supreme intelligence. In other words, the Absolute Truth is a supremely sentient being. The Absolute Truth emanates two energies: the inferior energy, called *prakṛti* in Sanskrit and characterized by inanimate matter; and the superior energy, which is composed of *ātmās,* living entities. The *ātmās* are called the superior energy because they possess consciousness, which is the main feature that distinguishes life from matter.

The behavior of inanimate matter can be described to some extent in terms of the push-pull mechanisms operating on molecular, atomic, and subatomic levels, and these push-pull mechanisms can in turn be described by using simple mathematical equations. As we have already pointed out, however, there are no mathematical laws that can describe the phenomena of life and its variegated activities. Therefore, life is clearly transcendental to material laws and can be defined, according to the *Vedas,* as "the nonphysical, fundamental particle called the *ātmā,* which is characterized by consciousness."

Since life is nonphysical and nonchemical, the mathematical laws that govern the activities of inert matter do not apply to life. However, it is reasonable to suppose that there must be some laws that govern life. According to the *Bhagavad-gītā,* these are higher-order natural laws incorporating free will. (As we shall see, free will plays a very important role in reincarnation.) It is clear that the existing scientific models and tools cannot grasp these higher-order natural laws, but it is conceivable that the parapsychological experiments now underway in many quarters may provide at least some clue as to the nature of these laws. Thus there is a vast area for further research in the fields of parapsychology and psychology that may help us understand the science of life and its variegated activities.

The Properties of Life (the Ātmā)

There are innumerable *ātmās* (living entities), each being a quantum of consciousness. Each *ātmā* resides temporarily in an ephemeral biological form, according to the *ātmā's* consciousness. This consciousness is due to the *ātmā* alone, but the content of the *ātmā's* consciousness is due to its interactions with the particular body it occupies. The material body can be divided into two categories: the gross and the subtle. The subtle body is made up of mind, intelligence, and the apparent self (or the false identification of one's self with the material body). The gross body is made up of the five gross elements – solid matter, liquids, radiant energy, gases, and ethereal substances. The interaction of the individual *ātmā* with the gross and subtle bodies produces inconceivably complex reactions, which cannot be explained by simple chemistry and physics in the living cell. That is why chemistry and physics cannot explain why there is so much difference between a living body and a dead one. Simply put, when the individual living being leaves the body, the live body becomes dead matter – although all the chemicals necessary for the functioning of the living organism are still present.

Consciousness and the Biological Forms

According to the information given in the *Vedas*, the varieties of life forms are products of the combinations and permutations of the three modes of material nature (goodness, passion, and ignorance). The life forms are just like temporary houses or apartments of various sizes, shapes, and colors, in which the eternal self, or living being, resides temporarily. The biological forms, governed by the three modes, put a constraint on the qualities and activities of the living beings' consciousness. Thus the individual being in a tiger's body will roar loudly and kill animals for food, while the living being in a swan's body will fly gracefully and swim on the surface of lakes. Even in the same family we see differences caused by the activities of the three modes of nature. Although all animals are in the mode of ignorance, they are influenced by the modes of goodness and passion in varying degrees. Cows, for example, are very simple, and their behavior is very mild; they are influenced by the mode of goodness to some extent. The ferocious nature of lions and tigers, on the other hand, reveals their passionate consciousness, while camels are almost completely in the mode of ignorance. In a similar manner, in the family of birds the swans are very noble and gracious, showing symptoms of goodness; hawks, eagles, and peacocks are predominantly in the mode of passion; and vultures and crows are predominantly in the mode of ignorance. Although the biological forms in the same family are similar in nature, the consciousness and behavior of these birds and animals are different. Thus there are millions of forms where the eternal self, or living being, temporarily resides, displaying its behavior according to how the three modes of material nature affect its consciousness.

Reincarnation and the Change of Body

Now the question arises: "What determines the particular biological form and type of consciousness that a living being acquires?" To answer this question, let us first investigate the transformations of form and consciousness that occur within one lifetime.

As mentioned earlier, consciousness and biological form are interrelated, due to the influence of the modes of nature. Thus a child's body and its conscious development are different from those of its youthful stage, and so on. In principle, then, as the body changes from boyhood to old age, the living being, or *ātmā*, actually passes through many bodies of various ages and varieties of conscious development. Thus the body changes, but the eternal living being within the body – the self – remains the same. Biological science confirms this. In his book *The Human Brain*, John Pfeiffer points out, "Your body does not contain a single one of the molecules that it contained seven years ago." The movement of the living entity through numerous bodies within one lifetime – something we can all verify by a little introspection – can be termed internal (or continuous) reincarnation or transmigration.

But what about the living being's passage to a new body at the time of death? To the author's knowledge, reports in the literature on the study of reincarnation are based primarily on some scattered data regarding some children's memories of previous lives. This information comes mainly from northern India, Sri Lanka, Burma, Thailand, Vietnam, and some areas of western Asia.* Although this information certainly supports the theory of reincarnation, it does not provide us with a scientific foundation from which to study it, because the vast majority of people cannot remember their past lives. Therefore we must consult a source of information more reliable than haphazard memory. That information is available in the *Vedas*. In the *Bhagavad-gītā* Lord Kṛṣṇa very clearly explains reincarnation to His friend and devotee Arjuna. The Lord says, "Just as a person puts on new garments, giving up old ones, similarly the individual living entity accepts new material bodies, giving up the old and useless ones." (*Gītā* 2.22) "Just as the embodied living entity passes, in one body, from boyhood to youth to old age, so the living entity similarly passes into another body at death." (*Gītā* 2.13) Lord Kṛṣṇa further explains that the mind is the mechanism underlying all these transmigrations: "Whatever state of being one remembers when he quits his body, that state he will attain without fail in his next life." (*Gītā*

* Ian Stevenson, "The Explanatory Value of the Idea of Reincarnation," *The Journal of Nervous and Mental Disease*, vol. 164 (1977), number 5, p. 308.

8.6) So, the living entity in a man's body could go into the body of an animal, a bird, an insect, a plant, another human, and so on. This journey of the self, or living entity, into different bodies can be referred to as external (or discontinuous) reincarnation or transmigration.

To illustrate how external reincarnation works, we will briefly relate the story of King Bharata, one of the great personalities in Vedic history, from the *Śrīmad-Bhāgavatam,* the foremost of the eighteen *Purāṇas.*

One day, after King Bharata had taken his bath as usual in the river Gaṇḍakī, he was chanting his mantra when he saw a pregnant deer come to the riverbank to drink water. Suddenly the thundering roar of a lion resounded throughout the forest. The deer was so frightened that it immediately gave birth to its fawn. It crossed the river, but then died immediately thereafter. Bharata took compassion on the motherless calf, rescued it from the water, took it to his *āśrama,* and cared for it affectionately. He gradually became attached to the young deer, and he always thought of it lovingly.

As it grew up, the deer became Bharata's constant companion, and he always took care of it. Gradually he became so absorbed in thinking of this deer that his mind became agitated, he reduced his meditative disciplines, and he fell away from his mystic yoga practice. Once, when the deer was absent, Bharata was so disturbed that he began to search for it. While searching and lamenting the deer's absence, Bharata fell down and died. Because his mind was fully absorbed in thinking of the deer, he naturally took his next birth in the womb of a deer.

As has been mentioned earlier, there is a subtle body, made up of mind, intelligence, and apparent self. In either kind of reincarnation, internal or external, the living being is carried by the subtle body under the laws of karma. The word karma is a Sanskrit term that can be defined as "the function and activity of the living entity within the framework of his free will and under the influence of the three modes of material nature over a span of time." For every action that an individual living being performs, he must undergo an appropriate reaction. For example, if someone is very charitable toward educational institutions, in his next life he may be very wealthy and receive an excellent education. On the other hand, if one performs or has an abortion, he or she will suffer the same fate in the next life. Thus we arrive at a definition of reincarnation, or transmigration, according to the Vedic information: "the continuous journey of the living entity, from one body to another, either internally or externally, under the stringent laws of his individual karma."

Evolution and Devolution of Consciousness

Darwinian evolution, or in modern times chemical evolution, assumes that it is strictly the morphology of an organism that evolves. The Vedic literatures, however, give us the information that it is not the body that evolves but rather the living being's consciousness. And this evolution of consciousness takes place by the process of the living being's transmigration from one body to another. Those living entities that are below the human form of life never violate the laws of nature; they have no choice but to follow them. So their transmigration is strictly unidirectional – from less conscious forms to more conscious forms. Thus microbes, plants, birds, and animals all evolve until they reach the human form of life.

However, when the individual living being comes to the human form of life, his consciousness is fully developed, and along with it his free will. Thus the individual being in the human form can be obstinately rebellious against the laws of nature, or he can be completely harmonious with the laws of nature. In other words, he can exercise his free will either to evolve to a higher plane of consciousness or to revert to a lower stage. From the human form of life, if the individual living being desires, he can escape the continuous cycle of transmigration from one form of body to another. This can be done by using his free will properly.

On the other hand, if he exercises his free will improperly, then he can go back to the lower species. And this is called devolution of consciousness – the passage of the living being from higher consciousness to lower consciousness – which intelligent men wish to avoid.

Reincarnation and the Science of Self-Realization

The eternal wisdom of the *Vedas* instructs us that the goal of all knowledge is to break free from the repeated cycle of birth and death. The intelligence of all forms of life below human beings is insufficiently developed to understand the science of self-realization. Therefore the *Vedānta-sūtra* says that in the human form of life one must inquire into the nature of the Absolute Truth.

We must begin by asking such questions as these: "Who am I?" "Where do I come from?" "What is the purpose of my existence?" "How can I get out of the cycle of repeated birth and death?" We should investigate the answers to all these questions very thoroughly. This is the beginning of the science of self-realization, or the science of the study of life.

Bhakti-yoga: The Process for Breaking the Chain of Birth and Death

The systematic process for studying the self is called *bhakti-yoga*. *Bhakti-yoga* is, once again, a Sanskrit term meaning "the spiritual discipline by which one links up with the Absolute Truth, the Supreme Person, in love." The basic tenet of *bhakti-yoga* is that in order to get accurate knowledge concerning the Absolute Truth, one must train the mind properly so that it is eligible to receive the knowledge coming from the higher source. We have already discussed how our new scientific paradigm describes the Absolute Truth as supremely sentient, and that everything – matter, life, knowledge, and so on – comes from that absolute source. In order to receive real knowledge, one's mind must be free from the contamination of the lower modes of nature. One of the main impurities is the false pride, or hubris, that impels us to believe we can understand everything by the process of experimental knowledge. We must give up this hubris, control the mind, and make it harmonious with nature. To control and train the mind, we must follow certain disciplines, one of the most basic of which is to hear proper sound vibrations. These sound vibrations are called mantras, which literally means "sound vibrations that can deliver the mind." The most important mantra given in the *Vedas* is the Hare Kṛṣṇa mantra: Hare Kṛṣṇa, Hare Kṛṣṇa, Kṛṣṇa Kṛṣṇa, Hare Hare/ Hare Rāma, Hare Rāma, Rāma Rāma, Hare Hare. Chanting this mantra regularly is the easiest and most effective method for purifying the mind of all influences of the lower modes of nature.

The gold we obtain from a gold mine is usually in a very impure state, but by a purificatory chemical process we can refine pure gold from it. Similarly, when the mind is contaminated by the material modes of nature, it becomes impure. We have to remove these impurities by chanting the Hare Kṛṣṇa mantra. Gradually our consciousness will become purer and purer, and our real identity will be revealed to us.

Thus by developing pure consciousness we can revive our original identity as purely spiritual beings, uncontaminated by the modes of nature. In this stage we do not identify ourselves any longer with the body, gross or subtle, and we are on the plane of God consciousness, or Kṛṣṇa consciousness. Thus we are free of reincarnation once and for all.

The Science of Knowing God

Navīna Śyāma Dāsa

Can the investigation of God through the method of Kṛṣṇa consciousness really be called scientific?

~

God: The Evidence; The God Delusion; God: The Failed Hypothesis; The Language of God: A Scientist Presents Evidence for Belief. Apparently, writing about God is the latest rage among scientists, both theistic and atheistic. Many of these authors have also been invited to speak to college crowds, and they are causing quite a stir. But is this really the best way to approach the question of God's existence? Conventional science, particularly in its "hard" forms such as physics and biology, doesn't seem to offer the right tools and techniques with which to come up with a definitive answer. On the other hand, many religious approaches seem to preclude the rigorous application of reason and the opportunity for individual experimentation. Between these two less than satisfactory alternatives, the Vedic literature of ancient India offers what could be a promising third option. To satisfy ourselves that this is so, we'll first have to look at why conventional science can't get the job done, and then move on to understand how the spiritual science of the Vedic literature succeeds in this task without compromising what modern people like about science.

Two cardinal doctrines present major obstacles to conventional science as a way to know God. First is the doctrine of naturalism, the assumption that all natural phenomena have natural causes. (*Natural* in this context means empirically observable, or perceivable through the five senses.) This is a foundational assumption of scientific research, and its acceptance in effect rules out any reality beyond the reach of the senses.

That being said, there are somewhat softer interpretations of this doctrine. Some scientists distinguish between metaphysical and methodological naturalism. Metaphysical naturalism is the view, described above, that behind everything in the world is an empirical cause. According to this view, the sun rises because of the rotation of the earth, and certainly not because it is pulled along by an imperceptible entity riding a golden chariot. Methodological naturalism, however, merely limits how we *study* the world to empirical observations (things we can touch, see, feel, and so on), while not necessarily ruling out supernatural explanations for these observations. According to this view, a chariot could possibly pull the sun, but the only acceptable way to test this proposition would be to use telescopes and similar instruments. Thus, supernatural phenomena may exist, but supernatural means are not permitted as a way to verify them. Although this perspective is more accommodating, we'll see below that it is still unnecessarily restrictive for one serious about investigating the existence of God.

The second hindrance is the doctrine of falsification. Popularized by the philosopher of science Karl Popper, this doctrine holds that for a statement to be considered scientific, one must be able to prove it false. In other words, if scientist A makes some claim but there is no way for scientist B to show that it is wrong, then the claim is considered unscientific. It can't be tested, so it's disregarded. An interesting consequence of accepting such a criterion for science, and one we'll explore more fully later, is that it becomes impossible to prove anything. One is only able to disprove.

Nevertheless, such is the functioning of science under the doctrine of falsification. Science accepts a theory if it can be used to reliably explain and predict natural phenomena and if no data contradict it. If it is refuted at some point, then another theory is accepted, and so the cycle continues. While the mercurial knowledge produced from such an approach might be acceptable for other purposes, it is not a proper basis for understanding God.

Double Blinders

Why do these twin doctrines of conventional science – naturalism and falsification – become so problematic when applied to the study of the divine? Because they're unwarranted blinders. Let's perform a thought experiment to find out how. Suppose vehement and gifted theists, peerless in their execution of conventional scientific investigation and consummate in their dedication to an omnipotent divine being, suddenly took over all the great research universities and institutes. Given decades of time, what is the farthest such God-fearing geniuses could take us? They could surely discredit every scientific theory ever proposed that did not include a rigorous conception of God. They could also propose elaborate models of their own that both centered on God and perfectly accorded with every piece of empirical data ever observed. But the million-dollar question is, Would they have *proven* the existence of God?

The answer is no. They would certainly have turned atheism into an unreasonable stance that no intelligent person could hope to justify. And they would have elaborated a comprehensive picture of the world as dependent on God in every way. But they would not have proven that God exists. Naturalism would prevent them from introducing data and evidence that transcend the five senses, and falsification would prevent them from establishing any kind of conclusive truth. Shackled by these ideological handcuffs of conventional science that limit it to disproving theories using natural data, they would never be able to produce positive evidence of a supernatural entity.

So where does that leave us, the spiritually inquisitive rationalists? If even in such an ideal scenario, conventional science could not give us the satisfaction of knowing that God exists, are we left with only blind faith in what the authorities tell us? Is there no way to employ rational methods of observation and experimentation to understand the Supreme? As it happens, the Vedic scriptures of ancient India provide us with just such an alternative.

Enlightenment Roots

To appreciate the value of what the Vedic literature offers, we must first understand that the scientific establishment cherishes naturalism and falsification because these help distinguish science from pseudoscience. Today's researchers are intellectual descendants of the Enlightenment, a movement in eighteenth-century Europe that shifted the gaze of humanity from the heavens to the earth and whose proponents esteemed reason and progress over dogma and tradition. As such, members of the scientific community constantly seek to delimit science as a way to explore the world with reason and the intellect, a way that is open to individual endeavor and initiative. In contrast, they vigilantly expel to the realm of pseudoscience any approaches they see as dependent on subjective emotion or passive reception, which for them usually includes religion of any kind. Both naturalism and falsification aid such a separation, and hence mainstream researchers have come to accept them as doctrines.

Granting that the motive underlying their acceptance is bona fide – distinguishing disciplined inquiry from whimsical allegation – a critical question is whether these doctrines are the only means to achieve this end. Not if we engage the Vedic wisdom. While avoiding the pitfalls that naturalism and falsification present, the Vedic literature gives a way to get knowledge that is nevertheless rigorous, systematic, and verifiable. Indeed, the traditional Vedic method of knowing God (as presented in scriptures like *Bhagavad-gītā* and *Śrīmad-Bhāgavatam*) is a model of good science, albeit a science adapted in unavoidable ways to the study of spirit.

Methods of the Soft Sciences

The first (rather unremarkable) adaptation is the realization that God is a person who must be dealt with accordingly, not an inert substratum of the universe that we can dig up and put on a microscope slide. Therefore if we are to look to science as a model, we must look to the social rather than the natural sciences.

Certainly many "hard" scientists scoff at the idea of disciplines like psychology, sociology, and economics being considered science at all, but that has not stopped legions of thoughtful people from trying to apply the scientific method to the study of human beings and their societies. These social scientists are simply forced to take into account qualities in their subjects, such as self-awareness and self-determination, that natural scientists, who research inert matter or subhuman species, generally take the liberty of ignoring. Since even the study of humans as conscious agents is a matter for social science, why would we use the methods of the natural sciences to study God? If anything, He is superhuman.

How then might we define the spiritual social science of the Vedic literature? We can define conventional science, social or otherwise, as "the objective observation of the natural realm by the senses and their extensions." But given that God is known in the Vedic literature as Adhokṣaja ("beyond the reach of the senses") and Acintya ("inconceivable"), the need to adapt this definition to the study of transcendence becomes obvious. A definition of spiritual science that takes God's transcendental nature into account might be "the subjective experience of the transcendental realm by the consciousness, in accordance with the direction of revealed scripture."

Is this new definition no longer scientific? Śrīla Prabhupāda apparently didn't think so; he referred to the practice of spiritual life as the science of self-realization. Let's review the components of this "science of self-realization" and see if such a perspective is justified.

To begin with, our new definition of science involves subjectivity rather than objectivity. But then, modern science (through the Heisenberg Uncertainty Principle and quantum mechanics) has brought the observer into the equations of physics and prevented him or her from remaining safely on the sidelines. Thus, the presence and perceptions of the person doing the measuring color every act of measurement, and there is no such thing as knowledge independent of the knower. Yes, these truths operate on the infinitesimal quantum scale, but the point is that conventional science has essentially shown objectivity to be illusory, so we can hardly be criticized for talking about a science based on subjective experience.

The next component of our definition of spiritual science is the use of consciousness, rather than our physical senses, as our primary research instrument. This obviously violates the doctrine of methodological naturalism, which restricts measurements to instruments that extend the senses. But is our definition still scientific in meaningful ways?

Isomorphism

Consider the principle of isomorphism, which dictates that the instrument used to measure a certain phenomenon should be appropriately matched to that phenomenon. To depend solely on the five senses (and their mechanical extensions) in our search for God violates this principle; they can only perceive matter, whereas our subject is spiritual. Considering this limitation, it is only reasonable to replace them with a more appropriate measuring tool. To dogmatically cling to only those instruments with which one is comfortable or familiar – in the face of their obvious inappropriateness – is the sign of an irrational researcher, not a good scientist. As the famous chemist John Platt wrote several decades ago in the journal *Science:*

> Beware of the man of one method or one instrument, either experimental or theoretical. He tends to become method-oriented rather than problem-oriented. The method-oriented man is shackled; the problem-oriented man is at least reaching freely toward what is most important.

If we are to successfully research the existence of God, as good scientists we must use whatever method is best suited to the problem at hand. The Vedic literature informs us that to understand the supreme spirit, the supreme consciousness, the supreme self, the only suitable instrument is our own spirit, our own consciousness, our own self. Indeed, only in our capacity as portions of His divinity can we connect with God.

Using Consciousness to Investigate God

Having sagaciously chosen consciousness as our instrument, how should we employ it? This is where the guidance of revealed scripture becomes crucial. Following scripture essentially means studying God on His own terms, for He is the ultimate source of scripture.

Adapting to the needs and demands of a subject is not alien to conventional social science research. Consent and access are of paramount importance, because human beings cannot be manipulated against their will as if they were mere vials of chemicals or laboratory chimpanzees. If these considerations are critical in studying ordinary people, we should not be surprised to find they are important in studying God. If we are to succeed, we need Him to consent to our study and grant us access to Him. We might find this subordinate status unpalatable, but we must accept that we are trying to meet with the busiest, richest, most powerful, and most famous person in existence.

Social science researchers often speak of critically positioned persons who can help them make important contacts as "gatekeepers." As it turns out, God has his own gatekeepers, and we need to work through them to gain an audience with God, just as we would work through a corporate hierarchy to arrange a meeting with a CEO.

Fortunately for us, in the *Bhagavad-gītā* God has elaborately presented the procedures by which we can gain access to Him. Among these the most foundational is the need to accept a guru. Is such a move unscientific? Not at all. Just as any doctoral student learns the art of research from an advisor, so too the spiritual aspirant must take instruction from an expert. Seasoned researchers, of either spirit or matter, can pass on finer points of technique and practice.

The Vedic approach to knowing God thus violates the doctrine of naturalism in its reliance on supernatural methods, yet it is surprisingly consistent with the spirit of science, and even many of its essential principles. It is an improved science, however, in that it allows access to an entirely different dimension of reality, systematically and with repeatability.

What of the other impediment to conventional scientific knowledge of God, the doctrine of falsification? How does the science of the Vedic literature address this limitation?

Two Perspectives on Knowledge

Once again a bit of background discussion is needed before we can answer such questions. Conventional science and Vedic science have dramatically divergent perspectives on knowledge. The former holds that human beings can't know anything positively or independently. Rather, based on the empirical data we gather by observing and interacting with the physical world, we constantly refine what we consider truth. Our knowledge base is thus relative and ever changing.

Ultimately, such a state of affairs really means we don't *know* anything. I may say I know that the sun will rise tomorrow or that there is a country called China halfway around the world from the U.S., but my so-called knowledge is based only on my experience. If tomorrow the sun doesn't rise or I fly to China only to find out it doesn't exist, I would simply revise what I considered truth. Today's dependable knowledge would become tomorrow's mythology. In light of such an understanding of knowledge, the doctrine of falsification makes sense. We can't really know what is true, so let's just spend our time showing what is definitely *not* true, and take what's left over as good enough for now.

The Vedic scriptures present a different view of knowledge. They claim that we can know things for certain, intrinsically and independently. This absolute knowledge is not subject to the fluxes of our ever-changing world. Not surprisingly, this principle applies most powerfully and most gloriously to the one question we should most want to answer: Is there a God? Sounds wonderful, we may say, but is this purportedly absolute knowledge scientific? It certainly seems so. Although presented in revealed scripture, one need not accept it blindly, based solely on someone else's word or experience. True to the spirit of scientific inquiry, it can be verified by individual endeavor.

More Scientific than Science

In fact, one could argue that this process is even more scientific than conventional science. After all, why do many people choose science, rather than, say, religion, as a means to acquire knowledge? I assume it is because if they are going to have to rely on information from some outside source, over some sort of authority figure, they prefer their own senses (which are an outside source in that I am different from my eyes, which can and do deceive me). At least then they are involved in the process and not merely passive recipients. But the Vedic literature boldly declares that you don't have to rely on any outside source – you can know for yourself. Knowledge does not have to stay externally dependent, on either an authority figure or our own senses, but can become something genuinely internal. What could be more satisfying to people who want to see for themselves?

In this way the Vedic method allows us to transcend the restrictions of falsification and acquire true positive knowledge, but in a way harmonious with scientific ideals like independent observation and verification.

Of course, we begin by accepting the version of scripture on faith, but again, is that really so unscientific? Every conventional research investigation begins with a hypothesis, a formulation of what the researcher expects to find. This hunch can come from theory, observation, previous research, life experience, intuition – just about anywhere. As long as the methods used in investigating the hypothesis are rigorous, its source is irrelevant. So why *not* start from scripture?

Indeed, even before we begin our investigation, scripture plays an important role. Lest we have trouble imagining what it feels like to have such positive knowledge, the Vedic scriptures use analogies to inspire us. Lord Kṛṣṇa explains in the opening of the most confidential chapter of the *Bhagavad-gītā* (chapter 9) that the knowledge He is about to describe gives "direct experience" (*pratyakṣa*). Although the subject being discussed is clearly spiritual, the Sanskrit word used is the same as that used in physical sensation. And if that doesn't give us enough of an idea, the *Śrīmad-Bhāgavatam* (11.2.42) assures us:

> Devotion, direct experience of the Supreme Lord, and detachment from other things – these three occur simultaneously for one who has taken shelter of the Supreme Personality of Godhead, in the same way that pleasure, nourishment, and relief from hunger come simultaneously and increasingly, with each bite, for a person engaged in eating.

By faithfully following the procedures God has given in the Vedic literature, we can expect to experience Him in as tangible a way as we experience a meal. And it doesn't stop at the internal. Rather, both the *Bhagavad-gītā* (6.30) and the *Śrīmad-Bhāgavatam* (11.2.45) inform us that at a certain stage of advancement, we'll see God in everything and everyone.

At this point it should be clear that what the Vedic literature offers is a genuinely scientific way to know God. Rather than invoking mere sentimentality or blind faith, it sets forth a coherent process that incorporates both reason and individual endeavor, and then invites willing souls to make their own investigation. So, for those of us who truly want to research the existence of God, the predicament is clear: Running on the two rails of naturalism and falsification, the locomotive of conventional science can take us some distance in the right direction. But sooner or later we have to board the airplane of Vedic science to reach our desired destination. So why wait until the end of the line?

Chapter Four

The "Love" Vacuum

On Sex and Suffering

A conversation between His Divine Grace
A.C. Bhaktivedanta Swami Prabhupāda and his disciples

One class of philosophers says that suffering cannot be dismissed and therefore we must be strong to tolerate it, and another class of philosophers says that since life is full of suffering, we should make life zero. But neither class has any information that there is real life where there is no suffering.

~

Devotee: Śrīla Prabhupāda, here in California the divorce rate is nearly 50%. Why do you think that is so?

Śrīla Prabhupāda: In India there is a saying that he who is married laments and he who is not married also laments. The married man laments, "Why did I marry? I could have remained free." And he who is not married laments, "Oh, why didn't I accept a wife? I would have been happy." [*Laughter.*] By sex one begets a child, and as soon as there is a child there is suffering. The child suffers and the parents also suffer to take care of him. But again they have another child. Therefore it is said in *Śrīmad-Bhāgavatam, tṛpyanti neha kṛpaṇā bahu-duḥkha-bhājaḥ*. In connection with this child-producing there is so much difficulty and trouble, but although one *knows* that, one again does the same thing.

Sex is the main happiness in this material world. That is the main happiness, and it is very abominable. What is this happiness? *Kaṇḍūyanena karayor iva duḥkha-duḥkham.* It is like the rubbing of two hands together to relieve an itch. Sex produces so many bad results, but still one is not satisfied. Now there are contraceptives, abortion – so many things. *Māyā* [illusion] is so strong; she says, "Yes, do this and be implicated."

Therefore the *Bhāgavatam* says, *kaṇḍūtivan manasijam viṣaheta dhīraḥ.* A man who is *dhīra,* sober and sane, tolerates this itching sensation of sex desire. One who can tolerate the itching sensation saves so much trouble, but one who cannot is immediately implicated. Whether illicit or legitimate, sex is trouble.

Devotee: Śrīla Prabhupāda, this is the first time we've walked this way. Everything looks different and new.

Śrīla Prabhupāda: [*Laughs.*] This is material life. We are wandering sometimes this way, sometimes that way, and we are thinking, "Oh, this is new." *Brahmāṇḍa bhramite:* we are wandering all over the universe trying to find out something new. But nothing is new: everything is old.

When a man becomes old he generally thinks, "Oh, this life is so troublesome." So he is allowed to change to a new body, a child's body. The child is taken care of and he thinks, "Now I've got such a comfortable life." But again he becomes old and disgusted. So Kṛṣṇa is so kind: "All right," He says, "change your body." This is *punaḥ punaś carvita-carvaṇānām,* chewing the chewed. Kṛṣṇa gives the living entity many facilities: "All right, become a tree. All right, become a serpent. All right, become a demigod. All right, become a king. Become a cobbler. Go to the heavenly planets. Go to the hellish planets." There are so many varieties of life, but in all of them the living entity is packed up in this material world. He's looking for freedom, but he does not know that freedom is available only under the shelter of Kṛṣṇa. That he will not accept.

Seeing the suffering in this material world, the Māyāvādīs [impersonalists] want to make life variety-less (*nirviśeṣa*) and the

Buddhists want to make it zero (*śūnyavādī*). But neither proposition is possible. You may remain variety-less for some time, but again you will want varieties. Big, big *sannyāsīs* [renunciants] preach so much about *brahma satyaṁ jagan mithyā* ["The impersonal Absolute is true; this universe is false"], but again they come down from Brahman to do political and social work. They cannot remain in Brahman for long, so they have to accept this material variety, because variety is the mother of enjoyment. Therefore our proposition is this: Come to the real variety, Kṛṣṇa consciousness. Then your life will be successful.

Devotee: Most people are trying to enjoy so much in this life that they don't even think about the next life.

Śrīla Prabhupāda: They do not know what the next life is, so they make it zero. They say, "There is no next life," and in that way they are satisfied. When a rabbit sees some danger it closes its eyes and thinks there is no danger. These rascals are like that. It is all ignorance.

Devotee: There is a philosophy called stoicism that says that since life is meant for suffering, one should just become very sturdy and suffer a great deal.

Śrīla Prabhupāda: So, their idea is that one who can suffer without any protest – he is a first-class man. Believing in such a philosophy means that one does not know how to *stop* suffering. One class of philosophers says that suffering cannot be dismissed and therefore we must be strong to tolerate it, and another class of philosophers says that since life is full of suffering, we should make life zero. But neither class has any information that there is real life where there is no suffering. That is Kṛṣṇa consciousness. There is *life,* but no suffering. *Ānanda-mayo 'bhyāsāt:* simply bliss. Dancing, eating, and chanting, with no suffering. Would anybody refuse that? Is there any such fool?

Devotee: People deny that such a life exists.

Śrīla Prabhupāda: But suppose there is such a life, where you can simply dance, eat, and live happily for eternity. Would you not like to accept it?

Devotee: Anyone would like to accept it. But people think it doesn't exist.

Śrīla Prabhupāda: So our first proposition should be that there is a life like this – only happiness, with no suffering. Everyone will say, "Yes, I would like it." They will accept it. Unfortunately, because people have been cheated again and again, they think that this is another cheating. Therefore, preaching Kṛṣṇa consciousness means to convince people that there is a life full of happiness, with no suffering.

Devotee: What will convince them that we are not cheating also?

Śrīla Prabhupāda: Invite them to come to our temple and see our devotees. We are chanting, dancing, and eating nicely. This is practical proof.

Devotee: But doesn't one have to be purified before one can realize these things?

Śrīla Prabhupāda: No. We say, "Come and chant Hare Kṛṣṇa with us; you'll become purified. We don't want anything from you. We shall give you food – we shall give you everything. Simply come and chant with us." This is our message.

Immortal Longings

Ravīndra Svarūpa Dāsa

We are possessed by an unremitting desire for pleasure, by the conviction that happiness is our right. This conflicts with the reality of our condition.

~

No one likes to be the bearer of bad news. Not only is it unpleasant; it can be dangerous. Kings routinely used to kill on the spot hapless messengers bringing word of defeat.

Even so, most people still acknowledge that truth, however unpalatable, is preferable to illusion, however cheering. This is, after all, only practical, for the facts as they affect us have a certain implacable stubbornness to which even the most compelling illusions must eventually yield. Facts always win – simply because they are facts.

You have probably gathered that I have some fairly unpleasant things to say.

Indeed, the illusion I want to destroy is perhaps the most deeply rooted and pervasive of all human convictions. It is the idea that we can achieve happiness through the enjoyment of our senses, especially through that prototype of all pleasure, sex and sexual love. Certainly no effort has been pursued as doggedly, and yet produced a record of such consistent failure, as this one. The wonder is that this history of universal defeat has in no way dampened the hope of imminent victory.

Certainly, with the disintegration of traditional religions and the official establishment of secular philosophies, this illusion has gained the force of an obsession. If we are no more than sophisticated animals, if our existence as individual conscious subjects is something haphazardly thrown up between two infinities of nothingness, then we would be foolish not to mine our allotment of endurance for as much sensual bliss as possible. Since this is all we have, we had better give it our best effort.

Sexual Fantasy

Such sentiments have greatly contributed to the presently widespread movement toward a full sensual awakening through the liberation of sexuality. Given that the body provides our only access to happiness, we must extirpate those constraints upon our fulfillment, those internal impediments inculcated by discarded, life-denying religions and moralities – the repression of desires, the consciousness of guilt, the fear and hatred of the body. Now one cultivates a liberated and expansive life, free from all repressions; one aspires to drink deeply at the wells of pure pleasure, unpolluted by guilt or shame, healed and whole in spirit through a joyous acceptance and celebration of the body.

It shouldn't take much experience of the actual conduct of sexual relations for an alert person to recognize that this vision of unrestrained, joyous sex is an unrealizable fantasy. Nevertheless, the fantasy still seems to exercise an irresistible fascination. I suppose that people must blame its disappointments on repressions still unpurged, residual guilt and shame, and a lack of trust in and surrender to the body itself.

But in fact none of us can wholeheartedly trust in and surrender to the body, because we know, beneath the bluff and the bravado, that our bodies are frail and weak and dying and that the greatest pleasure it gives us is heartbreakingly brief. We find ourselves bound within a complexity of muscle and vein that nature can dismantle at any moment, in any of thousands of horrible ways. Our strength and beauty leak away in daily increments. Our body disintegrates before our eyes and becomes itself a major source of our suffering, and then we die.

Therefore, no one can help but be horrified by his body (even though the mind must repress those feelings in self-defense). This horror is not an artificial hate or fear imposed by some life-denying religion. It is only a sensible reaction to a correct perception.

Our position is intrinsically divided. We are not whole. We are endowed with a developed consciousness that makes our incarceration in bodies like those of animals agonizing for us. We can imagine, abstract, generalize, range far beyond the narrow limits of local place and time. Our minds continually search for the first principles behind all things, for the one that underlies the many, for the permanent that persists through all change, for the eternal beyond the temporal. Meanwhile we struggle fitfully in a dying body. Our spirits reach for the infinite; our molars rot.

The consciousness that gives us such strong intimations of immortality also forces us to be acutely aware of our helplessness before nature, our fragility before the huge weight of the universe, and the constant threat of death under which we live. Even a small child draws the connection between the bleeding cut on his finger and the animals he sees exploded in gore upon the roadside.

All the same, we are possessed by an unremitting desire for pleasure, by the conviction that happiness is our right. This conflicts with the reality of our condition. Therefore, the mind represses with great power our perception of reality and our horror at our situation. Any person will verbally admit to you that he knows he is going to die, but the admission rings curiously hollow. It is as if he were talking about someone else. At heart, he refuses to believe it. This is how he lives a "happy" life – at least for a time.

We should recognize that most of human culture is a

complicity to sustain our vital delusion, a skillful artifice to keep ourselves unconscious. We erect and vie for artificial or symbolic goals so that we can prove to ourselves our strength and power, our endurance and invulnerability; we have thousands of ways of patting ourselves and each other on the back. But of course, nature grinds relentlessly on and pays no heed to our fine and tender feelings, our banners and our flags, our list of conquests and victories. While we keep ourselves resolutely preoccupied and distracted, absorbed in our illusory enterprises, death comes, to our great surprise.

We dismiss death from our minds to be happy, but it doesn't really work. On the contrary, since in this world life and death are bound tightly together, to retreat from death is to retreat from life. One cannot become selectively unconscious.

This explains the loss of that pristine and glorious vision of the world we knew as a child, a loss poets ceaselessly lament. Somehow we fall from grace, and thereafter we experience life with a deadened spirit and narrowed consciousness, a diminished capacity for feeling. Adulthood fully initiates us into the established system of illusions, into a life of intense effort toward makeshift goals whose real purpose is to keep us from thought. Such a life is necessarily thin, grey, tasteless, and it has an undercurrent of constant, nagging despair, for which most societies provide some sort of anesthetic – intoxicants, television, or the like. All the while, the wonder and splendor of the edenic world of our childhood lies shining all about us, but we have turned away from it in fear, for we have learned that it is a place of death.

This discovery begins early enough, but our retreat into organized unreality takes time. Yet there is one thing more than anything else that seals it. This is sex.

The Ultimate Failure

My assertion, of course, goes quite counter to the tenet of the sexual liberation movement that through surrender to sex we can gain a new innocence and thus enter a world radiant with intense and joyous experience. But such a liberated posture ignores that the body, which is the vehicle of sexual pleasure, is also the vehicle of pain and disease and senescence and death.

The initiation into sex, that experience of overwhelming subjugation to the body for pleasure, is precisely that experience which contributes most to the diminished capacity for living. This is not so hard to see. Our first sexual act precipitates a tenacious identification with the body, forges a fast bond to it. Thereafter, we are committed to the project of seeking happiness through the senses. At the same time, we awaken to a deep and abiding dread:

We have sealed our pact with mortality. As sex deadens the spirit, it quickens all the senses. It becomes the center of all material enjoyment. Yet sensual pleasures depend entirely upon the favorable arrangement of circumstances, and so the more a person is committed to pursuing these pleasures, the greater his anxiety. Most of all he needs money. Sex indentures him to ceaseless labor. Securing attractive sexual partners is at best an elaborate and troublesome pursuit, fraught with dangers to one's self-esteem. As a person becomes older, the pursuit becomes harder and depends almost entirely upon his ability to maintain his social prestige and display his opulence and generosity. There is no end to worry and to fear.

On the other hand, we may try to withdraw from the anxieties of the sexual marketplace and take the advice of countless popular songs by seeking the one we "love" and who "loves" us in return. Such a discovery is rare enough, but it hardly ends our sufferings. On the contrary, nothing can compare to our anguish when we lose the object of our love – or that one's love for us. Love is no shelter. And we have discovered that as people increasingly demand sexual fulfillment from marriage, the less durable such relationships are becoming.

Our inability to sustain relationships is at the heart of our predicament. All our happiness and our achievement depend upon our successfully perpetuating relationships, and our ultimate failure to do so is called death. Small losses prefigure the larger one. We want to live, to expand our organism, to increase the power of our being – in short, to overcome death. As sex is the act of creation of life, we turn to it to commune with the energy of life itself and to prove our vital power. This power becomes embodied in offspring. Our family becomes the nucleus of a fortification composed of real estate, money, social connections, privilege, and power. We feed our vital force by competing with enemies and destroying them. In this way we prosper and gloriously expand. Yet all these activities have a desperate and driven character. We are trying to fool ourselves. For at heart we know very well that nothing can protect us, that all our powerful friends, aristocratic relatives, and sweet-faced children are fallible soldiers in the war, and that all of us are doomed.

Revolt Against Death

I think I have drawn an honest picture of our human predicament, and I am afraid that by now you must be thinking I am willfully obtuse. You may indeed be willing to admit that all of us have to settle for less happiness in life than we want (as Freud put it, the "reality principle" replaces the "pleasure principle"), and you might admit that sex never really does live up to its promise. All the same, it still gives us *some* pleasure, and with the pain and suffering we have to face, why shouldn't we at least accept this pleasure?

Sex is a biological drive; it is fundamental to life itself. We cannot be free of it, and so even though it is not without difficulties, even worse are the difficulties of suppression and frustration. So what can we do? It is simply perverse to keep harping on the dark side of things, and all this bad news is pointless.

But there is, I assure you, a point. I would like you to consider the possibility that our revolt against the sentence of death imposed by the body, our intuitive consciousness that we are meant for more than casual destruction, may have a justification in dimly apprehended, obscured fact. Our developed human consciousness, which keeps us from being comfortable in an animal body, may indicate or symptomize a fundamental feature of existence.

To put it another way, consider the possibility that our involvement in sex, and in the whole frantic enterprise of sensual life that expands from it, constitutes a kind of intoxication or stupefaction of awareness that occludes our normal consciousness of our real nature – a nature that is in fact not subject at all to death. If this is so, there is a prospect for realizing, through the excavation of that eternal self, an inherent and inalienable happiness absolutely independent of the states of the body. One can achieve this, however, only if one can remove the stupefaction of consciousness by directing his energies away from the project of material satisfaction that centers on sex.

The project of uncovering the eternal self that I am proposing should not be confused with the repressive programs that have been propagated in the name of religion. The project of self-realization does not call for enduring a bleak *life* of frustration and deprivation to attain a future heavenly enjoyment. Nor does it propose that we seek happiness as a neutral "peace," the mere absence of pain, through atrophy of the affections. On the contrary, I propose that our desire to possess an unending existence of uninterrupted, ever-intensifying bliss is legitimate, and that there is a practical way we can fulfill it immediately, a way so natural, powerful, and attractive that all other engagements lose their allure.

Fundamental Ignorance

You may be thinking, however, that if there were anything to this it would have already been accepted by our intellectual and political leaders and embedded in educational policy. The problem is that a person's knowledge is relative to his situation. When a person is habituated to sensual enjoyment and to sex, his instruments of perception malfunction, and so he is unable to comprehend or experience his own eternal nature, no matter how outstanding he may otherwise be. Such people are sunk in an ignorance so profound, so fundamental, that even their greatest knowledge is really a kind of advancement in ignorance. In spite of repeated failures, they perpetually put forward hopeless and quixotic schemes to bring happiness, and they seem to have an animallike obliviousness to the essential character of the world. Even though they mislead others, however, they are ultimately not worthy of anger or scorn: they suffer like everyone else.

Knowledge concerning the eternal self and the method of freeing it can come only from one who is himself free. This implies that if there is such a person there must have been a historical succession of them passing down the teaching. In fact, such traditions have appeared in many countries, and often enough – although the usual course is that it will flourish for a while, become compromised by the spirit of material enjoyment, and then look absurd and be rejected.

I was taught the science of self-realization by His Divine Grace A.C. Bhaktivedanta Swami Prabhupāda, who follows from a historical tradition going back thousands of years in India. The teachings of that tradition, recorded in ancient Sanskrit texts like *Bhagavad-gītā* and *Śrīmad-Bhāgavatam,* recognize a variety of methods for self-realization, but recommend strongly, above all others, the method called *bhakti-yoga.*

To help explain this method of freeing the self, let me first set out a more detailed account of the self and its relation to matter and to other selves.

There are two categories of selves. All selves are eternal and of the nature of pure cognition and bliss, but one category contains numberless selves, and the other category contains one self alone. The one self is called the supreme self because it completely sustains the many. The one is infinite and self-sufficient; the many are infinitesimal and dependent. (You may call the many infinitesimal selves "souls" and the one infinite self "God," but I have avoided these terms because speculative philosophy and theology have burdened them with such misinformation, controversy, and a general bad name that I would rather start here with a verbal clean slate.) You may compare the supreme self to the sun and the subordinate selves to the atomic particles of sunshine; so we can speak of the one supreme self as the energetic and of the multitudinous subordinate selves as the energy. Just as the atoms of sunshine are a part of the sun, though removed from it, so the individual selves are separated particles of the supreme self, and accordingly they are qualitatively identical with the supreme, even though they are quantitatively minute. Each fragmental self possesses a tiny allotment of all the qualities of the complete self.

The milieu in which the supreme self eternally dwells with the subordinate selves is called the spiritual, or internal, energy. In that atmosphere, the supreme self is the unwavering object of love for the subordinate selves because He is supremely attractive – for this reason, He is called "Kṛṣṇa" ("the all-attractive one"). Each act of the subordinate selves expresses their uninterrupted, ever-increasing love for Kṛṣṇa, who returns His own feelings in the same way. Thus each self is fully satisfied because he is fully absorbed in an eternal loving relationship with the supremely lovable person, the source of all beauty. Kṛṣṇa returns the love of the subordinate selves without reservation, in a relationship that time cannot sunder. This is the natural condition of the selves.

As the origin of everything, the supreme self is the supreme enjoyer, and the subordinate selves derive their own sustenance and bliss by participating in His enjoyment. They cannot enjoy independently. Yet it happens that some selves want this one thing. Having everything, an eternal life of bliss and knowledge, they nevertheless want to controvert their own essential nature as subordinate, dependent beings. They want to become the supreme self. Instead of serving, they would like to be served. Thus they want to abrogate their relationship with Kṛṣṇa; since they have a minute amount of the independence the supreme possesses in full, they can do it.

Kṛṣṇa does not transgress the small independence of His fragmental parts, and He accedes to their desire. For them – that is to say, for us – He creates another milieu, called the material, or external, energy. Of course, it is logically impossible for the supreme self to grant subordinate selves their desire to be the supreme, for by definition there can be only one supreme. It is the essential nature of the subordinate selves to serve, to be controlled by, the supreme. That nature cannot be changed, but in the material energy the tiny selves can have the illusion that they are independent, that they are the supreme, that they are the enjoyers and the controllers. All the same, they remain inescapably under the control of Kṛṣṇa's material energy, which they cannot overcome.

Returning to a Pure Existence

Selves are beings that experience, centers of consciousness, subjects. Matter does not experience; it is without subjectivity; it is completely an object. Selves live; matter is lifeless. When the selves enter the alien, material energy, they acquire and animate bodies made out of lifeless matter. Driven by a desire to forget Kṛṣṇa and their relation to Him, they identify themselves with bodies of matter. In this way the self becomes a divided being. Now the self thinks of itself as a product of nature, as an object created and destroyed in time. As the body is damaged by disease and injury, as it disintegrates with age, and as it dies, the self thinks, "This is happening to me." Thus the self enters the interminable horror of material existence, a nightmare of carnage from which it cannot awake. As one body is destroyed, nature transfers him to another, to undergo a similar destruction.

The self moves blindly through these bodies, driven by an overwhelming appetite for enjoyment. In its original condition, the self is filled with a ceaseless love for the supreme, all-attractive self. This love is constitutional; it cannot be removed; it is the self's very life. Therefore, when the self turns aside from the proper object of his love, that love is not annihilated but becomes transmuted or redirected. When the self contacts the material energy, his love for Kṛṣṇa is transformed into lust, just as milk in contact with acid turns into curd.

So the erotic drive is indeed part of our essential makeup. But it is a transformation of what is in fact our love for Kṛṣṇa. Desire, therefore, cannot possibly be annihilated, nor can it be successfully repressed or suppressed. However, it can be reverted to its original state.

Yet as long as we are impelled by the erotic drive, we take on a succession of bodies of matter. We move up the hierarchy of beings. In the lower stages of our evolution, in plant and then animal bodies, our consciousness is heavily covered. We are only dimly and fitfully sentient. When at last we acquire human bodies, our consciousness, that effulgence of the eternal self, becomes uniquely uncovered. This fuller manifestation of the eternal self in beings that still inhabit material bodies creates a problematical situation, full of the tensions of a divided nature, and provides a kind of suffering that ignorant animals do not experience. The gift of uncovered consciousness causes us to wonder: Who am I? Why am I here? What is my purpose? Why must I die? Such questions lead us toward self-realization. If we do not at least begin upon this course, then we must take another. The revelation of our spiritually conscious nature shows us the incongruities of our position in matter, and the proper response is to seek freedom from material entanglement and thus resolve the sufferings that arise from duality. Unfortunately, too many people respond to the illuminations of a higher consciousness by frantically trying to snuff it out by pursuing intense animal satisfactions that produce a narrow, excited awareness, and by seeking the oblivion of drugs. This course drops the self again into animal bodies, in which it will devour and be devoured, until it at last returns to human form and once more confronts its eternal nature.

If we seize the chance of human consciousness, we can solve the problem of existence by cultivating knowledge of the self, become freed from encagement in matter, and return to our pure existence in intimate, eternal love with Kṛṣṇa.

Our return to our normal condition is engineered by Kṛṣṇa. While we have forgotten Him, He has not forgotten us; He has remained close by our side through all our wanderings in darkness and in pain, waiting for us to show the first flicker of a desire to abandon our illusory project of becoming the supreme. When, in the hidden depths of our being, we start to yearn for Kṛṣṇa and to regret our folly in turning away, Kṛṣṇa immediately arranges for us to meet one of His self-realized representatives. This person tells us explicitly about the conditions of material existence, about our eternal nature, and about our relation with Kṛṣṇa, thus reviving our latent knowledge. He also initiates us onto the path of spiritual restoration with direct practical instructions. We would probably think that freedom from material conditions was some unrealizable idea, if we did not have Kṛṣṇa's representative before us as a living testament to its factuality.

The Flavor of Natural Love

The essence of the program to return the self to its pure state consists of bringing that self into direct contact with Kṛṣṇa. The simplest and most effective way of doing this is through sound. The sounds that name or describe Kṛṣṇa are of a totally different nature from sounds that name or describe material things. This is because Kṛṣṇa is absolute, or nondual. The duality of the material world entails that a substance and its name have nothing intrinsic in common. If, for example, I say "water, water, water," my thirst is not slaked. On the other hand, if I say "Kṛṣṇa, Kṛṣṇa, Kṛṣṇa," or any other personal name of the Supreme Self, I come directly into contact with Him. By thus using our tongue to utter and ear to hear the names and glorification of the supreme, we are united with Him. That contact is potent. Kṛṣṇa is the supreme pure, and His association is purifying. We are qualitatively one with Kṛṣṇa, and His association revives that original character, reawakens our native consciousness. Quickly, then, we begin to experience our eternal nature and to taste the remarkable flavor of our natural love, and as we do so we lose interest in the material substitutes that used to attract us. Our lust begins to be transformed back into love again. Thus, the revival of pure consciousness is based not on the repression or suppression of desire, but on its respiritualization.

This is different from sublimation. Sublimation is an artificial replacement of a gross physical urge with a more refined substitute, and the satisfaction it affords is never as intense and absorbing as the satisfaction of the original urge. But when, by contrast, our love is returned to Kṛṣṇa, it gains immeasurably in intensity and in power, for it has found its proper object, and it is now free from the fear of change and death that block its investment in material things. Our love for Kṛṣṇa begins to flow effortlessly, unchecked and unimpeded. It exfoliates without limit. Since Kṛṣṇa includes all other selves, our love expands to encompass them also. As one begins to live and breathe the atmosphere of unconditioned and uninterrupted love for Kṛṣṇa, he sees the whole world in a new light, and his former attempts to exploit it for his own pleasure seem perverse.

From the very beginning of Kṛṣṇa consciousness one gains the positive taste for spiritual existence, and so the addictions of the senses become relatively easy to give up. The four greatest impediments to spiritual life – illicit sex, intoxication, meat-eating, and gambling – can be abandoned with surprising ease. When one has the real thing, a real life of unceasing bliss and knowledge, there is no difficulty in putting aside the counterfeits.

Unconditional love for Kṛṣṇa is manifest in unconditional engagement in the service of Kṛṣṇa, in service that has no desire for reward and no interruption. This is the characteristic that distinguishes love from its perverted material transformation, lust, in which personal gain is the motive. Even the sexual union of a man and a woman can be used in the service of Kṛṣṇa. It is extremely good fortune for a child to be born from parents engaged in self-realization, for from his earliest moments he lives in an atmosphere uncontaminated by lust and greed, and he takes in the principles of spiritual life with his mother's milk. Such children can be conceived only when the parents unite specifically for that purpose and insure the good qualities of their offspring through their own purification of consciousness. The first duty of parents is to be able to deliver their children from death, and family life dedicated to that purpose is conducive to self-realization and as such need not be artificially renounced.

But sex for any other purpose – sex to exploit the body for enjoyment, to fuel the delusions of the ego – is the cause of death. Sex more than anything else fixes our false identification of our selves with the body, rivets us into the flesh, and addicts us to material aggrandizement. Sexual desire can never be satisfied, for it grows by what it feeds on. This permanently frustrated desire causes a deep and abiding rage, which deepens our illusion. The twin delusions of desire and hate drive us on through interminable bodily incarcerations, hurtling us over and over into forms that fill us with fear, suffer the ceaseless onslaught of injury and disease, disintegrate while we still occupy them, and are destroyed. In reality none of this happens to us, but we have erroneously identified ourselves with the body and have thereby taken these torments upon us. Death is an illusion we have imposed upon ourselves by our desire to enjoy this world. Sex is the essence of that desire. Sex, therefore, is death.

It is only right that we struggle against the sentence of death. It is only proper that we seek a life of uninterrupted and unending pleasure uncompromised by shame or fear. It is only natural that we want to be whole and at one with ourselves, uncompromised by duality. The most deadly delusion is that sex is a way to these goals, for in fact it is the greatest single impediment. It is the cause of our disease, which we embrace as the cure.

The restrictions upon sexual activity enjoined by religions were originally meant to assist in overcoming this greatest block to human happiness. Unfortunately, now only the restrictions and negations survive, while the real reason for them has been forgotten.

But the viable path of self-realization is once again open. It may seem to you that, whatever good intentions you may have, the sexual drive is too powerful for you to overcome. It is true that it is too strong for artificial suppression. But I know from experience that if you simply begin by taking up the positive practices of *bhakti-yoga,* especially the reciting of the name of Kṛṣṇa in the form of the Hare Kṛṣṇa mantra, you will find that what seemed so formidable a barrier becomes easy to cross and that your authentic life, beyond the world of birth and death, is at hand.

Four No-Nonsense Facts of Life

Viśākhā Devī Dāsī

"What is the most amazing thing?" a sagacious king was once asked. "The most amazing thing," the king responded, "is that although everyone knows he is destined to die, just as his relatives and friends have died, no one prepares for his own death. He acts as if he will live forever."

~

You may have heard Kṛṣṇa's devotees use the term *conditioned soul,* and you may have wondered what it meant. A conditioned soul is one controlled by the insurmountable forces of material nature, especially the miseries of birth, aging, disease, and death.

For us conditioned souls in the material world, all the rewards and pleasantries of life – the tender love of our friends and relatives, our homes, hobbies, studies, dinners at eight, and tennis on Sundays – all are fleeting because of these relentless impositions of nature. Some souls, desiring to attain lasting pleasure, try to become unconditioned, free from the influence of material nature.

To do this they require a qualified spiritual teacher, as well as guidebooks, like *Bhagavad-gītā* and *Śrīmad-Bhāgavatam,* elaborate treatises on material and spiritual knowledge. *Bhagavad-gītā* describes one aspect of knowledge as "the perception of the evil of birth, death, old age, and disease." This unabashedly pessimistic view of material life is an impetus for those who want to become unconditioned.

In the Third Canto of the *Śrīmad-Bhāgavatam,* this impetus is strengthened through a discussion between Lord Kapila, an incarnation of the Supreme Personality of Godhead, and His mother, Devahūti.

"Devahūti said: My dear Lord, please describe in detail, both for myself and for people in general, the continual process of birth and death, for by hearing of such calamities we may become detached from the activities of this material world."

In answer to her question, Lord Kapila explained in detail how the life force, the soul, enters the womb of a woman through a particle of male semen during sexual intercourse, how the fetus develops over the weeks and months of pregnancy, and how it suffers.

Owing to the mother's eating bitter pungent food, or food which is too salty or too sour, the body of the child incessantly suffers pains which are almost intolerable. Covered outside by the intestines, the child remains lying on one side of the abdomen, his head turned toward his belly and his back arched like a bow. The child thus remains just like a bird in a cage, without freedom of movement.

Although scientific researchers have confirmed many of the *Śrīmad-Bhāgavatam's* statements about the development of the fetus, they have yet to discover how much it suffers. As we have forgotten the pain of injuries or illnesses we suffered years ago, we have similarly forgotten the pain of the fetal condition.

And what to speak of the birth itself! "Pushed downward all of a sudden by the wind that helps parturition," Kapila describes, "the child comes out with great trouble, head downward, breathless, and deprived of memory due to severe agony."

As any mother knows, the infant's miseries continue after birth. The helpless babe can't express what he wants, nor can he refuse the undesirables given him. He can't scratch himself or even move properly, and he cries from indigestion, colic, teething, teasing, and from pains that only he knows.

Just as a farmer neglects his old and worn-out animals, so, in Lord Kapila's words, "seeing the old man unable to support them, his family members do not treat him with the same respect as before." Thus old people, regarded by their relatives as too difficult to live with and care for, languish in homes for the aged. If they do stay home, "they remain just like a pet dog and eat whatever is negligently given to them." Afflicted with many illnesses, Kapila explains, they eat only small morsels of food and remain idle invalids, while their bodies dwindle and deteriorate under the imperceptible yet indomitable influence of time. The old person's body becomes a time-ravaged shell, like an abandoned house, a barren structure without facilities or comfort.

In the form of old age, time serves a summons of death that no one can refuse. But instead of preparing for death, senior citizens erect a lackluster facade of painted wrinkles, dyed hair, and sporty clothes. Living on their "golden years'" retirement funds, they enjoy shuffleboard, mild surf, and shopping expeditions – until death comes and their body, along with its facade, returns to dust.

Despite extensive medical research, sophisticated hospitals, and hard-working doctors, disease has not decreased. Just as the body must take birth and must die, so it must be wracked by one or more of myriad diseases – from arthritis to AIDS, from muscle sprains to mental imbalance. Though considered an abnormal condition, disease is actually the normal condition imposed on the bodies of all conditioned souls subjected to the impositions of nature.

"What is the most amazing thing?" a sagacious king was once asked. "The most amazing thing," the king responded, "is that although everyone knows he is destined to die, just as his relatives and friends have died, no one prepares for his own death. He acts as if he will live forever."

Time vanquishes everything material. With each rising and setting of the sun, with each passing moment, the balance of our life is being snatched away. Each passing birthday means one year closer to death.

Lord Kapila describes a dying man's final moments:

> In his diseased condition, the old man's eyes bulge due to the pressure of air from within, and his glands become congested with mucus. He has difficulty breathing, and upon exhaling and inhaling he produces a sound like *ghura-ghura*, a rattling within the throat. In this way he comes under the clutches of death and lies down, surrounded by lamenting friends and relatives, and although he wants to speak to them, he no longer can. Thus he dies pitiably, in inconceivable pain and grief.

Unable to finish his plans, dissatisfied with the provisions he's made for his family, and unaware of his own fate, the dying man is as helpless as a newborn.

Our brief lifetime is likened to a bubble in the ocean. The tossing of ocean waves produces many small bubbles that stay together for some time and then separate, never to reunite. Similarly, our family, friends, and countrymen cluster like bubbles, only to be separated by death.

Although all conditioned souls, as eternal spiritual beings, are not meant to die, they are subject to death because their existence is intertwined with material nature. But it is possible to become disentangled, to solve the problem of death.

"The saints and sages," Devahūti said, "being freed from all the disturbances of the senses and mind, meditate upon the Supreme Personality of Godhead, for by His mercy only can one become free from the clutches of material nature."

Lord Kapila appreciated her realization and said,

> The path of devotional service is very easy. You can execute this system without difficulty, and by following it you shall very soon be liberated, even within your present body.

> Persons who are not conversant with this method of devotional service to the Supreme Lord certainly cannot get out of the cycle of birth and death.

Since the conditioned soul doesn't know of the spiritual science called devotional service, he works hard and neglects to look philosophically at the causes of and cures for his miseries. But the unconditioned soul withdraws his senses from material activities and, well equipped with knowledge and detachment, engages them fully in the service of the Supreme Lord. Anyone whose only aim is to serve the Supreme Lord under the direction of a bona fide spiritual master is liberated even within the material body. Although he will still have to satisfy the body's basic needs, he is not disturbed by the forces of material nature.

"You mean an unconditioned soul doesn't grow old, get diseases, or die?" you may ask in disbelief. Of course, from an external viewpoint he does experience these conditions. But in a higher, spiritual sense he doesn't, because he has realized that he's not the material body but the spirit soul within. Just as my wearing an old coat and blouse won't make me old, similarly the conditions of the body and mind can never actually affect the eternal soul.

So even death – the ultimate material condition – has no influence on the liberated soul. For example, when a cat holds a rat in its mouth, the rat feels terror, knowing that death is near. But when that same cat holds its kitten in its mouth, the kitten feels comfort. Similarly, when death comes for a conditioned soul, he's terrified, but for an unconditioned soul "death" means that the Lord has come to carry him back to Godhead, back to the spiritual world.

Liberation to a Higher Pleasure

His Divine Grace A.C. Bhaktivedanta Swami Prabhupāda

"Everyone is inviting, 'Come on, enjoy sex.' But no matter how hard you try to enjoy sex, you cannot be satisfied. That is certain. Unless you come to the spiritual platform of enjoyment, you will never be satisfied." In this explanation of a Bengali song written several centuries ago by a great Kṛṣṇa conscious spiritual master, Śrīla Prabhupāda proposes that there is a pleasure higher than sex and tells us how to begin experiencing it.

~

Narottama dāsa Ṭhākura, who has written this song, is a famous *ācārya* [spiritual master], and his compositions are accepted as Vedic truth. In this song he represents himself as a common man, as one of us. He laments, appealing to Hari, Lord Kṛṣṇa, *hari hari biphale janama goṅāinu:* "My dear Lord, I have uselessly spoiled my life, because I have not worshiped You."

People do not know that they are spoiling their life. They are thinking, "I've got a very nice apartment, a very nice car, a very nice wife, a very nice income, a very nice social position." All these material attractions make us forget the purpose of our life – to worship Kṛṣṇa.

In one verse, the *Śrīmad-Bhāgavatam* summarizes the material attractions:

> *puṁsaḥ striyā mithunī-bhāvam etaṁ*
> *tayor mitho hṛdaya-granthim āhuḥ*
> *ato gṛha-kṣetra-sutāpta-vittair*
> *janasya moho 'yam ahaṁ mameti*

The basic principle of material attraction is sex: *puṁsaḥ striyā mithunī-bhāvam etam.* A man hankers after a woman, and a woman hankers after a man. And when they actually engage in sex, they become very much attracted to each other: *tayor mitho hṛdaya-granthim āhuḥ. Hṛdaya* means "heart," and *granthim* means "hard knot." So when a man and a woman engage in sex, the hard knot in the heart is tied. "I cannot leave you," he says. "You are my life and soul." And she says, "I cannot leave you. You are my life and soul."

For a few days. Then divorce.

But the beginning is sex. The basic principle of material attraction is sex. We have organized sex life in many social conventions. Marriage is a social convention that gives sex a nice finishing touch, that's all. Sometimes it is said that marriage is legalized prostitution. But for keeping up social relations one has to accept some regulative principles, some restrictions on sense gratification. Therefore civilized human beings recognize that there is a difference between sex in marriage and sex outside of marriage, which is just like sex between animals.

In any case, when two people unite some way or other, their next demand is a nice apartment (*gṛha*) and some land (*kṣetra*). Then children (*suta*). When you have an apartment and a wife, the next requirement is to have children, because without children no home life is pleasant. *Pūtra-hīnaṁ gṛhaṁ śūnyam:* "Home life without children is just like a desert." Children are the real pleasure of home life. Finally there is the circle of relatives, or society (*āpta*).

And all these paraphernalia have to be maintained with money (*vittaiḥ*). So money is required.

In this way one becomes entangled in the material world and covered by illusion. Why illusion? Why are such important things – wife, children, money – illusion? Because although at the present moment you may think everything is all right – you have a nice arrangement of home life, apartment, wife, children, society, and position – as soon as your body is finished everything is finished. You're forced to leave everything and move on to your next platform. And you do not know what your next platform will be. Your next body may be that of a human being or a cat or a dog or a demigod or anything. You do not know. But whatever it is, as soon as you leave your present body you will forget everything. There will be no remembrance of who you were, who your wife was, what your home was like, how big your bank balance was, and so on. Everything will be finished.

Everything will be finished in a flash, just like a bubble bursting in the ocean. The thrashing of the waves in the ocean generates millions and billions of bubbles, but the next moment they are all finished. Finished.

In this way material life is going on. The living entity travels through many species of life, many planets, until he comes to the human form of life. Human life is an opportunity to understand how we are transmigrating from one place to another, from one life to another, and simply wasting our time, not understanding what our constitutional position is and why we are suffering so much distress.

These things are to be understood in this human form of life. But instead of inquiring about our real position, we are simply engaged with *mithunī-bhāvam* and *gṛha-kṣetra-sutāpta-vittaiḥ* – sex, wife, home, property, children, society, money, and position. We are captivated with these things, and we are spoiling our life.

So Narottama dāsa Ṭhākura, representing us, is lamenting, "My dear Lord, I have spoiled my life." Why? *Mānuṣya-janama pāiyā rādhā-kṛṣṇa nā bhajiyā:* "This human form of life is meant for understanding Rādhā-Kṛṣṇa [the Lord and His energy] and worshiping Rādhā-Kṛṣṇa. But instead of making contact with Rādhā-Kṛṣṇa, I am simply spoiling my life in sense gratification."

Then his lament goes on. *Golokera prema-dhana hari-nāma-saṅkīrtana rati nā janmilo kene tāy:* "Alas, why have I no attraction for chanting Hare Kṛṣṇa?" The chanting of the Hare Kṛṣṇa mantra is a transcendental vibration; it is not a material thing. It is imported from the transcendental abode of Kṛṣṇa. From there the transcendental sound of Hare Kṛṣṇa has come. This sound is like the sunshine coming from the sun. Although you cannot go to the sun – it is far, far beyond your reach – you can understand that the sunshine is coming from the sun globe. There is no doubt about it. Similarly, the vibration of the Hare Kṛṣṇa mantra is coming from Kṛṣṇa's planet, Goloka (*golokera prema-dhana*). And this chanting produces love of Kṛṣṇa. (*Prema-dhana* means "the treasure of love for Kṛṣṇa.")

Narottama dāsa Ṭhākura laments, *hari-nāma-saṅkīrtana rati nā janmilo kene tāy:* "Alas, why do I have no attachment for the chanting of Hare Kṛṣṇa?" Why should one be attached to this chanting? That is explained in the next line. *Saṁsāra-biṣānale dibā-niśi hiyā jale jurāite:* "Chanting Hare Kṛṣṇa is the only remedy to relieve the heart from the burning poison of sense gratification." *Hiyā* means "heart." Our heart is always burning. Why? Because it is in touch with the sense-gratificatory process. No sense-gratificatory process can give me satisfaction, even though I try this way and that way, this way and that way. People are trying sense gratification in so many ways, and now they have come to the last point: the naked dance and… What is that short skirt?

Devotee: Miniskirt.

Śrīla Prabhupāda: Miniskirt, yes. [*Laughs.*] So, because in the material world the basic principle is sex, everyone is inviting, "Yes, come on, enjoy sex. Come on, enjoy sex." But no matter how you try to enjoy sex, you cannot be satisfied. That is certain, because sense gratification is not your real platform of enjoyment. You are a spirit soul, and unless you come to the spiritual platform you will never be satisfied by any sense gratification. You'll simply go on hankering after pleasure, but you will find no satisfaction.

Therefore, Narottama dāsa Ṭhākura says we are suffering in *saṁsāra-biṣānale. Saṁsāra* indicates our material demands for eating, sleeping, mating, and defending. These are just like fiery poison. Then he says, "My heart is burning from this poison, but I have not searched out the means of relief: the chanting of Hare Kṛṣṇa. I have no attachment for this chanting, and therefore I have spoiled my life."

Then he says, *vrajendra-nandana jei śacī-suta hoilo sei.* The chanting of Hare Kṛṣṇa was introduced by Lord Kṛṣṇa Himself, Vrajendra-nandana, in the form of Lord Caitanya, Śacī-suta. Kṛṣṇa took the part of the son of Mahārāja Nanda, the king of Vṛndāvana. Therefore Kṛṣṇa is called Vrajendra-nandana. And Lord Caitanya took the role of the son of mother Śacī; so He is known as Śacī-suta. The Supreme Lord takes pleasure when He is addressed with His devotee's name, with His energy's name. (His devotees are also His energy.) Although He has no father – He is the father of everyone – He accepts some devotee as His father when He appears on earth. When a pure devotee wants Kṛṣṇa as his son, Kṛṣṇa accepts the devotee as His parent.

So Narottama dāsa Ṭhākura says that Vrajendra-nandana (Śrī Kṛṣṇa) has now appeared as Śacī-suta (Lord Caitanya), and Balarāma (Kṛṣṇa's brother) has become Nitāi. And what is Their business? *Dīna-hīna-jata chilo hari-nāme uddhārilo:* saving all kinds of wretched, sinful conditioned souls by teaching them the chanting of Hare Kṛṣṇa. In this age, Kali-yuga, you cannot find a pious man or a saintly person. Everyone is addicted to sinful activities. But simply by distributing the chanting of Hare Kṛṣṇa, Lord Caitanya saved everyone, however fallen he might have been. "Come on!" He said. "Chant Hare Kṛṣṇa and be delivered."

What is the evidence that Lord Caitanya saved even the most fallen? *Tāra sākṣī jagāi mādhāi.* Jagāi and Mādhāi were two brothers who engaged in all kinds of sinful affairs. They were born into a very high *brāhmaṇa* family, but by bad association they became sinful. Similarly, in the present age, although the people of the West are descending from Āryan families, very nice families, by association they have become fallen. Their environment is full of illicit sex, intoxication, meat-eating, and gambling. So Jagāi and Mādhāi are specimens of the modern population, and Lord Caitanya delivered them simply by inducing them to chant the Hare Kṛṣṇa mantra.

So chanting Hare Kṛṣṇa will actually deliver all fallen souls, without doubt. This is not bogus propaganda. Whatever his past life, anyone who takes to this chanting process will become saintly. He will become a pure, Kṛṣṇa conscious person.

Chanting Hare Kṛṣṇa will purify our heart, our burning heart. Then we will understand, "I am an eternal servant of the Supreme Lord, Kṛṣṇa." Ordinarily we can come to this understanding only after many, many births, as Kṛṣṇa confirms in the *Bhagavad-gītā*. *Bahūnāṁ janmanām ante jñānavān māṁ prapadyate:* "After many, many births, when a person becomes a man of wisdom, he surrenders unto Me." Why? *Vāsudevaḥ sarvam iti:* Because he knows that Vāsudeva, Kṛṣṇa, is everything. But that kind of great soul is very rare (*sa mahātmā su-durlabhaḥ*).

But Lord Caitanya has made it easy to become such a great soul. How? Simply by chanting Hare Kṛṣṇa. Therefore at the end of his song Narottama dāsa Ṭhākura says, *hā hā prabhu nanda-suta vṛṣabhānu-sutā-juta koruṇā karoho ei-bāro:* "My dear Lord Kṛṣṇa, You are now present before me with Your internal potency, Your pleasure potency, Rādhārāṇī. Please be merciful to me. Don't neglect me because I am so sinful. My past life is so black, but don't neglect me. Please accept me. Don't kick me away. I surrender unto You."

So, all of us should follow in the footsteps of Narottama dāsa Ṭhākura. The purificatory process is chanting Hare Kṛṣṇa. And as soon as our heart is purified, we will become completely convinced that Kṛṣṇa is the Supreme Lord and that we are His eternal servants. We have forgotten this. We are serving, but instead of serving the Lord we are serving our senses. We have never become the master. We are not the masters of our senses; we are the servants of our senses. That is our position.

So why not become the servant of the Supreme Lord instead of remaining the servant of your senses? Actually, you can become the master of your senses only when you become the servant of Kṛṣṇa. Otherwise, it is not possible. Either *godāsa* or *gosvāmī:* that is your choice. A person who is the servant of his senses is called *godāsa,* and a person who is the master of his senses is called *gosvāmī.* He controls his senses. When his tongue wants to eat something that is not offered to Kṛṣṇa, he thinks, "O tongue, you cannot taste this thing. It is not *kṛṣṇa-prasāda* [food offered to Kṛṣṇa]." In this way one becomes a *gosvāmī,* a master of his senses.

When a person does not allow his senses to do anything for sense gratification but acts only for the service of Kṛṣṇa, that is called devotional service. *Hṛṣīkeṇa hṛṣīkeśa-sevanaṁ bhaktir ucyate:* Devotional service means to engage your senses in satisfying the master of the senses. The supreme master of the senses is Kṛṣṇa. Now we are trying to use our senses for our personal service. This is called *māyā,* illusion. But when we engage the same senses in the service of Kṛṣṇa, that is perfection. We don't stop the activities of the senses, but we purify the senses by engaging them in the service of the Lord. This is Kṛṣṇa consciousness.

Thank you very much. Any questions?

Devotee: Śrīla Prabhupāda, how is it that Lord Jesus is called the son of God? If Kṛṣṇa is usually the son, how is Jesus –

Śrīla Prabhupāda: Not "usually." Kṛṣṇa is the supreme father, but He becomes His devotee's son out of His love. Being a son is not Kṛṣṇa's constitutional position; being the father is His constitutional position (*ahaṁ bīja-pradaḥ pitā*). But sometimes He voluntarily becomes a son to taste His devotee's fatherly or motherly love for Him.

When a pure devotee prays, "My dear Lord, I want You for my son," Kṛṣṇa accepts his prayer. Vasudeva and Devakī became Kṛṣṇa's parents in this way. In a previous life they underwent severe austerities. They were married, but they had no sex. They were determined that unless they could get the Lord as their son they would not have a child. So they performed severe austerities for many thousands of years. Then the Lord appeared to them and asked, "What do you want?"

"Sir, we want a son like You."

"How can you get a son like Me? I'll become your son!"

So Kṛṣṇa, the Lord, is the father of everyone, but He voluntarily becomes the son of His devotee. Otherwise, His position is always the supreme father.

Devotee: Śrīla Prabhupāda, I read in the *Śrīmad-Bhāgavatam* that when one becomes a liberated soul he attains perfect freedom and that sometimes his freedom is on the same level as Kṛṣṇa's or even more than Kṛṣṇa's. Can you explain this?

Śrīla Prabhupāda: Yes. Take Vasudeva, for example. He's more than Kṛṣṇa. Or Mother Yaśodā. You have seen the picture of Yaśodā binding Kṛṣṇa?

Devotee: Kṛṣṇa looks like a little baby?

Śrīla Prabhupāda: Yes. The Supreme Personality of Godhead is feared by everyone, but He becomes fearful of Mother Yaśodā: "My dear mother, kindly do not bind Me. I shall obey your orders."

So Mother Yaśodā has become more than God, more than Kṛṣṇa. The Māyāvādī [impersonalistic] philosophers want to become one with the Lord, but our philosophy is to become more than Kṛṣṇa. Why one with Kṛṣṇa? *More* than Kṛṣṇa. And, actually, Kṛṣṇa does make His devotee more than Himself. Another example is Arjuna. Kṛṣṇa took the part of his chariot driver. Kṛṣṇa was actually the hero of the Battle of Kurukṣetra, but He gave that position to His devotee: "Arjuna, you become the hero. I shall be your charioteer."

Kṛṣṇa is just like a father who wants to see his son become more than himself. If the father has an M. A., he wants to see his son get a Ph. D. Then the father is satisfied. He'll not tolerate an outsider's becoming more than him, but he's glad if his son becomes more than him. Similarly, Kṛṣṇa, the Supreme Lord, wants to see His devotee become more than Himself. That is His pleasure.

Kṛṣṇa, Enchanter of the Soul

His Divine Grace A. C. Bhaktivedanta Swami Prabhupāda

A man is attracted by a woman, a woman is attracted by a man, and when they are united in sex, their attachment for this material world increases more and more.... But our business is not to be attracted by the glimmer of this material world; our business is to be attracted by Kṛṣṇa. And when we become attracted by the beauty of Kṛṣṇa, we will lose our attraction for the false beauty of this material world.

~

In this material world everyone is attracted by sex. This is a fact. As the *Śrīmad-Bhāgavatam* [7.9.45] says, *yan maithunādi-gṛhamedhi-sukhaṁ hi tuccham:* "The happiness – the so-called happiness – of household life begins from *maithuna,* or sexual intercourse."

Generally, a man marries to satisfy sex desire. Then he begets children. Then, when the children are grown up, the daughter marries a boy and the son marries a girl for the same purpose: sex. Then grandchildren.

In this way, material happiness expands as *śry-aiśvarya-prajepsavaḥ*. *Śrī* means "beauty," *aiśvarya* means "wealth," and *prajā* means "children." People think they are successful if they have a beautiful wife, a good bank balance, and good sons, daughters, daughters-in-law, and so on. If one's family consists of beautiful women and riches and many children, one is supposed to be a most successful man.

What is this success? The scripture says this success is simply an expansion of sexual intercourse. That's all. We may polish it in different ways, but this same sex happiness is also there in the hogs. The hogs eat the whole day, here and there – "Where is stool? Where is stool?" – and then have sex without any discrimination. The hog does not discriminate whether he has sex with his mother, sister, or daughter.

So the scripture says we are encaged in this material world only for sex. In other words, we are victims of Cupid. Cupid, or Madana, is the god of sex. Unless one is induced by Madana one cannot be engladdened in sex life. And one of Kṛṣṇa's names is Madana-mohana, "He who vanquishes Cupid." In other words, one who is attracted to Kṛṣṇa will forget the pleasure derived from sex. This is the test of advancement in Kṛṣṇa consciousness.

Another meaning of *madana* is "to intoxicate or madden." Everyone is maddened by the force of sex desire. The *Śrīmad-Bhāgavatam* says, "The whole material world is going on because of the attraction between male and female." A man is attracted by a woman, a woman is attracted by a man, and when they are united in sex their attachment for this material world increases more and more. After marriage, the man and woman seek a nice home and a job or some land for farming, because they have to earn money to get food and other things. Then come children, friends and relatives, and wealth. In this way the attraction for the material world becomes tighter and tighter. And it all begins with our attraction for *madana,* the pleasure of sex.

But our business is not to be attracted by the glimmer of this material world; our business is to be attracted by Kṛṣṇa. And when we become attracted by the beauty of Kṛṣṇa, we will lose our attraction for the false beauty of this material world. As Śrī Yāmunācārya says,

yad-avadhi mama cetaḥ kṛṣṇa-pādāravinde
nava-nava-rasa-dhāmany udyataṁ rantum āsīt
tad-avadhi bata nārī-saṅgame smaryamāṇe
bhavati mukha-vikāraḥ suṣṭhu niṣṭhīvanaṁ ca

"Since I have been attracted by the beauty of Kṛṣṇa and have begun to serve His lotus feet, I am getting newer and newer pleasure, and as soon as I think of sexual intercourse my mouth immediately turns aside and I spit."

So Kṛṣṇa is Madana-mohana, the conqueror of Madana, or Cupid. Madana is attracting everyone, but when one is attracted by Kṛṣṇa, Madana is defeated. And as soon as Madana is defeated, we conquer this material world. Otherwise, it is very difficult. As Kṛṣṇa says in the *Bhagavad-gītā,*

daivī hy eṣā guṇamayī
mama māyā duratyayā
mām eva ye prapadyante
māyām etāṁ taranti te

This material world is very difficult to overcome, but if one surrenders unto Kṛṣṇa and catches His lotus feet very strongly – "Kṛṣṇa, save me!" – Kṛṣṇa promises, "Yes, I'll save you. Don't worry, I shall save you." *Kaunteya pratijānīhi na me bhaktaḥ praṇaśyati:* "My dear Arjuna, you can declare to the world that I will protect My devotee who has no other desire but to serve Me."

Unfortunately, people do not know that our only business is to take shelter of the lotus feet of Kṛṣṇa. We have no other business. Any other business we may do simply entangles us in this material world. The aim of human life is to get out of the clutches of the material world. But, as the *Bhāgavatam* says, *na te viduḥ svārtha-gatiṁ hi viṣṇum:* "People do not know that their ultimate goal in life is to realize Viṣṇu, or Kṛṣṇa."

It is very difficult to turn people to Kṛṣṇa consciousness in this age. Still, Caitanya Mahāprabhu has ordered us to distribute this knowledge all over the world. So let us try. Even if the people do not take our instruction, that is no disqualification for us. Our only qualification is simply to try our best. *Māyā* [illusion] is very strong. Therefore to take the living entities out of the clutches of *māyā* is not a very easy thing. My Guru Mahārāja had so many temples all over India, and sometimes he would say, "If by selling all these temples I could turn one man to Kṛṣṇa consciousness, my mission would be successful." He used to say that.

Our purpose is not to construct big, big buildings, although that is sometimes required for spreading Kṛṣṇa consciousness and for giving shelter to people. But our main business is to turn the faces of the bewildered conditioned souls toward Kṛṣṇa. That is our main purpose. Therefore Bhaktivinoda Ṭhākura and other Vaiṣṇavas have warned us to be careful about constructing too many big temples because our attention may be diverted toward material things. In other words, we may become forgetful of Kṛṣṇa.

Of course, ultimately nothing is material. Thinking something is material is simply an illusion. Actually, there is nothing but spirit. How can there be anything material? The Supreme Lord is the Supreme Spirit, and since everything is coming from Him, what we call the material energy is also coming from Him and is thus ultimately spiritual.

But the difficulty is that in this material world, Kṛṣṇa's inferior energy, there is the possibility of forgetting Kṛṣṇa. People are engaged in so many activities – we can see this very clearly in the Western countries – and they are inventing so many modern facilities, but the result is that they are forgetting Kṛṣṇa. That is material – this forgetfulness of Kṛṣṇa.

Actually, there is nothing except Kṛṣṇa and His energies. As Nārada Muni says, *idaṁ hi viśvaṁ bhagavān ivetaraḥ:* "This world is Kṛṣṇa, Bhagavān." But to those in ignorance it appears different from Bhagavān. For a *mahā-bhāgavata,* a pure devotee, there is no conception of material and spiritual because he sees Kṛṣṇa everywhere. As soon as he sees anything we call material, he sees it as a transformation of Kṛṣṇa's energy (*pariṇāma-vāda*). Lord Caitanya gave the following example: A pure devotee may see a tree, but he forgets the tree and sees the energy of Kṛṣṇa. And as soon as he sees the energy of Kṛṣṇa, he sees Kṛṣṇa. Therefore, instead of seeing the tree he sees Kṛṣṇa.

Another example is the sun and the sunshine. As soon as you see the sunshine you can immediately think of the sun. Is that not so? In the morning, as soon as you see the sunshine shining in your window, you can immediately remember the sun. You are confident the sun is there because you know that without the sun there cannot be any sunshine. Similarly, whenever we see something we should immediately think of Kṛṣṇa with reference to that particular thing, because that thing is a manifestation of Kṛṣṇa's energy. And because the energy is not different from the energetic, those who have understood Kṛṣṇa along with His energies do not see anything except Kṛṣṇa. Therefore for them there is no material world. To a perfect devotee, everything is spiritual (*sarvaṁ khalv idaṁ brahma*).

So we have to train our eyes to see Kṛṣṇa everywhere. And this training is devotional service to Kṛṣṇa, which is a process of purification:

sarvopādhi-vinirmuktaṁ
tat-paratvena nirmalam
hṛṣīkeṇa hṛṣīkeśa-
sevanaṁ bhaktir ucyate

As soon as we are in Kṛṣṇa consciousness, we give up our false designations, and our seeing, touching, smelling, and so on become *nirmala,* or purified, by being engaged in the service of Kṛṣṇa. Then we can immediately see Kṛṣṇa everywhere. As long as our eyes are not purified we cannot see Kṛṣṇa, but as soon as they are purified by the process of devotional service we will see nothing but Kṛṣṇa.

Cupid is one of the agents of the illusory, material energy, but if we are perfectly in Kṛṣṇa consciousness, Cupid cannot pierce our heart with his arrows. It is not possible. A good example is Haridāsa Ṭhākura. When Haridāsa Ṭhākura was a young man, a nicely dressed young prostitute came to him in the middle of the night and revealed her desire to unite with him. Haridāsa Ṭhākura said, "Yes, please sit down. I shall fulfill your desire, but just let me finish my chanting of Hare Kṛṣṇa." Just see! It's the dead of night, and in front of Haridāsa Ṭhākura is a beautiful young girl proposing to have sex with him. But still he's steady, chanting Hare Kṛṣṇa, Hare Kṛṣṇa, Kṛṣṇa Kṛṣṇa, Hare Hare/ Hare Rāma, Hare Rāma, Rāma Rāma, Hare Hare. But he never finished his chanting, so her plan was unsuccessful.

Cupid cannot pierce our heart when we are fully absorbed in Kṛṣṇa consciousness. There may be thousands of beautiful women before a devotee, but they cannot disturb him. He sees them as energies of Kṛṣṇa. He thinks, "They are Kṛṣṇa's; they are meant for His enjoyment."

A devotee's duty is to try to engage all beautiful women in the service of Kṛṣṇa, not to try to enjoy them. A devotee is not pierced by the arrows of Cupid because he sees everything in relationship with Kṛṣṇa. That is real renunciation. He does not accept anything for his own sense gratification but engages everything and everyone in the service of Kṛṣṇa. This is the process of Kṛṣṇa consciousness.

Thank you very much.

Chapter Five

Ancient Wisdom, Modern Times

Advice to the United Nations

A conversation between His Divine Grace
A.C. Bhaktivedanta Swami Prabhupāda and Mr. C. Hennis
of the UN's International Labour Organization in Geneva

How can society be organized for the peace and well-being of all? In this conversation with a member of the United Nations, Śrīla Prabhupāda discusses the importance of the social body having a brain.

~

Śrīla Prabhupāda: The social body should have a class of men who act as the brain and guide everyone so that everyone can become happy. That is the purpose of our movement.

Mr. Hennis: That's a valid point, because it has always been affirmed in every society that there is a need for a priestly class or a class of philosophical leaders.

Śrīla Prabhupāda: But now the so-called priestly class is amending the biblical injunctions according to their whims. For instance, the Bible enjoins, "Thou shalt not kill." But the priestly class is like the other classes – sanctioning slaughterhouses. So how can they guide?

Mr. Hennis: But the animal world is entirely composed of beings that eat one another. I suppose that the justification people have for maintaining slaughterhouses is that it is just a cleaner way of killing than for a lion to jump on the back of an antelope.

Śrīla Prabhupāda: But as a human being you should have discrimination. You should be guided by your brain, and society should be guided by the "brain class" of priestly, thoughtful men. Nature has given human beings the fruits, the vegetables, the grains, milk – all of which have great nutritional value. Human beings should be satisfied with these wholesome foods. Why should they maintain slaughterhouses? And how can they think they will be happy by being sinful, by not following God's commandments? This means society has no brain.

Mr. Hennis: My organization isn't directly concerned with giving people brains.

Śrīla Prabhupāda: Your organization may not be directly concerned, but if human society is brainless, then no matter how much you may try to organize, society can never become happy. That is my point.

Mr. Hennis: My organization is concerned with taking away the obstacles that prevent people from attaining a proper brain. One of the obstacles is just plain poverty.

Śrīla Prabhupāda: No. The main thing is, society must learn to discriminate between pious and sinful activities. Human beings must engage in pious activities, not sinful activities. Otherwise, they have no brain. They are no better than animals. And from the moral point of view, do you like sending your mother to the slaughterhouse? You are drinking the milk of the cow – so she is your mother – and after that you are sending her to the slaughterhouse. That is why we ask, Where is society's brain?

Mr. Hennis: Of course, when you speak of the distinctions that are made between pious activities and sinful activities –

Śrīla Prabhupāda: Today practically no one is making this distinction. We are making it, and we have introduced these ideas by establishing farm communities and protecting our cows. Our cows are winning awards for giving the most milk because they are so jubilant. They know, "These people will not kill me." They know it, so they are very happy. Nor do we kill their calves. At other farms, soon after the cow gives birth to a calf, they pull her calf away for slaughter. You see? This means society has no brain. You may create hundreds of organizations, but society will never be happy. That is the verdict.

Mr. Hennis: Well, we can't be accused of engaging in sinful activities when we don't think what we are doing is sinful.

Śrīla Prabhupāda [*Laughing*]: Oh? You don't think you can be accused of breaking the state law just because you don't know what the state law is? The point is, if your priestly class has no knowledge of what is sinful they may instruct you, "Don't do anything sinful," but what good is that? You must have a priestly class who knows what is sinful so that they can teach you. And then you must give your sinful activities up. When these young people came to me I told them, "Flesh-eating, illicit sex, gambling, and intoxication – these things are sinful. You must give them up." If we do not give up these sinful activities, nature punishes us. So we must know the laws of nature – what nature wants. At the very least, nature wants that we human beings stop our sinful activities. If we do not, then we must be punished.

Mr. Hennis: We are just trying to give people a fair share of the material things of life: proper wages, decent homes, and decent opportunities for leisure.

Śrīla Prabhupāda: That is all right, but people must know what is sinful and what is pious.

Mr. Hennis: Yes, but I don't think you can properly expect to indoctrinate people. At least, you can't expect an international organization to indoctrinate people.

Śrīla Prabhupāda: As an international organization for peace and well-being, the United Nations should maintain a class of men who can act as society's brain. Then everything will be all right. Simply legs and hands working without any direction, without any brain – that is not very good. The United Nations was organized for the total benefit of human society, but it has no department that can actually be called the brain organization.

Mr. Hennis: That's true, that's true. They are servants of the membership, servants of the various states of the world. We are only the servants of these people. What we try and do is let them get together and help them understand their problems.

Śrīla Prabhupāda: Yes, help them understand. At the very least, help them understand what they should do and what they should not do. At least do this much.

Mr. Hennis: This we do try to do to the extent that it is possible for the secretariat to shape and evolve a philosophy. We try to do it. But of course, we can't adopt a completely radical approach. We do what we can, in the manner of a good servant and the manner of a good steward, to try, and we hope the leaders are on the right path and the right direction.

Śrīla Prabhupāda: If society does not know what is sinful and what is pious, it is all useless. If your body has no brain, then your body is dead. And if the social body has no brain, then it is dead.

The Failure of Liberation Movements

Hridayānanda Dāsa Goswami

When you have no knowledge of God and the soul, your struggle for freedom ends in bondage. This article, originally published in 1983 in Back to Godhead *magazine, addresses a topic that is perennially relevant in a world constantly struggling for peace.*

~

Modern history is full of liberation movements. Even the American Revolution and the formation of the American nation can be seen as a type of liberation movement that signaled the eventual collapse of European colonialism.

Americans have continued to create liberation movements that seek to free blacks, women, Latinos, homosexuals, and other groups from the social dominance and economic exploitation of majority groups. Unfortunately, almost all these liberation movements seem to reinforce rather than transcend a materialistic view of personal identity and thus unwittingly contain within their ideology the seeds of further prejudice, exploitation, and bondage – the very things they are fighting against. This can be explained as follows.

Modern materialism, often under the rubric of "science," tends to define reality exclusively in terms of matter and the laws that govern it. Biologist John Maynard Smith of the University of Sussex declares, "The individual is simply a device constructed by the genes to insure the production of more genes like themselves." According to Dr. Richard L. Thompson, a mathematician at the State University of New York at Binghamton, "This statement conveys in a nutshell what modern science has to say about the meaning of human life."

Unfortunately, modern liberation movements, perhaps unconsciously, seem to accept this superficial definition of life. Thus in the Unity Statement of the Women's Pentagon Action, we find the following statement: "We are made of blood and bone, we are made of ... water."

Obviously, we are not blood, bone, and water, since blood, bone, and water are unconscious material elements that would hardly march to the Pentagon to secure political and economic rights. We are consciousness, and therefore we are aware of, or conscious of, the blood, bone, water, and so on that make up our body. We conscious beings march to Washington to demand our rights. We, who are consciousness, form liberation movements because *it is the nature of consciousness to seek freedom.*

If we misidentify ourselves as mere material machines, then wittingly or unwittingly we destroy the real basis of a peaceful, virtuous society: respect for the ultimate spiritual identity of all living beings.

Unfortunately, most liberation movements emphasize our different bodily identities in terms of race, gender, ethnicity, and even species and thus intensify rather than transcend our false identification with the material body. Through this "balkanization" of life, we learn to conceive of life as a perpetual battle between competing body types.

As vividly demonstrated in the bizarre history of Communism, so-called liberation based on a divisive, mundane ideology tends to exacerbate rather than ameliorate the world's strife.

Let us further analyze this syndrome. The material body desires sex, food, shelter, and defense, while the material mind seeks to gratify its pride and vanity by imagining that one is better than others. A person attached to and controlled by the material body and mind will seek to gratify the body's desires and the mind's vanity. Such a person will tend to be an exploiter or manipulator of the material world, being driven to seek personal pleasure and superiority, either as an individual or through a material collective identity such as family, community, nation, ideology, or even sectarian religion.

The first stage of liberation is understanding that I am not a bag of molecules; I am not a bodily machine. I am pure consciousness. The *Bhagavad-gītā* teaches us our spiritual identity and gives the following example to illustrate our existence beyond the material body: In this life we first have the body of a baby, then of a child, an adolescent, and finally an adult. Though the body replaces its physical components every seven years, forming in this time span a new physical entity, we remain the same person. That continuous person is the self, or the soul.

In this way I free myself from the illusion of being a biomachine, the illusion that my existence as a conscious person is not ultimately real since it can be reduced to impersonal, unconscious entities like atoms and molecules. I free myself from the exploitative, self-centered desires that plague the material body and mind. This is real liberation.

Liberated persons can satisfy their basic material and spiritual needs without seeking, mentally or physically, to utilize other persons as instruments of that satisfaction. Thus the liberated soul satisfies Kant's categorical imperative that we treat each person as an end in themselves and not as a means to our ends.

A liberated person sees all the earthly creatures, those in bodies of human beings, animals, birds, fish, insects, plants, or whatever, as eternal spiritual entities temporarily encased in diverse material coverings. Thus a liberated person sees that every living entity is spiritually equal to oneself and is worthy of respect and concern. A liberated soul does not see any creature, even those in animal bodies, as mere objects of cruel consumption or manipulation. A liberated person opposes the inexplicable brutality of the slaughterhouse and the general devastation of the earth for selfish, unnecessary human gratification.

How should we practically proceed to achieve such a state of consciousness? First we should free ourselves from the illusion that we are material machines. Next we should free ourselves from the selfish desires that pollute the material body and mind. And finally we should free ourselves from the misunderstanding that we are meant to be lords of the earth. The earth does not belong to human beings either individually or collectively. It belongs to God. The experience of God is immediately available to any person who chants His holy name.

Systematic exploitation of the earth, the bodies of others, or even one's own body constitutes grave irresponsibility and duplicity since we have no evidence that this world or even our own bodies ultimately belong to us. Upon arriving in a particular country, our duty is to understand the laws that govern that place. Similarly, knowledge of the laws that govern the universe is of primary concern to every human being. It would be absurd and self-destructive to put aside such questions.

If we dedicate ourselves to bodily happiness, without understanding the soul and God, we are unreasonably presupposing two things:

1. We presuppose that the body and not consciousness, or the soul, is our essential identity, worthy of our ultimate if not exclusive concern. We assume that we are bodies and that perhaps we have a soul, rather than understanding that we are consciousness, or self or soul, and that we are living in a body.

2. We presuppose that if there is a God, He is not a participant in or a controller of human affairs, and therefore satisfaction of such a God is irrelevant or unnecessary to the progressive improvement of the human condition. Implicit in this misapprehension is the presumption that human beings potentially may control the affairs of the earth or even other worlds. This implies

human proprietorship of the earth and possibly other planets, a concept rife with selfish intentions and devoid of real certainty.

In fact there is a God, and His laws govern the universe. Violation of God's laws disturbs the entire world directly or indirectly, just as an ordinary crime, apart from its specific victim, weakens the entire system of peaceful coexistence and is thus socially undesirable for all citizens. Violation of the laws of God violates society in general. Violation of God's laws, which are instituted for the universal happiness and flourishing of all souls, thus violates the cosmic order. We take without giving back – the most basic act of injustice.

On the other hand, if God does not create our body, and if there is no divine soul within, then one person's control or manipulation of another is merely a biophysical event without ultimate moral value, meaning, or consequences. On this account, morality and justice are mere inventions of self-righteous entities, who are merely expressing the dictates of their genes or perhaps their own fantasies of an objective moral order.

In such a godless, soul-less reality, attempts by a people or social class to free itself from oppression or to achieve justice would be mere tests of political strength for personal gratification, a playing out of social Darwinism with no ultimate meaning beyond human wishes.

If we claim that God is useless or nonexistent because millions of innocent people suffer in the face of an all-powerful God, then we accept the primitive concept that the soul is created in the present life and therefore cannot be guilty for his or her suffering as an infant, child, or adult since the suffering soul has no activities prior to this birth. This concept of soul-creation, and of the soul's single chance at salvation, has greatly exacerbated the so-called "problem of evil," in response to which some theologians have been driven to declare the suffering of innocents an inscrutable religious mystery. This naturally weakens one's hope in a reasonable spiritual explanation of life. The Vedic and indeed Buddhist notion of karma and reincarnation according to reasonable moral principles offers a more rational approach to this perennial theological problem.

We living beings dwell in our bodies as eternal conscious souls. We perceive only our own and each other's bodies and thus we misunderstand ourselves to be material entities whose real home is in this material world. We then seek to exploit the body for selfish gratification rather than to engage it in God's service. Thus the ignorant, greedy, and competing souls of this world become entangled in endless conflicts and miseries.

The real tyranny is the tyranny of illusion – the illusion that conceals our eternal spiritual nature. A Kṛṣṇa conscious soul works for justice in this world based on the spiritual equality of all living things. Real liberation entails extracting the conscious self from the cycle of birth, death, disease, and old age. Liberation that ignores our permanent life, our ultimate happiness, and our supreme wisdom is but a shadow of real freedom.

A world of a few big exploiters or of many little exploiters will produce the same confusion and conflict. It is ludicrous to seek peace on a planet full of billions of competing gods. The urge to exploit matter for bodily or mental gratification, and thereby to gratify one's false ego, is like a germ. As long as a single cell of this germ remains in one's mind, it will eventually grow and undermine our efforts to achieve liberation.

Many liberation movements directly or indirectly, consciously or unwittingly, nullify the very basis of respect among all creatures: recognition of the sanctity of all life forms. They do this by embracing a gross material concept of life, ignoring the transcendental source of existence, that supreme conscious entity who alone embodies the authority to establish an irrefutable imperative of nonexploitative social intercourse.

A Formula for Peace

His Divine Grace A. C. Bhaktivedanta Swami Prabhupāda

This article by Śrīla Prabhupāda was first published in 1956 in New Delhi, India, in Back to Godhead, *the magazine he founded in 1944. Appealing to his Indian readers to "employ everything in transcendental service for the interest of the Lord," he concludes that "this alone can bring the desired peace."*

~

In the revealed scriptures the Supreme Lord is described as *sac-cid-ānanda-vigraha. Sat* means "eternal," *cit* means "fully cognizant," *ānanda* means "joyful," and *vigraha* means "a specific personality." Therefore the Lord, or the Supreme Godhead, who is one without a second, is an eternal, joyful personality with a full sense of His own identity. That is a concise description of the Supreme Lord, and no one is equal to or greater than Him.

The living entities, or *jīvas,* are minute samples of the Supreme Lord, and therefore we find in their activities the desire for eternal existence, the desire for knowledge of everything, and an urge for seeking happiness in diverse ways. These three qualities of the living being are minutely visible in human society, but they are increased and enjoyed one hundred times more by the beings who reside in the upper planets, which are called Bhūrloka, Svarloka, Janaloka, Tapoloka, Maharloka, Brahmaloka, and so forth.

But even the standard of enjoyment on the highest planet in the material world, which is thousands and thousands of times superior to what we enjoy on this earth, is also described as insignificant in comparison to the spiritual bliss enjoyed in the company of the Supreme Lord. His loving service in different mellows (relationships) makes even the enjoyment of merging with the impersonal spiritual effulgence as insignificant as a drop of water compared with the ocean.

Every living being is ambitious to have the topmost level of enjoyment in the material world, and yet one is always unhappy here. This unhappiness is present on all the above-mentioned planets in spite of a long life span and high standards of comfort.

That is the law of material nature. One can increase the duration of life and standard of comfort to the highest capacity, and yet by the law of material nature one will be unhappy. The reason is that the quality of happiness suitable for our constitution is different from the happiness derived from material activities. The living entity is a minute particle of *sac-cid-ānanda-vigraha,* and therefore he necessarily has a propensity for joyfulness that is spiritual in quality. But he is vainly trying to derive his spiritual joyfulness from the foreign atmosphere of the material nature.

A fish that is taken out of the water cannot be happy by any arrangement for happiness on the land – it must have an aquatic habitation. In the same way, the minute *sac-cid-ānanda* living entity cannot be really happy through any amount of material planning conceived by his illusioned brain. Therefore, the living entity must be given a different type of happiness, a transcendental happiness, which is called spiritual bliss. Our ambitions should be aimed at enjoying spiritual bliss and not material happiness.

The ambition for spiritual bliss is good, but the method of attaining this standard is not merely to negate material happiness. Theoretical negation of material activities, as propounded by Śrīpāda Śaṅkarācārya, may be relevant for an insignificant section of men, but the devotional activities propounded by Śrī Caitanya

Mahāprabhu are the best and surest way of attaining spiritual bliss. In fact, they change the very face of material nature.

Hankering after material happiness is called lust, and in the long run lustful activities are sure to meet with frustration. The body of a venomous snake is very cool. But if a man wants to enjoy the coolness of the snake's body and therefore garlands himself with the snake, then surely he will be killed by the snake's bite. The material senses are like snakes, and indulging in so-called material happiness surely kills one's spiritual self-awareness. Therefore a sane man should be ambitious to find the real source of happiness.

Once, a foolish man who had no experience of the taste of sugarcane was told by a friend to taste its sweetness. When the man inquired about sugarcane's appearance, the friend imperfectly informed him that sugarcane resembles a bamboo stick. The foolish man thus began trying to extract sugarcane juice from a bamboo stick, but naturally he was baffled in his attempt.

That is the position of the illusioned living being in his search for eternal happiness within the material world, which is not only full of miseries but also transient and flickering. In the *Bhagavad-gītā*, the material world is described as full of miseries. The ambition for happiness is good, but the attempt to derive it from inert matter by so-called scientific arrangements is an illusion. Befooled persons cannot understand this. The *Gītā* describes how a person driven by the lust for material happiness thinks, "So much wealth do I have today, and I will gain more according to my schemes. So much is mine now, and it will increase in the future."

The atheistic, or godless, civilization is a huge affair of sense gratification, and everyone is now mad after money to keep up an empty show. Everyone is seeking money because that is the medium of exchange for sense-gratificatory objects. To expect peace in such an atmosphere of gold-rush pandemonium is a utopian dream. As long as there is even a slight tinge of madness for sense gratification, peace will remain far, far away. The reason is that by nature everyone is an eternal servitor of the Supreme

Lord, and therefore we cannot enjoy anything for our personal interest. We have to employ everything in transcendental service for the interest of the Lord. This alone can bring about the desired peace. A part of the body cannot make itself satisfied; it can only serve the whole body and derive satisfaction from that service. But now everyone is busy in self-interested business, and no one is prepared to serve the Lord. That is the basic cause of material existence.

From the highest executive administrator down to the lowest sweeper in the street, everyone is working with the thought of unlawful accumulation of wealth. But to work merely for one's self-interest is unlawful and destructive. Even the cultivation of spiritual realization merely for one's self-interest is unlawful and destructive.

As a result of all the unlawful moneymaking, there is no scarcity of money in the world. But there is a scarcity of peace. Since the whole of our human energy has been diverted to this moneymaking, the moneymaking capacity of the total population has certainly increased. But the result is that such an unrestricted and unlawful inflation of money has created a bad economy and has enabled us to manufacture huge, costly weapons that threaten to destroy the very result of such moneymaking.

Instead of enjoying peace, the leaders of big moneymaking countries are now making big plans how they can save themselves from the modern destructive weapons, and yet a huge sum of money is being thrown into the sea for experiments with such dreadful weapons. Such experiments are being carried out not only at huge monetary costs, but also at the cost of many poor lives, thereby binding such nations to the laws of karma. That is the illusion of material nature. As a result of the impulse for sense gratification, money is earned by spoiled energy, and it is then spent for the destruction of the human race. The energy of the human race is thus spoiled by the law of nature because that energy is diverted from the service of the Lord, who is actually the owner of all energies.

Wealth derives from Mother Lakṣmī, or the goddess of fortune. As the Vedic literatures explain, the goddess of fortune is meant to serve Lord Nārāyaṇa, the source of all the *naras,* or living beings. The *naras* are also meant to serve Nārāyaṇa, the Supreme Lord, under the guidance of the goddess of fortune. The living being cannot enjoy the goddess of fortune without serving Nārāyaṇa, or Kṛṣṇa, and therefore whoever desires to enjoy her wrongly will be punished by the laws of nature, and the money itself will become the cause of destruction instead of being the cause of peace and prosperity.

Such unlawfully accumulated money is now being snatched away from the miserly citizens by various methods of state taxation for the various national and international war funds, which spend the money in a wasteful manner. The citizen is no longer satisfied with just enough money to maintain his family nicely and cultivate spiritual knowledge, both of which are essential in human life. He now wants money unlimitedly for satisfying insatiable desires, and in proportion to his unlawful desires his accumulated money is now being taken away by the agents of the illusory nature in the shape of medical practitioners, lawyers, tax collectors, societies, institutions, and so-called religionists, as well as by famines, earthquakes, and many other such calamities.

One miser who, under the dictation of the illusory nature, hesitated to purchase a copy of *Back to Godhead,* spent $2500 for a week's supply of medicine and then died. A similar thing happened when a man who refused to spend a cent for the service of the Lord wasted $3500 in a legal suit between the members of his household. That is the law of nature. If money is not devoted to the service of the Lord, by the law of nature it must be spent as spoiled energy in the fight against legal problems, diseases, and so on. Foolish people have no eyes to see such facts, so necessarily the laws of the Supreme Lord befool them.

The laws of nature do not allow us to accept more money than is required for proper maintenance. There is ample arrangement by the law of nature to provide every living being with his due share of food and shelter, but the insatiable lust of the human being has disturbed the whole arrangement of the almighty father of all species of life.

By the arrangement of the Supreme Lord, there is an ocean of salt, because salt is necessary for the living being. In the same manner, God has arranged for sufficient air and light, which are also essential for the living being. One can collect any amount of salt from the storehouse, but one cannot take more salt than he needs. If he takes more salt he spoils the broth, and if he takes less salt his eatables become tasteless. On the other hand, if he takes only what he absolutely requires, the food is tasty and he is healthy. So ambition for wealth, for more than we need, is harmful, just as eating more salt than we absolutely need is harmful. That is the law of nature.

Spiritual Advice to Businessmen

His Divine Grace A.C. Bhaktivedanta Swami Prabhupāda

On January 30, 1973, in Calcutta, Śrīla Prabhupāda speaks to the Bharata Chamber of Commerce, a group of the region's leading businessmen. "We should not be satisfied with becoming a big businessman. We must know what our next life is.... If you cultivate this knowledge and at the same time go on doing your business, your life will be successful."

~

Mr. President, ladies, and gentlemen, I thank you very much for kindly inviting me. I'll serve you to the best of my ability.

Today's subject is "Culture and Business." We understand business to mean "occupational duty." According to our Vedic culture there are different types of business. As described in *Bhagavad-gītā*, *cātur-varṇyaṁ mayā sṛṣṭaṁ guṇa-karma-vibhāgaśaḥ*. The four divisions of the social system, based on people's qualities and types of work, are the *brāhmaṇas* [intellectuals and teachers], the *kṣatriyas* [military men and state leaders], the *vaiśyas* [farmers and merchants], and the *śūdras* [laborers]. Before doing business one must know what kinds of work there are and who can do what kind of work. People have different capabilities, and there are different types of work, but now we have created a society where everyone takes up everyone else's business. That is not very scientific.

Society has natural cultural divisions, just as there are natural divisions in the human body. The whole body is one unit, but it has different departments – for example, the head department, the arm department, the belly department, and the leg department. This is scientific. So in society the head department is represented by the *brāhmaṇa,* the arm department by the *kṣatriya,* the belly department by the *vaiśya,* and the leg department by the *śūdra.* Business should be divided scientifically in this way.

The head department is the most important department, because without the head the other departments – the arm, the belly, and the leg – cannot function. If the arm department is lacking, business can still go on. If the leg department is lacking, business can go on. But if the head department is not there – if your head is cut off from your body – then even though you have arms, legs, and a belly, they are all useless.

The head is meant for culture. Without culture every type of business creates confusion and chaos. And that is what we have at the present moment because of jumbling of different types of business. So there must be one section of people, the head department, who give advice to the other departments. These advisors are the intelligent and qualified *brāhmaṇas.*

śamo damas tapaḥ śaucaṁ
kṣāntir ārjavam eva ca
jñānaṁ vijñānam āstikyaṁ
brahma-karma svabhāva-jam

"Peacefulness, self-control, austerity, purity, tolerance, honesty, knowledge, wisdom, and religiousness – these are the natural qualities by which the *brāhmaṇas* work."

The *brāhmaṇas,* the head of the social body, are meant to guide society in culture. Culture means knowing the aim of life. Without understanding the aim of life, a man is a ship without a rudder. But at the present moment we are missing the goal of life because there is no head department in society. The whole human society is now lacking real *brāhmaṇas* to give advice to the other departments.

Arjuna is a good example of how a member of the *kṣatriya* department should take advice. He was a military man; his business was to fight. In the Battle of Kurukṣetra he engaged in his business, but at the same time he took the advice of the *brahmaṇya-deva,* Lord Kṛṣṇa. As it is said,

namo brahmaṇya-devāya
go-brāhmaṇa-hitāya ca
jagad-dhitāya kṛṣṇāya
govindāya namo namaḥ

"Let me offer my respectful obeisances unto Lord Kṛṣṇa, who is the worshipable Deity for all brahminical men, who is the well-wisher of cows and *brāhmaṇas,* and who is always benefiting the whole world. I offer my repeated obeisances to the Personality of Godhead, known as Kṛṣṇa and Govinda."

In this verse the first things taken into consideration are the cows and the *brāhmaṇas* (*go-brāhmaṇa*). Why are they stressed? Because a society with no brahminical culture and no cow protection is not a human society but a chaotic, animalistic society. And any business you do in a chaotic condition will never be perfect. Business can be done nicely only in a society following a proper cultural system.

Instructions for a perfect cultural system are given in *Śrīmad-Bhāgavatam.* At a meeting in the forest of Naimiṣāraṇya, where many learned scholars and *brāhmaṇas* had assembled and Śrīla Sūta Gosvāmī was giving instructions, he stressed the *varṇāśrama* social system (*ataḥ pumbhir dvija-śreṣṭhā varṇāśrama-vibhāgaśaḥ*). The Vedic culture organizes society into four *varṇas* [occupational divisions] and four *āśramas* [spiritual stages of life]. As mentioned before, the *varṇas* are the *brāhmaṇa, kṣatriya, vaiśya,* and *śūdra.* The *āśramas* are the *brahmacārī-āśrama* [celibate student life], *gṛhastha-āśrama* [family life], *vānaprastha-āśrama* [retired life], and *sannyāsa-āśrama* [renounced life]. Unless we take to this institution of *varṇāśrama-dharma*, the whole society will be chaotic.

And the purpose of *varṇāśrama-dharma* is to satisfy the Supreme Lord. As stated in the *Viṣṇu Purāṇa*,

varṇāśramācāravatā
puruṣeṇa paraḥ pumān
viṣṇur ārādhyate panthā
nānyat tat-toṣa-kāraṇam

According to this verse, one has to satisfy the Supreme Lord by properly performing one's prescribed duties according to the system of *varṇa* and *āśrama*. In a state, you have to satisfy your government. If you don't you are a bad citizen and cause chaos in society. Similarly, in the cosmic state – that is, in this material creation as a whole – if you do not satisfy the Supreme Lord, the proprietor of everything, then there will be a chaotic condition. Our Vedic culture teaches that whatever you do you must satisfy the Supreme Lord. That is real culture.

Sva-karmaṇā tam abhyarcya siddhiṁ vindati mānavaḥ. You may do any business – the *brāhmaṇa's* business, the *kṣatriya's* business, the *vaiśya's* business, or the *śūdra's* business – but by your business you should satisfy the Supreme Personality of Godhead. You may be a merchant, a professional man, a legal advisor, a medical man – it doesn't matter. But if you want perfection in your business, then you must try to satisfy the Supreme Personality of Godhead. Otherwise you are simply wasting your time.

In *Bhagavad-gītā* Lord Kṛṣṇa says *yajñārthāt karmaṇaḥ*. The word *yajña* refers to Viṣṇu, or Kṛṣṇa, the Supreme Lord. You have to work for Him. Otherwise you become bound by the reactions of your activities (*anyatra loko 'yaṁ karma-bandhanaḥ*). And as long as you are in the bondage of karma, you have to transmigrate from one body to another.

Unfortunately, at the present moment people do not know that there is a soul and that the soul transmigrates from one body to another. As stated in *Bhagavad-gītā, tathā dehāntara-prāptiḥ:* When the body dies, the soul transmigrates to another body. I've talked with big, big scientists and professors who do not know that there is life after death. They do not know. But according to our Vedic information, there is life after death. And we can experience transmigration of the soul in this present life. It is a very common thing: A baby soon gets the body of a boy, the boy then gets the body of a young man, and the young man gets the body of an old man. Similarly, the old man, after the annihilation of his body, will get another body. It is quite natural and logical.

Actually, we have two bodies, the gross body and the subtle body. The gross body is made up of our senses and the bodily elements – bones, blood, and so on. When we change our body at death, the present gross body is destroyed, but the subtle body, made of mind, intelligence, and ego, is not. The subtle body carries us to our next gross body.

It is just like what happens when we sleep. At night we forget about the gross body, and the subtle body alone works. As we dream we are taken away from our home, from our bed, to some other place, and we completely forget the gross body. When our sleep is over we forget about the dream and become attached again to the gross body. This is going on in our daily experience.

So we are the observer, sometimes of the gross body and sometimes of the subtle body. Both bodies are changing, but we are the unchanging observer, the soul within the bodies. Therefore, our inquiry should be, "What is my position? At night I forget my gross body, and during the daytime I forget my subtle body. Then what is my real body?" These are the questions we should ask.

So you may do your business, as Arjuna did his business. He was a fighter, a *kṣatriya*, but he did not forget his culture, hearing *Gītā* from the master. But if you simply do business and do not cultivate your spiritual life, then your business is a useless waste of time (*śrama eva hi kevalam*).

Our Kṛṣṇa consciousness movement is being spread so that you do not forget your cultural life. We do not say that you stop your business and become a *sannyāsī* like me and give up everything. We do not say that. Nor did Kṛṣṇa say that. Kṛṣṇa never said, "Arjuna, give up your fighting business." No, He said, "Arjuna, you are a *kṣatriya*. You are declining to fight, saying, 'Oh, it is very abominable.' You should not say that. You *must* fight." That was Kṛṣṇa's instruction.

Similarly, we Kṛṣṇa conscious people are also advising everyone, "Don't give up your business. Go on with your business, but simply hear about Kṛṣṇa." Caitanya Mahāprabhu also said this, quoting from *Śrīmad-Bhāgavatam: sthāne sthitāḥ śruti-gatāṁ tanu-vāṅ-manobhiḥ*. Caitanya Mahāprabhu never said, "Give up your position." Giving up one's position is not very difficult. But to cultivate spiritual knowledge while one stays in his position – that is required. Among the animals there is no cultivation of spiritual life. That is not possible; the animals cannot cultivate this knowledge. Therefore, if human beings do not cultivate spiritual knowledge, they're exactly like animals (*dharmeṇa hīnāḥ paśubhiḥ samānāḥ*).

So we should be very conscious about our eternal existence. We, the spirit soul within the body, are eternal (*na hanyate hanyamāne śarīre*). We are not going to die after the annihilation of our body. This is the cultivation of knowledge, or *brahma-jijñāsā,* which means inquiry about one's self. Caitanya Mahāprabhu's first disciple, Sanātana Gosvāmī, was formerly finance minister in the government of Nawab Hussein Shah. Then he retired and approached Caitanya Mahāprabhu and humbly said, "My dear Lord, people call me *paṇḍita*." (Because he was a *brāhmaṇa* by caste, naturally he was called *paṇḍita,* meaning "a learned person.") "But I am such a *paṇḍita*," he said, "that I do not even know who or what I am."

This is the position of everyone. You may be a businessman or you may be in another profession, but if you do not know what you are, wherefrom you have come, why you are under the tribulations of the laws of material nature, and where you are going in your next life – if you do not know these things, then whatever you are doing is useless. As stated in *Śrīmad-Bhāgavatam,*

dharmaḥ svanuṣṭhitaḥ puṁsāṁ
viṣvaksena-kathāsu yaḥ
notpādayed yadi ratiṁ
śrama eva hi kevalam

"The occupational activities a man performs according to his own position are only so much useless labor if they do not provoke attraction for the message of the Personality of Godhead." Therefore our request to everyone is that while you engage in your business, in whatever position Kṛṣṇa has posted you, do your duty nicely, but do not forget to cultivate Kṛṣṇa knowledge.

Kṛṣṇa knowledge means God consciousness. We must know that we are part and parcel of God (*mamaivāṁśo jīva-loke jīva-bhūtaḥ sanātanaḥ*). We are eternally part and parcel of Kṛṣṇa, or God, but we are now struggling with the mind and senses (*manaḥ ṣaṣṭhānīndriyāṇi prakṛti-sthāni karṣati*). Why this struggle for existence? We must inquire about our eternal life beyond this temporary life. Suppose in this temporary life I become a big businessman for, say, twenty years or fifty years or at the utmost one hundred years. There is no guarantee that in my next life I'm going to be a big businessman. No. There is no such guarantee. But this we do not care about. We are taking care of our present small span of life, but we are not taking care of our eternal life. That is our mistake.

In this life I may be a very great businessman, but in my next life, by my karma, I may become something else. There are 8,400,000 forms of life. *Jalajā nava-lakṣāṇi sthāvarā lakṣa-viṁśatiḥ:* There are 900,000 forms of life in the water, and 2,000,000 forms of trees and other plants. Then, *kṛmayo rudra-saṅkhyakāḥ pakṣiṇāṁ daśa-lakṣaṇam*: There are 1,100,000 species of insects and reptiles, and 1,000,000 species of birds. Finally, *triṁsāl-lakṣāni paśavaḥ catur-lakṣāni mānuṣaḥ:* There are 3,000,000 varieties of beasts and 400,000 human species. So we must pass through 8,000,000 different forms of life before we come to the human form of life.

Therefore Prahlāda Mahārāja says,

kaumāra ācaret prājño
dharmān bhāgavatān iha
durlabhaṁ mānuṣaṁ janma
tad apy adhruvam arthadam

"One who is sufficiently intelligent should use the human form of body from the very beginning of life – in other words, from the tender age of childhood – to practice the activities of devotional service. The human body is most rarely achieved, and although temporary like other bodies, it is meaningful because in human life one can perform devotional service. Even a slight amount of sincere devotional service can give one complete perfection." This human birth is very rare. We should not be satisfied simply with becoming a big businessman. We must know what our next life is, what we are going to be.

There are different kinds of men. Some are called *karmīs*, some are called *jñānīs*, some are called *yogīs*, and some are called *bhaktas*. The *karmīs* are after material happiness. They want the best material comforts in this life, and they want to be elevated to the heavenly planets after death. The *jñānīs* also want happiness, but being fed up with the materialistic way of life, they want to merge into the existence of Brahman, the Absolute. The *yogīs* want mystic power. And the *bhaktas*, the devotees, simply want the service of the Lord. But unless one understands who the Lord is, how can one render service to Him? So cultivating knowledge of God is the highest culture.

There are different kinds of culture: the culture of the *karmīs*, the culture of the *jñānīs*, the culture of the *yogīs*, and the culture of the *bhaktas*. Actually, all of these people are called *yogīs* if they are doing their duty sincerely. Then they are known as *karma-yogīs*, *jñāna-yogīs*, *dhyāna-yogīs*, and *bhakti-yogīs*. But in *Bhagavad-gītā* Kṛṣṇa says,

yoginām api sarveṣāṁ
mad-gatenāntarātmanā

śraddhāvān bhajate yo māṁ
sa me yuktatamo mataḥ

Who is the first-class *yogī*? Kṛṣṇa answers, "He who is always thinking of Me." This means the Kṛṣṇa conscious person is the best *yogī*. As already mentioned, there are different kinds of *yogīs* (the *karma-yogī*, the *jñāna-yogī*, the *dhyāna-yogī*, and the *bhakti-yogī*), but the best *yogī* is he who always thinks of Kṛṣṇa within himself with faith and love. One who is rendering service to the Lord – he is the first-class *yogī*.

So we request everyone to try to know what he is, what Kṛṣṇa is, what his relationship with Kṛṣṇa is, what his real life is, and what the goal of his life is. Unless we cultivate all this knowledge, we are simply wasting our time, wasting our valuable human form of life. Although everyone will die – that's a fact – one who dies after knowing these things is benefited. His life is successful.

The cat will die, the dog will die – everyone will die. But one who dies knowing Kṛṣṇa – oh, that is a successful death. As Kṛṣṇa says in *Bhagavad-gītā*,

janma karma ca me divyam
evaṁ yo vetti tattvataḥ
tyaktvā dehaṁ punar janma
naiti mām eti so 'rjuna

"One who knows in truth the transcendental nature of My appearance and activities does not, upon leaving the body, take his birth again in this material world, but attains My eternal abode, O Arjuna."

So wherever we go all over the world, our only request is, "Please try to understand Kṛṣṇa. Then your life is successful." It doesn't matter what your business is. You have to do something to live. Kṛṣṇa says, *śarīra-yātrāpi ca te na prasiddhyed akarmaṇaḥ:* If you stop working your life will be hampered. One has to do something for his livelihood, but at the same time he has to cultivate knowledge for the perfection of his life. The perfection of life is simple: try to understand Kṛṣṇa. This is what we are prescribing all over the world. It is not very difficult. If you read *Bhagavad-gītā As It Is* you will come to understand Kṛṣṇa. Kṛṣṇa explains everything.

For the neophytes, Kṛṣṇa says, *raso 'ham apsu kaunteya prabhāsmi śaśi-sūryayoḥ:* "My dear Kaunteya, I am the taste of water, and I am the light of the sun and the moon." There is no need to say, "I cannot see God." Here is God: the taste of water is God. Everyone drinks water, and when one tastes it he is perceiving God. Then why do you say, "I cannot see God"? Think as God directs and then gradually you'll see Him. Simply remember this one instruction from *Bhagavad-gītā, raso 'ham apsu kaunteya prabhāsmi śaśi-sūryayoḥ:* "I am the taste of water; I am the shining illumination of the sun and moon." Who has not seen the sunlight? Who has not seen the moonlight? Who has not tasted water? Then why do you say, "I have not seen God"? If you simply practice this *bhakti-yoga,* as soon as you taste water and feel satisfied you will think, "Oh, here is Kṛṣṇa." Immediately you will remember Kṛṣṇa. As soon as you see the sunshine, you will remember, "Oh, here is Kṛṣṇa." As soon as you see the moonshine, you will remember, "Oh, here is Kṛṣṇa." And *śabdaḥ khe:* As soon as you hear some sound in the sky, you will remember, "Here is Kṛṣṇa."

In this way, you will remember Kṛṣṇa at every step of your life. And if you remember Kṛṣṇa at every step of life, you become the topmost *yogī*. And above all, if you practice the chanting of Hare Kṛṣṇa, Hare Kṛṣṇa, Kṛṣṇa Kṛṣṇa, Hare Hare/ Hare Rāma, Hare Rāma, Rāma Rāma, Hare Hare, you will easily remember Kṛṣṇa. There is no tax. There is no loss to your business. If you chant the Hare Kṛṣṇa mantra, if you remember Kṛṣṇa while drinking water, what is your loss? Why don't you try it? This is the real culture of knowledge. If you cultivate this knowledge and at the same time go on doing your business, your life will be successful. Thank you very much.

Are You More than Green, Righteous, and Dead?

Jayādvaita Swami

Caring about the environment makes you feel good about yourself. Is feeling good sufficient?

~

Twenty years ago, no one gave a damn. You could gum up a river with factory sludge, chop down rain forests wholesale, spray fluorocarbons into the air like a kid sprinkling confetti, and no one would say boo.

No longer. Grade-school kids want to grow up to be ecologists. New York tycoons sort their trash to recycle. Rock singers play concerts to save prairies and wetlands. Political candidates tell us they're worried about the fate of the three-toed baboon.

Caring about the environment helps you feel good about yourself. At the supermarket you choose paper instead of plastic. You write your thank-you notes on cards made from ground-up newsprint and cotton waste. You chip in a few dollars for Greenpeace. Hey, you care about the earth. You're a righteous human being.

Yet too often our concern for the earth lacks a metaphysical grounding. Intuitively, living in harmony with the earth feels right. If the earth is the house we're going to live in, why litter the rooms with beer cans or pee all over the carpet?

But in an ultimate sense, so what? If life is just a series of chemical reactions, what does it matter if the chemicals go messy? Species come and species go. Why get all mushy and teary-eyed if a few berserk bipeds wipe out some hundred thousand kinds of their neighbors? The earth may be our mother, but sooner or later she's going to blow to atomic dusting powder anyway. And from a cosmic point of view that's just a few mega-moments down the line. So why all the fuss?

You can say it's for our children, it's for future generations. But they're also just a flash in eternity. Why bother for them?

Guardians of the green remind us urgently that dirtying and devouring the earth is short-sighted. But to be far-sighted we have to look beyond what seems clean, pleasant, and harmonious on a physical spot of earth on a brief ride through the universe. We have to ask ourselves not only how well we're treating the earth but why we're on it and where we are ultimately going.

Otherwise, though ecologically aware, we're metaphysically dead.

Chapter Six

Spiritual Traditions & Teachers

The Four Noble Truths of Buddhism

Satyarāja Dāsa

How well does Vaiṣṇava philosophy align with the fundamental principles of Buddhism?

~

Revered participants: I stand before you as a representative of the Vaiṣṇava tradition, though, I must admit, I lack the qualities and realizations of the ideal Vaiṣṇava. Still, I will try to present the teachings of this prestigious and time-honored tradition as it has been conveyed to me by one of its most exalted teachers: His Divine Grace A.C. Bhaktivedanta Swami Prabhupāda, the founder and spiritual preceptor of the International Society for Krishna Consciousness. His Divine Grace also happens to be my spiritual master.

The Venerable Bodhi Santosh Roshi, leader and spiritual director of your Society, has asked me to speak about the Four Noble Truths of Buddhism. This will be a distinct honor, since these same truths lie at the basis of Vaiṣṇava thought. In this brief talk I will explain how this is so.

Before beginning, however, I would like to briefly mention just what these truths are. Please correct me if I am inaccurate in how

I express them: (1) the truth of suffering, of the universality of suffering; (2) the truth of the origin of suffering, which is related to suffering as an ontological reality; (3) the truth of the cessation of suffering; and (4) the truth of the Path, which is integrally related to the cessation of suffering.

If there are no objections, then, I would like to begin by exploring the first two of the Four Noble Truths: the truth of suffering and the truth of the origin of suffering.

First and Second Noble Truths

In both Buddhism and Vaiṣṇavism, we think deeply about life and material nature – not just the beauty of nature, but also the harsh reality of existence. Contrary to what many might think, to take a good, hard look at the difficult aspects of being is not necessarily negative. Rather, when guided by a self-realized teacher it can be a first step toward spiritual enlightenment. Unless we are frightfully aware of the distasteful side of life we are likely to become its victims. Once victimized by material existence, pursuing higher matters is difficult.

The plain fact is this: All happiness or pleasure in this world is temporary; it must come to an end. So suffering, to one degree or another, is unavoidable. Therefore, far from being a sour grapes sort of philosophy, to acknowledge and even explore the implications of pain and suffering is simply realistic. Most of the world's spiritual traditions, therefore, recommend cultivating knowledge of nescience and transcendence side by side, so that one can gradually rise beyond the mundane and become situated in a life of true goodness.

This is a gradual evolution that takes time – from ignorance, to passion, to goodness, to pure goodness, or transcendence. To this end, Buddhism and Vaiṣṇavism in particular do not shy away from educating adherents about the stark miseries of material life. Fundamental meditations in both Buddhist and Vaiṣṇava traditions are meant to make practitioners aware of the inevitability of

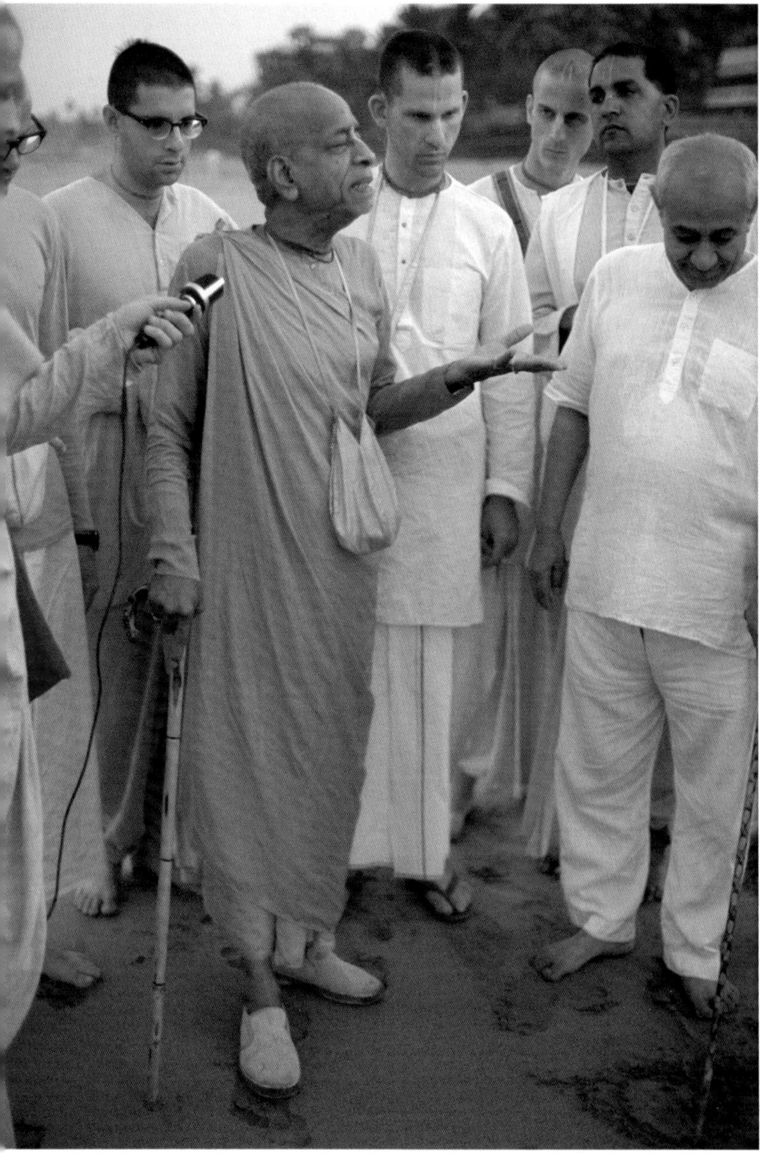

His Divine Grace A. C. Bhaktivedanta Swami Prabhupāda (Founder-*Ācārya* of the International Society for Krishna Consciousness) and followers in discussion on a beach in Mumbai, India.

Śrīla Prabhupāda and his disciples walk with Father Emmanuel Jungclaussen of Niederalteich Monastery, Germany.

Śrīla Prabhupāda discussing Kṛṣṇa consciousness with Dr. Stillson Judah, Professor Emeritus, History of Religions, Graduate Theological Union, California.

Śrīla Prabhupāda meeting with American reporters.

‹ṛṣṇa, the Supreme Personality of Godhead, is the ever-youthful, ıll-attractive reservoir of love. When we stimulate our original love or Kṛṣṇa, that love expands out into this world and beyond and ›ecomes an expression of our eternal nature.

There is another nature beyond this material one – the world of anti-matter, or the eternal kingdom of God, where trees, animals, flowers, and people all exist in intimate loving relationships with Kṛṣṇa. Each of us has a place in that spiritual world, for it is our eternal home.

Mother Yaśodā in her ecstasy of loving motherhood runs after her child, Kṛṣṇa. In the most intimate expressions of love of God, pure *bhakti*, the devotees forget that Kṛṣṇa is the father of all living beings and instead act as His parents, friends, and lovers.

The law of karma is as strict, relentless, and impartial as the laws of motion and gravity. Good begets good, and evil begets evil. If we slaughter animals to fill our dinner plates, we can expect human society to be filled with violence in equal measure.

From the time Sukla Gupta was a year and a half old and barely able to talk, she began to tell memories of her past life as a woman named Mana. Cases of past-life remembrance strongly point to the existence of reincarnation. (pp. 67—76)

The *Bhagavad-gītā* tells us that while the individual is the master of his or her body, Kṛṣṇa, as the Supersoul, is the supreme master of every body. The indwelling Supersoul sits in everyone's heart, ready to give us the wisdom to find our way back to the spiritual world.

The *Bhagavad-gītā* says, "Whatever state of being one remembers when he quits his body, that state he will attain without fail in his next life." King Bharata, his consciousness at death absorbed in his pet deer, transmigrated into the body of a deer. (p. 133)

Whether boss or laborer, master or servant, president or prisoner, everyone is under the tight control of the three modes of material nature (goodness, passion, and ignorance), which compete within us for supremacy and push us from one material situation to the next.

While speaking the *Bhagavad-gītā* Kṛṣṇa showed Arjuna His universal form, containing all of existence. Seeing Arjuna's fear at this vision of infinity, He then showed him His four-armed form, and at last, the beautiful form Arjuna held so dear.

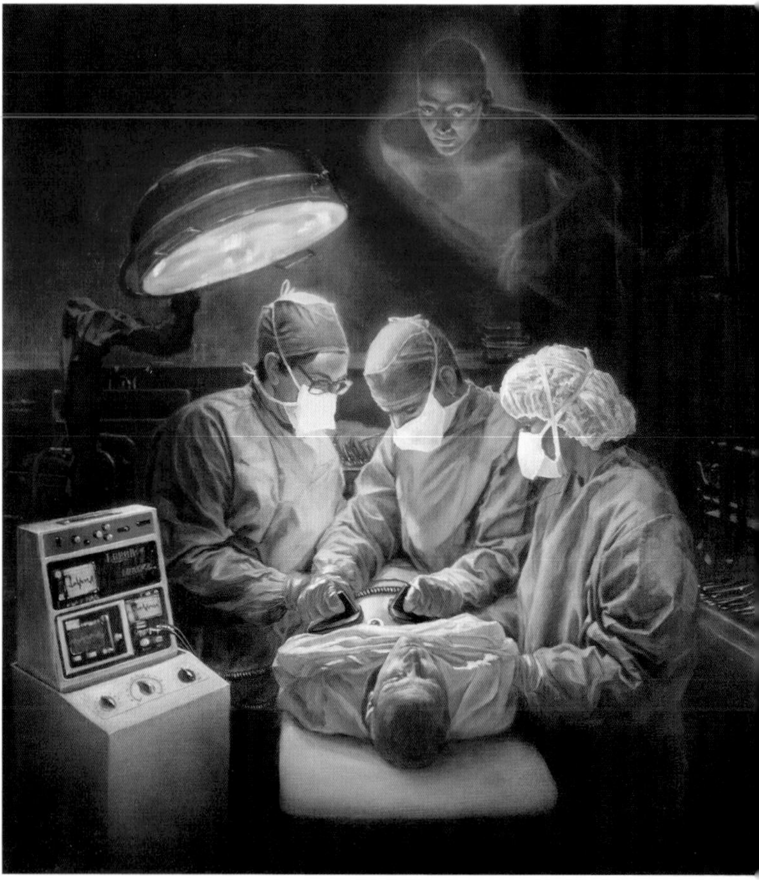

As near-death experiences indicate, there is one constant element in us that permeates our body. That "conscious observer," or self, does not change when we are awake or asleep – or even at death – because it is nonmaterial.

"As the embodied soul continuously passes, in this body, from boyhood to youth to old age, the soul similarly passes into another body at death. A sober person is not bewildered by such a change." (*Gītā* 2.13)

Kṛṣṇa (center) is the original Personality of Godhead, but He has many transcendental forms, each of which appears in this world for a particular purpose. The most famous of His forms are known as *līlā-avatāras,* "pastime incarnations," and their stories are told throughout the Vedic literature. His ten most prominent pastime incarnations are (counterclockwise, from the upper left-hand corner): (1) Mātsya; (2) Kūrma; (3) Varāha; (4) Nṛsiṁha; (5) Vāmana; (6) Paraśurāma; (7) Rāmacandra; (8) Kṛṣṇa Himself; (9) Buddha; (10) Kalki.

Rādhā and Kṛṣṇa, the Divine Couple, enjoy pure love for one another in the spiritual world. Śrīmatī Rādhārāṇī is the embodiment of perfect devotional service and, as Kṛṣṇa's spiritual potency, She is nondifferent from Him.

When Kṛṣṇa came as Lord Caitanya five hundred years ago, He and His associates gave an easy process by which to clear the heart of unhappiness and absorb it in love of God: the congregational chanting of Kṛṣṇa's transcendental names.

birth, death, old age, and disease, for example, and how these phenomena affect people's lives. Knowledge of these things can serve as a catalyst to move beyond materialism and to pursue divinity in earnest.

Regarding birth, death, old age, and disease, the Buddha story is familiar to everyone here today: Siddhārtha Gautama, the Buddha, was a noble prince, and in his youth he was sheltered from the miseries of life. When the prince traveled out of his kingdom for the first time and saw a dying person, a person giving birth, a diseased person, and an aged person, he asked his servant if such hardship, or suffering, was common. His servant responded by telling him that these calamities, in one way or another, necessarily afflict man in his sojourn through life. At that moment the Buddha resolved to find the solution to suffering.

The ancient Vedic texts of India home in on three kinds of suffering: suffering caused by one's own body and mind, suffering caused by the bodies and minds of others, and suffering that comes from natural calamities. In Sanskrit suffering is known as *duḥkha,* a word that carries implications of "pain," "distress," "grief," "affliction," and "frustration." I believe you use this same term. In your tradition you say that *duḥkha* comes from *avidyā,* or "ignorance." We say the same thing. My spiritual master, Śrīla Prabhupāda, began his work in the West with the notion that people are suffering due to want of knowledge. He claimed that spiritual knowledge was the only thing that could lessen their suffering. For this reason he tirelessly labored to translate ancient Vedic texts and to personally teach how to live a life of spiritual fervor – he felt deeply the suffering of others and wanted to help them rise beyond such suffering.

Ignorance begins with bodily identification. When the life-force, or the soul within the body, misidentifies with the aggregate of material elements – which is only the body, even if we see it as our actual selves – it begins a life of illusion, and this is the seed of all suffering to follow. The *Bhagavad-gītā,* a central text for the Vaiṣṇava tradition, boldly declares that the body and soul are different and that ignorance, illusion, and, consequently, suffering, come from the soul's erroneous identification with matter.

I realize that this is a touchy subject in Buddhist teaching. Bodhi Santosh Roshi and I have spent much time discussing the intricacies of Buddhist thought on the soul and reincarnation. It is beyond the scope of this lecture to definitively talk about the various Buddhist positions on this point. I will, however, say – and I know that Bodhi Santosh Roshi agrees – that the earliest forms of Indian Buddhism accept the Vedic conclusion about the nature of the soul and reincarnation. This is true, too, of most forms of northern Buddhism, or Mahayana Buddhism, and it is fundamental to Tibetan Buddhism as well.

But even those forms of Buddhism that reject the idea of a soul are adamant that illusion, and thus suffering, comes from the body. Such forms of Buddhism merely start from the next step. That is, rather than focus on the difference between the body and the self, they ask, "What are the implications of bodily identification?"

So let us use that as a starting point. What are the implications of bodily identification? Well, for one, bodily identification breeds desire, or craving. In Buddhism, this is called *tāṅha* or *tṛṣṇa,* words that imply "greediness" and "pandering to the senses." If you have a body, it is natural to be concerned for its needs. But most people go far beyond the body's needs. They become absorbed in excessive sense gratification. Prabhupāda compared sense gratification to using salt in a food preparation: If you add too much you will spoil it, and if you add too little you will spoil it as well.

Thus both Buddhism and Vaiṣṇavism propose a "middle path," if you will, a path that does not deny the senses but does not overly indulge them either. As the *Gītā's* second chapter informs us, all misery begins when one contemplates the objects of the senses. This contemplation leads to attachment and, eventually, selfish desire. This gives rise to anger. Why anger? Because the pleasures of this world are temporary, as we have noted, and so they inevitably come to an end – we eventually lose the objects of our attachment. This makes us angry. When we are angry, the *Gītā* says, we can't think straight. We become bewildered. This leads to loss of memory. At this point, intelligence is lost. (The *Gītā* defines intelligence as good memory and fine discretion.) Naturally, in such a state of mind one can't pursue spiritual life. So these are some introductory ideas about suffering and the causes of suffering.

Third Noble Truth

The third Noble Truth is that of the cessation of suffering. If all suffering comes from desire, then the cessation of suffering comes from the extinguishing of desire. This is somewhat problematic. Where there is self, there is self-interest. It is thus natural to desire. We want the best for ourselves and our loved ones. This is natural. The question, then, is not desire, but rather inordinate desire, or that desire which, again, is unnecessary or excessive. The Buddhist and the Vaiṣṇava both work at quieting unnecessary passions or desires, and, conversely, cultivating desires of the spirit, pursuing passion for truth.

To dedicate one's life to the path of Buddhism or Vaiṣṇavism requires commitment, determination, and, yes, passion. One must desire the goal of Buddhism or Vaiṣṇavism, of one's chosen path. Someone may put forth the Zenlike idea that one only reaches the goal when one ceases to pursue it. But this is only partly true. If one pursues truth for truth itself, devoid of ego, this is entirely appropriate. In other words, one must pursue it for the right reasons. Then it is okay. If one does not desire enlightenment, at least on some level, one will never achieve it.

The point is to get beyond selfish cravings, self-interested desires, and by so doing to realize one's bonding with all that exists. In Vaiṣṇavism this is called the *brahma-bhūta* stage, wherein one sees all living beings equally and does not distinguish between them or judge them because of material differences. If one can reach this level of enlightenment, one can raise oneself beyond all material suffering. In Buddhism, it is said that this is achieved by following the Path – which means different things to different people.

Fourth Noble Truth

In Buddhism, the Path tells us to do things in "the right way" – it is the Eightfold Path, consisting of the right view, right thought, right speech, right action, right livelihood, right effort, right mindfulness, and right concentration. In Vaiṣṇavism this is called the mode of goodness, and it is difficult to achieve. Indeed, in this age few are able to truly act properly, and if, after much practice, they find that they can, they will be doing a great thing for themselves and for the world around them. The Eightfold Path is thus the most noble of goals.

I must say, however, that, in my opinion, if one actually achieves this goal – if one achieves it to perfection – one will be acting in Kṛṣṇa consciousness, or Vaiṣṇavism. You see, my understanding of Vaiṣṇavism is not some sectarian religion that pits itself against all other religions. No. Rather, I see Vaiṣṇavism as *sanātana-dharma*, or the eternal function of the soul. Thus, I see all bona fide spiritual traditions as but various expressions of Vaiṣṇavism. It is for this reason that, when I contemplate the Eightfold Path of Buddhism, I can only see it as acting for God, for Kṛṣṇa, because to do something in the right way, as I understand it, means doing it for Him. Ultimately, to act properly is to act for our source. To behave in the right way is to behave in the way in which our creator intended.

This is a touchy issue, I know. Buddhism does not traditionally deal with God or His nature. But the God question haunts us even if we find Him irrelevant or not necessary for liberation, as is often the case in Buddhistic thought. When we deal with questions of ontology and teleology – the questions concerning where everything comes from and where everything is going – we can't help but consider the existence of God. What religion in general, and Vaiṣṇavism in particular, has to offer is this: positive information about the world beyond suffering. Both Buddhism and Vaiṣṇavism agree that this is a world of suffering, but what lies beyond this world? In Vaiṣṇava tradition, we learn of Vaikuṇṭha, the spiritual realm, a place where the chief characteristics are eternity, knowledge, and bliss – the exact opposite of temporality, ignorance, and suffering. Although the material world is a land of exploitation, the spiritual realm is described as the land of dedication, the land of love.

There are Buddhist traditions, too, that speak of higher realms – lands of demigods and higher beings. But, to my knowledge, only in the Vaiṣṇava tradition does one find exacting details about the abode of Kṛṣṇa, the Supreme Personality of Godhead, and how to get there. This is where I would like to go if I ever achieve perfection on my path, and that is perhaps why I have chosen the path of Vaiṣṇavism. Recently, when the Dalai Lama was in New York, I was fortunate enough to hear him lecture. After explaining that he respected all spiritual paths and that all paths have merit, he admitted that he was particularly partial to Buddhism, and that is why he is a Buddhist. I must confess that I too share a similar prejudice. While I acknowledge that all revealed traditions are respect-worthy and have a good deal to offer, I can only attempt to approach the truth through the Vaiṣṇava tradition. This is my approach to spiritual life, and I hope you will indulge me that preference. Thank you very much.

Addendum: Buddha in the Bhāgavatam

"Then, in the beginning of Kali-yuga, the Lord will appear as Lord Buddha, the son of Añjanā, in the province of Gayā, just for the purpose of deluding those who are envious of the faithful theists."

Śrīmad-Bhāgavatam 1.3.24

> Lord Buddha, a powerful incarnation of the Personality of Godhead, appeared in the province of Gayā (Bihar) as the son of Añjanā, and he preached his own conception of

nonviolence and deprecated even the animal sacrifices sanctioned in the *Vedas*. At the time when Lord Buddha appeared, the people in general were atheistic and preferred animal flesh to anything else. On the plea of Vedic sacrifice, every place was practically turned into a slaughterhouse, and animal-killing was indulged in unrestrictedly. Lord Buddha preached nonviolence, taking pity on the poor animals. He preached that he did not believe in the tenets of the *Vedas* and stressed the adverse psychological effects incurred by animal-killing. Less intelligent men of the age of Kali, who had no faith in God, followed his principle, and for the time being they were trained in moral discipline and nonviolence, the preliminary steps for proceeding further on the path of God realization. He deluded the atheists because such atheists who followed his principles did not believe in God, but they kept their absolute faith in Lord Buddha, who himself was the incarnation of God. Thus the faithless people were made to believe in God in the form of Lord Buddha. That was the mercy of Lord Buddha: he made the faithless faithful to him.

Kṛṣṇa, Christos, Christ

A conversation between His Divine Grace
A.C. Bhaktivedanta Swami Prabhupāda
and Father Emmanuel Jungclaussen

In 1974, near ISKCON's center in Frankfurt am Main, West Germany, Śrīla Prabhupāda and several of his disciples took a morning walk with father Emmanuel Jungclaussen, a Benedictine monk from Niederalteich Monastery. Noticing that Śrīla Prabhupāda was carrying meditation beads similar to the rosary, Father Emmanuel explained that he also chanted a constant prayer: "Lord Jesus Christ, be merciful unto us." The following conversation ensued.

~

Śrīla Prabhupāda: What is the meaning of the word Christ?
Father Emmanuel: *Christ* comes from the Greek word Christos, meaning "the anointed one."
Śrīla Prabhupāda: Christos is the Greek version of the word Kṛṣṇa.
Father Emmanuel: This is very interesting.
Śrīla Prabhupāda: When an Indian person calls on Kṛṣṇa, he often says, "Kṛṣṭa." Kṛṣṭa is a Sanskrit word meaning "attraction." So when we address God as "Christ," "Kṛṣṭa," or "Kṛṣṇa," we indicate the same all-attractive Supreme Personality of Godhead. When Jesus said, "Our Father, who art in heaven, sanctified be Thy name," that name of God was "Kṛṣṭa" or "Kṛṣṇa." Do you agree?

Father Emmanuel: I think Jesus, as the son of God, has revealed to us the actual name of God: Christ. We can call God "Father," but if we want to address Him by His actual name, we have to say "Christ."

Śrīla Prabhupāda: Yes. "Christ" is another way of saying Kṛṣṭa, and "Kṛṣṭa" is another way of pronouncing Kṛṣṇa, the name of God. Jesus said that one should glorify the name of God, but yesterday I heard one theologian say that God has no name – that we can call Him only "Father." A son may call his father "Father," but the father also has a specific name. Similarly, "God" is the general name of the Supreme Personality of Godhead, whose specific name is Kṛṣṇa. Therefore whether you call God "Christ," "Kṛṣṭa," or "Kṛṣṇa," ultimately you are addressing the same Supreme Personality of Godhead.

Father Emmanuel: Yes, if we speak of God's actual name, then we must say, "Christos." In our religion, we have the Trinity: the Father, Son, and the Holy Spirit. We believe we can know the name of God only by revelation from the Son of God. Jesus Christ revealed the name of the father, and therefore we take the name Christ as the revealed name of God.

Śrīla Prabhupāda: Actually, it doesn't matter – Kṛṣṇa or Christ – the name is the same. The main point is to follow the injunctions of the Vedic scriptures that recommend chanting the name of God in this age. The easiest way is to chant the *mahā-mantra:* Hare Kṛṣṇa, Hare Kṛṣṇa, Kṛṣṇa Kṛṣṇa, Hare Hare/ Hare Rāma, Hare Rāma, Rāma Rāma, Hare Hare. Rāma and Kṛṣṇa are names of God, and Hare is the energy of God. So when we chant the *mahā-mantra,* we address God together with His energy. This energy is of two kinds, the spiritual and the material. At present we are in the clutches of the material energy. Therefore we pray to Kṛṣṇa that He may kindly deliver us from the service of the material energy and accept us into the service of the spiritual energy. That is our whole philosophy. Hare Kṛṣṇa means, "O energy of God, O God [Kṛṣṇa], please engage me in Your service." It is our nature to render service. Somehow or other we have come to the service of material things, but when this service is transformed into the service of the spiritual energy, then our life is perfect. To practice *bhakti-yoga* [loving service to God] means to become free from designations like "Hindu," "Muslim," "Christian," this or that, and simply to serve God. We have created Christian, Hindu, and Muhammadan religions, but when we come to a religion without designations, in which we don't think we are Hindus or Christians or Muhammadans, then we can speak of pure religion, or *bhakti*.

Father Emmanuel: *Mukti*?

Śrīla Prabhupāda: No, *bhakti*. When we speak of *bhakti, mukti* [liberation from material miseries] is included. Without *bhakti* there is no *mukti*, but if we act on the platform of *bhakti*, then *mukti* is included. We learn this from the *Bhagavad-gītā* [14.26]:

māṁ ca yo 'vyabhicāreṇa
bhakti-yogena sevate
sa guṇān samatītyaitān
brahma-bhūyāya kalpate

"One who engages in full devotional service, unfailing in all circumstances, at once transcends the modes of material nature and thus comes to the level of Brahman."

Father Emmanuel: Is Brahman Kṛṣṇa?

Śrīla Prabhupāda: Kṛṣṇa is Para-brahman. Brahman is realized in three aspects: as impersonal Brahman, as localized Paramātmā, and as personal Brahman. Kṛṣṇa is personal, and He is the Supreme Brahman, for God is ultimately a person. In the *Śrīmad-Bhāgavatam* [1.2.11], this is confirmed:

vadanti tat tattva-vidas
tattvam yaj jñānam advayam
brahmeti paramātmeti
bhagavān iti śabdyate

"Learned transcendentalists who know the Absolute Truth call this nondual substance Brahman, Paramātmā, or Bhagavān." The feature of the Supreme Personality is the ultimate realization of

God. He has all six opulences in full: He is the strongest, the richest, the most beautiful, the most famous, the wisest, and the most renounced.

Father Emmanuel: Yes, I agree.

Śrīla Prabhupāda: Because God is absolute, His name, His form, and His qualities are also absolute, and they are nondifferent from Him. Therefore to chant God's holy name means to associate directly with Him. When one associates with God, one acquires godly qualities, and when one is completely purified, one becomes an associate of the Supreme Lord.

Father Emmanuel: But our understanding of the name of God is limited.

Śrīla Prabhupāda: Yes, we are limited, but God is unlimited. And because He is unlimited, or absolute, He has unlimited names, each of which is God. We can understand His names as much as our spiritual understanding is developed.

Father Emmanuel: May I ask a question? We Christians also preach love of God, and we try to realize love of God and render service to Him with all our heart and all our soul. Now, what is the difference between your movement and ours? Why do you send your disciples to the Western countries to preach love of God when the gospel of Jesus Christ is propounding the same message?

Śrīla Prabhupāda: The problem is that the Christians do not follow the commandments of God. Do you agree?

Father Emmanuel: Yes, to a large extent you're right.

Śrīla Prabhupāda: Then what is the meaning of the Christians' love for God? If you do not follow the orders of God, then where is your love? Therefore we have come to teach what it means to love God: if you love Him, you cannot be disobedient to His orders. And if you're disobedient, your love is not true.

All over the world, people love not God but their dogs. The Kṛṣṇa consciousness movement is therefore necessary to teach people how to revive their forgotten love for God. Not only the Christians, but also the Hindus, the Muhammadans, and all others are guilty. They have rubber-stamped themselves "Christian," "Hindu," or "Muhammadan," but they do not obey God. That is the problem.

Visitor: Can you say in what way the Christians are disobedient?

Śrīla Prabhupāda: Yes. The first point is that they violate the commandment "Thou shalt not kill" by maintaining slaughterhouses. Do you agree that this commandment is being violated?

Father Emmanuel: Personally, I agree.

Śrīla Prabhupāda: Good. So if the Christians want to love God, they must stop killing animals.

Father Emmanuel: But isn't the most important point –

Śrīla Prabhupāda: If you miss one point, there is a mistake in your calculation. Regardless of what you add or subtract after that, the mistake is already in the calculation, and everything that follows will also be faulty. We cannot simply accept that part of the scripture we like, and reject what we don't like, and still expect to get the result. For example, a hen lays eggs with its back part and eats with its beak. A farmer may consider, "The front part of the hen is very expensive because I have to feed it. Better to cut it off." But if the head is missing there will be no eggs anymore, because the body is dead. Similarly, if we reject the difficult part of the scriptures and obey the part we like, such an interpretation will not help us. We have to accept all the injunctions of the scripture as they are given, not only those that suit us. If you do not follow the first order, "Thou shalt not kill," then where is the question of love of God?

Visitor: Christians take this commandment to be applicable to human beings, not to animals.

Śrīla Prabhupāda: That would mean that Christ was not intelligent enough to use the right word: murder. There is killing, and there is murder. Murder refers to human beings. Do you think Jesus was not intelligent enough to use the right word – murder – instead of the word killing? Killing means any kind of killing, and especially animal killing. If Jesus had meant simply the killing of humans, he would have used the word murder.

Father Emmanuel: But in the Old Testament the commandment

"Thou shalt not kill" does refer to murder. And when Jesus said, "Thou shalt not kill," he extended this commandment to mean that a human being should not only refrain from killing another human being, but should also treat him with love. He never spoke about man's relationship with other living entities, but only about his relationship with other human beings. When he said, "Thou shalt not kill," he also meant in the mental and emotional sense – that you should not insult anyone or hurt him, treat him badly, and so on.

Śrīla Prabhupāda: We are not concerned with this or that testament but only with the words used in the commandments. If you want to interpret these words, that is something else. We understand the direct meaning. "Thou shalt not kill" means, "The Christians should not kill." You may put forth interpretations in order to continue the present way of action, but we understand very clearly that there is no need for interpretation. Interpretation is necessary if things are not clear. But here the meaning is clear. "Thou shalt not kill" is a clear instruction. Why should we interpret it?

Father Emmanuel: Isn't the eating of plants also killing?

Śrīla Prabhupāda: The Vaiṣṇava philosophy teaches that we should not even kill plants unnecessarily. In the *Bhagavad-gītā* [9.26] Kṛṣṇa says:

patraṁ puṣpaṁ phalaṁ toyaṁ
yo me bhaktyā prayacchati
tad ahaṁ bhakty-upahṛtam
aśnāmi prayatātmanaḥ

"If someone offers Me with love and devotion a leaf, a flower, a fruit, or a little water, I will accept it." We offer Kṛṣṇa only the kind of food He demands, and then we eat the remnants. If offering vegetarian food to Kṛṣṇa were sinful, then it would be Kṛṣṇa's sin, not ours. But God is *apāpa-viddha* – sinful reactions are not applicable to Him. He is like the sun, which is so powerful that it can purify even urine – something impossible for us to do. Kṛṣṇa is also like a king, who may order a murderer to be hanged but who himself is beyond punishment because he is very powerful. Eating food first offered to the Lord is also something like a soldier's killing during wartime. In a war, when the commander orders a man to attack, the obedient soldier who kills the enemy will get a medal. But if the same soldier kills someone on his own, he will be punished. Similarly, when we eat only *prasāda* [the remnants of food offered to Kṛṣṇa], we do not commit any sin. This is confirmed in the *Bhagavad-gītā* [3.13]:

yajña-śiṣṭāśinaḥ santo
mucyante sarva-kilbiṣaiḥ
bhuñjate te tv aghaṁ pāpā
ye pacanty ātma-kāraṇāt

"The devotees of the Lord are released from all kinds of sins because they eat food that is offered first for sacrifice. Others, who prepare food for personal sense enjoyment, verily eat only sin."

Father Emmanuel: Kṛṣṇa cannot give permission to eat animals?

Śrīla Prabhupāda: Yes – in the animal kingdom. But the civilized human being, the religious human being, is not meant to kill and eat animals. If you stop killing animals and chant the holy name Christ, everything will be perfect. I have not come to teach you, but only to request you to please chant the name of God. The Bible also demands this of you. So let's kindly cooperate and chant, and if you have a prejudice against chanting the name Kṛṣṇa, then chant "Christos" or "Kṛṣṭa" – there is no difference. Śrī Caitanya said: *nāmnām akāri bahudhā nija-sarva-śaktiḥ*. "God has millions and millions of names, and because there is no difference between God's name and Himself, each one of these names has the same potency as God." Therefore, even if you accept designations like "Hindu," "Christian," or "Muhammadan," if you simply chant the name of God found in your own scriptures, you will attain the spiritual platform. Human life is meant for self-realization – to learn how to love God. That is the actual beauty of man. Whether you discharge this duty as a Hindu, a Christian, or a Muhammadan, it doesn't matter – but discharge it!

Father Emmanuel: I agree.

Śrīla Prabhupāda [*pointing to a string of 108 meditation beads*]: We always have these beads, just as you have your rosary. You are chanting, but why don't the other Christians also chant? Why should they miss this opportunity as human beings? Cats and dogs cannot chant, but we can, because we have a human tongue. If we chant the holy names of God, we cannot lose anything; on the contrary, we gain greatly. My disciples practice chanting Hare Kṛṣṇa constantly. They could also go to the cinema or do so many other things, but they have given everything up. They eat neither fish nor meat nor eggs, they don't take intoxicants, they don't drink, they don't smoke, they don't partake in gambling, they don't speculate, and they don't maintain illicit sexual connections. But they do chant the holy name of God. If you would like to co-operate with us, then go to the churches and chant "Christ," "Kṛṣṭa," or "Kṛṣṇa." What could be the objection?

Father Emmanuel: There is none. For my part, I would be glad to join you.

Śrīla Prabhupāda: No, we are speaking with you as a representative of the Christian Church. Instead of keeping the churches closed, why not give them to us? We would chant the holy name of God there twenty-four hours a day. In many places we have bought churches that were practically closed because no one was going there. In London I saw hundreds of churches that were closed or used for mundane purposes. We bought one such church in Los Angeles. It was sold because no one came there, but if you visit this same church today, you will see thousands of people. Any intelligent person can understand what God is in five minutes; it doesn't require five hours.

Father Emmanuel: I understand.

Śrīla Prabhupāda: But the people do not. Their disease is that they don't want to understand.

Visitor: I think understanding God is not a question of intelligence, but a question of humility.

Śrīla Prabhupāda: Humility means intelligence. The humble and meek own the kingdom of God. This is stated in the Bible, is it not? But the philosophy of the rascals is that everyone is God, and today this idea has become popular. Therefore no one is humble and meek. If everyone thinks that he is God, why should he be humble and meek? Therefore I teach my disciples how to become humble and meek. They always offer their respectful obeisances in the temple and to the spiritual master, and in this way they make advancement. The qualities of humbleness and meekness lead very quickly to spiritual realization. In the Vedic scriptures it is said, "To those who have firm faith in God and the spiritual master, who is His representative, the meaning of the Vedic scriptures is revealed."

Father Emmanuel: But shouldn't this humility be offered to everyone else, also?

Śrīla Prabhupāda: Yes, but there are two kinds of respect: special and ordinary. Śrī Kṛṣṇa Caitanya taught that we shouldn't expect honor for ourselves, but should always respect everyone else, even if he is disrespectful to us. But special respect should be given to God and His pure devotee.

Father Emmanuel: Yes, I agree.

Śrīla Prabhupāda: I think the Christian priests should cooperate with the Kṛṣṇa consciousness movement. They should chant the name Christ or Christos and should stop condoning the slaughter of animals. This program follows the teachings of the Bible; it is not my philosophy. Please act accordingly and you will see how the world situation will change.

Father Emmanuel: I thank you very much.

Śrīla Prabhupāda: Hare Kṛṣṇa.

"Thou Shalt Not Kill" or "Thou Shalt Not Murder"?

A conversation between His Divine Grace
A.C. Bhaktivedanta Swami Prabhupāda
and Cardinal Jean Daniélou

At a monastic retreat near Paris, in July of 1973, Śrīla Prabhupāda talked with Jesuit Cardinal Jean Daniélou of the Académie Francaise about the sacredness of both human and animal life and the importance of nonviolence for those wishing to love God. The discussion focused on the biblical commandment, "Thou shalt not kill": "[T]he Bible does not simply say, 'Do not kill the human being.' It says broadly, 'Thou shalt not kill.' ... why do you interpret this to suit your own convenience?"

~

Śrīla Prabhupāda: Jesus Christ said, "Thou shalt not kill." So why is it that the Christian people are engaged in animal killing?
Cardinal Daniélou: Certainly in Christianity it is forbidden to kill, but we believe that there is a difference between the life of a human being and the life of the beasts. The life of a human being is sacred because man is made in the image of God; therefore, to kill a human being is forbidden.

Śrīla Prabhupāda: But the Bible does not simply say, "Do not kill the human being." It says broadly, "Thou shalt not kill."
Cardinal Daniélou: We believe that only human life is sacred.
Śrīla Prabhupāda: That is your interpretation. The commandment is "Thou shalt not kill."
Cardinal Daniélou: It is necessary for man to kill animals in order to have food to eat.
Śrīla Prabhupāda: No. Man can eat grains, vegetables, fruits, and milk.
Cardinal Daniélou: No flesh?
Śrīla Prabhupāda: No. Human beings are meant to eat vegetarian food. The tiger does not come to eat your fruits. His prescribed food is animal flesh. But man's food is vegetables, fruits, grains, and milk products. So how can you say that animal killing is not a sin?
Cardinal Daniélou: We believe it is a question of motivation. If the killing of an animal is for giving food to the hungry, then it is justified.
Śrīla Prabhupāda: But consider the cow: we drink her milk; therefore, she is our mother. Do you agree?
Cardinal Daniélou: Yes, surely.
Śrīla Prabhupāda: So if the cow is your mother, how can you support killing her? You take the milk from her, and when she's old and cannot give you milk, you cut her throat. Is that a very humane proposal? In India those who are meat-eaters are advised to kill some lower animals like goats, pigs, or even buffalo. But cow killing is the greatest sin. In preaching Kṛṣṇa consciousness we ask people not to eat any kind of meat, and my disciples strictly follow this principle. But if, under certain circumstances, others are obliged to eat meat, then they should eat the flesh of some lower animal. Don't kill cows. It is the greatest sin. And as long as a man is sinful, he cannot understand God. The human being's main business is to understand God and to love Him. But if you remain sinful, you will never be able to understand God – what to speak of loving Him.

Cardinal Daniélou: I think that perhaps this is not an essential point. The important thing is to love God. The practical commandments can vary from one religion to the next.
Śrīla Prabhupāda: So, in the Bible God's practical commandment is that you cannot kill; therefore killing cows is a sin for you.
Cardinal Daniélou: God says to the Indians that killing is not good, and he says to the Jews that...
Śrīla Prabhupāda: No, no, no. Jesus Christ taught that "Thou shalt not kill." Why do you interpret this to suit your own convenience?
Cardinal Daniélou: But Jesus allowed the sacrifice of the Paschal Lamb.
Śrīla Prabhupāda: But he never maintained a slaughterhouse.
Cardinal Daniélou: [*Laughs.*] No, but he did eat meat.
Śrīla Prabhupāda: When there is no other food, someone may eat meat in order to keep from starving. That is another thing. But it is most sinful to regularly maintain slaughterhouses just to satisfy your tongue. Actually, you will not even have a human society until this cruel practice of maintaining slaughterhouses is stopped. And although animal killing may sometimes be necessary for survival, at least the mother animal, the cow, should not be killed. That is simply human decency. In the Kṛṣṇa consciousness movement our practice is that we don't allow the killing of any animals. Kṛṣṇa says, *patraṁ puṣpaṁ phalaṁ toyaṁ yo me bhaktyā prayacchati:* "Vegetables, fruits, milk, and grains should be offered to Me in devotion." [*Gītā* 9.26] We take only the remnants of Kṛṣṇa's food (*prasāda*). The trees offer us many varieties of fruits, but the trees are not killed. Of course, one living entity is food for another living entity, but that does not mean you can kill your mother for food. Cows are innocent; they give us milk. You take their milk – and then kill them in the slaughterhouse. This is sinful.
Student: Śrīla Prabhupāda, Christianity's sanction of meat-eating is based on the view that lower species of life do not have a soul like the human being's.

Śrīla Prabhupāda: That is foolishness. First of all, we have to understand the evidence of the soul's presence within the body. Then we can see whether the human being has a soul and the cow does not. What are the different characteristics of the cow and the man? If we find a difference in characteristics, then we can say that in the animal there is no soul. But if we see that the animal and the human being have the same characteristics, then how can you say that the animal has no soul? The general symptoms are that the animal eats, you eat; the animal sleeps, you sleep; the animal mates, you mate; the animal defends, and you defend. Where is the difference?

Cardinal Daniélou: We admit that in the animal there may be the same type of biological existence as in men, but there is no soul. We believe that the soul is a human soul.

Śrīla Prabhupāda: Our *Bhagavad-gītā* says *sarva-yoniṣu,* "In all species of life the soul exists." The body is like a suit of clothes. You have black clothes; I am dressed in saffron clothes. But within the dress you are a human being, and I am also a human being. Similarly, the bodies of the different species are just like different types of dress. They are soul, a part and parcel of God. Suppose a man has two sons, not equally meritorious. One may be a Supreme Court judge and the other may be a common laborer, but the father claims both as his sons. He does not make the distinction that the son who is a judge is very important and the worker-son is not important. And if the judge-son says, "My dear father, your other son is useless; let me cut him up and eat him," will the father allow this?

Cardinal Daniélou: Certainly not, but the idea that all life is part of the life of God is difficult for us to admit. There is a great difference between human life and animal life.

Śrīla Prabhupāda: That difference is due to the development of consciousness. In the human body there is developed consciousness. Even a tree has a soul, but a tree's consciousness is not very developed. If you cut a tree it does not resist. Actually, it does resist, but only to a very small degree. There is a scientist named

Jagadish Chandra Bose who has made a machine which shows that trees and plants are able to feel pain when they are cut. And we can see directly that when someone comes to kill an animal, it resists, it cries, it makes a horrible sound. So it is a matter of the development of consciousness. But the soul is there within all living beings.

Cardinal Daniélou: But metaphysically, the life of man is sacred. Human beings think on a higher platform than the animals do.

Śrīla Prabhupāda: What is that higher platform? The animal eats to maintain his body, and you also eat in order to maintain your body. The cow eats grass in the field, and the human being eats meat from a huge slaughterhouse full of modern machines. But just because you have big machines and a ghastly scene, while the animal simply eats grass, this does not mean that you are so advanced that only within your body is there a soul and that there is not a soul within the body of the animal. That is illogical. We can see that the basic characteristics are the same in the animal and the human being.

Cardinal Daniélou: But only in human beings do we find a metaphysical search for the meaning of life.

Śrīla Prabhupāda: Yes. So metaphysically search out why you believe that there is no soul within the animal – that is metaphysics. If you are thinking metaphysically, that's all right. But if you are thinking like an animal, then what is the use of your metaphysical study? Metaphysical means "above the physical" or, in other words, "spiritual." In the *Bhagavad-gītā* Kṛṣṇa says, *sarva-yoniṣu kaunteya:* "In every living being there is a spirit soul." That is metaphysical understanding. Now either you accept Kṛṣṇa's teachings as metaphysical, or you'll have to take a third-class fool's opinion as metaphysical. Which do you accept?

Cardinal Daniélou: But why does God create some animals who eat other animals? There is a fault in the creation, it seems.

Śrīla Prabhupāda: It is not a fault. God is very kind. If you want to eat animals, then He'll give you full facility. God will give you the body of a tiger in your next life so that you can eat flesh very freely. "Why are you maintaining slaughterhouses? I'll give you fangs and claws. Now eat." So the meat-eaters are awaiting such punishment. The animal-eaters become tigers, wolves, cats, and dogs in their next life – to get more facility.

Divine Culture

His Divine Grace A.C. Bhaktivedanta Swami Prabhupāda

People should not think that we are preaching a sectarian religion. No. We are simply preaching how to love God.

~

There is a misconception that the Kṛṣṇa consciousness movement represents the Hindu religion. In fact, however, Kṛṣṇa consciousness is in no way a faith or religion that seeks to defeat other faiths or religions. Rather, it is an essential cultural movement for the entire human society and does not consider any particular sectarian faith. This cultural movement is especially meant to educate people in how they can love God.

Sometimes Indians both inside and outside of India think that we are preaching the Hindu religion, but actually we are not. One will not find the word *Hindu* in the *Bhagavad-gītā*. Indeed, there is no such word as *Hindu* in the entire Vedic literature. This word has been introduced by the Muslims from provinces next to India, such as Afghanistan, Baluchistan, and Persia. There is a river called Sindhu bordering the northwestern provinces of India, and since the Muslims there could not pronounce Sindhu properly, they instead called the river Hindu, and the inhabitants of this tract of land they called Hindus. In India, according to the Vedic language, the Europeans are called *mlecchas* or *yavanas*. Similarly, Hindu is a name given by the Muslims.

India's actual culture is described in the *Bhagavad-gītā*, where it is stated that according to the different qualities or modes of nature there are different types of men, who are generally classified into four social orders and four spiritual orders. This system of social and spiritual division is known as *varṇāśrama-dharma*. The four *varṇas*, or social orders, are *brāhmaṇa, kṣatriya, vaiśya,* and *śūdra*. The four *āśramas*, or spiritual orders, are *brahmacarya, gṛhastha, vānaprastha,* and *sannyāsa*. The *varṇāśrama* system is described in the Vedic scriptures known as the *Purāṇas*. The goal of this institution of Vedic culture is to educate every man for advancement in knowledge of Kṛṣṇa, or God. That is the entire Vedic program.

When Lord Caitanya talked with the great devotee Rāmānanda Rāya, the Lord asked him, "What is the basic principle of human life?" Rāmānanda Rāya answered that human civilization begins when *varṇāśrama-dharma* is accepted. Before coming to the standard of *varṇāśrama-dharma* there is no question of human civilization. Therefore, the Kṛṣṇa consciousness movement is trying to establish this right system of human civilization, which is known as Kṛṣṇa consciousness, or *daiva-varṇāśrama* – divine culture.

In India, the *varṇāśrama* system has now been taken in a perverted way, and thus a man born in the family of a *brāhmaṇa* (the highest social order) claims that he should be accepted as a *brāhmaṇa*. But this claim is not accepted by the *śāstra* (scripture). One's forefather may have been a *brāhmaṇa* according to *gotra*, or the family hereditary order, but real *varṇāśrama-dharma* is based on the factual quality one has attained, regardless of birth or heredity. Therefore, we are not preaching the present-day system of the Hindus, especially those who are under the influence of Śaṅkarācārya, for Śaṅkarācārya taught that the Absolute Truth is impersonal, and thus he indirectly denied the existence of God.

Śaṅkarācārya's mission was special; he appeared to reestablish the Vedic influence after the influence of Buddhism. Because Buddhism was patronized by Emperor Aśoka, 2600 years ago the Buddhist religion practically pervaded all of India. According to the Vedic literature, Buddha was an incarnation of Kṛṣṇa who had a special power and who appeared for a special purpose. His system of thought, or faith, was accepted widely, but Buddha rejected the authority of the *Vedas*. While Buddhism was spreading, the Vedic culture was stopped both in India and in other places. Therefore, since Śaṅkarācārya's only aim was to drive away Buddha's system of philosophy, he introduced a system called Māyāvāda.

Strictly speaking, Māyāvāda philosophy is atheism, for it is a process in which one imagines that there is God. This Māyāvāda system of philosophy has been existing since time immemorial. The present Indian system of religion or culture is based on the Māyāvāda philosophy of Śaṅkarācārya, which is a compromise with Buddhist philosophy. According to Māyāvāda philosophy there actually is no God, or if God exists He is impersonal and all-pervading and can therefore be imagined in any form. This conclusion is not in accord with the Vedic literature. That literature names many demigods, who are worshiped for different purposes, but in every case the Supreme Lord, the Personality of Godhead, Viṣṇu, is accepted as the supreme controller. That is real Vedic culture.

The philosophy of Kṛṣṇa consciousness does not deny the existence of God and the demigods, but Māyāvāda philosophy denies both; it maintains that neither the demigods nor God exists. For the Māyāvādīs, ultimately all is zero. They say that one may imagine any authority – whether Viṣṇu, Durgā, Lord Śiva, or the sun god – because these are the demigods generally worshiped in society. But the Māyāvāda philosophy does not in fact accept the existence of any of them. The Māyāvādīs say that because one cannot concentrate one's mind on the impersonal Brahman, one may imagine any of these forms. This is a new system, called *pañcopāsanā*. It was introduced by Śaṅkarācārya, but the *Bhagavad-*

gītā does not teach any such doctrines, and therefore they are not authoritative.

The *Bhagavad-gītā* accepts the existence of the demigods. The demigods are described in the *Vedas,* and one cannot deny their existence, but they are not to be understood or worshiped according to the way of Śaṅkarācārya. The worship of demigods is rejected in the *Bhagavad-gītā*. The *Gītā* (7.20) clearly states:

kāmais tais tair hṛta jñānāḥ
prapadyante 'nya-devatāḥ
taṁ taṁ niyamam āsthāya
prakṛtyā niyatāḥ svayā

"Those whose minds are distorted by material desires surrender unto demigods and follow the particular rules and regulations of worship according to their own natures." Furthermore, in the *Bhagavad-gītā* (2.44), Lord Kṛṣṇa states:

bhogaiśvarya-prasaktānāṁ
tayāpahṛta-cetasām
vyavasāyātmikā buddhiḥ
samādhau na vidhīyate

"In the minds of those who are too attached to sense enjoyment and material opulence, and who are bewildered by such things, the resolute determination for devotional service does not take place." Those who are pursuing the various demigods have been described as *hṛta jñānāḥ,* which means "those who have lost their sense." That is also further explained in the *Bhagavad-gītā* (7.23):

antavat tu phalaṁ teṣāṁ
tad bhavaty alpa-medhasām
devān deva-yajo yānti
mad-bhaktā yānti mām api

"Men of small intelligence worship the demigods, and their fruits are limited and temporary. Those who worship the demigods go to the planets of the demigods, but My devotees ultimately reach My supreme abode." The rewards given by the demigods are temporary, because any material facility must act in connection with the temporary body. Whatever material facilities one gets, whether by modern scientific methods or by deriving benedictions from the demigods, will be finished with the body. But spiritual advancement will never be finished.

People should not think that we are preaching a sectarian religion. No. We are simply preaching how to love God. There are many theories about the existence of God. The atheist, for example, will never believe in God. Atheists like Professor Jacques Monod, who won the Nobel Prize, declare that everything is chance (a theory already put forward long ago by atheistic philosophers of India such as Cārvāka). Then other philosophies, such as the *karma-mīmāṁsā* philosophy, accept that if one goes on doing his work nicely and honestly, automatically the result will come, without need for one to refer to God. For evidence, the proponents of such theories cite the argument that if one is diseased with an infection and takes medicine to counteract it, the disease will be neutralized. But our argument in this connection is that even if one gives a man the best medicine, he still may die. The results are not always predictable. Therefore, there is a higher authority, *daiva-netreṇa,* a supreme director. Otherwise, how is it that the son of a rich and pious man becomes a hippie in the street or that a man who works very hard and becomes rich is told by his doctor, "Now you may not eat any food, but only barley water"?

The *karma-mīmāṁsā* theory holds that the world is going on without the supreme direction of God. Such philosophies say that everything takes place by lust (*kāma-haitukam*). By lust a man becomes attracted to a woman, and by chance there is sex and the woman becomes pregnant. There is actually no plan to make the woman pregnant, but by a natural sequence when a man and a woman unite, a result is produced. The atheistic theory, which is described in the sixteenth chapter of the *Bhagavad-gītā* as asuric, or demoniac, is that actually everything is going on in this way because of chance and resulting from natural attraction. This demoniac theory supports the idea that if one wants to avoid children, he may use a contraceptive method.

Actually, however, there is a great plan for everything: the Vedic plan. The Vedic literature gives directions regarding how men and women should unite, how they should beget children, and what the purpose of sex life is. Kṛṣṇa says in the *Bhagavad-gītā* that sex life sanctioned by the Vedic order, or sex life under the direction of the Vedic rules and regulations, is bona fide and is acceptable to Him. But chance sex life is not acceptable. If by chance one is sexually attracted and there are children, they are called *varṇa-saṅkara,* unwanted population. That is the way of the lower animals; it is not acceptable for humans. For humans, there is a plan. We cannot accept the theory that there is no plan for human life or that everything is born of chance and material necessity.

Śaṅkarācārya's theory that there is no God and that one can go on with his work and imagine God in any form just to keep peace and tranquility in society is also more or less based on this idea of chance and necessity. Our way, however, which is completely different, is based on authority. It is this divine *varṇāśrama-dharma* that Kṛṣṇa recommends, not the caste system as it is understood today. This modern caste system is now condemned in India also, and it *should* be condemned, for the classification of different types of men according to birth is not the Vedic or divine caste system.

There are many classes of men in society – some men are engineers, some are medical practitioners, some are chemists, tradesmen, businessmen, and so on. These varieties of classes are not to be determined by birth, however, but by quality. No such thing as the caste-by-birth system is sanctioned by the Vedic literature, nor do we accept it. We have nothing to do with the caste system, which is also at present being rejected by the public in India. Rather, we give everyone the chance to become a *brāhmaṇa* and thus attain the highest status of life.

Because at the present moment there is a scarcity of *brāhmaṇas,* spiritual guides, and *kṣatriyas,* administrative men, and because the entire world is being ruled by *śūdras,* or men of the manual laborer class, there are many discrepancies in society. It is to mitigate all these discrepancies that we have taken to this Kṛṣṇa consciousness movement. If the *brāhmaṇa* class is actually reestablished, the other orders of social well-being will automatically follow, just as when the brain is perfectly in order, the other parts of the body, such as the arms, the belly, and the legs, all act very nicely.

The ultimate goal of this movement is to educate people in how to love God. Caitanya Mahāprabhu approves the conclusion that the highest perfection of human life is to learn how to love God. The Kṛṣṇa consciousness movement has nothing to do with the Hindu religion or any system of religion. No Christian gentleman will be interested in changing his faith from Christian to Hindu. Similarly, no Hindu gentleman of culture will be ready to change to the Christian faith. Such changing is for men who have no particular social status. But everyone will be interested in understanding the philosophy and science of God and taking it seriously. One should clearly understand that the Kṛṣṇa consciousness movement is not preaching the so-called Hindu religion. We are giving a spiritual culture that can solve all the problems of life, and therefore it is being accepted all over the world.

Yoga for the Modern Age

His Divine Grace A.C. Bhaktivedanta Swami Prabhupāda

In a lecture given in Los Angeles, California, on February 19, 1969, Śrīla Prabhupāda takes his listeners through five verses of the Bhagavad-gītā *(6.30–34) that describe the* yogī's *battle to conquer the mind – and how the mind can easily be conquered by practicing* bhakti-yoga.

~

arjuna uvāca
yo 'yaṁ yogas tvayā proktaḥ
sāmyena madhusūdana
etasyāhaṁ na paśyāmi
cañcalatvāt sthitiṁ sthirām

"Arjuna said: O Madhusūdana, the system of yoga which You have summarized appears impractical and unendurable to me, for the mind is restless and unsteady." [*Gītā* 6.33]

This is the crucial test of the eightfold *aṣṭāṅga-yoga* system expounded by Lord Śrī Kṛṣṇa. It has already been explained that one must sit in a certain way and concentrate the mind on the form of Viṣṇu seated within the heart. According to the *aṣṭāṅga-yoga* system, first of all one has to control the senses, follow all the rules and regulations, practice the sitting posture and the breathing process, concentrate the mind on the form of Viṣṇu within the heart, and then become absorbed in that form. There are eight processes in this *aṣṭāṅga-yoga* system, but here Arjuna says quite frankly that this *aṣṭāṅga-yoga* system is very difficult. Indeed, he says that it "appears impractical and unendurable to me."

Actually, the *aṣṭāṅga-yoga* system is not impractical, for were it impractical, Lord Kṛṣṇa would not have taken so much trouble to describe it. It is not impractical, but it *appears* impractical. What may be impractical for one man may be practical for another. Arjuna is representative of the common man in the sense that he is not a mendicant or a *sannyāsī* or a scholar. He is on the battlefield fighting for his kingdom, and in this sense he is an ordinary man engaged in a worldly activity. He is concerned with earning a livelihood, supporting his family, and so on. Arjuna has many problems, just as the common man, and generally this system of *aṣṭāṅga-yoga* is impractical for the ordinary common man. That is the point being made. It is practical for one who has already completely renounced everything and can sit in a secluded, sacred place on the side of a hill or in a cave. But who can do this in this age? Although Arjuna was a great warrior, a member of the royal family, and a very advanced person, he proclaims this yoga system impractical. And what are we in comparison to Arjuna? If we attempt this system, failure is certain.

Therefore this system of mysticism described by Lord Kṛṣṇa to Arjuna beginning with the words *śucau deśe* and ending with *yogī paramaḥ* is here rejected by Arjuna out of a feeling of inability. As stated before, it is not possible for an ordinary man to leave home and go to a secluded place in the mountains or jungles to practice yoga in this age of Kali. The present age is characterized by a bitter struggle for a life of short duration. As Kali-yuga progresses, our life span gets shorter and shorter. Our forefathers lived for a hundred years or more, but now people are dying at the age of sixty or seventy. Gradually the life span will decrease even further. Memory, mercy, and other good qualities will also decrease in this age.

In Kali-yuga, people are not serious about self-realization even by simple, practical means, and what to speak of this difficult yoga system, which regulates the mode of living, the manner of sitting, selection of place, and detachment of the mind from material engagements. As a practical man, Arjuna thought it was impossible to follow this system of yoga, even though he was favorably endowed in many ways. He was not prepared to become a pseudo *yogī* and practice some gymnastic feats. He was not a pretender but a soldier and a family man. Therefore he frankly admitted that for him this system of yoga would be a waste of time. Arjuna belonged to the royal family and was highly elevated in terms of numerous qualities; he was a great warrior, he had great longevity, and, above all, he was the most intimate friend of Lord Kṛṣṇa, the Supreme Personality of Godhead. Five thousand years ago, when Arjuna was living, the life span was very long. At that time, people used to live up to one thousand years. In the present age of Kali-yuga, the life span is limited to a hundred years; in Dvāpara-yuga, the life span was a thousand years; in Tretā-yuga, the life span was ten thousand years; and in Satya-yuga, the life span was one hundred thousand years. Thus as the *yugas* degenerate, the life span decreases. Even though Arjuna was living at a time when one would live and practice meditation for a thousand years, he still considered this system impossible.

Five thousand years ago Arjuna had much better facilities than we do now, yet he refused to accept this system of yoga. In fact, we do not find any record in history of his practicing it at any time. Therefore, this system must be considered generally impossible in this age of Kali. Of course, it may be possible for some very few, rare men, but for the people in general it is an impossible proposal. If this were so five thousand years ago, what of the present day? Those who are imitating this yoga system in different so-called schools and societies, although complacent, are certainly wasting their time. They are completely ignorant of the desired goal.

Since this *aṣṭāṅga-yoga* system is considered impossible, the *bhakti-yoga* system is recommended for everyone. Without training or education, one can automatically participate in *bhakti-yoga*.

Even a small child can clap at *kīrtana*. Therefore Lord Caitanya Mahāprabhu has proclaimed *bhakti-yoga* the only system practical for this age.

harer nāma harer nāma
harer nāmaiva kevalam
kalau nāsty eva nāsty eva
nāsty eva gatir anyathā

"In this age of quarrel and hypocrisy the only means of deliverance is chanting the holy name of the Lord. There is no other way. There is no other way. There is no other way." Chanting is very simple, and one will feel the results immediately. *Pratyakṣāvagamaṁ dharmyam*. If we attempt to practice other yoga systems we will remain in darkness; we will not know whether or not we are making progress. In *bhakti-yoga* one can understand, "Yes, now I am making progress." This is the only yoga system by which one can quickly attain self-realization and liberation in this life. One doesn't have to wait for another lifetime.

cañcalaṁ hi manaḥ kṛṣṇa
pramāthi balavad dṛḍham
tasyāhaṁ nigrahaṁ manye
vāyor iva suduṣkaram

"The mind is restless, turbulent, obstinate, and very strong, O Kṛṣṇa, and to subdue it, I think, is more difficult than controlling the wind." [*Gītā* 6.34] By chanting Hare Kṛṣṇa, one captures the mind immediately. Just by saying the name *Kṛṣṇa* and hearing it, the mind is automatically fixed on Kṛṣṇa. This means that the yoga system is immediately attained. The entire yoga system aims at concentration on the form of Viṣṇu, and Kṛṣṇa is the original personality from whom all these Viṣṇu forms are expanded. Kṛṣṇa is like the original candle from which all other candles are lit. If one candle is lit, one can light any number of candles, and there is no doubt that each candle is as powerful as the original candle. Nonetheless, one has to recognize the original candle as the original. Similarly, from Kṛṣṇa millions of Viṣṇu forms expand, and each Viṣṇu form is as good as Kṛṣṇa, but Kṛṣṇa remains the original. Thus one who concentrates his mind on Lord Śrī Kṛṣṇa, the original Supreme Personality of Godhead, immediately attains the perfection of yoga.

śrī-bhagavān uvāca
asaṁśayaṁ mahā-bāho
mano durnigrahaṁ calam
abhyāsena tu kaunteya
vairāgyeṇa ca gṛhyate

"Lord Śrī Kṛṣṇa said: O mighty-armed son of Kuntī, it is undoubtedly very difficult to curb the restless mind, but it is possible by suitable practice and by detachment." [*Gītā* 6.35] Kṛṣṇa does not say that it is not difficult. Rather, He admits that it *is* difficult, but possible by means of constant practice. Constant practice means engaging ourselves in some activities that remind us of Kṛṣṇa. In this Society for Krishna Consciousness we therefore have many activities – *kīrtana,* temple activities, *prasāda,* publications, and so on. Everyone is engaged in some activity with Kṛṣṇa at the center. Therefore whether one is typing for Kṛṣṇa, cooking for Kṛṣṇa, chanting for Kṛṣṇa, or distributing literature for Kṛṣṇa, he is in the yoga system and he is also in Kṛṣṇa. We engage in activities just as in material life, but these activities are molded in such a way that they are directly connected with Kṛṣṇa. Thus through every activity, Kṛṣṇa consciousness is possible, and perfection in yoga follows automatically.

asaṁyatātmanā yogo
duṣprāpa iti me matiḥ
vaśyātmanā tu yatatā
śakyo 'vāptum upāyataḥ

"For one whose mind is unbridled, self-realization is difficult work. But he whose mind is controlled and who strives by appropriate means is assured of success. That is My opinion." [*Gītā* 6.36]

The Supreme Personality of Godhead declares that one who does not accept the proper treatment to detach the mind from material engagement can hardly achieve success in self-realization. Trying to practice yoga while engaging the mind in material enjoyment is like trying to ignite a fire while pouring water on it. Similarly, yoga practice without mental control is a waste of time. I may sit down to meditate and focus my mind on Kṛṣṇa, and that is very commendable, but there are many yoga societies that teach their students to concentrate on the void or on some color. That is, they do not recommend concentration on the form of Viṣṇu. Trying to concentrate the mind on the impersonal or the void is very difficult and troublesome. It is stated by Śrī Kṛṣṇa in the twelfth chapter of *Bhagavad-gītā,*

kleśo 'dhikataras teṣām
avyaktāsakta-cetasām
avyaktā hi gatir duḥkhaṁ
dehavadbhir avāpyate

"For those whose minds are attached to the unmanifested, impersonal feature of the Supreme, advancement is very troublesome. To make progress in that discipline is always difficult for those who are embodied."

In the temple, the devotee tries to concentrate on the form of Kṛṣṇa. Concentrating on nothingness, on void, is very difficult, and naturally the mind is very flickering. Therefore instead of concentrating on the void, the mind searches out something else. The mind must be engaged in thinking of something, and if it is not thinking of Kṛṣṇa, it must be thinking of *māyā*. Therefore, pseudo-meditation on the impersonal void is simply a waste of time. Such a show of yoga practice may be materially lucrative, but useless as far as spiritual realization is concerned. I may open a class in yogic meditation and charge people money for sitting down and pressing their nose this way and that, but if my students do not attain the real goal of yoga practice, they have wasted their time and money and I have cheated them.

Therefore one has to concentrate his mind steadily and constantly on the form of Viṣṇu, and that is called *samādhi*. In Kṛṣṇa consciousness the mind is controlled by engaging it constantly in the transcendental loving service of the Lord. Unless one is engaged in Kṛṣṇa consciousness, he cannot steadily control the mind. A Kṛṣṇa conscious person easily achieves the result of yoga practice without separate endeavor, but a yoga practitioner cannot achieve success without becoming Kṛṣṇa conscious.

The Gītā Condensed

Kalakaṇṭha Dāsa

In 1968 His Divine Grace A.C. Bhaktivedanta Swami Prabhupāda published the Bhagavad-gītā As It Is, *which has since sold tens of millions of copies in dozens of languages. As a lifetime devotee of Kṛṣṇa and a consummate Sanskritist, Śrīla Prabhupāda spells out the clear conclusions of the* Gītā *that are often obscured by arms-length commentators with their own agendas. Śrīla Prabhupāda's purports (commentaries) illuminate for us the verses spoken by Kṛṣṇa and Arjuna. The following condensed version of their historic conversation combines key points from the verses and purports in the same sequence as the original. These are not direct quotes and thus cannot replace the complete* Bhagavad-gītā As It Is. *Instead, this version provides an overview of the philosophical thread of the* Gītā.

~

Part 1: Action

Arjuna: Kṛṣṇa, please drive my chariot between the two armies. Let me see which followers of that criminal Duryodhana have come here to fight.

Kṛṣṇa (*steering the fine golden chariot between the two huge armies facing each other on the vast, flat battlefield*): Just see, cousin, all the great warriors assembled here.

Arjuna (*aghast*): Kṛṣṇa, I can't fight all these dear relatives, teachers, and elders. My whole family would be destroyed. I'd rather die, or just live as a beggar.

Kṛṣṇa (*smiling kindly*): You forget that everyone is an eternal soul, not a physical body. You can kill the body but not the soul.

Arjuna: Kṛṣṇa, how could I kill these worshipable men? Any victory would be tainted with their blood. I don't know what to do. Please instruct me.

Kṛṣṇa: My friend, you're a warrior. Fight, but not for yourself. Fight for the Supreme. Then you're acting as the eternal soul you truly are. Fight all varieties of materialism and be a *yogī*.

Arjuna: What do *yogīs* do? How do they behave?

Kṛṣṇa: *Yogīs* perform their external duties without attachment because they have mastered their mind and senses. They enjoy an inner happiness that is lost to most people.

Arjuna: You're telling me to be happy within and fight at the same time. That's a contradiction.

Kṛṣṇa: You can't live without acting, Arjuna. Instead of acting for yourself, turn what you do into a sacrifice for the Supreme. Then you'll be happy.

Arjuna: What is this power pushing me toward acting selfishly?

Kṛṣṇa: Lust, Arjuna, born of festering desire. Lust destroys your ability to think clearly. For a long time I've been teaching people how to use yoga to conquer lust. I taught the sun god, who taught his son, who started a long chain of teachers. Somehow, though, the original knowledge has been lost, so today, dear friend, I'll teach it to you Myself.

Arjuna: How could You teach the sun god, who's so much older than You?

Kṛṣṇa: Ordinary bodies age and die, Arjuna, but My body is spiritual and never deteriorates. From time to time I appear in society to help the good people and to vanquish the bad. Good people get rid of their lust and turn their love to Me. But there are many kinds of people, and I respond to everyone individually.

Act for My sake, Arjuna. When you do, everything involved – your work, your equipment, your knowledge – becomes part of a blissful offering, a sacrifice for the Supreme. There are many ways to sacrifice, Arjuna, so you need to find a truly enlightened guru to help you sort them out.

Acting without attachment and acting for Me are both forms of yoga. However, by acting for Me you automatically act without attachment. Remember that I'm your friend, that I own everything, that all action is meant for Me. Then you'll have endless inner peace. You'll do your duty in perfect yoga, or union with Me. To do this you may find it helpful to perform the long austerities involved with the mystic process of yoga and meditation.

Arjuna: Making the mind sit still is like trying to control the wind. Mystic yoga seems too hard for me.

Kṛṣṇa: Yes, it is hard, but it's possible.

Arjuna: What if I start the path of yoga and fail? Then I'm a loser, materially and spiritually.

Kṛṣṇa: If you do the right thing, how can you lose? At least in your next lifetime you'll be better off. On the other hand, if you simply learn to serve Me with love, at death you'll come to Me and leave this horrible world.

Part 2: Devotion

Kṛṣṇa: Arjuna, just listen. You're one of the rare souls who want to know the truth. Just try to understand these points: Everything comes from Me, Arjuna, even the three types of materialism, which affect everyone except Me, their creator.

People who are materialistic, arrogant, falsely wise, or dull ignore Me. People turn to Me when they're curious, desperate, sad, or wise.

People who think I'm just a mouthpiece for Brahman, the formless spirit, never get to know Me personally. But wise people who serve Me come to Me after death.

Arjuna: Tell me about this formless spirit, please, as well as the gods, the soul, karma, and Your presence in my heart. And, please, how do I know You at death?

Kṛṣṇa: The formless spirit, or Brahman, is My spiritual effulgence, and the sparklike individual spirit souls are of the same spiritual substance. By nature, the individual souls serve, but if they choose to serve this endlessly changing world of matter they suffer karma. As for the gods, I create them to manage this material world. And yes, I do live in your heart as the Supersoul, Arjuna.

As for remembering Me at death, practice by thinking of Me as you fight. At other times think of Me as both ancient and fresh, grand and minuscule, but always as a person, shining like the sun. Mystic *yogīs* train themselves with long, deep, mechanical meditation to leave their bodies at just the right time. That helps them proceed to Me in the spiritual world – the only world free of the extended misery of birth and death. But you can get there simply by remembering Me. In fact, by serving Me you gain whatever you might achieve from study, austerity, charity, renunciation, or any sort of religion.

Let Me tell you more. These lessons comprise the king of education, Arjuna. Because you have no envy toward Me you're able to understand them. You must simply listen with faith.

I create the universe and everything in it, but I remain an individual, untouched by My creation. Fools see Me as an ordinary man, but great souls bow to Me and serve Me with love. Some offer great sacrifices to the gods instead, for they like the material enjoyment the gods can give them. But if one lovingly offers Me a little water or a flower or some vegetarian food, I accept it.

Even if you make a mistake, I'll still accept you; I'm equal to everyone but partial to My devotees. Be My devotee, and I promise you'll come to Me.

In short, just know that I create everything. Always serve Me and speak about Me, and you'll be happy, for I, sitting in your heart, shall shine the lamp of knowledge and destroy all the ignorance in your life.

Arjuna: I love listening to You, Kṛṣṇa. It seems that only You can truly know Yourself. How can I know You?

Kṛṣṇa: When you see the best of anything – the shark among the fish or lion among beasts, for example – think of Me. Yet anything wonderful you see in this world is just a spark of My true splendor.

Arjuna: Kṛṣṇa, You have kindly dispelled my illusion. Although I see You now as You are, if You think I am able to behold it, please show me Your form in which You are the universe and everything within it.

Kṛṣṇa: Yes, Arjuna. I shall give you divine eyes to see this divine vision.

Arjuna (*amazed*): Kṛṣṇa, I see the huge gods with their weapons and jewels, dispersed on every planet, dazzling with every imaginable color. The blazing glory of it all surrounds and blinds me. And yet the gods bow in fear before You. Truly You are everything, Kṛṣṇa! You see everything with Your eyes, which are the sun and moon.

(*fearful*) Now I see You crushing the bodies of every living being with Your terribly sharp teeth. My relatives, my enemies – everyone is rushing into Your mouth! Why are You doing this?

Kṛṣṇa: I am time, the death of all. All these warriors are already as good as dead, Arjuna. Fight as My weapon and win your fame!

Arjuna (*trembling*): Almighty Lord, I bow to You from every side! Every living thing should glorify You, but I have foolishly treated You as a friend. Please forgive me, as a father forgives a son or a wife forgives a husband. And please, let me see You again as Kṛṣṇa.

Kṛṣṇa: My universal form has frightened you, Arjuna. Be calm. Now see Me in the form you hold dear. Arjuna, even by performing every kind of good deed, a person will not see Me like this, as I am, as Kṛṣṇa. Only by loving devotion can I be truly seen.

Arjuna: My Lord, should I contemplate You as Kṛṣṇa or as infinite, formless spirit?

Kṛṣṇa: Some people meditate on Me as an endless spirit. That kind of meditation is troublesome, but eventually they may achieve Me. But if you directly think of Me, I swiftly rescue you from the sea of birth and death.

If you can't always think of Me, then hear and chant about Me in the practice of *bhakti,* or devotional yoga. If you can't do that, then work for Me, or at least work for charity, because detachment brings peace – more so than mere knowledge.

Those who think of Me in devotion show wonderful qualities of kindness, tolerance, steadiness, and determination. They love Me, and I love them.

Part 3: Spiritual Knowledge

Arjuna: Kṛṣṇa, what is the relationship of the body and the soul?
Kṛṣṇa: The body is like a field of action for the soul. An ordinary soul interacts with the body by using the senses and by feeling emotions such as lust and hate. However, taking help from a guru, a wise soul becomes detached from the material body. Such a person is humble, equipoised, and truly independent.

As the Supersoul, I offer guidance to all souls, however wise or unwise they may be. Each soul can choose between Me and materialism. Those who choose materialism suffer repeated birth and death in different species. Those who choose Me come to see the whole situation – the compassionate Supersoul and the plight of a spiritual soul encased in dull matter.

Let Me tell you more about matter. It comes in three varieties, or modes: goodness, passion, and ignorance. As the seed-giving father, I bring dead matter to life by implanting the soul. Then the modes take over. Goodness forces the soul to happiness, passion to ambition, and ignorance to delusion. The three modes compete for supremacy, knocking you, the eternal soul, from one material situation to the next. Only when you are free of their control can you taste real happiness.
Arjuna: How does one rise above the three modes, and having conquered them, how does one behave?
Kṛṣṇa: To conquer the modes and be free of karma, simply love and serve Me in every circumstance. Then as the modes come and

go you'll observe them without loving or hating them. At that point you'll be unshakably calm and treat everyone equally.

Arjuna, imagine this world as a great, ancient banyan tree with branches that grow down to become roots. No one can figure out where such a tree begins or ends. If you want to escape its entangling branches, you must cut it down. Then you can enter My self-illumined abode, where there is no need of sunlight or electricity. When you go there, you won't miss this mortal banyan tree.

I want everyone to come to My abode, so I sit in every heart as the Supersoul, offering guidance. I also write the Vedic literature so that people can understand Me. I exist beyond both the materialist and the enlightened soul. If you know Me, you'll be wise and everything you do will come out perfect.

I've told you something about enlightened souls; they're honest, pure, self-controlled, and detached. You are such a person, Arjuna, but I'd like you to hear something about the materialistic, atheistic demons.

Demons don't know what to do or what not to do. They're unclean, dishonest, and preoccupied with sex. Thinking My creation to be their personal property, they build costly, destructive weapons and feel powerful and proud. Their occasional pretenses of religion or charity are meaningless, for lust enslaves them. Chained to materialism by greed and anger, they fall into lower species of life birth after birth.

The Vedic scriptures, which could save them from such a fate, are of no interest to demons.

Arjuna: What becomes of those who don't refer to the *Vedas* but make up their own ways of worship?

Kṛṣṇa: Religion by imagination is a product of the three modes. In goodness one worships the gods, in passion, powerful demons, and in ignorance, ghosts.

The three modes affect everything – even your food. Juicy, fatty, wholesome foods are in goodness; bitter, salty, pungent foods are in passion; and stale, cold, putrid foods are in ignorance. The modes also influence what kind of charity you give and what kind of discipline you impose on yourself. Still, you should not renounce charity or penance.

Arjuna: What does it mean, then, for one to be renounced?

Kṛṣṇa: Renunciation means detachment from the fruits of your work. One in the mode of goodness works dutifully but renounces the result. One in the mode of passion renounces work when it grows troublesome. One in ignorance renounces work out of laziness or confusion.

By seeing others as souls and acting with that understanding, you will stay in goodness. That takes a determined mind, but the initial trouble will later bring you happiness. Happiness in passion seems splendid at the start but ends up being painful. Happiness in ignorance, such as taking intoxicants, is bitter from beginning to end.

Those who work in goodness, or *brāhmaṇas,* are often judges, teachers, or priests. *Kṣatriyas,* those who work in passion, are often administrators, police, or soldiers. Passion and ignorance combine to produce *vaiśyas,* business people or farmers. Those largely in ignorance are called *śūdras,* and they work as artisans, laborers, or servants.

Regardless of the kind of work that best suits you, by doing your work for the Supreme you turn it to yoga and become enlightened. For that reason it's better to do your own work imperfectly than someone else's perfectly.

My dear Arjuna, here is a final summary of what I have been teaching you:

By serving Me you will learn to act and live in simple wisdom, controlling your mind and senses and renouncing the fruits of your work. Soon you will enjoy peace and insight as you achieve unprecedented happiness and appreciation for everyone. In such a state of mind you will attain My abode.

Think about Me and stay with My devotees; I will clear every obstacle from your path. If you become egoistic and think that you can make it on your own, you'll be lost.

You're a warrior, Arjuna; because of your nature you'll fight no matter what. Fight for Me and you'll return to your original home in My abode.

Now I've told you the secrets of perfection. Think over what I've said, and then do whatever you wish to do.

Since you are very, very dear to Me, I'll conclude with this:

Think about Me always. Become My devotee. Worship Me and give Me homage, and you will return to Me. Give up all other duties, Arjuna, and submit yourself to Me. Don't worry; I'll free you from the results of any past mistakes.

Please repeat these words of Mine, but only to pious people. That too shall ensure that you will return to Me, for no one is dearer to Me than one who shares this message. And anyone who hears it faithfully, without envy, attains to the worlds of the pious.

Arjuna, do you understand?

Arjuna (*firmly*): Infallible Kṛṣṇa, You have destroyed my illusions and doubts. By Your kindness I have remembered who I really am. Now, according to Your instructions, I shall fight.

Chapter Seven

East–West Dialogues

Here in this section is a series of conversations between Śrīla Prabhupāda and several of his disciples trained in philosophy. These conversations do not represent an exhaustive treatment of the philosophers under discussion. After all, these philosophers, some of the most prominent in the West, wrote voluminously and created a complex system of thought outlining an original worldview. Instead, what you'll find here is a fascinating series of insights into some of their most salient ideas and a concise yet thorough presentation of the basics of *bhakti-yoga*.

Socrates

A conversation between His Divine Grace
A. C. Bhaktivedanta Swami Prabhupāda and his disciples

Socrates (c. 470–c. 399 BC) was a thorn in the side of the leaders of ancient Athens, who saw him as a corruptor of young men. The problem was that he was uncompromising in his search for an objective understanding of such moral virtues as justice, courage, and piety, and he passed on this spirit to his students, most notably Plato. And in the process, the leaders contended, he neglected the gods of the state. He taught all who would listen to engage in self-examination and tend to their souls. Even today, many have heard of Socrates' instruction to "know thyself," but what does it mean? Here Śrīla Prabhupāda explains that to really know the self one must know the Supreme Self, Kṛṣṇa.

~

Disciple: Socrates strongly opposed the Sophists, a group of speculators who taught that the standards of right and wrong and of truth and falsity were completely relative, being established solely by individual opinion or social convention. Socrates, on the other hand, seemed convinced that there was an absolute, universal truth, or good, beyond mere speculation and opinion, that could be known clearly and with certainty.

Śrīla Prabhupāda: He was correct. For our part, we accept Kṛṣṇa, God, as the supreme authority, the Absolute Truth. Kṛṣṇa is by definition supreme perfection, and philosophy is perfect when it is in harmony with Him. This is our position. The philosophy of the Kṛṣṇa consciousness movement is religious in the sense that it is concerned with carrying out the orders of God. That is the sum and substance of religion. It is not possible to manufacture a religion. In the *Bhagavad-gītā* and *Śrīmad-Bhāgavatam,* manufactured religion is called *kaitava-dharma,* just another form of cheating.

Our basic principle is *dharmaṁ tu sākṣād bhagavat-praṇītam.* The word *dharma* refers to the orders given by God, and if we follow those orders we are following *dharma.* An individual citizen cannot manufacture laws since laws are given by the government. Our perfection lies in following the orders of God cent percent. Those who have no conception of God or His orders may manufacture religious systems, but our system is different.

Disciple: The Socratic dialectic usually sought to gradually arrive at an understanding of the essence of a particular moral virtue – for example, self-control, piety, courage, or justice – by examining proposed definitions for completeness and consistency. Socrates wanted to establish more than just a list of universal definitions, however. He tried to show that any particular virtue, when understood in depth, was not different from all the others. The unity of the virtues thus implied the existence of a single absolute good. For Socrates, the goal of life is to rise by means of the intellect to a realization of this absolute good. A person who had attained such knowledge of the good would be self-realized in that he would always do the good without fail. A soul who had thus realized the good was said to be in a healthy or sound state, or to have attained wisdom. Socrates' name for the single absolute good was "knowledge."

Could one say that Socrates was a kind of *jñāna-yogī*?

Śrīla Prabhupāda: Socrates was a *muni,* a great thinker. However, the real truth comes to such a *muni* after many, many births. As Kṛṣṇa says in the *Bhagavad-gītā:*

bahūnāṁ janmanām ante
jñānavān māṁ prapadyate
vāsudevaḥ sarvam iti
sa mahātmā su-durlabhaḥ

"After many births and deaths, one who is actually in knowledge surrenders unto Me, knowing Me to be the cause of all causes and all that is. Such a great soul is very rare."

People like Socrates are known as *jñānavān*, wise men, and after many births they surrender themselves to Kṛṣṇa. They do not do so blindly, but knowing that the Supreme Personality of Godhead is the source of everything. However, this process of self-searching for knowledge takes time. If we take the instructions of Kṛṣṇa directly and surrender unto Him, we save time and many, many births.

Disciple: Socrates terms his method *maieutic*, that is, "like that of a midwife." He thought that a soul could not really come to knowledge of the good by the imposition of information from an external source. Rather, such knowledge had to be awakened within the soul itself. The teacher's business is to direct, encourage, and prod a soul until it gives birth to the truth. The maieutic method therefore suggests that since the soul is able to bring the truth out of itself, knowledge is really a kind of recollection or remembrance. If so, then there must have been a previous life in which the soul possessed the knowledge it has forgotten. This suggests, then, that the soul (understood as something involving intelligence and memory) exists continuously through many lives and, indeed, is eternal.*

Śrīla Prabhupāda: Yes, the soul is eternal. And because the soul is eternal, the intelligence, mind, and senses are also eternal. However, they are all now covered by a material coating, which must

* Scholars disagree about whether Socrates explicitly taught the doctrine of remembrance. Even if the doctrine was Plato's, Plato clearly thought it inherent in Socrates' maieutic method itself.

be cleansed. Once this material coating is washed away, the real mind, intelligence, and senses will emerge. That is stated in the *Nārada-pañcarātra: tat-paratvena nirmalam.* The purificatory process takes place when one is in touch with the transcendental loving service of the Lord and is chanting the Hare Kṛṣṇa *mahā-mantra*. Caitanya Mahāprabhu said, *ceto-darpaṇa-mārjanam:* one must cleanse the heart. All misconceptions come from misunderstanding one's real nature and one's relationship with God. We are all part and parcel of God, yet somehow or other we have forgotten this. Previously we rendered service to God, but now we are rendering service to something illusory. This is *māyā*. Whether we are liberated or conditioned, our constitutional position is to render service. In the material world we work according to our different capacities – as a politician, a thinker, a poet, or whatever. But if we are disconnected from Kṛṣṇa, all of this is *māyā*. When we perform our duty in order to develop Kṛṣṇa consciousness, our duty enables liberation from this bondage.

Disciple: It is interesting that nowadays we find the kind of relativism taught by the Sophists to be again very widespread: "If you believe it, then it's true for you." Socrates took up the task of vigorously combating this position, trying to demonstrate by strong arguments that there must be an absolute truth that is distinguishable from the relative and that must be categorically acknowledged by everyone.

Śrīla Prabhupāda: That is what we are also doing. The Absolute Truth is true for everyone, and the relative truth is relative to a particular position. The relative truth depends on the Absolute Truth, which is the *summum bonum*. God is the Absolute Truth, and the material world is relative truth. Because the material world is God's energy, it appears to be real or true, just as the reflection of the sun in water emits some light. But that reflection is not independent of the sun, and as soon as the sun sets, that light will disappear. The Absolute Truth is Kṛṣṇa, and this cosmos is relative truth, a manifestation of Kṛṣṇa's external energy. If Kṛṣṇa withdrew His energy, the cosmos would not exist.

In another sense, Kṛṣṇa and Kṛṣṇa's energy are not different. We cannot separate heat from fire; heat is also fire, yet heat is not fire. This is the position of relative truth. As soon as we experience heat, we understand that there is fire. Yet we cannot say that heat is fire. Relative truth is like heat because it stands on the strength of the Absolute Truth, just as heat stands on the strength of fire. Because the Absolute is true, relative truth also appears to be true, although it has no independent existence. A mirage appears to be water because in actuality there is such a thing as water. Similarly, this material world appears attractive because there is actually an all-attractive spiritual world.

Disciple: Socrates held that the highest duty of man was to "care for his soul," that is, to cultivate that healthy state of soul which is true knowledge, the attainment of the good. When a man becomes fixed in such knowledge he will as a matter of course act correctly in all affairs, he will be beyond the dictates of the passions, and he will remain peaceful and undisturbed in every circumstance. Socrates himself seems to have attained such a state, as his own behavior at the time of his death illustrates: he calmly drank the poison hemlock rather than give up his principles. He seems to have realized knowledge of at least some aspect of the Absolute Truth, although we must add that he never spoke of it as a person or gave it a personal name.

Śrīla Prabhupāda: That is the preliminary stage of understanding the Absolute, known as Brahman realization, realization of the impersonal feature. One who advances further attains Paramātmā realization, realization of the localized feature, whereby one realizes that God is everywhere. It is a fact that God is everywhere, but at the same time God has His own abode (*goloka eva nivasaty akhilātma-bhūtaḥ*). God is a person, and He has His own abode and associates. Although He is in His abode, He is present everywhere, within every atom (*andāntara-stha-paramāṇu-cayāntara-stham*). Like other impersonalists, Socrates cannot understand how God, through His potency, can remain in His own abode and simultaneously be present in every atom. The material world is His expansion, His energy (*bhūmir āpo 'nalo vāyuḥ khaṁ mano buddhir eva ca*). Because His energy is expanded everywhere, He can be present everywhere. Although the energy and the energetic are nondifferent, we cannot say that they are not distinct. They are simultaneously one and different. This is the perfect philosophy of *acintya-bhedābheda-tattva,* inconceivable simultaneous oneness and difference.

Disciple: Socrates held that "all the virtues are one thing: knowledge." He saw goodness and knowledge as inseparable. This union of the two seems to reflect features of *sattva-guṇa* as described in the *Bhagavad-gītā.*

Śrīla Prabhupāda: *Sattva-guṇa,* the mode of goodness, is a position from which we can receive knowledge. Knowledge cannot be received from the platform of passion and ignorance. If we hear about Kṛṣṇa, or God, we are gradually freed from the clutches of darkness and passion. Then we can come to the platform of *sattva-guṇa,* and when we are perfectly situated there, we are beyond the lower modes. In the words of *Śrīmad-Bhāgavatam:*

naṣṭa-prāyeṣv abhadreṣu nityaṁ bhāgavata-sevayā
bhagavaty uttama-śloke bhaktir bhavati naiṣṭhikī
tadā rajas-tamo-bhāvāḥ kāma-lobhādayaś ca ye
ceta etair anāviddhaṁ sthitaṁ sattve prasīdati

"For one who regularly attends classes on *Śrīmad-Bhāgavatam* and renders service to the pure devotee, all that is troublesome to the heart is almost completely destroyed, and loving service unto the Personality of Godhead, who is praised with transcendental songs, is established as an irrevocable fact. As soon as irrevocable loving service is established in the heart, the effects of nature's modes of passion and ignorance, such as lust, desire, and hankering, disappear from the heart. Then the devotee is established in goodness, and he becomes completely happy."

This process may be gradual, but it is certain. The more we hear about Kṛṣṇa, the more we become purified. Purification means freedom from the attacks of greed and passion. Then we can become happy. From this platform of purity, known as the *brahma-bhūta* platform, we can realize ourselves and then realize God. So before realizing the Supreme Good, we must first come to the platform of *sattva-guṇa,* goodness. Therefore we have regulations prohibiting illicit sex, meat-eating, intoxication, and gambling. Ultimately we must transcend even the mode of goodness through *bhakti.* Then we become liberated, gradually develop love of God, and regain our original state (*muktir hitvānyathā rūpam*). This means giving up all material engagements and rendering full service to Kṛṣṇa. Then we attain the state where *māyā* cannot touch us. If we keep in touch with Kṛṣṇa, *māyā* has no jurisdiction. *Māyām etāṁ taranti te.* This is perfection.

Disciple: Socrates took the oracular *gnothi seauton,* "know thyself," to enjoin "care of the soul." Care of the soul, as we have seen, involved an intense intellectual endeavor, a kind of introspective contemplation or meditation. It gradually purified the self, detaching it more and more from the body and its passions. Thus through the contemplative endeavor entailed by "know thyself," a person attained knowledge and self-control, and with that he also became happy.

Śrīla Prabhupāda: Yes, that is a fact. Meditation means analyzing the self and searching for the Absolute Truth. That is described in the Vedic literatures: *dhyānāvasthita-tad-gatena manasā paśyanti yaṁ yoginaḥ.* Through meditation the *yogī* sees the Supreme Truth (Kṛṣṇa, or God) within himself. Kṛṣṇa is there. The *yogī* consults with Kṛṣṇa, and Kṛṣṇa advises him. That is the relationship Kṛṣṇa has with the *yogī. Dadāmi buddhi-yogaṁ tam.* When one is purified, he is always seeing Kṛṣṇa within himself. This is confirmed in the *Brahma-saṁhitā:*

premāñjana-cchurita-bhakti-vilocanena
santaḥ sadaiva hṛdayeṣu vilokayanti
yaṁ śyāmasundaram acintya-guṇa-svarūpaṁ
govindam ādi-puruṣaṁ tam ahaṁ bhajāmi

"I worship the primeval Lord, Govinda, who is always seen by the devotee whose eyes are anointed with the pulp of love. He is seen in His eternal form of Śyāmasundara, situated within the heart of the devotee."

Thus an advanced saintly person is always seeing Kṛṣṇa. In this verse the word *śyāmasundara* means "blackish but at the same time extraordinarily beautiful." Being the Supreme Personality of Godhead, Kṛṣṇa is of course very beautiful. The word *acintya* means that He has inconceivable, unlimited qualities. Although He is situated everywhere, as Govinda He is always dancing in Vṛndāvana with the *gopīs*. There He plays with His friends and sometimes, acting as a naughty boy, teases His mother. These pastimes of the Supreme Person are described in the *Śrīmad-Bhāgavatam*.

Disciple: As far as we know, Socrates himself had no teacher in philosophy. Indeed, he refers to himself as "self-made." Do you believe that one can be self-taught? Can self-knowledge be attained through one's own meditation or introspection?

Śrīla Prabhupāda: Yes. Ordinarily everyone thinks according to the bodily conception. If I begin to study the different parts of my body and seriously begin to consider what I am, I will gradually arrive at the study of the soul. If I ask myself, "Am I this hand?" the answer will be "No, I am not this hand. Rather, this is my hand." I can thus continue analyzing each part of the body and discover that all the parts are mine but that I am different. Through this method of self-study, any intelligent man can see that he is not the body. This is the first lesson of the *Bhagavad-gītā:*

dehino 'smin yathā dehe
kaumāraṁ yauvanaṁ jarā
tathā dehāntara-prāptir
dhīras tatra na muhyati

"As the embodied soul continuously passes, in this body, from boyhood to youth to old age, the soul similarly passes into another body at death. A sober person is not bewildered by such a change."

At one time I had the body of a child, but now that body no longer exists. Nonetheless, I am aware that I possessed such a body; therefore from this I can deduce that I am something other than the body. I may rent an apartment, but I do not identify with it. The body may be mine, but I am not the body. By this kind of introspection, a man can teach himself the distinction between the body and the soul.

As far as being completely self-taught, according to the *Bhagavad-gītā* and the Vedic conception, life is continuous. Since we are always acquiring experience, we cannot actually say that Socrates was self-taught. Rather, in his previous lives he had cultivated knowledge, and this knowledge was simply continuing. That is a fact. Otherwise, why is one person intelligent and another ignorant? This is due to continuity of life through the process of transmigration of the soul.

Disciple: Socrates believed that through intellectual endeavor a person can attain knowledge or wisdom, which is nothing else but the possession of all the virtues in their unity. Such a person always acts in the right way and thus is happy. Therefore the enlightened man is meditative, knowledgeable, and virtuous. He is also happy because he acts properly.

Śrīla Prabhupāda: Yes, that is confirmed in the *Bhagavad-gītā*. *Brahma-bhūtaḥ prasannātmā na śocati na kāṅkṣati:* when one is self-realized, he immediately becomes happy, joyful (*prasannātmā*). This is because he is properly situated. One may labor a long time under some mistaken idea, but when he finally comes to the proper conclusion, he becomes very happy. He thinks, "Oh, what a fool I was, going on so long in such a mistaken way!" Thus a self-realized person is happy.

Happiness means that one no longer has to think of attaining things. For instance, Dhruva Mahārāja told the Lord, *svāmin kṛtārtho 'smi varaṁ na yāce:* "Having seen You, my Lord, I don't want any material benediction." Prahlāda Mahārāja also said, "My Lord, I don't want material benefits. I have seen my father – who was such a big materialist that even the demigods were afraid of him – destroyed by You within a second. Therefore I am not after these things."

So real knowledge means that one no longer hankers for anything. The *karmīs, jñānīs,* and *yogīs* are all hankering after something. The *karmīs* want material wealth, beautiful women, and good positions. If one is not hankering for what one does not have, he is lamenting for what he has lost. The *jñānīs* are also hankering, expecting to become one with God and merge into His existence. And the *yogīs* are hankering after some magical powers to befool others into thinking that they have become God. In India some *yogīs* convince people that they can manufacture gold and fly in the sky, and foolish people believe them. Even if a *yogī* can fly, what is his great achievement? There are many birds flying. What is the difference? An intelligent person can understand this. If a person says that he will walk on water, thousands of fools will come to see him. People will even pay ten rupees just to see a man bark like a dog, not thinking that there are many dogs barking anyway. In any case, people are always hankering and lamenting, but the devotee is fully satisfied in the service of the Lord. He doesn't hanker for anything, nor does he lament.

Disciple: Through *jñāna,* the search for truth, Socrates may have realized Brahman. Could he have also realized Paramātmā?

Śrīla Prabhupāda: Yes.

Disciple: But what about the realization of Bhagavān, Kṛṣṇa? I thought that Kṛṣṇa can be realized only through *bhakti,* devotion.

Śrīla Prabhupāda: Yes, one cannot enter into Kṛṣṇa's abode without being a purified devotee. Kṛṣṇa states this in the *Bhagavad-gītā, bhaktyā mām abhijānāti:* "One can understand Me as I am only by devotional service." Kṛṣṇa never says that He can be understood by *jñāna, karma,* or yoga. The personal abode of Kṛṣṇa is especially reserved for the *bhaktas,* and the *jñānīs, yogīs,* and *karmīs* cannot go there.

Disciple: Now, although Socrates described himself as "self-made," he believed not only in the value of insight or meditation but also in the idea that knowledge can be imparted from one person to another. He therefore believed in the role of a guru, or teacher, which he himself was for many people.

Prabhupāda: Yes, this is the standard Vedic principle – that to learn the truth one must approach a guru, or spiritual master. In the *Bhagavad-gītā* Kṛṣṇa gives the same instruction:

tad viddhi praṇipātena
paripraśnena sevayā
upadekṣyanti tad jñānaṁ
jñāninas tattva-darśinaḥ

"Just try to learn the truth by approaching a spiritual master. Inquire from him submissively and render service unto him. The self-realized souls can impart knowledge unto you because they have seen the truth." Here "seen the truth" means the spiritual master is constantly seeing the Lord within his heart. In other words, within his heart he can constantly see the Supreme Lord as the Supersoul and take advice from Him. In the *Bhagavad-gītā* Kṛṣṇa confirms that He enlightens the pure devotee from within. He says, *dadāmi buddhi-yogaṁ tam,* "I give him intelligence." These are the qualifications of a real spiritual master.

So it seems that Socrates would give his disciples a chance to develop their understanding. That is a good process, and it is natural. It is just like when a father teaches his child to walk. First of all he helps the child, taking his hand: "Now walk, walk. Let me see how you walk." Although the child sometimes falls down, the father will encourage, "Oh, you are doing very nicely. Now stand up again and walk." Similarly, a genuine spiritual master gives his disciple a chance to develop his intelligence so he can think properly how to go back home, back to Godhead.

Disciple: What does it mean to "think properly how to go back home, back to Godhead"?

Śrīla Prabhupāda: To always think of Kṛṣṇa. We should act in such a way that we have to think of Kṛṣṇa all the time. For instance, we are discussing Socratic philosophy in order to strengthen our

Kṛṣṇa consciousness. Therefore the ultimate goal is Kṛṣṇa; otherwise we are not interested in criticizing or accepting anyone's philosophy. We are neutral.

Disciple: So the proper use of intelligence is to guide everything in such a way that we become Kṛṣṇa conscious?

Śrīla Prabhupāda: That's it. Without Kṛṣṇa consciousness, we remain on the mental platform. Being on the mental platform means hovering. On that platform, we are not fixed. It is the business of the mind to accept this and reject that, but when we are fixed in Kṛṣṇa consciousness we are no longer subjected to the mind's acceptance or rejection.

Disciple: Right conduct then becomes automatic?

Śrīla Prabhupāda: Yes, as soon as the mind wanders, we should immediately drag it back to concentrate on Kṛṣṇa. While chanting, our mind sometimes wanders far away, but when we become conscious of this, we should immediately bring the mind back to hear the sound vibration of "Hare Kṛṣṇa." That is called *yoga-abhyāsa,* the practice of yoga. We should not allow our mind to wander elsewhere. We should simply chant and hear the Hare Kṛṣṇa mantra; that is the best yoga system.

Disciple: Socrates could have avoided the death penalty if he had compromised his convictions. He refused to do this and so became a martyr for his beliefs.

Śrīla Prabhupāda: It is good that he stuck to his point yet regrettable that he lived in a society in which he could not think independently. Therefore he was obliged to die. In that sense, Socrates was a great soul because although he appeared in a society that was not very advanced, he was still such a great philosopher.

Plato

A conversation between His Divine Grace
A.C. Bhaktivedanta Swami Prabhupāda and his disciples

Plato (c. 428–c. 347 BC) was one of the most creative and influential thinkers in Western philosophy. The chief student of Socrates, he founded the Academy in Athens in 387 BC, beginning an institution that continued for almost a thousand years and came to be known as the first European university. There are some striking similarities between Plato's ideal state and the one Kṛṣṇa outlines in the Bhagavad-gītā. *But, as Śrīla Prabhupāda points out, Plato erred in his conception of the soul and of the goal of education.*

~

Disciple: In the *Republic,* Plato's major work on political theory, Plato wrote that society can enjoy prosperity and harmony only if it places people in working categories or classes according to their natural abilities. He thought people should find out their natural abilities and use those abilities to their fullest capacity – as administrators, as military men, or as craftsmen. Most important, the head of state should not be an average or mediocre man. Instead, society should be led by a very wise and good man – a "philosopher king" – or a group of very wise and good men.
Śrīla Prabhupāda: This idea appears to be taken from the *Gītā,* where Kṛṣṇa says that the ideal society has four divisions:

brāhmaṇas, kṣatriyas, vaiśyas, and *śūdras.* These divisions come about by the influence of the modes of nature. Everyone, both in human society and in animal society, is influenced by the modes of material nature [*sattva-guṇa, rajo-guṇa,* and *tamo-guṇa,* or goodness, passion, and ignorance]. By scientifically classifying men according to these qualities, society can become perfect. But if we place a man in the mode of ignorance in a philosopher's post, or put a philosopher to work as an ordinary laborer, havoc will result.

In the *Bhagavad-gītā* Kṛṣṇa says that the *brāhmaṇas* – the most intelligent men, who are interested in transcendental knowledge and philosophy – should be given the topmost posts, and under their instructions the *kṣatriyas* should work. The administrators should see that there is law and order and that everyone is doing his duty. The next section is the productive class, the *vaiśyas,* who engage in agriculture and cow protection. And finally there are the *śūdras,* common laborers who help the other sections. This is Vedic civilization – people living simply, on agriculture and cow protection. If you have enough milk, grain, fruits, and vegetables, you can live very nicely.

The *Śrīmad-Bhāgavatam* compares the four divisions of society to the different parts of the body – the head, the arms, the belly, and the legs. Just as all parts of the body cooperate to keep the body fit, in the ideal state all sections of society cooperate under the leadership of the *brāhmaṇas.* Comparatively, the head is the most important part of the body, since it gives directions to the other parts. Similarly, the ideal state functions under the directions of the *brāhmaṇas,* who are not personally interested in political affairs or administration because they have a higher duty. At present this Kṛṣṇa consciousness movement is training *brāhmaṇas.* If the administrators take our advice and conduct the state in a Kṛṣṇa conscious way, there will be an ideal society throughout the world.

Disciple: How does modern society differ from the Vedic ideal?

Śrīla Prabhupāda: Now there is large-scale industrialization, which means exploitation of one person by another. Such industry was unknown in Vedic civilization – it was unnecessary. In addition, modern civilization has taken to slaughtering and eating animals, which is barbarous. It is not even human.

In Vedic civilization, when a person was unfit to rule he was deposed. For instance, King Vena proved to be an unfit king. He was simply interested in hunting. Of course, *kṣatriyas* are allowed to hunt, but not whimsically. They are not allowed to kill many birds and beasts unnecessarily as King Vena was doing and as people do today. At that time the intelligent *brāhmaṇas* objected and immediately killed him with a curse. Formerly, the *brāhmaṇas* had so much power that they could kill simply by cursing; weapons were unnecessary.

At present, however, because the head of the social body is missing it is a dead body. The head is very important, and our Kṛṣṇa consciousness movement is attempting to create some *brāhmaṇas* who will form the head of society. Then the administrators will be able to rule very nicely under the instructions of the philosophers and theologians – that is, under the instructions of God conscious people. A God conscious *brāhmaṇa* would never advise opening slaughterhouses. But now, the many rascals heading the government allow animal slaughter. When Mahārāja Parīkṣit saw a degraded man trying to kill a cow, he immediately drew his sword and said, "Who are you? Why are you trying to kill this cow?" He was a real king. Nowadays, unqualified men have taken the presidential post. And although they may pose themselves as very religious, they are simply rascals. Why? Because under their noses thousands of cows are being killed, while they collect a good salary. Any leader who is at all religious should resign his post in protest if cow slaughter goes on under his rule. Since people do not know that these administrators are rascals, they are suffering. And the people are also rascals because they are voting for these bigger rascals. It is Plato's view that the government should be ideal, and this is the ideal: The saintly philosophers should be at the head of the state; according to their advice the politicians should rule; under the protection of the politicians, the productive class should protect the cows and provide the necessities of life; and the laborer class should help. This is the scientific division of society that Kṛṣṇa advocates in the *Bhagavad-gītā*, where He says, *cātur-varṇyaṁ mayā sṛṣṭaṁ guṇa-karma-vibhāgaśaḥ:* "According to the three modes of material nature and the work ascribed to them, the four divisions of human society were created by Me."

Disciple: Plato also observed social divisions. However, he advocated three divisions. One class consisted of the guardians, men of wisdom who governed society. Another class consisted of the warriors, who were courageous and who protected the rest of society. And the third class consisted of the artisans, who performed their services obediently and worked only to satisfy their appetites.

Śrīla Prabhupāda: Yes, human society does have this threefold division, also. The first-class man is in the mode of goodness, the second-class man is in the mode of passion, and the third-class man is in the mode of ignorance.

Disciple: Plato's understanding of the social order was based on his observation that man has a threefold division of intelligence, courage, and appetite. He said that the soul has these three qualities.

Śrīla Prabhupāda: That is a mistake. The soul does not have any material qualities. The soul is pure, but because of his contact with the different qualities of material nature, he is "dressed" in various bodies. This Kṛṣṇa consciousness movement aims at removing this material dress. Our first instruction is "You are not this body." It appears that in his practical understanding Plato identified the soul with the bodily dress, and that does not show very good intelligence.

Disciple: Plato believed that man's position is marginal – between matter and spirit – and therefore he also stressed the development of the body. He thought that everyone should be educated from an early age, and that part of that education should be gymnastics – to keep the body fit.

Śrīla Prabhupāda: This means that in practice Plato very strongly identified the self as the body. What was Plato's idea of education?

Disciple: To awaken the student to his natural position – whatever his natural abilities or talents are.
Śrīla Prabhupāda: And what is that natural position?
Disciple: The position of moral goodness. In other words, Plato thought everyone should be educated to work in whatever way is best suited to awaken his natural moral goodness.
Śrīla Prabhupāda: But moral goodness is not enough, because simple morality will not satisfy the soul. One has to go above morality – to Kṛṣṇa consciousness. Of course, in this material world morality is taken as the highest principle, but there is another platform, which is called the transcendental (*vāsudeva*) platform. Man's highest perfection is on that platform, and this is confirmed in *Śrīmad-Bhāgavatam*. However, because Western philosophers have no information of the *vāsudeva* platform, they consider the material mode of goodness to be the highest perfection and the end of morality. But in this world even moral goodness is infected by the lower modes of ignorance and passion. You cannot find pure goodness (*śuddha-sattva*) in this material world because pure goodness is the transcendental platform. To come to the platform of pure goodness, which is the ideal, one has to undergo austerities (*tapasā brahmacaryeṇa śamena ca damena ca*). One has to practice celibacy and control the mind and senses. If one has money, one should distribute it in charity. Also, one should always be very clean. In this way one can rise to the platform of pure goodness.

There is another process for coming to the platform of pure goodness – and that is Kṛṣṇa consciousness. If one becomes Kṛṣṇa conscious, all good qualities automatically develop in him. Automatically he leads a life of celibacy, controls his mind and senses, and has a charitable disposition. In this Age of Kali, people cannot possibly be trained to engage in austerity. Formerly, a *brahmacārī* would undergo austere training. Even though he might be from a royal or learned family, a *brahmacārī* would humble himself and serve the spiritual master as a menial servant. He would immediately do whatever the spiritual master ordered. The *brahmacārī* would beg alms from door to door and bring them to the spiritual master, claiming nothing for himself. Whatever he earned he would give to the spiritual master because the spiritual master would not spoil the money by spending it for sense gratification – he would use it for Kṛṣṇa. This is austerity. The *brahmacārī* would also observe celibacy, and because he followed the directions of the spiritual master, his mind and senses were controlled.

Today, however, this austerity is very difficult to follow, so Śrī Caitanya Mahāprabhu has given the process of taking to Kṛṣṇa consciousness directly. In this case, one need simply chant Hare Kṛṣṇa, Hare Kṛṣṇa, Kṛṣṇa Kṛṣṇa, Hare Hare/ Hare Rāma, Hare Rāma, Rāma Rāma, Hare Hare and follow the regulative principles given by the spiritual master. Then one immediately rises to the platform of pure goodness.

Disciple: Plato thought the state should train citizens to be virtuous. His system of education went like this: For the first three years of life, the child should play and strengthen his body. From three to six, the child should learn religious stories. From seven to ten, he should learn gymnastics; from ten to thirteen, reading and writing; from fourteen to sixteen, poetry and music; from sixteen to eighteen, mathematics. And from eighteen to twenty, he should undergo military drill. From twenty to thirty-five, those who are scientific and philosophical should remain in school and continue learning, and the warriors should engage in military exercises.

Śrīla Prabhupāda: Is this educational program for all men, or are there different types of education for different men?

Disciple: No, this is for everyone.

Śrīla Prabhupāda: This is not very good. If a boy is intelligent and inclined to philosophy and theology, why should he be forced to undergo military training?

Disciple: Well, Plato said that everyone should undergo two years of military drill.

Śrīla Prabhupāda: But why should someone waste two years? No one should waste even two days. This is nonsense – imperfect ideas.

Disciple: Plato said this type of education reveals what category a person belongs to. He did have the right idea that one belongs to a particular class according to his qualification.

Śrīla Prabhupāda: Yes, that we also say, but we disagree that everyone should go through the same training. The spiritual master should judge the tendency or disposition of the student at the start of his education. He should be able to see whether a boy is fit for military training, administration, or philosophy, and then he should fully train the boy according to his particular tendency. If one is naturally inclined to philosophical study, why should he waste his time in the military? And if one is naturally inclined to military training, why should he waste his time with other things? Arjuna belonged to a *kṣatriya* family. He and his brothers were never trained as philosophers. Droṇācārya was their master and teacher, and although he was a *brāhmaṇa,* he taught them *Dhanur Veda,* not *brahma-vidyā. Brahma-vidyā* is theistic philosophy. No one should be trained in everything; that is a waste of time. If one is inclined toward production, business, or agriculture he should be trained in those fields. If one is philosophical he should be trained as a philosopher. If one is militaristic he should be trained as a warrior. And if one has ordinary ability he should remain a *śūdra,* or laborer. This is stated by Nārada Muni in *Śrīmad-Bhāgavatam* when he says *yasya yal-lakṣaṇaṁ proktam:* the four classes of society are recognized by their symptoms and qualifications. Nārada Muni also says that one should be selected for training according to his qualifications. Even if one is born in a *brāhmaṇa* family he should be considered a *śūdra* if his qualifications are those of a *śūdra.* And if one is born in a *śūdra* family he should be accepted as a *brāhmaṇa* if his symptoms are brahminical. The spiritual master should be expert enough to recognize the tendencies of the student and immediately train him in that line. This is perfect education.

Disciple: Plato believed that the student's natural tendency would not come out unless he practiced everything.

Śrīla Prabhupāda: No, that is wrong – because the soul is continuous and therefore everyone has some tendency from his previous birth. I think Plato didn't realize this continuity of the soul from body to body. According to the Vedic culture, immediately after a boy's birth astrologers should calculate what category he belongs to. Astrology can help if there is a first-class astrologer. Such an astrologer can tell what line a boy is coming from and how he should be trained. Plato's method of education was imperfect because it was based on speculation.

Disciple: Plato observed that a particular combination of the three modes of nature is acting in each individual.

Śrīla Prabhupāda: Then why did he say that everyone should be trained in the same way?

Disciple: Because he claimed that the person's natural abilities will not manifest unless he is given a chance to try everything. He saw that some people listen primarily to their intelligence, and he said they are governed by the head. He saw that some people have an aggressive disposition, and he said such courageous types are governed by the heart – by passion. And he saw that some people, who are inferior, simply want to feed their appetites. He said these people are animalistic, and he believed they are governed by the liver.

Śrīla Prabhupāda: That is not a perfect description. Everyone has a liver, a heart, and all the bodily limbs. Whether one is in the mode of goodness, passion, or ignorance depends on one's training and on the qualities he acquired during his previous life. According to the Vedic process, at birth one is immediately given a classification. Psychological and physical symptoms are considered, and generally it is ascertained from birth that a child has a particular tendency. However, this tendency may change according to circumstances, and if one does not fulfill his assigned role he can be transferred to another class. One may have had brahminical training in a previous life, and he may exhibit brahminical symptoms in this life, but one should not think that because he has taken birth in a *brāhmaṇa* family he is automatically a *brāhmaṇa*. A person may be born in a *brāhmaṇa* family and be a *śūdra*. It is a question not of birth but of qualification.

Disciple: Plato also believed that one must qualify for his post. His system of government was very democratic. He thought everyone should be given a chance to occupy the different posts.
Śrīla Prabhupāda: Actually, we are the most democratic because we are giving everyone a chance to become a first-class *brāhmaṇa*. The Kṛṣṇa consciousness movement is giving even the lowest member of society a chance to become a *brāhmaṇa* by becoming Kṛṣṇa conscious. *Caṇḍālo 'pi dvija-śreṣṭho hari-bhakti-parāyaṇaḥ:* Although one may be born in a family of *caṇḍālas,* as soon as he becomes God conscious, Kṛṣṇa conscious, he can be elevated to the highest position. Kṛṣṇa says that everyone can go back home, back to Godhead. *Samo 'haṁ sarva-bhūteṣu:* "I am equal to everyone. Everyone can come to Me. There is no hindrance."
Disciple: What is the purpose of the social orders and the state government?
Śrīla Prabhupāda: The ultimate purpose is to make everyone Kṛṣṇa conscious. That is the perfection of life, and the entire social structure should be molded with this aim in view. Of course, not everyone can become fully Kṛṣṇa conscious in one lifetime, just as not all students in a university can attain the PhD degree in one attempt. But the idea of perfection is to pass the PhD examination, and therefore the PhD courses should be maintained. Similarly, an institution like this Kṛṣṇa consciousness movement should be maintained so that at least some people can attain and everyone can approach the ultimate goal, Kṛṣṇa consciousness.
Disciple: So the goal of the state government is to help everyone become Kṛṣṇa conscious?
Śrīla Prabhupāda: Yes, Kṛṣṇa consciousness is the highest goal. Therefore, everyone should help this movement and take advantage of it. Regardless of his work, everyone can come to the temple. The instructions are for everyone, and *prasāda* is distributed to everyone. Therefore, there is no difficulty. Everyone can contribute to this Kṛṣṇa consciousness movement. The *brāhmaṇas* can contribute their intelligence, the *kṣatriyas* their charity, the *vaiśyas* their grain, milk, fruits, and flowers, and the *śūdras* their

bodily service. By such joint effort, everyone can reach the same goal – Kṛṣṇa consciousness, the perfection of life.

Disciple: In a very famous allegory in the *Republic,* Plato describes representatives of humanity chained in a dark cave and able to see only shadows cast by the light of a fire. One person breaks free and sees the outside world, and he returns to the cave to tell the people there that they are living in darkness. But the cave dwellers consider him crazy.

Śrīla Prabhupāda: This is just like our story of Dr. Frog. He had never gone out of his dark well, so he thought, "Here is everything." When he was informed about the vast Atlantic Ocean, he could not conceive of a body of water so expansive.

Similarly, those who are in the dark well of this material world cannot conceive of the light outside, in the spiritual world. But that world is a fact. Suppose someone has fallen into a well and he cries out, "I have fallen into this well! Please save me!" Then a man outside drops down a rope and calls, "Just catch hold of this rope and I will pull you out!" But no, the fallen man has no faith in the man outside and does not catch hold of the rope. Similarly, we are telling everyone in the material world, "You are suffering. Just take up this Kṛṣṇa consciousness and all your suffering will be relieved." Unfortunately, people refuse to catch hold of the rope, or they do not even admit they are suffering.

But one who is fortunate will catch hold of the rope of Kṛṣṇa consciousness, and then the spiritual master will help him out of this dark world of suffering and bring him to the illuminated, happy world of Kṛṣṇa consciousness.

Origen

A conversation between His Divine Grace
A. C. Bhaktivedanta Swami Prabhupāda and his disciples

Origen of Alexandria (c. 185–c. 254 AD) was one of the most influential founders of the Christian Church and ranks among the most prolific writers and teachers in the history of the Church. Known as the father of Christian mysticism, he taught reincarnation, a doctrine that later Church authorities rejected. Though many of Origen's teachings seem to derive from the Vedic literatures, Śrīla Prabhupāda notes here that he was mistaken to think that the soul was created at some point.

~

Disciple: Origen is generally considered the founder of formal Christian philosophy because he was the first to attempt to establish Christianity on the basis of philosophy as well as faith. He believed that the ultimate spiritual reality consists of the supreme, infinite person, God, as well as individual personalities. Ultimate reality may be defined as the relationships of persons with one another and with the infinite person Himself. In this view, Origen differs from the Greeks, who were basically impersonalists.
Śrīla Prabhupāda: Our Vedic conception is almost the same. Individual souls, which we call living entities, are always present, and

each one of them has an intimate relationship with the Supreme Personality of Godhead. In material, conditioned life, the living entity has forgotten this relationship. By rendering devotional service, he attains the liberated position and at that time revives his relationship with the Supreme Personality of Godhead.

Disciple: Origen ascribed to a doctrine of the Trinity, in which God the Father is supreme. God the Son, called the Logos, is subordinate to the Father. It is the Son who brings the material world into existence. That is, God the Father is not the direct creator; rather, it is the Son who creates directly, like Lord Brahmā. The third aspect of the Trinity is the Holy Spirit, who is subordinate to the Son. According to Origen, all three of these aspects are divine and coeternal. They have always existed simultaneously as the Trinity of God.

Śrīla Prabhupāda: According to the *Vedas,* Kṛṣṇa is the original Personality of Godhead. As He confirms in the *Bhagavad-gītā, ahaṁ sarvasya prabhavaḥ:* "I am the source of all spiritual and material worlds." Whether you call this origin the Father or the Holy Spirit, it doesn't matter. The Supreme Personality of Godhead is the origin. According to the Vedic conception there are two types of expansions: God's personal expansions, called *viṣṇu-tattva,* and His partial part-and-parcel expansions, called *jīva-tattva.* There are many varieties of personal expansions: *puruṣa-avatāras, śaktyāveśa-avatāras, manvantara-avatāras,* and so on. For the creation of this material world the Lord expands as Brahmā, Viṣṇu, and Maheśvara [Śiva]. Viṣṇu is a personal expansion and Brahmā is a *jīva-tattva* expansion. Between the personal *viṣṇu-tattva* expansions and the *jīva-tattva* expansions is a kind of intermediate expansion called Śiva, or Maheśvara. The material ingredients are given, and Brahmā creates each universe. Viṣṇu maintains the creation, and Lord Śiva annihilates it. It is the nature of the external potency to be created, maintained, and dissolved. More detailed information is given in the *Śrīmad-Bhāgavatam* and *Caitanya-caritāmṛta.*

In any case, the *jīvas,* or living entities, are all considered sons of God. They are situated in one of two positions: liberated or conditioned. Those who are liberated can personally associate with the Supreme Personality of Godhead, and those who are conditioned within this material world have forgotten the Supreme Lord. Therefore they suffer here in different bodily forms. They can be elevated, however, through the practice of Kṛṣṇa consciousness under the guidance of the *śāstras* and the bona fide guru.

Disciple: Origen believed that it is through the combined working of divine grace and man's free will that the individual soul attains perfection, which consists of attaining a personal relationship with the infinite person.

Śrīla Prabhupāda: Yes, and that is called *bhakti-mārga,* the path of devotional service to the Supreme Personality of Godhead, Bhagavān. The Absolute Truth is manifested in three features: Brahman, Paramātmā, and Bhagavān. Bhagavān is the personal feature, and the Paramātmā, situated in everyone's heart, may be compared to the Holy Spirit. The Brahman feature is present everywhere. The highest perfection of spiritual life includes the understanding of the personal feature of the Lord. When one understands Bhagavān, one engages in His service. In this way the living entity is situated in his original, constitutional position and is eternally blissful.

Disciple: Origen considered that just as man's free will precipitated his fall, man's free will can also bring about his salvation. Man can return to God by practicing material detachment. Such detachment can be made possible by help from the Logos, the Christ.

Śrīla Prabhupāda: Yes, that is also our conception. The fallen soul is transmigrating within this material world, up and down in different forms of life. When his consciousness is sufficiently developed, he can be enlightened by God, who gives him instructions in the *Bhagavad-gītā.* Through the spiritual master's help he can attain full enlightenment. When he understands his transcendental position of bliss, he automatically gives up material bodily attachments. Then he attains freedom. The living entity attains his normal, constitutional position when he is properly situated in his spiritual identity and engaged in the service of the Lord.

Disciple: Origen believed that all the elements found in the material body are also found in the spiritual body, which he called the "interior man." Origen writes, "There are two men in each of us.... As every exterior man has for homonym the interior man, so it is for all his members, and one can say that every member of the exterior man can be found under this name in the interior man." Thus for every sense that we possess in the exterior body, there is a corresponding sense in the interior body, or spiritual body.

Śrīla Prabhupāda: The spirit soul is now within this material body, but originally the spirit soul had no material body. The spiritual body of the spirit soul is eternally existing. The material body is simply a coating of the spiritual body. The material body is cut, like a suit, according to the spiritual body. The material elements – earth, water, air, fire, etc. – become like a clay when mixed together, and they coat the spiritual body. It is because the spiritual body has a shape that the material body also takes a shape. In actuality, the material body has nothing to do with the spiritual body; it is but a kind of contamination causing the suffering of the spirit soul. As soon as the spirit soul is coated with this material contamination he identifies himself with the coating and forgets his real spiritual body. That is called *māyā,* ignorance or illusion. This ignorance continues as long as we are not fully Kṛṣṇa conscious. When we become fully Kṛṣṇa conscious, we understand that the material body is but the external coating and that we are different. When we attain this uncontaminated understanding we arrive at what is called the *brahma-bhūta* platform. When the spirit soul, which is Brahman, is under the illusion of the material bodily conditioning, we are on the *jīva-bhūta* platform. *Brahma-bhūta* is attained when we no longer identify with the material body but with the spirit soul within. When we come to this platform, we become joyful.

brahma-bhūtaḥ prasannātmā
na śocati na kāṅkṣati
samaḥ sarveṣu bhūteṣu
mad-bhaktiṁ labhate parām

"One who is thus transcendentally situated at once realizes the Supreme Brahman and becomes fully joyful. He never laments or desires to have anything. He is equally disposed toward every living entity. In that state he attains pure devotional service unto Me." In this position one sees all living entities as spirit souls; he does not see the outward covering. When he sees a dog he sees a spirit soul covered by the body of a dog. This state is also described in *Bhagavad-gītā.*

vidyā-vinaya-sampanne
brāhmaṇe gavi hastini
śuni caiva śva-pāke ca
paṇḍitāḥ sama-darśinaḥ

"The humble sages, by virtue of true knowledge, see with equal vision a learned and gentle *brāhmaṇa,* a cow, an elephant, a dog, and a dog-eater [outcaste]." When one is in the body of an animal, he cannot understand his spiritual identity. This identity can best be realized in a human civilization in which the *varṇāśrama* system is practiced. This system divides life into four *āśramas* (*brāhmaṇa, kṣatriya, vaiśya,* and *śūdra*) and four *varṇas* (*brahmacārī, gṛhastha, vānaprastha,* and *sannyāsa*). The highest position is that of a *brāhmaṇa-sannyāsī,* a platform from which one may best realize his original, constitutional position, act accordingly, and thus attain deliverance, or *mukti. Mukti* means understanding our constitutional position and acting accordingly. Conditioned life, a life of bondage, means identifying with the body and acting on the bodily platform. On the *mukti* platform, our activities differ from those enacted on the conditioned platform. Devotional service is rendered from the *mukti* platform. If we engage in devotional service, we maintain our spiritual identity and are therefore liberated, even though inhabiting the conditioned, material body.

Disciple: Origen also believed that the interior man, or the spiritual body, has spiritual senses that enable the soul to taste, see, touch, and contemplate the things of God.

Śrīla Prabhupāda: Yes. That is devotional life.

Disciple: During his lifetime, Origen was a famous teacher and was very much in demand. For him, preaching meant explaining the words of God and no more. He believed that a preacher must first be a man of prayer and must be in contact with God. He should not pray for material goods but for a better understanding of the scriptures.

Śrīla Prabhupāda: Yes, that is a real preacher. As explained in Vedic literatures: *śravaṇaṁ kīrtanam.* First of all, we become perfect by hearing. This is called *śravaṇam.* When we are thus situated by hearing perfectly from an authorized person, our next stage begins: *kīrtanam,* preaching. In this material world, everyone is hearing something from someone else. In order to pass examinations, a student must hear his professor. Then, in his own right, he can become a professor himself. If we hear from a bona fide spiritual master, we become perfect and can become real preachers. We should preach about Kṛṣṇa for Kṛṣṇa, not for any person within this material world. We should hear and preach about the Supreme Person, the transcendental Personality of Godhead. That is the duty of a liberated soul.

Disciple: As far as contradictions and seeming absurdities in scripture are concerned, Origen considered them to be stumbling blocks permitted to exist by God in order for man to pass beyond the literal meaning. He writes that "everything in scripture has a spiritual meaning, but not all of it has a literal meaning."

Śrīla Prabhupāda: Generally speaking, every word in scripture has a literal meaning, but people cannot understand it properly because they do not hear from the proper person. They interpret instead. There is no need to interpret the words of God. Sometimes the words of God cannot be understood by an ordinary person; therefore we may require the transparent medium of the guru. Since the guru is fully cognizant of the words spoken by God, we are advised to receive the words of the scriptures through the guru. There is no ambiguity in the words of God, but due to our imperfect knowledge, we sometimes cannot understand. Not understanding, we try to interpret, but because we are imperfect, our interpretations are also imperfect. The purport is that the words of God, the scriptures, should be understood from a person who has realized God.

Disciple: Origen did not believe that the individual soul has been existing from all eternity. It was created. He writes: "The rational natures that were made in the beginning did not always exist; they came into being when they were created."

Śrīla Prabhupāda: That is not correct. Both the living entity and God are simultaneously eternally existing, and the living entity is part and parcel of God. Although eternally existing, the living entity is changing his body. *Na hanyate hanyamāne śarīre.* One body after another is being created and destroyed, but the living being himself exists eternally. So we disagree when Origen says that the soul is created. Our spiritual identity is never created. That is the difference between spirit and matter. Material things are created, but spirit is without beginning.

na tv evāhaṁ jātu nāsaṁ
na tvaṁ neme janādhipāḥ
na caiva na bhaviṣyāmaḥ
sarve vayam ataḥ param

"Never was there a time when I did not exist, nor you, nor all these kings; nor in the future shall any of us cease to be."

Disciple: Origen differed from later Church doctrine in his belief in transmigration. Although he believed that the soul was originally created, he also believed that it transmigrated because it could always refuse to give itself to God. So he saw the individual soul as possibly rising and falling perpetually on the evolutionary scale. Later Church doctrine held that one's choice for eternity is made in this one lifetime. As Origen saw it, the individual soul, falling short of the ultimate goal, is reincarnated again and again.

Śrīla Prabhupāda: Yes, that is the Vedic version. Unless one is liberated and goes to the kingdom of God he must transmigrate from one material body to another. The material body grows, remains for some time, reproduces, grows old, and becomes useless. Then the living entity has to leave one body for another. Once in a new body he again attempts to fulfill his desires, and again he goes through the process of dying and accepting another material body. This is the process of transmigration.

Disciple: It is interesting that neither Origen nor Christ rejected transmigration. It wasn't until Augustine that it was denied.

Śrīla Prabhupāda: Transmigration is a fact. A person cannot wear the same clothes all of his life. Our clothes become old and useless and we have to change them. The living being is certainly eternal, but he has to accept a material body for material sense gratification, and such a body cannot endure perpetually. All of this is thoroughly explained in the *Bhagavad-gītā:*

dehino 'smin yathā dehe
kaumāraṁ yauvanaṁ jarā
tathā dehāntara-prāptir
dhīras tatra na muhyati

"As the embodied soul continuously passes, in this body, from boyhood to youth to old age, the soul similarly passes into another body at death. A sober person is not bewildered by such a change."

śarīraṁ yad avāpnoti
yac cāpy utkrāmatīśvaraḥ
gṛhītvaitāni saṁyāti
vāyur gandhān ivāśayāt

"The living entity in the material world carries his different conceptions of life from one body to another as the air carries aromas. Thus he takes one kind of body and again quits it to take another."

So this process of transmigration will continue until one attains liberation and goes back home, back to Godhead.

John Stuart Mill

A conversation between His Divine Grace
A. C. Bhaktivedanta Swami Prabhupāda and his disciples

The Briton John Stuart Mill (1806–1873) belonged to a school of philosophy called utilitarianism. An economist as well as a philosopher, Mill had a great impact on 19th-century British thought, not only in philosophy and economics but also in the areas of political science, logic, and ethics. His motto: "The greatest good for the greatest number." Here Śrīla Prabhupāda points out the glaring fallacy: Who's to say what "the greatest good" is?

~

Disciple: Mill claimed that the world, or nature, can be improved by man's efforts, but that perfection is not possible.
Śrīla Prabhupāda: In one sense, that is correct. This world is so made that although you make it perfect today, tomorrow it will deteriorate. Nonetheless, the world can be improved by Kṛṣṇa consciousness. You can better the world by bringing people to Kṛṣṇa consciousness and delivering the message of Kṛṣṇa to whomever you meet. That is the best social activity you can perform.
Disciple: The goal of the utilitarians was more specifically to obtain whatever the people desire or require. Their motto is "The greatest good for the greatest number."

Śrīla Prabhupāda: The people desire happiness. The utilitarians try to give people artificial happiness, happiness separate from Kṛṣṇa, but we are trying to give direct happiness, happiness that is connected with Kṛṣṇa. If we purify our existence, we can attain eternal happiness, spiritual bliss. Everyone is working hard for happiness, but how can happiness be attained in a diseased condition? The material disease is an impediment to happiness. This disease has to be cured.

Disciple: Mill felt that virtues like courage, cleanliness, and self-control are not instinctive in man but have to be cultivated. In *Nature* he writes, "The truth is that there is hardly a single point of excellence belonging to human character which is not decidedly repugnant to the untutored feelings of human nature...."

Śrīla Prabhupāda: Yes. Therefore there are educational systems in human society. Men should be educated according to the instructions given in the Vedic literatures. The *Bhagavad-gītā* is the grand summation of all Vedic literature, and therefore everyone should read it. But they should read it as it is, without interpretation.

Disciple: For Mill, there are several ways to ascertain knowledge. For instance, we can determine the cause and the effects of things by determining whether the phenomena under investigation have only one circumstance in common. If so, we can conclude that the circumstance alone is the cause of the effect.

Śrīla Prabhupāda: Certainly there is the natural law of cause and effect, but if we go further to determine the ultimate cause, we arrive at Kṛṣṇa. Everything has an original source, a cause. If you try to find out the cause of this and that and conduct research, that is called *darśana,* which means "to find the cause." Therefore philosophy is called *darśana-śāstra,* which means "finding the ultimate cause." If we continue to search out the ultimate cause, we arrive at Kṛṣṇa, the original cause of everything.

Disciple: But what kind of test can we apply to phenomena to find out the cause? How can we determine that God is the cause behind everything?

Śrīla Prabhupāda: For every phenomenon there is a cause, and we know that God is the ultimate cause. Mill may give many methods for studying immediate causes, but we are interested in the ultimate cause of everything. The ultimate cause has full independence to do anything and everything beyond our calculation. Everything that we see is but an effect of His original push.

Disciple: If we see rain falling and want to prove that God is the cause of rain, what test can we apply?

Śrīla Prabhupāda: The *śāstras*, the Vedic literatures. We are advised to see through the *śāstras* because we cannot see directly. Since our senses are defective, direct perception has no value. Therefore we have to receive knowledge through authoritative instruction.

Disciple: In other words, when we see an apple fall from a tree we have to see through the eyes of the *śāstras* in order to see God in that act?

Śrīla Prabhupāda: God has made His laws so perfect that one cause effects one thing, and that in turn effects another, and so on. We may see an apple grow and explain it as "nature," but this nature is working according to certain laws. An apple has a certain color and taste because it is following specific laws set down by Kṛṣṇa. Kṛṣṇa's energies are perfect and are working perfectly. Everything is being carried out under systematic laws, although we may not perceive these laws.

Disciple: Scientists admit that nothing can come out of nothing.

Śrīla Prabhupāda: If something emerges, there must be a cause in the background. We say that the root cause of everything is the Supreme Brahman, the Absolute Truth, or the Supreme Personality of Godhead.

Disciple: Mill would certainly not agree that God is the cause of everything because one of the things we see in this world is evil, and he considered God to be at war with it. Man's role, he thought, is to help God end this war. He writes, "If Providence is omnipotent, Providence intends whatever happens, and the fact of its happening proves that Providence intended it. If so, everything which a human being can do is predestined by Providence and is a fulfillment of its designs. But if, as is the more religious theory, Providence intends not all which happens, but only what is good, then indeed man has it in his power, by his voluntary actions, to aid the intentions of Providence."

Śrīla Prabhupāda: Providence desires only the good. The living entity is in this material world due to the improper utilization of his will. Because the living entity wants to enjoy this material world, God is so kind that He gives him facilities and directions. When a child wants to play in a certain way he is guided by some nurse or servant hired by the parents. Our position is something like that. We have given up the company of God to come to this material world to enjoy ourselves. So God has allowed us to come here, saying, "All right, enjoy this experience, and when you understand that this material enjoyment is ultimately frustrating you can come back." Thus the Supreme Lord is guiding the enjoyment of all living beings, especially human beings, so that they may again return home, back to Godhead. Nature is the agent acting under the instructions of God. If the living entity is overly addicted to misusing his freedom, he is punished. This punishment is a consequence of the living entity's desire. God does not want a human being to become a village hog, but when one develops such a mentality by eating anything and everything, God gives the facility by providing the body of a hog so that he can even eat stool. God is situated in everyone's heart and is noting the desires of the living entity from within. According to one's desires, God orders material nature to provide a particular body. In this way one continues transmigrating from body to body, in various species of life.

Disciple: Mill further writes, "Limited as, on this showing, the divine power must be by inscrutable but insurmountable obstacles, who knows what man could have been, created without desires which never are to be, and even which never ought to be, fulfilled?" Thus Mill concludes that the existence of evil, or pain and death, excludes the existence of an omnipotent God. He sees man in a position to "aid the intentions of Providence" by surmounting his evil instincts. God is not infinite in His power because if He were there would be no evil.

Śrīla Prabhupāda: Evil is undoubtedly created by God, but this was necessary due to the human being's misuse of his free will. God gives man good directions, but when man is disobedient, evil is naturally there to punish him. Evil is not desired by God, yet it is created because it is necessary. The government constructs prisons not because it wants to but because they are necessary. The government prefers to construct universities so that people can attain an education and become highly enlightened. But because some people misuse their independence and violate the state laws, prisons are necessary. We suffer due to our own evil activities. Thus God, being supreme, punishes us. When we are under the protection of God nothing is evil; everything is good. God does not desire to create evil, but man's evil activities provoke God to create an evil situation.

Disciple: In the Judeo-Christian tradition, God is at war with Satan. In the Vedic literature, there are also wars between the demigods and the demons, as well as Kṛṣṇa and the demons, but these wars do not seem to be taken as serious confrontations between God and His enemies. Isn't Kṛṣṇa's mood always playful?

Śrīla Prabhupāda: Since Kṛṣṇa is all-powerful, when He is fighting with demons He is actually playing. This fighting does not affect His energy. It is like a father fighting with his small child. The father may seem to be fighting seriously, but he is only playing: one slap is sufficient to subdue the child. Similarly, Kṛṣṇa sometimes plays by giving the demons a chance to fight Him, but one strong slap is sufficient. There is no question of fighting with God on an equal level. He is omnipotent. However, when a living entity is disobedient and harasses the devotees, God kills him. When Kṛṣṇa descends on this earth He chastises the demons and protects His devotees (*paritrāṇāya sādhūnāṁ vināśāya ca duṣkṛtām*). Whenever there is a fight between the demons and the demigods, God takes the side of the demigods.

Disciple: Mill saw it more like an actual struggle between God and Satan, or evil.

Śrīla Prabhupāda: There is struggle because the demons are always transgressing God's rules. A demon is one who rejects God's rules, and a demigod is one who accepts them. That is the main difference, as stated in the *śāstras*.

Disciple: But Mill pictures God Himself as struggling hard in the fight to conquer the demons.

Śrīla Prabhupāda: God has no reason to struggle. According to the *Vedas* He is so powerful that He has nothing to strive for (*na tasya kāryaṁ karaṇaṁ ca vidyate*). Just as a king may have many servants, ministers, and soldiers to carry out his desires, Kṛṣṇa has many energies that act according to His order. Kṛṣṇa Himself has nothing to do but play on His flute and enjoy Himself. That is why the *Vedas* declare, *ānanda-mayo 'bhyāsāt:* "God is always blissful."

So God has no reason to struggle for anything because nobody is equal to or greater than Him (*na tat-samaś cābhyadikaś ca dṛśyate*). But if God is not working hard, then how are things happening? *Parāsya śaktir vividhaiva śrūyate:* Through the agency of God's multi-energies everything is going on systematically and naturally (*svābhāvikī jñāna-bala-kriyā ca*). For example, by God's order the sun rises early in the morning, exactly on time. So although God is enjoying Himself, the universe is going on in accordance with His orders. There is no question of God struggling against evil. His various agents can kill all the evil elements in the world easily enough.

Disciple: Mill believed that God is good but that He is involved in a world not of His own making.

Śrīla Prabhupāda: Is God to be judged by Mr. Mill? God is good, but not as good as Mr. Mill thinks He ought to be? Is this his opinion of God? Is God good in all conditions? Or is God only good when Mr. Mill considers Him good? What is God's position?

Disciple: Mill says that the presence of evil indicates that if God were everything, He would not be completely good.

Śrīla Prabhupāda: Therefore God has to depend on the opinion of Mr. Mill. Is it that Mr. Mill does not approve of all God's activities?
Disciple: He maintains that God is good but that He is limited in His power. If His power were absolute, everything would be good.
Śrīla Prabhupāda: How nonsensical! Everything *is* good! That is our philosophy. When God kills a demon, immediately flowers are showered from the sky. Whatever God does is good. Kṛṣṇa danced with other men's wives in the dead of night, and this activity is worshiped as *rāsa-līlā*. However, if an ordinary man does this he is immediately condemned as a debauchee. In all circumstances God is good and worshipable. It is not that we subject God to our judgment, saying, "Oh, yes, You are good, but not *so* good." Fools think, "I am better than God. I can create my own God." God creates us; we cannot create God. Unfortunately, Mill did not know what is evil and what is good. He should have known that whatever is created by God is good, even if it appears to be evil to us. We may think that such-and-such is evil, but actually it is good. If we do not know how it is good, that is our fault. God cannot be placed under our judgment. In all circumstances, God is good.
Disciple: Mill was particularly interested in the role of authority. In *Utility of Religion* he writes, "Consider the enormous influence of authority on the human mind.... Authority is the evidence on which the mass of mankind believe everything which they are said to know except facts of which their own senses have taken cognizance. It is the evidence on which even the wisest receive all those truths of science, or facts in history or in life, of which they have not personally examined the proofs."
Śrīla Prabhupāda: You can neither defy nor deny real authority. We are presenting our Kṛṣṇa consciousness movement on this principle. We should carry out the orders of the authority, and Kṛṣṇa, or God, is the supreme authority. Whatever He says must be accepted without interpretation. In this way, everyone can be happy. Those who are sane do not hesitate to accept God's authority, and they become happy abiding by His orders. Those who exactly follow the instructions of the supreme authority are also authorities.

The spiritual master is the authoritative servant and God is the authoritative master. If we follow the instructions of the authoritative servant, we in turn become authoritative servants of the spiritual master.

Disciple: Concerning morality, Mill writes, "Belief, then, in the supernatural, great as are the services which it rendered in the earlier stages of human development, cannot be considered to be any longer required either for enabling us to know what is right and wrong in social morality, or for supplying us with motives to do right and to abstain from wrong."

Śrīla Prabhupāda: Morality means abiding by the orders of God. That is real morality. Other moralities are manufactured, and they differ in different countries. Religion and real morality, however, function according to the same principle. Religion means carrying out the orders of God, and morality means following those principles whereby we can fulfill the desires of God. Before the Battle of Kurukṣetra Arjuna considered killing to be immoral, but when he understood from the instructions of Kṛṣṇa that the fight was necessary, he decided to carry out his duty as a *kṣatriya*. So this is morality. Ultimately, morality means carrying out the desires of God.

Disciple: For Mill, there are two moral sanctions of conduct. One is internal, which is our conscience and sense of duty.

Śrīla Prabhupāda: What does he mean by conscience? A sense of duty is different from the conscience. It is our duty to receive instructions from higher personalities. If we do not, how can we know our duty?

Disciple: Mill felt that our duty is that which produces the most good for the most people.

Śrīla Prabhupāda: That is all so vague. What if everyone wants to take drugs? Is it our duty to help them? How can a rascal understand what his duty is? One has to be trained to know.

Disciple: Mill would say that there is a rational or guiding principle for action, and this is the golden rule of the Christians: "Do unto others as you would have them do unto you."

Śrīla Prabhupāda: This means that you have to approach Christ. You cannot manufacture golden rules yourself. You have to abide by the orders of Christ, and that means approaching a superior authority.

Disciple: The second sanction of moral conduct is external: the fear of displeasing other men or God. We hope to win favor through acting morally.

Śrīla Prabhupāda: This also means accepting authority. Therefore the *Vedas* tell us that if we want to be really learned we must approach a guru. Did John Stuart Mill have a guru?

Disciple: His father, James Mill, was also a great philosopher.

Śrīla Prabhupāda: In any case, we must accept some authority, be it Christ or Kṛṣṇa. Our duty lies in following the orders of the higher authority. Of course, we accept Kṛṣṇa, the Supreme Personality of Godhead, as our authority.

Disciple: Mill himself rejected many basic Christian tenets, and he even believed that there is no intrinsic value in the belief in the immortality of the soul. He writes, "Those who believe in the immortality of the soul generally quit life with fully as much if not more reluctance as those who have no such expectation."

Śrīla Prabhupāda: We have daily experience of how the soul continues even though the body changes. In our own family we can see that the body of an infant changes into the body of a boy, a young man, a middle-aged man, and then an old man. In any condition the soul is the same. Why is it difficult to understand the immortality of the soul? If we cannot understand it, we are not very intelligent.

yasyātma-buddhiḥ kuṇape tri-dhātuke
sva-dhīḥ kalatrādiṣu bhauma ijya-dhīḥ
yat-tīrtha-buddhiḥ salile na karhicij
janeṣv abhijñeṣu sa eva go-kharaḥ

"A human being who identifies this body made of three elements with his self, who considers the by-products of the body to be his kinsmen, who considers the land of his birth worshipable, and who goes to a place of pilgrimage simply to take a bath rather than meet men of transcendental knowledge there, is to be considered like an ass or a cow." If a person does not understand the immortality of the soul, he is an animal. There is no question of belief. It is a fact. If a man says, "I don't believe I will grow old," he is ignorant of the facts. If he does not die when he is young, he necessarily grows old. This is a question of common sense, not of beliefs. In the *Bhagavad-gītā* Kṛṣṇa says that there was never a time when we did not exist nor will there ever be a time when we will cease to exist. The soul is immortal; it never takes birth and never dies. This is the beginning of knowledge. First of all we must understand what we are. If we do not, we will surely be wrongly directed. We will take care of the body just as a foolish man might take care of a birdcage and neglect the bird within it.

Disciple: Mill was not only a utilitarian but a humanist, and he felt that a humanistic religion can have a greater effect than a supernatural religion. A humanistic religion would foster unselfish feelings and would have man at the center.

Śrīla Prabhupāda: Without God, how can it be a religion? As I have already explained, religion means carrying out the orders of God.

Disciple: Concerning immortality, Mill asserts that there is no evidence for the immortality of the soul and none against it.

Śrīla Prabhupāda: What does he need to be convinced? There is a great deal of evidence. It is mankind's misfortune that a person like Mill cannot understand a simple truth that even a child can understand.

Disciple: Ultimately, Mill considered the whole domain of the supernatural to be removed from the region of belief into that of simple hope.

Śrīla Prabhupāda: It is neither hope nor belief but a fact. At any rate, to those who are Kṛṣṇa conscious it is a fact. Kṛṣṇa came and gave Arjuna instructions, and those instructions are recorded.

Disciple: Mill was such a staunch humanist that he wrote, "I will call no being good who is not what I mean when I apply that epithet to my fellow creatures, and if such a being can sentence me to hell for not so calling him, to hell I will go."

Śrīla Prabhupāda: God is always good, and if one does not know the goodness of God he is imperfect. According to all Vedic literatures God is always good and always great. What does Mill consider to be a good man?

Disciple: One who works for what he calls "the greatest happiness principle" – that is, the greatest happiness for everyone on earth.

Śrīla Prabhupāda: Is there any man who can do good for all?

Disciple: Christ said that no man is good, that there is only one good, and that is God.

Śrīla Prabhupāda: Yes, that is a fact. You may think that such-and-such man is good, but he is limited in his power. He may still think in terms of his nation or society. Only a pure devotee of Kṛṣṇa can be good because he abides by the order of the Supreme Good. Even if one has the desire to be a good man, it is not possible independent of God. In any case, these are all mental concoctions – good and bad. One who is not God conscious is necessarily bad, and one who is God conscious is good. This should be the only criterion.

Disciple: But what of Mill's contention that the good gives the greatest pleasure to the greatest number of people?

Śrīla Prabhupāda: And what if the people are fools and rascals? The greatest number of people may say that cigarettes are very nice, but does this mean that they are desirable?

Disciple: Mill makes a distinction between the quality and the quantity of pleasure. Certain pleasures are superior to others.

Śrīla Prabhupāda: When you have quality, the quantity naturally decreases. For instance, ordinary people take pleasure in eating, sleeping, mating, drinking, smoking, and so on. The pleasure of Kṛṣṇa consciousness is a transcendental pleasure, but the people who take to it are very few. Generally, since conditioned souls are fools, the pleasure that is most popular is the one followed by the greatest number of fools. According to our Vedic philosophy man is born a fool, but he can be made intelligent through education and culture.

Disciple: Mill advocated utilizing those principles that can give the pleasure of highest quality to the maximum people. He also wrote, "It is better to be a human being dissatisfied than a pig satisfied. It is better to be Socrates dissatisfied than a fool satisfied."

Śrīla Prabhupāda: But how often will you find a Socrates? You cannot find Socrates loitering on every street. There will only be one in millions. There is no question of the maximum number of people enjoying pleasure as Socrates did. Men of Socrates' caliber are a minimum. In the *Bhagavad-gītā* Kṛṣṇa says,

manuṣyāṇāṁ sahasreṣu
kaścid yatati siddhaye
yatatām api siddhānāṁ
kaścin māṁ vetti tattvataḥ

"Out of many thousands of men, one may endeavor for perfection, and of those who have achieved perfection, hardly one knows Me in truth." This is not a question of quantity but of quality.

Disciple: Mill felt that the highest quality of pleasure might also be enjoyed by a larger number. All men should be trained to find pleasure according to this higher standard.

Śrīla Prabhupāda: This means that the maximum pleasure should be introduced to the maximum number of people. Unfortunately, it is not accepted by the greatest number but only by a few. The Kṛṣṇa consciousness movement, for instance, cannot be understood by the masses. Only a few who are fortunate can understand. There may be millions of stars in the sky, but there is only one moon, and that is sufficient to drive away the darkness. It is not possible to have many moons, although there may be many glowworms.

Disciple: Mill was trying to ascertain that standard of pleasure that is most desirable.

Śrīla Prabhupāda: That he does not know. That he has to learn from the devotees of Kṛṣṇa. Ordinary men take sex to be the highest pleasure, and the entire material world is existing because of sex, but how long does this sex pleasure last? Only a few minutes. A wise man wants pleasure that doesn't end in only a few minutes but that continues perpetually. As Kṛṣṇa says in the *Bhagavad-gītā:*

bāhya-sparśeṣv asaktātmā
vindaty ātmani yat sukham
sa brahma-yoga-yuktātmā
sukham akṣayam aśnute

ye hi saṁsparśa-jā bhogā
duḥkha-yonaya eva te
ādy-antavantaḥ kaunteya
na teṣu ramate budhaḥ

Here the word *akṣayam* means "eternal," and *sukham* means "pleasure." Here Kṛṣṇa states that those who are intelligent are not interested in transient pleasure but in eternal pleasure. They know their constitutional position; they know they are not the body. The pleasures of the body are transient and are sought by rascals. If one identifies with the body, he naturally seeks bodily pleasure. One who knows that he is not the body but eternal spirit soul seeks eternal spiritual pleasure through *bhakti-yoga.*

Disciple: Mill believed that a small amount of a higher type of pleasure is superior to a greater amount of a lower type.

Śrīla Prabhupāda: Yes, that is our philosophy. In the *Bhagavad-gītā* Kṛṣṇa says,

nehābhikrama-nāśo 'sti
pratyavāyo na vidyate
sv-alpam apy asya dharmasya
trāyate mahato bhayāt

"In *bhakti-yoga* there is no loss or diminution, and a little advancement on this path can protect one from the most dangerous type of fear." Even if one falls down from Kṛṣṇa consciousness, he still gains from what little he has experienced. On the other hand, if one works very hard but does not take to devotional service, all his labors go in vain. There are many students who come to Kṛṣṇa consciousness for a few days and then go away, but they return again because the quality is so great. Kṛṣṇa consciousness is so potent. Except for Kṛṣṇa consciousness, everything is being dissipated by time. Everything in this world is transient, but because we are eternal spirit souls, we should accept only that which has permanent value. It is foolishness to be satisfied with anything else.

Karl Marx

A conversation between His Divine Grace
A. C. Bhaktivedanta Swami Prabhupāda and his disciples

With his Communist Manifesto *– beginning with the ominous "A specter is haunting Europe – the specter of communism" and ending with the clarion call "Workers of the world, unite!" – the German philosopher Karl Marx (1818–1883) launched the communist movement. In the following dialogue, Śrīla Prabhupāda focuses on why those who have tried to put Marx's philosophy into practice have been frustrated in their attempts to eradicate greed from human nature and society at large.*

~

Disciple: Karl Marx contended that philosophers have only interpreted the world; the point is to change it. His philosophy is often called "dialectical materialism" because it comes from the dialectic of George Hegel – thesis, antithesis, and synthesis. When applied to society, his philosophy is known as communism. His idea is that for many generations the bourgeoisie have competed with the proletariat, and that this conflict will terminate in the communist society. In other words, the workers will overthrow the capitalistic class and establish a so-called dictatorship of the proletariat, which will finally become a classless society.

Śrīla Prabhupāda: But how is a classless society possible? Men naturally fall into different classes. Your nature is different from mine, so how can we artificially be brought to the same level?
Disciple: His idea is that human nature, or ideas, are molded by the means of production. Therefore everyone can be trained to participate in the classless society.
Śrīla Prabhupāda: Then training is required?
Disciple: Yes.
Śrīla Prabhupāda: And what will be the center of training for this classless society? What will be the motto?
Disciple: The motto is "From each according to his ability, to each according to his need." The idea is that everyone would contribute something, and everyone would get what he needed.
Śrīla Prabhupāda: But everyone's contribution is different. A scientific man contributes something and a philosopher contributes something else. The cow contributes milk and the dog contributes service as a watchdog. Even the trees, the birds, the beasts – everyone is contributing something. So by nature a reciprocal arrangement is already there among social classes. How can there be a classless society?
Disciple: Well, Marx's idea is that the means of production will be owned in common. No one would have an advantage over anyone else, and thus one person could not exploit another. Marx is thinking in terms of profit.
Śrīla Prabhupāda: First we must know what profit actually is. For example, the American hippies already had "profit." They were from the best homes, their fathers were rich – they had everything. Yet they were not satisfied; they rejected it. No, this idea of a classless society based on profit-sharing is imperfect. Besides, the communists have not created a classless society. We have seen in Moscow how a poor woman will wash the streets while her boss sits comfortably in his car. So where is the classless society? As long as society is maintained, there must be some higher and lower classification. But if the central point of society is one, then whether one works in a lower or a higher position, he doesn't care.

For example, our body has different parts – the head, the legs, the hands – but everything works for the stomach.

Disciple: Actually, the Russians supposedly have the same idea: they claim the common worker is just as glorious as the top scientist or manager.

Śrīla Prabhupāda: But in Moscow we have seen that not everyone is satisfied. One boy who came to us was very unhappy because in Russia young boys are not allowed to go out at night.

Disciple: The Russian authorities would say that he has an improper understanding of Marxist philosophy.

Śrīla Prabhupāda: That "improper understanding" is inevitable. They will never be able to create a classless society because, as I have already explained, everyone's mentality is different.

Disciple: Marx says that if everyone is engaged according to his abilities in a certain type of production, and everyone works for the central interest, then everyone's ideas will become uniform.

Śrīla Prabhupāda: Therefore we must find out the real central interest. In our International Society for Krishna Consciousness everyone has a central interest in Kṛṣṇa. Therefore one person is speaking, another person is typing, another is going to the press or washing the dishes, and no one is begrudging, because they are all convinced they are serving Kṛṣṇa.

Disciple: Marx's idea is that the center is the state.

Śrīla Prabhupāda: But the state cannot be perfect. If the Russian state is perfect, then why was Khrushchev driven from power? He was elected premier. Why was he driven from power?

Disciple: Because he was not fulfilling the aims of the people.

Śrīla Prabhupāda: Well, then, what is the guarantee the next premier will do that? There is no guarantee. The same thing will happen again and again. Because the center, Khrushchev, was imperfect, people begrudged their labor. The same thing is going on in noncommunist countries as well. The government is changed, the prime minister is deposed, the president is impeached. So what is the real difference between Russian communism and other political systems? What is happening in other countries is also happening in Russia, only they call it by a different name. When we talked with Professor Kotovsky of Moscow University, we told him he had to surrender: either he must surrender to Kṛṣṇa or to Lenin, but he must surrender. He was taken aback by this.

Disciple: From studying history Marx concluded that the characteristics of culture, the social structure, and even the thoughts of the people are determined by the means of economic production.

Śrīla Prabhupāda: How does he account for all the social disruption in countries like America, which is so advanced in economic production?

Disciple: He says that capitalism is a decadent form of economic production because it relies on the exploitation of one class by another.

Śrīla Prabhupāda: But there is exploitation in the communist countries also. Khrushchev was driven out of power because he was exploiting his position. He was giving big government posts to his son and son-in-law.

Disciple: He was deviating from the doctrine.

Śrīla Prabhupāda: But since any leader can deviate, how will perfection come? First the person in the center must be perfect, then his dictations will be correct. Otherwise, if the leaders are all imperfect men, what is the use of changing this or that? The corruption will continue.

Disciple: Presumably the perfect leader would be the one who practiced Marx's philosophy without deviation.

Śrīla Prabhupāda: But Marx's philosophy is also imperfect! His proposal for a classless society is unworkable. There must be one class of men to administer the government and one class of men to sweep the streets. How can there be a classless society? Why should a sweeper be satisfied seeing someone else in the administrative post? He will think, "He is forcing me to work as a sweeper in the street while he sits comfortably in a chair." In our International Society I am also holding the superior post: I am sitting in a chair, and you are offering me garlands and the best food.

Why? Because you see a perfect man whom you can follow. That mentality must be there. Everyone in the society must be able to say, "Yes, here is a perfect man. Let him sit in a chair and let us all bow down and work like menials." Where is that perfect man in the communist countries?

Disciple: The Russians claim that Lenin is a perfect man.

Śrīla Prabhupāda: Lenin? But no one is following Lenin. Lenin's only perfection was that he overthrew the czar's government. What other perfection did he show? The people are not happy simply reading Lenin's books. I studied the people in Moscow. They are unhappy. The government cannot force them to be happy artificially. Unless there is a perfect, ideal man in the center, there cannot possibly be a classless society.

Disciple: Perhaps they see the workers and the managers in the same way that we do – in the absolute sense. Since everyone is serving the state, the sweeper is as good as the administrator.

Śrīla Prabhupāda: But unless the state gives perfect satisfaction to the people, there will always be distinctions between higher and lower classes. In the Russian state, that sense of perfection in the center is lacking.

Disciple: Their goal is the production of material goods for the enhancement of human well-being.

Śrīla Prabhupāda: That is useless! Economic production in America has no comparison in the world, yet still people are dissatisfied. The young men are confused. It is nonsensical to think that simply by increasing production everyone will become satisfied. No one will be satisfied. Man is not meant simply for eating. He has mental necessities, intellectual necessities, spiritual necessities. In India many people sit alone silently in the jungle and practice yoga. They do not require anything. How will increased production satisfy them? If someone were to say to them, "If you give up this yoga practice, I will give you two hundred bags of rice," they would laugh at the proposal. It is animalistic to think that simply by increasing production everyone will become satisfied. Real happiness does not depend on either production or starvation, but upon peace of mind. For example, if a child is crying but the mother does not know why, the child will not stop simply by giving him some milk. Sometimes this actually happens: the mother cannot understand why her child is crying, and though she is giving him her breast, he continues to cry. Similarly, dissatisfaction in human society is not caused solely by low economic production. That is nonsense. There are many causes of dissatisfaction. The practical example is America, where there is sufficient production of everything, yet the young men are becoming hippies. They are dissatisfied, confused. No, simply by increasing economic production people will not become satisfied. Marx's knowledge is insufficient. Perhaps because he came from a country where people were in scarcity, he had that idea.

Disciple: Yes, now we've seen that production of material goods alone will not make people happy.

Śrīla Prabhupāda: Because they do not know that real happiness comes from spiritual understanding. That understanding is given in the *Bhagavad-gītā:* God is the supreme enjoyer, and He is the proprietor of everything. We are not actually enjoyers; we are all workers. These two things must be there: an enjoyer and a worker. For example, in our body the stomach is the enjoyer and all other parts of the body are workers. So this system is natural: there must always be someone who is the enjoyer and someone who is the worker. It is present in the capitalist system also. In Russia there is always conflict between the managers and the workers. The workers say, "If this is a classless society, why is that man sitting comfortably and ordering us to work?" The Russians have not been able to avoid this dilemma, and it cannot be avoided. There must be one class of men who are the directors or enjoyers and another class of men who are the workers. Therefore the only way to have a truly classless society is to find that method by which both the managers and the workers will feel equal happiness. For example, if the stomach is hungry and the eyes see some food, immediately the brain will say, "O legs, please go there!" and "Hand, pick it up," and "Now please put it into the mouth." Immediately the food goes into the stomach, and as soon as the stomach is satisfied, the eyes are satisfied, the legs are satisfied, and the hand is satisfied.

Disciple: But Marx would use this as a perfect example of communism.

Śrīla Prabhupāda: But he has neglected to find out the real stomach.

Disciple: His is the material stomach.

Śrīla Prabhupāda: But the material stomach is always hungry again; it can never be satisfied. In the Kṛṣṇa consciousness movement we have the substance for feeding our brains, our minds, and our souls. *Yasya prasādād bhagavat-prasādaḥ*. If the spiritual master is satisfied, then Kṛṣṇa is satisfied, and if Kṛṣṇa is satisfied, then everyone is satisfied. Therefore you are all trying to satisfy your spiritual master. Similarly, if the communist countries can come up with a dictator who, if satisfied, automatically gives satisfaction to all the people, then we will accept such a classless society. But this is impossible. A classless society is possible only when Kṛṣṇa is in the center. For the satisfaction of Kṛṣṇa, the intellectual can work in his own way, the administrator can work in his way, the merchant can work in his way, and the laborer can work in his way – and they can all be perfectly satisfied in their own position. This is truly a classless society.

Disciple: How is this different from the communist country, where all sorts of men contribute for the same central purpose, which is the state?

Śrīla Prabhupāda: The difference is that if the state is not perfect, no one will willingly contribute to it. They may be forced to contribute, but they will not voluntarily contribute unless there is a perfect state in the center. For example, the hands, legs, and brain are working in perfect harmony for the satisfaction of the stomach. Why? Because they know without a doubt that by satisfying the stomach they will all share the energy and also be satisfied. Therefore, unless the people have this kind of perfect faith in the leader of the country, there is no possibility of a classless society.

Disciple: The communists theorize that if the worker contributes to the central fund, he will get satisfaction in return.
Śrīla Prabhupāda: Yes, but if he sees imperfection in the center, he will not work enthusiastically because he will have no faith that he will get full satisfaction. That perfection of the state will never be there, and therefore the workers will always remain dissatisfied.
Disciple: The propagandists play upon this dissatisfaction and tell the people that foreigners are causing it.
Śrīla Prabhupāda: But if the people were truly satisfied they could not be influenced by outsiders. If you are satisfied that your spiritual master is perfect – that he is guiding you nicely – will you be influenced by outsiders?
Disciple: No.
Śrīla Prabhupāda: Because the communist state will never be perfect, there is no possibility of a classless society.
Disciple: Marx examines history and sees that in Greek times, in Roman times, and in the Middle Ages slaves were always required for production.
Śrīla Prabhupāda: The Russians are also creating slaves – the working class. Joseph Stalin stayed in power simply by killing all his enemies. He killed so many men that he is recorded in history as the greatest criminal. He was certainly imperfect, yet he held the position of dictator, and the people were forced to obey him.
Disciple: His successors have denounced him.
Śrīla Prabhupāda: That's all well and good, but his successors should also be denounced. The point is that in any society there must be a leader, there must be directors, and there must be workers, but everyone should be so satisfied that they forget the difference.
Disciple: No envy.
Śrīla Prabhupāda: Ah, no envy. But that perfection is not possible in the material world. Therefore Marx's theories are useless.
Disciple: But on the other hand, the capitalists also make slaves of their workers.

Śrīla Prabhupāda: Wherever there is materialistic activity, there must be imperfection. But if they make Kṛṣṇa the center, then all problems will be resolved.
Disciple: Are you saying that any materialistic system of organizing the means of production is bound to be full of exploitation?
Śrīla Prabhupāda: Yes, certainly, certainly! The materialistic mentality means exploitation.
Disciple: Then what is the solution?
Śrīla Prabhupāda: Kṛṣṇa consciousness!
Disciple: How is that?
Śrīla Prabhupāda: Just make Kṛṣṇa the center and work for Him. Then everyone will be satisfied. As it is stated in the *Bhāgavatam:*

yathā taror mūla-niṣecanena
tṛpyanti tat-skandha-bhujopaśākhāḥ
prāṇopahārāc ca yathendriyāṇāṁ
tathaiva sarvārhaṇam acyutejyā

If you simply pour water on the root of a tree, all the branches, twigs, leaves, and flowers will be nourished. Similarly, everyone can be satisfied simply by *acyutejyā. Acyuta* means Kṛṣṇa, and *ijyā* means worship. So this is the formula for a classless society: Make Kṛṣṇa the center and do everything for Him. There are no classes in our International Society for Krishna Consciousness. Now you are writing philosophy, but if I want you to wash dishes, you will do so immediately because you know that whatever you do, you are working for Kṛṣṇa and for your spiritual master. In the material world different kinds of work have different values, but in Kṛṣṇa consciousness everything is done on the absolute platform. Whether you wash dishes or write books or worship the Deity, the value is the same because you are serving Kṛṣṇa. That is a classless society. Actually, the perfect classless society is Vṛndāvana. In Vṛndāvana, some are cowherd boys, some are cows, some are trees, some are fathers, some are mothers, but the center is Kṛṣṇa, and everyone is satisfied simply by loving Him. When all people become Kṛṣṇa conscious and understand how to love Him, then there will be a classless society. Otherwise it is not possible.

Disciple: Marx's definition of communism is "The common or public ownership of the means of production, and the abolition of private property." In our International Society for Krishna Consciousness, don't we have the same idea? We also say, "Nothing is mine." We have also abolished private property.

Śrīla Prabhupāda: While the communist says, "Nothing is mine," he thinks everything belongs to the state. The state, however, is simply an extended "mine." For example, if I am the head of a family, I might say, "I do not want anything for myself, but I want many things for my children." Mahatma Gandhi, who sacrificed so much to drive the English out of India, was at the same time thinking, "I am a very good man; I am doing national work." Therefore, this so-called nationalism or so-called communism is simply extended selfishness. The quality remains the same. The real change occurs when we say, "Nothing belongs to me; everything belongs to God, Kṛṣṇa, and therefore I should use everything in His service." That is factual abolition of private property.

Disciple: Marx says that the capitalists are parasites living at the cost of the workers.

Śrīla Prabhupāda: But the communists are also living at the cost of the workers: the managers are drawing big salaries, and the common workers are dissatisfied. Indeed, their godless society is becoming more and more troublesome. Unless everyone accepts God as the only enjoyer and himself simply as His servant, there will always be conflict. In the broad sense, there is no difference between the communists and the capitalists because God is not accepted as the supreme enjoyer and proprietor in either system. Actually, no property belongs to either the communists or the capitalists. Everything belongs to God.

Disciple: Marx condemns the capitalists for making a profit. He says that profit-making is exploitation and that the capitalists are unnecessary for the production of commodities.

Śrīla Prabhupāda: Profit-making may be wrong, but that exploitative tendency is always there, whether it is a communist or a capitalist system. In Bengal it is said that during the winter season the bugs cannot come out because of the severe cold. So they become dried up, being unable to suck any blood. But as soon as the summer season comes, the bugs get the opportunity to come out, so they immediately bite someone and suck his blood to their full satisfaction. Our mentality in this material world is the same: to exploit others and become wealthy. Whether you are a communist in the winter season or a capitalist in the summer season, your tendency is to exploit others. Unless there is a change of heart, this exploitation will go on.

I once knew a mill worker who acquired some money. Then he became the proprietor of the mill and took advantage of his good fortune to become a capitalist. Henry Ford is another example. He was an errand boy, but he got the opportunity to become a capitalist. There are many such instances. So to a greater or lesser degree, the propensity is always there in human nature to exploit others and become wealthy. Unless this mentality is changed, there is no point in changing from a capitalist to a communist society. Material life means that everyone is seeking some profit, some adoration, and some position. By threats the state can force people to curb this tendency, but for how long? Can they change everyone's mind by force? No, it is impossible. Therefore, Marx's proposition is nonsense.

Disciple: Marx thinks the minds of people can be changed by forced conditioning.

Śrīla Prabhupāda: That is not possible. Even a child cannot be convinced by force, what to speak of a mature, educated man. We have the real process for changing people's minds: chanting the Hare Kṛṣṇa mantra. *Ceto-darpaṇa-mārjanam:* This process cleanses the heart of material desires. We have seen that people in Moscow are not happy. They are simply waiting for another revolution. We talked to one working-class boy who was very unhappy. When a pot of rice is boiling, you can take one grain and press it between your fingers, and if it is hot you can understand all the rice is boiling. Thus we can understand the position of the Russian people from the sample of that boy. We could also get further ideas by talking with Professor Kotovsky from the India Department of Moscow University. How foolish he was! He said that after death everything is finished. If this is his knowledge, and if that young boy is a sample of the citizenry, then the situation in Russia is very bleak. They may theorize about so many things, but we could not even purchase sufficient groceries in Moscow. There were no vegetables, fruits, or rice, and the milk was of poor quality. If that Madrasi gentleman had not contributed some *dāl* and rice, then practically speaking we would have starved. The Russians' diet seemed to consist of only meat and liquor.

Disciple: The communists play upon this universal profit motive. The worker who produces the most units at his factory is glorified by the state or receives a small bonus.

Śrīla Prabhupāda: Why should he get a bonus?

Disciple: To give him some incentive to work hard.

Śrīla Prabhupāda: Just to satisfy his tendency to lord it over others and make a profit, his superiors bribe him. This Russian communist idea is very good provided the citizens do not want any profit. But that is impossible, because everyone wants profit. The state cannot destroy this tendency either by law or by force.

Disciple: The communists try to centralize everything – money, communications, and transport – in the hands of the state.

Śrīla Prabhupāda: But what benefit will there be in that? As soon as all the wealth is centralized, the members of the central government will appropriate it, just as Khrushchev did. These are all useless ideas as long as the tendency for exploitation is not reformed. The Russians have organized their country according to Marx's theories, yet all their leaders have turned out to be cheaters. Where is their program for reforming this cheating propensity?

Disciple: Their program is to first change the social condition, and then, they believe, the corrupt mentality will change automatically.

Śrīla Prabhupāda: Impossible. Such repression will simply cause a reaction in the form of another revolution.

Disciple: Are you implying that the people's mentality must first be changed, and then a change in the social structure will naturally follow?

Śrīla Prabhupāda: Yes. But the leaders will never be able to train all the people to think that everything belongs to the state. This idea is simply utopian nonsense.

Disciple: Marx has another slogan: "Human nature has no reality." He says that man's nature changes through history according to material conditions.

Śrīla Prabhupāda: He does not know the real human nature. It is certainly true that everything in this cosmic creation, or *jagat,* is changing. Your body changes daily. Everything is changing, just like waves in the ocean. This is not a very advanced philosophy. Marx's theory is also being changed; it cannot last. But man does have a fundamental nature that never changes: his spiritual nature. We are teaching people to come to the standard of acting according to their spiritual nature, which will never change. Acting spiritually means serving Kṛṣṇa. If we try to serve Kṛṣṇa now, we will continue to serve Kṛṣṇa when we go to Vaikuṇṭha, the spiritual world. Therefore, loving service to Lord Kṛṣṇa is called *nitya,* or eternal. As Kṛṣṇa says in the *Bhagavad-gītā, nitya-yukta upāsate:* "My pure devotees perpetually worship Me with devotion."

The communists give up Kṛṣṇa and replace Him with the state. Then they expect to get the people to think, "Nothing in my favor; everything in favor of the state." But people will never accept this idea. It is impossible; let the rascals try it! All they can do is simply force the people to work, as Stalin did. As soon as he found someone opposed to him, he immediately cut his throat. The same disease is still there today, so how will their program be successful?

Disciple: As I mentioned, their idea is that human nature has no reality of its own. It is simply a product of the material environment. Thus, by putting a man in the factory and making him identify with the state and something like scientific achievement, they think they can transform him into a selfless person.
Śrīla Prabhupāda: But because he has the basic disease, envy, he will remain selfish. When he sees that he is working so hard but that the profit is not coming to him, his enthusiasm will immediately slacken. In Bengal there is a proverb: "As a proprietor I can turn sand into gold, but as soon as I am no longer the proprietor, the gold becomes sand." The Russian people are in this position. They are not as rich as the Europeans or the Americans, and because of this they are unhappy.
Disciple: One of the methods the authorities in Russia use is to constantly whip the people into believing there may be a war at any moment. Then they think, "To protect our country, we must work hard."
Śrīla Prabhupāda: If the people cannot make any profit on their work, however, they will eventually lose all interest in the country. The average man will think, "Whether I work or not, I get the same result. I cannot adequately feed and clothe my family." Then he will begin to lose his incentive to work. A scientist will see that despite his high position, his wife and children are dressed just like the common laborer.
Disciple: Marx says that industrial and scientific work is the highest kind of activity.
Śrīla Prabhupāda: But unless the scientists and the industrialists receive sufficient profit, they will be reluctant to work for the state.
Disciple: The Russian goal is the production of material goods for the enhancement of human well-being.
Śrīla Prabhupāda: Their "human well-being" actually means, "If you don't agree with me, I'll cut your throat." This is their "well-being." Stalin had his idea of "human well-being," but anyone who disagreed with his version of it was killed or imprisoned. They may say that a few must suffer for the sake of many, but

we have personally seen that Russia has achieved neither general happiness nor prosperity. For example, in Moscow none of the big buildings have been recently built. They are old and ravaged, or poorly renovated. Also, at the stores the people had to stand in long lines to make purchases. These are indications that economic conditions are unsound.

Disciple: Marx considered religion an illusion that must be condemned.

Śrīla Prabhupāda: The divisions between different religious faiths may be an illusion, but Marx's philosophy is also an illusion.

Disciple: Do you mean that it's not being practiced?

Śrīla Prabhupāda: In the sixty years since the Russian Revolution, his philosophy has become distorted. On the other hand, Lord Brahmā began the Vedic religion countless years ago, and though foreigners have been trying to devastate it for the last two thousand years, it is still intact. Vedic religion is not an illusion, at least not for India.

Disciple: Here is Marx's famous statement about religion. He says, "Religion is the sigh of the oppressed creature, the heart of the heartless world, just as it is the spirit of the spiritless situation. It is the opium of the people."

Śrīla Prabhupāda: He does not know what religion is. His definition is false. The *Vedas* state that religion is the course of action given by God. God is a fact, and His law is also a fact. It is not an illusion. Kṛṣṇa gives the definition of religion in *Bhagavad-gītā: sarva-dharmān parityajya mām ekaṁ śaraṇaṁ vraja.* To surrender unto God – this is religion.

Disciple: Marx believes everything is produced from economic struggle and that religion is a technique invented by the bourgeoisie or the capitalists to dissuade the masses from revolution by promising them a better existence after death.

Śrīla Prabhupāda: He himself has created a philosophy that is presently being enforced by coercion and killing.

Disciple: And he promised that in the future things will be better. So he is guilty of the very thing that he condemns religion for.

Śrīla Prabhupāda: As we have often explained, religion is that part of our nature which is permanent, which we cannot give up. No one can give up his religion. And what is that religion? Service. Marx desires to serve humanity by putting forward his philosophy. Therefore that is his religion. Everyone is trying to render some service. The father is trying to serve his family, the statesman is trying to serve his country, and the philanthropist is trying to serve all humanity. Whether you are Karl Marx or Stalin or Mahatma Gandhi, a Hindu, a Muslim, or a Christian, you must serve. Because we are presently rendering service to so many people and so many things, we are becoming confused. Therefore, Kṛṣṇa advises us to give up all this service and serve Him alone:

sarva-dharmān parityajya
mām ekaṁ śaraṇaṁ vraja
ahaṁ tvāṁ sarva-pāpebhyo
mokṣayiṣyāmi mā śucaḥ

"Abandon all varieties of service and just surrender unto Me. I shall deliver you from all sinful reactions. Do not fear."

Disciple: The communists – and even to a certain extent the capitalists – believe that service for the production of goods is the only real service. Therefore they condemn us because we are not producing anything tangible.

Śrīla Prabhupāda: How can they condemn us? We are giving service to humanity by teaching the highest knowledge. A high court judge does not produce any grains in the field. He sits in a chair and gets $75,000 or $100,000 a year. Does that mean he is not rendering any service? Of course he is. The theory that unless one performs manual labor in the factory or the fields he is not doing service would simply give credit to the peasant and the worker. It is a peasant philosophy.

There is a story about a king and his prime minister. Once the king's salaried workers complained, "We are actually working, and this minister is doing nothing, yet you are paying him such a large salary. Why is that?"

The king then called his minister in and also had someone bring in an elephant. "Please take this elephant and weigh it," the king said to his workers. The workers took the elephant to all the markets, but they could not find a scale large enough to weigh the animal.

When they returned to the palace the king asked, "What happened?"

One of the workers answered, "Sir, we could not find a scale large enough to weigh the elephant."

Then the king addressed his prime minister, "Will you please weigh this elephant?"

"Yes, sir," said the prime minister, and he took the elephant away. He returned within a few minutes and said, "It weighs 11,650 pounds."

The workers were astonished. "How did you weigh it so quickly?" they asked. "Did you find some very large scale?"

The minister replied, "No. It is impossible to weigh an elephant on a scale. I went to the river, took the elephant on a boat, and noted the watermark. After taking the elephant off the boat, I put weights in the boat until the same watermark was reached. Then I had the elephant's weight."

The king said to his workers, "Now do you see the difference?"

One who has intelligence has strength, not the fools and the rascals. Marx and his followers are simply fools and rascals. We don't take advice from them; we take advice from Kṛṣṇa or His representative.

Disciple: Religion isn't simply a force to keep people illusioned?

Śrīla Prabhupāda: No. Religion means to serve the spirit. That is religion. Everyone is rendering service, but no one knows where his service will be most successful. Therefore Kṛṣṇa says, "Serve Me, and you will serve the spiritual society." This is real religion. The Marxists want to build a so-called perfect society without religion, yet even up to this day, because India's foundation is religion, people all over the world adore India.

Disciple: Marx says that God does not create man; rather, man creates God.

Śrīla Prabhupāda: That is more nonsense. From what he says, I can tell he is a nonsensical rascal and a fool. One cannot understand that someone is a fool unless he talks. A fool may dress very nicely and sit like a gentleman amongst gentlemen, but we can tell the fools from the learned men by their speech.

Disciple: Marx's follower was Nikolai Lenin. He reinforced all of Marx's ideas and added a few of his own. He believed that revolution is a fundamental fact of history. He said that history moves in leaps, and that it progresses toward the communist leap. He wanted Russia to leap into the dictatorship of the proletariat, which he called the final stage of historical development.

Śrīla Prabhupāda: No. We can say with confidence – and they may note it carefully – that after the Bolshevik Revolution there will be many other revolutions, because as long as people live on the mental plane there will be only revolution. Our proposition is to give up all these mental concoctions and come to the spiritual platform. If one comes to the spiritual platform, there will be no more revolution. As Dhruva Mahārāja said, *nātaḥ paraṁ parama vedmi na yatra nādaḥ:* "Now that I am seeing God, I am completely satisfied. Now all kinds of theorizing processes are finished." So God consciousness is the final revolution. There will be repeated revolutions in this material world unless people come to Kṛṣṇa consciousness.

Disciple: The Hare Kṛṣṇa revolution.

Śrīla Prabhupāda: The Vedic injunction is that people are searching after knowledge, and that when one understands the Absolute Truth, he understands everything. *Yasmin vijñāte sarvam evaṁ vijñātaṁ bhavati.* People are trying to approach an objective, but they do not know that the final objective is Kṛṣṇa. They are simply trying to make adjustments with so many materialistic revolutions. They have no knowledge that they are spiritual beings and that unless they go back to the spiritual world and associate with the Supreme Spirit, God, there is no question of happiness. We are like fish out of water. Just as a fish cannot be happy unless he is in the water, we cannot be happy apart from the spiritual world. We are part and parcel of the Supreme Spirit, Kṛṣṇa, but we have left His association and fallen from the spiritual world because of our desire to enjoy this material world. So unless we reawaken the understanding of our spiritual position and go back home to the spiritual world, we can never be happy. We can go on theorizing for many lifetimes, but we will only see one revolution after another. The old order changes, yielding its place to the new. Or in other words, history repeats itself.

Disciple: Marx says that there are always two conflicting properties in material nature, and that the inner pulsation of opposite forces causes history to take leaps from one revolution to another. He claims that the communist revolution is the final revolution because it is the perfect resolution of all social and political contradictions.

Śrīla Prabhupāda: If the communist idea is spiritualized, then it will become perfect. As long as the communist idea remains materialistic, it cannot be the final revolution. They believe that the state is the owner of everything. But the state is not the owner; the real owner is God. When they come to this conclusion, then the communist idea will be perfect. We also have a communistic philosophy. They say that everything must be done for the state, but in our International Society for Krishna Consciousness we are actually practicing perfect communism by doing everything for Kṛṣṇa. We know Kṛṣṇa is the supreme enjoyer of the result of all work (*bhoktāraṁ yajña-tapasām*). The communist philosophy as it is now practiced is vague, but it can become perfect if they accept the conclusion of the *Bhagavad-gītā* – that Kṛṣṇa is the supreme proprietor, the supreme enjoyer, and the supreme friend of everyone. Then people will be happy. Now they mistrust the state, but if the people accept Kṛṣṇa as their friend, they will have perfect confidence in Him, just as Arjuna was perfectly confident in Kṛṣṇa on the Battlefield of Kurukṣetra. The great victory of Arjuna and his associates on the Battlefield of Kurukṣetra showed that his confidence in Kṛṣṇa was justified:

yatra yogeśvaraḥ kṛṣṇo
yatra pārtho dhanur-dharaḥ
tatra śrīr vijayo bhūtir
dhruvā nītir matir mama

"Wherever there is Kṛṣṇa, the master of all mystics, and wherever there is Arjuna, the supreme archer, there will also certainly be opulence, victory, extraordinary power, and morality. That is my opinion." So if Kṛṣṇa is at the center of society, then the people will be perfectly secure and prosperous. The communist idea is welcome, provided they are prepared to replace the so-called state with God. That is religion.

Sigmund Freud

A conversation between His Divine Grace
A. C. Bhaktivedanta Swami Prabhupāda and his disciples

The founder of psychoanalysis, Sigmund Freud (1856–1939) spent most of his life in Vienna investigating the intricacies of the human mind and formulating ideas that have largely guided the treatment of mental illness in the West up to the present day. Here Śrīla Prabhupāda points out that because Freud ignores the real craziness of materialistic life – the misidentification of the self with the body – all his analyses and treatments are ultimately futile.

~

Disciple: Sigmund Freud's idea was that many psychological problems originate with traumatic experiences in childhood or infancy. His method of cure was to have the patient try to recall these painful events and analyze them.

Śrīla Prabhupāda: But he did not know that one must again become an infant. After this life one will be put into another womb and the same traumatic experiences will happen again. Therefore it is the duty of the spiritual master and the parents to save the child from taking another birth. The opportunity of this human form of life is that we can understand the horrible experiences of birth, death, old age, and disease and act so that we shall not be forced to go through the same things again. Otherwise, after death we shall have to take birth in a womb and suffer repeated miseries.

Disciple: Freud treated many people suffering from neuroses. For instance, suppose a man is sexually impotent. By recalling his childhood he may remember some harmful experience with his father or mother that caused him to be repelled by women. In this way he can resolve the conflict and lead a normal sex life.

Śrīla Prabhupāda: However, even in the so-called normal condition, the pleasure derived from sexual intercourse is simply frustrating and insignificant. For ordinary men attached to the materialistic way of life, their only pleasure is sexual intercourse. But the *śāstras* say, *yan maithunādi-gṛhamedhi-sukhaṁ hi tuccham:* the pleasure derived from sexual intercourse is tenth-class at best. Because they have no idea of the pleasure of Kṛṣṇa consciousness the materialists regard sex as the highest pleasure. And how is it actually experienced? We have an itch, and when we scratch it we feel some pleasure. But the aftereffects of sexual pleasure are abominable. The mother has to undergo labor pains and the father has to take responsibility for raising the children nicely and giving them an education. Of course, if one is irresponsible like cats and dogs, that is another thing. But for those who are actually gentlemen, is it not painful to bear and raise children? Certainly. Therefore everyone is avoiding children by contraceptive methods. But much better is to follow the injunction of the *śāstras:* Simply try to tolerate the itching sensation and avoid so much pain. This is real psychology. That itching sensation can be tolerated if one practices Kṛṣṇa consciousness. Then one will not be very attracted by sex life.

Disciple: Freud's philosophy is that people have neuroses or disorders of their total personality – various conflicts and anxieties – and that all these originate with the sexual impulse.

Śrīla Prabhupāda: That we admit. An embodied living being must have hunger, and he must have the sex impulse. We find that even in the animals these impulses are there.

Disciple: Freud believed that the ego tries to restrain these primitive drives and that all anxieties arise from this conflict.

Śrīla Prabhupāda: Our explanation is as follows: Materialistic life is no doubt very painful. As soon as one acquires a material body he must always suffer three kinds of miseries: miseries caused by other living beings, miseries caused by the elements, and miseries caused by his own body and mind. So the whole problem is how to stop these miseries and attain permanent happiness. Unless one stops his materialistic way of life, with its threefold miseries and repeated birth and death, there is no question of happiness. The whole Vedic civilization is based on how one can cure this materialistic disease. If we can cure this disease, its symptoms will automatically vanish. Freud is simply dealing with the symptoms of the basic disease. When you have a disease, sometimes you have headaches, sometimes your leg aches, sometimes you have a pain in your stomach, and so on. But if your disease is cured, then all your symptoms disappear. That is our program.

Disciple: In his theory of psychoanalysis Freud states that by remembering and reevaluating emotional shocks from our childhood we can release the tension we are feeling now.

Śrīla Prabhupāda: But what is the guarantee that one will not get shocked again? He may cure the results of one shock, but there is no guarantee that the patient will not receive another shock. Therefore Freud's treatment is useless. Our program is total cure – no more shocks of any kind. If one is situated in real Kṛṣṇa consciousness he can face the most severe type of adversity and remain completely undisturbed. In our Kṛṣṇa consciousness movement we are giving people this ability. Freud tries to cure the reactions of one kind of shock, but other shocks will come one after another. This is how material nature works. If you solve one problem, another problem arises immediately. And if you solve that one, another one comes. As long as you are under the control of material nature these repeated shocks will come. But if you become Kṛṣṇa conscious, there are no more shocks.

Disciple: Freud's idea is that the basic instinct in the human personality is the sexual drive, or libido, and that if the expressions of a child's sexuality are inhibited, then his personality becomes disordered.

Śrīla Prabhupāda: Everyone has the sex appetite: this tendency is innate. But our *brahmacarya* system restricts a child's sex life from the earliest stages of his development and diverts his attention to Kṛṣṇa consciousness. As a result there is very little chance that he will suffer such personality disorders. In the Vedic age the leaders of society knew that if a person engaged in unrestricted sex indulgence, then the duration of his materialistic life would increase. He would have to accept a material body birth after birth. Therefore the *śāstras* enjoin that one may have sexual intercourse only if married and only for procreation. Otherwise it is illicit. In our Kṛṣṇa consciousness society, we prohibit illicit sex, but not legal sex. In the *Bhagavad-gītā* Kṛṣṇa says, *dharmāviruddho bhūteṣu kāmo 'smi bharatarṣabha:* "I am sexual intercourse that is not against religious principles." This means that sex must be regulated. Everyone has a tendency to have sex unrestrictedly – and in Western countries they are actually doing this – but according to the Vedic system, there must be restrictions. And not only must sex be restricted, but meat-eating, gambling, and drinking as well. So in our Society we have eliminated all these things, and our Western students are becoming pure devotees of Kṛṣṇa. The people at large, however, must at least restrict these sinful activities, as explained in the Vedic *śāstras.*

The Vedic system of *varṇāśrama-dharma* is so scientific that everything is automatically adjusted. Life becomes very peaceful, and everyone can make progress in Kṛṣṇa consciousness. If the Vedic system is followed by human society, there will be no more of these mental disturbances.

Disciple: Freud says that sexual energy is not only expressed in sexual intercourse but is associated with a wide variety of pleasurable bodily sensations such as pleasures of the mouth, like eating and sucking.

Śrīla Prabhupāda: That is confirmed in the *śāstras: yan maithunādi-*

gṛhamedhi-sukham. The only pleasure in this material world is sex. The word *ādi* indicates that the basic principle is *maithuna,* sexual intercourse. The whole system of materialistic life revolves around this sexual pleasure. But this pleasure is like one drop of water in the desert. The desert requires an ocean of water. If you find one drop of water in a desert, you can certainly say, "Here is some water." But what is its value? Similarly, there is certainly some pleasure in sex life, but what is the value of that pleasure? Compared to the unlimited pleasure of Kṛṣṇa consciousness, it is like one drop of water in the desert. Everyone is seeking unlimited pleasure, but no one is becoming satisfied. They are having sex in so many different ways, and the young girls walking on the street are almost naked. The whole society has become degraded. Every woman and girl is trying to attract a man, and the men take advantage of the situation. There is a saying in Bengal, "When milk is available in the marketplace, what is the use of keeping a cow?" So men are declining to keep a wife because sex is so cheap. They are deserting their families.

Disciple: Freud says that as the child grows up he begins to learn that by giving up immediate sensual satisfaction he can gain a greater benefit later on.

Śrīla Prabhupāda: But even this so-called greater benefit is illusory, because it is still based on the principle of material pleasure. The only way to entirely give up these lower pleasures is to take to Kṛṣṇa consciousness. As Kṛṣṇa states in the *Bhagavad-gītā, paraṁ dṛṣṭvā nivartate:* "By experiencing a higher taste, he is fixed in consciousness." And as Yāmunācārya said, "Since I have been engaged in the transcendental loving service of Kṛṣṇa, realizing ever-new pleasure in Him, whenever I think of sex pleasure I spit at the thought, and my lips curl in distaste." That is Kṛṣṇa consciousness. Our prescription is that in the beginning of life the child should be taught self-restraint (*brahmacarya*), and when he is past twenty he can marry. In the beginning he should learn how to restrain his senses. If a child is taught to become saintly, his semen rises to his brain, and he is able to understand spiritual values. Wasting semen decreases intelligence. So from the beginning, if he is a *brahmacārī* and does not misuse his semen, then he will become intelligent and strong and fully grown.

For want of this education everyone's brain and bodily growth are being stunted. After the boy has been trained as a *brahmacārī,* if he still wants to enjoy sex he may get married. And because he has been trained from childhood to renounce materialistic enjoyment, when he is fifty years old he can retire from household life. At that time naturally his firstborn son will be twenty-five years old, and he can take responsibility for maintaining the household. Household life is simply a license for sex life – that's all. Sex is not required, but one who cannot restrain himself is given a license to get married and have sex. This is the real program that will save society. By speculating on some shock that may or may not have occurred in childhood, one will never discover the root disease. The sex impulse, as well as the impulse to become intoxicated and to eat meat, is present from the very beginning of life. Therefore one must restrain himself. Otherwise he will be implicated.

Disciple: So the Western system of bringing up children seems artificial because the parents either repress the child too severely or don't restrict him at all.

Śrīla Prabhupāda: That is not good. The Vedic system is to give the child direction for becoming Kṛṣṇa conscious. There must be some repression, but our use of repression is different. We say the child must rise early in the morning, worship the Deity in the temple, and chant Hare Kṛṣṇa. In the beginning, force may be necessary. Otherwise the child will not become habituated. But the idea is to divert his attention to Kṛṣṇa conscious activities. Then, when he realizes he is not his body, all difficulties will disappear. As one increases his Kṛṣṇa consciousness, he becomes indifferent to all these material things. So Kṛṣṇa consciousness is the prime remedy – the panacea for all diseases.

Disciple: Freud divided the personality into three departments: the ego, the superego, and the id. The id is the irrational instinct for enjoyment. The ego is one's image of his own body, and is the instinct for self-preservation. The superego represents the moral restrictions of parents and other authorities.

Śrīla Prabhupāda: It is certainly true that everyone has some false egoism, or *ahaṅkāra*. For example, Freud thought he was Austrian. That is false ego, or identifying oneself with one's place of birth. We are giving everyone the information that this identification with a material body is ignorance. It is due to ignorance only that I think I am Indian, American, Hindu, or Muslim. This is egoism of the inferior quality. The superior egoism is "I am Brahman. I am an eternal servant of Kṛṣṇa." If a child is taught this superior egoism from the beginning, then automatically his false egoism is stopped.

Disciple: Freud says that the ego tries to preserve the individual by organizing and controlling the irrational demands of the id. In other words, if the id sees something, like food, it automatically demands to eat it, and the ego controls that desire in order to preserve the individual. The superego reinforces this control. So these three systems are always conflicting in the personality.

Śrīla Prabhupāda: But the basic principle is false, since Freud has no conception of the soul existing beyond the body. He is considering the body only. Therefore he is a great fool. According to *bhāgavata* philosophy, anyone in the bodily concept of life – anyone who identifies this body, composed of mucus, bile, and air, as his self – is no better than an ass.

Disciple: Then these interactions of the id, the ego, and the superego are all bodily interactions?

Śrīla Prabhupāda: Yes, they are all subtle bodily interactions. The mind is the first element of the subtle body. The gross senses are controlled by the mind, which in turn is controlled by the intelligence. And the intelligence is controlled by the ego. So if the ego is false, then everything is false. If I falsely identify with this body because of false ego, then anything based on this false idea is also false. This is called *māyā,* or illusion. The whole of Vedic education aims at getting off this false platform and coming to the real platform of spiritual knowledge, called *brahma-jñāna.* When one comes to the knowledge that he is spirit soul he immediately becomes happy. All his troubles are due to the false ego, and as soon as the individual realizes his true ego, the blazing fire of material existence is immediately extinguished. These philosophers are simply describing the blazing fire, but we are trying to get him out of the burning prison house of the material world altogether. They may attempt to make him happy within the fire, but how can they be successful? He must be saved from the fire. Then he will be happy. That is the message of Caitanya Mahāprabhu, and that is Lord Kṛṣṇa's message in the *Bhagavad-gītā*. Freud identifies the body with the soul. He does not know the basic principle of spiritual understanding, which is that we are not this body. We are different from this body and are transmigrating from one body to another. Without this knowledge, all his theories are based on a misunderstanding.

Not only Freud, but everyone in this material world is under illusion. In Bengal, a psychiatrist in the civil service was once called to give evidence in a case where the murderer was pleading insanity. The civil servant examined him to discover whether he was actually insane or not. In the courtroom he said, "I have tested many persons, and I have concluded that everyone is insane to some degree. In the present case, if the defendant is pleading insanity, then you may acquit him if you like, but as far as I know, everyone is more or less insane." And that is our conclusion as well. Anyone who identifies with his material body must be crazy, because his life is based on a misconception.

Disciple: Freud also investigated the problem of anxiety, which he said was produced when the impulses of the id threaten to overpower the rational ego and the moral superego.

Śrīla Prabhupāda: Anxiety will continue as long as one is in the material condition. No one can be free from anxiety in conditioned life.

Disciple: Is it because our desires are always frustrated?

Śrīla Prabhupāda: Yes. Your desires must be frustrated because you desire something that is not permanent. Suppose I wish to live forever, but since I have accepted a material body, there is no question of living forever. Therefore I am always anxious that death will come. I am afraid of death, when the body will be destroyed. This is the cause of all anxiety: acceptance of something impermanent as permanent.

Disciple: Freud says that anxiety develops when the superego represses the primitive desires of the id to protect the ego. Is such repression of basic instincts very healthy?

Śrīla Prabhupāda: Yes. For us repression means restraining oneself from doing something which in the long run is against one's welfare. For example, suppose you are suffering from diabetes and the doctor says, "Don't eat any sweet food." If you desire to eat sweets, you must repress that desire. Similarly, in our system of *brahmacarya* there is also repression. A *brahmacārī* should not sit down with a young woman or even look at one lustfully. He may desire to do so, but he must repress the desire. This is called *tapasya,* or voluntary repression.

Disciple: But aren't these desires given outlet in other ways? For instance, instead of looking at a beautiful woman, we look at the beautiful form of Kṛṣṇa.

Śrīla Prabhupāda: Yes, that is our process: *paraṁ dṛṣṭvā nivartate.* If you have a better engagement, you can give up an inferior engagement. When you are captivated by seeing the beautiful form of Kṛṣṇa, naturally you have no more desire to look at the so-called beautiful form of a young woman.

Disciple: What's the effect of childhood experiences on one's later development?

Śrīla Prabhupāda: Children imitate whoever they associate with. You all know the movie *Tarzan.* He was brought up by monkeys and he took on the habits of monkeys. If you keep children in good association their psychological development will be very good – they will become like demigods. But if you keep them in bad association they will turn out to be demons. Children are a blank slate. You can mold them as you like, and they are eager to learn.

Disciple: So a child's personality doesn't develop according to a fixed pattern?

Śrīla Prabhupāda: No. You can mold them in any way, like soft dough. However you put them into the mold, they will come out – like *badas, capātīs,* or *kachoris*. Therefore if you give children good association they will develop nicely, and if you put them in bad association they will develop poorly. They have no independent psychology.

Disciple: Actually, Freud had a rather pessimistic view of human nature. He believed that we are all beset with irrational and chaotic impulses that cannot be eliminated.

Śrīla Prabhupāda: This is not only pessimism but evidence of his poor fund of knowledge. He did not have perfect knowledge, nor was he trained by a perfect man. Therefore his theories are all nonsense.

Disciple: He concluded that it was impossible to be happy in this material world but that one can alleviate some of the conflicts through psychoanalysis. He thought one can try to make the path as smooth as possible, but it will always be troublesome.

Śrīla Prabhupāda: It is true that one cannot be happy in this material world. But if one becomes spiritually elevated – if his consciousness is changed to Kṛṣṇa consciousness – then he will be happy.

Betting on God: Pascal's Wager and the Spoils of Faith

Satyarāja Dāsa

Scientific discoveries are convincing intelligent people that betting on the existence of God is a reasonable gamble.

~

I read a recent statistic that was mind-boggling: According to a series of Gallup surveys, 94% of Americans believe in God, and 90% pray. Why, I wondered, in our modern age of science, do so many people still believe? This is a time when things not empirically proven are left by the wayside. Of course, a good number of believers have simple faith, and that's that. But there is also a burgeoning scientific community offering impetus for statistics like those above.

I happened upon the work of Patrick Glynn, a Harvard scholar, currently the associate director of the George Washington University Institute for Communitarian Policy Studies in Washington, D.C. He promotes the Anthropic Principle, which originated in the 1970s as the brainchild of Cambridge astrophysicists and cosmologists, including Brandon Carter, a colleague of people like Stephen Hawking and Roger Penrose. Glynn, however, made the theory popular through his book *God: The Evidence.*

Basically, the Anthropic Principle posits that "what we expect to observe in the universe must be restricted by the conditions necessary for our presence as observers." In other words, all the seemingly arbitrary and unrelated constants in physics have one strange thing in common: these are precisely the values you need if you want to have life in the universe. Moreover, the myriad laws of physics seem to have been fine-tuned from the very beginning of the universe for the existence of human beings.

According to Glynn, more and more scientists are subscribing to the Anthropic Principle, which heavily implies an ordered universe and a supreme controller, i.e., God. Because of this, Glynn tells us, "Pascal's Wager" is starting to really make sense.

"Who's what?" I asked myself.

I promptly went online to find out exactly what Pascal's Wager is all about.

Pascal's Wager

The seventeenth-century mathematician/philosopher Blaise Pascal formulated a pragmatic argument for justifying belief in God. Which is worth the risk of error, Pascal questioned, belief or non-belief? It is wise, he said, to "wager" on the existence of God, for the alternative, to put one's faith in faithlessness, is an inferior bet. And, more, if one believes in God but is eventually proven wrong, one loses nothing. But if one believes and is proven right, one gains just about everything. And what if one disbelieves in God and is proven wrong? What if one lives an atheistic life and then finds out there is a God? That's going to be trouble for sure.

Most philosophers think Pascal's Wager is the weakest of all the traditional arguments for believing in the existence of God. But Pascal thought it was the strongest. After completing his construction of the full argument in his work *Pensées*, he wrote, "This is conclusive, and if men are capable of any truth, this is it." This declaration was a rare moment of certainty for Pascal, one of the most skeptical thinkers of the modern era.

But here's how he saw it: Suppose a loved one is dying. You've tried everything, and all the specialists agree that there is no hope. Then a doctor comes along and offers a new "miracle drug." He says there's a 50–50 chance it can save your loved one's life. Would it be reasonable to try it, even if there were some expense? And what if it were free? Couldn't one conclude that it is entirely reasonable to try it and unreasonable not to?

Here's another analogy: Suppose you're at work and you hear a report that your house is on fire and your children inside. You don't know whether the report is true or false. What is the reasonable thing to do? Do you ignore the report, or do you take the time to check it out, either by going home or by phoning in?

"No reasonable person," wrote Pascal, "will be in doubt in such cases. Deciding whether to believe in God is a case like these. It is therefore the height of folly not to 'bet' on God, even if you have no certainty, no proof, no guarantee that your bet will win."

Śrīla Prabhupāda agreed with Pascal on this point. In *Dialectic Spiritualism: A Vedic View of Western Philosophy,* a series of dialogues between Prabhupāda and some of his disciples, he is apprised of Pascal's Wager. Here is the substance of the exchange:

> **Disciple:** Pascal claims that by faith we have to make a forced option, or what he calls a religious wager. We either have to cast our lot on the side of God – in which case we have nothing to lose in this life and everything to gain in the next – or we deny God and jeopardize our eternal position.
> **Prabhupada:** That is our argument. If there are two people, and neither has experience of God, one may say that there is no God, and the other may say that there is God. So both must be given a chance. The one who says there is no God dismisses the whole case, but the one who says there is a God must become cautious. He cannot work irresponsibly. If there is a God, he cannot run risks. Actually, both are taking risks because neither knows for certain that there is a God. However, it is preferable that one believe.

Disciple: Pascal says there is a fifty-fifty chance.
Prabhupada: Yes, so take the fifty percent chance in favor.
Disciple: Pascal also advocated that. We have nothing to lose and everything to gain.
Prabhupada: Yes. We also advise people to chant Hare Kṛṣṇa. Since you have nothing to lose and everything to gain, why not chant?

Of course, Pascal's Wager is not the best way to approach God. Obviously, if one has an inborn appreciation for God and serves Him out of natural love and devotion, that's best. If not, one should develop the sense of loving God by following the recommendations of one who does love God, along with the advice given by the scriptures and the sages. But, as the *Bhagavad-gītā* (chapter 12) tells us, people are rarely spontaneous lovers of God. Second best, says Lord Kṛṣṇa, is to fix one's mind on God. And if one can't do that, then one should follow the regulative principles of an established religious path. This would be Pascal's advice, too. In this way, the *Gītā* offers many options for those of us not born with a natural or innate love of God.

To understand Pascal's wager, it helps to understand its background. Pascal lived in a time of great skepticism. He was a Christian apologist looking for a way to explain God to skeptical peers. He saw faith and reason as two ladders to the Divine. What remaining options were there for those bereft of these ladders?

"Could there be a third ladder," he questioned, "out of the pit of unbelief and into the light of belief?"

Pascal's Wager claims to be that third ladder. Pascal was well aware that it was a low ladder.

"If your belief in God emerges as a bet," he wrote, "that is certainly not a deep, mature, or adequate faith. But it is something, it is a start, it is enough to dam the tide of atheism."

The Wager appeals not to a high ideal, like higher echelons of faith, hope, love, or even proof, but to a low one: the instinct for self-preservation, the desire to be happy and not unhappy. Bet on

God and you'll be happy; don't, and you won't. That's what it amounts to.

Counterarguments

Of course, atheistic philosophers are naturally critical of Pascal's Wager. The first problem, they say, is that the Wager implies the necessity of making a choice. But in fact, say Pascal's critics, we don't really have to. We can just adhere to the principle of agnosticism and admit that we don't really know if God exists or not. We can live our days with this lack of certainty. Period.

But on the battlefield of life, one simply must choose to go one way or the other. Consider Arjuna, the hero of the *Bhagavad-gītā*. At the onset of a civil war, right there on the battlefield he said, "I'm not going to fight." Like Arjuna, we sometimes pretend there is no battle, that we can live our lives without answering to one course of action or another, that we can live our lives without consequence. Clearly, this sort of denial is not advantageous. In Arjuna's case, armies were arrayed, waiting for battle. He had to choose. Pascal says we must bet for God or against Him, and this bet will determine exactly how we live our life, for better or for worse. One can be a good person without God, says Pascal, but it is far less likely.

Another problem put forward by critics of Pascal's Wager is that it focuses on accepting the God of Christianity, along with His rules as given through the biblical tradition. But why, they wonder, should the wager be that narrow? What if I bet on the Christian conception of God but that conception turns out to be wrong? What if God is someone else, with a whole other set of rules?

The fact is that God Himself may be unknowable in all His fullness, but His laws are certainly within our range of knowledge. Moral law and, higher, spiritual law are no secret to humanity. Despite what some may think, God's commandments vary little from religion to religion. *Sanatāna-dharma,* or the eternal function of the soul, is a thread that connects the mystical essence of religion. And the science of God focuses in on that. Kṛṣṇa consciousness teaches that betting on God is the prerogative of the human form of life. Pascal's Wager – even if only a fifty-fifty chance that God exists – is a wise choice.

God Is a Safe Bet

If God does not exist, it doesn't matter how you wager, for there is nothing to win after death and nothing to lose as well. But if God does exist, your only chance of winning eternal happiness is to believe – and to act on that belief – and your only chance of losing it is to refuse to believe.

But is it worth the price? This is the real question. What must be given up to wager that God exists? Let us remind ourselves that whatever we give up is only finite, and, as Pascal would say, it is most reasonable to wager something finite on the chance of winning something infinite. That's what the theistic enterprise is all about. Even if you have to give up certain deep-rooted habits or pleasures to wager on God, doesn't the possibility of a higher happiness make it worth it in the end? Patrick Glynn, mentioned earlier, deals with this at some length:

> Of course, the touchy issue here concerns what those who opt for belief must sacrifice in this life: Revelation teaches that they must, in Pascal's words, "curtail" their "passions." Pascal tried to minimize this sacrifice by pointing to the purely rational benefits of a life lived in conformity with the moral law. "Now, what harm will you come by," he wrote, "in making this choice? You will be faithful, honest, humble, grateful, generous, a sincere friend, truthful. Certainly, you will not enjoy those pernicious delights – glory and luxury; but will you not experience others?" The atheist and agnostic position has always been that Pascal had soft-pedaled the sacrifice end of the bargain. In giving up the pleasures

> and glories that religion teaches us to forgo, so the atheist argument has run, we are indeed sacrificing much. But modern research in psychology makes clear that the morally unrestrained life is not worth living. The crowning irony is this: Even if their beliefs were to be proved illusions, religiously committed people lead happier and healthier lives, as numerous studies show.
>
> But the larger point to recognize is that the modern secular psychological paradigm – the effort to give a complete account of the workings of the human mind without reference to God or spirit – has crumbled. Modernity failed to achieve its ambition of a comprehensive, materialistic alternative to the religious understanding of the human condition. A purely secular view of human mental life has been shown to fail not just at the theoretical, but also at the practical, level. The last thing that Freud would have predicted as the outcome of more than a half century's scientific psychological research and therapeutic experience was the rediscovery of the soul.

A God conscious life has much to offer, with spiritual bliss superseding any and all hardships. Sure, devotees rise early, commit to regulated chanting, and follow certain restrictive principles, like no meat-eating, no intoxication, no illicit sex, and no gambling. But these accoutrements of devotional life are not as hard as they seem, and they get easier as the years pass.

Actually, research shows that these things are good for you. Rising early and being regulated in one's habits are good for health, and so is vegetarianism and refraining from intoxication. Learning how to meditate on Kṛṣṇa's names and contemplating the philosophy of Kṛṣṇa consciousness are good for the brain, stimulating in ways that material pleasure can't even approach. Associating with devotees means being with the best people in the world. I've come to love many of my copractitioners, for they exhibit higher qualities and are some of the best people I've ever met. And chanting the holy name in *kīrtana* – at home, at the temple, or in the streets – has to be the highest pleasure known to man! The spoils of faith definitely outweigh the difficulties of devotion. And if Pascal were here today, he would clearly have reason to increase his odds.

Chapter Eight

Vedic Principles for Modern Life

Dharma – Nature, Duty, and Divine Service

The Meaning of Dharma According to A. C. Bhaktivedanta Swami Prabhupāda

Graham M. Schweig, PhD

The concept of dharma *is difficult to translate into Western terms, but* dharma *is interwoven through all aspects of life. Understanding it, therefore, is essential to deep spiritual practice.*

~

The concept of *dharma* is of central importance in Vaiṣṇava philosophy and practice. So important is the concept that His Divine Grace A. C. Bhaktivedanta Swami Prabhupāda actually defines the central teaching of Vaiṣṇava philosophy, *bhakti,* in terms of *dharma.* Therefore, if one desires to understand *bhakti,* an understanding of *dharma* is essential. The purpose of this study is to examine the dimensions of *dharma* that contribute to an understanding of the genuine experience of *bhakti.*

The concept of *dharma* is difficult for the Westerner to understand. Many a student and scholar of Indian religion and philosophy has failed to arrive at a full sense of its meaning and has put forward incomplete and faulty interpretations, thus demonstrating *dharma's* seeming foreignness. Because the West has no experience that is the equivalent of *dharma,* we have neither a direct nor adequate English translation of the word. To account for the complexity of this concept, and for the difficulty Westerners have in understanding it, I will analyze the various dimensions of *dharma* as they are exhibited in the extensive writings and translations of Śrīla Prabhupāda.

The Problem of Translation

The various specific meanings of *dharma,* which emerge through the context in which the word is found, reveal the richness of the concept and will gradually introduce us to a unique experience. In his writings, Śrīla Prabhupāda often translates *dharma* simply as "religion." But he indicates that he uses this particular translation for convenience and for want of a better single English term, and he expresses dissatisfaction with a translation that could be misleading. In the introduction to his translation of the *Bhagavad-gītā,* Śrīla Prabhupāda notes that the word *religion* "conveys the idea of faith, and faith may change." If a person's religion can change, then it is not eternal but temporary, and therefore material. Thus in his introduction to the *Gītā* he cautions the reader that *dharma* translated as "religion" is intended to mean truly spiritual religion, which is eternal, changeless.

At the same time, Śrīla Prabhupāda also mentions that the word *dharma* appears sometimes in the traditional Hindu context of the four *puruṣarthas,* or standard, worldly aims of life: *dharma* (religiosity), *artha* (economic development), *kāma* (sense gratification), and *mokṣa* (liberation). Here Śrīla Prabhupāda translates *dharma* as "mundane religion." He rejects this sense of *dharma* for the same reason that he objects to the sense of religion as "changeable faith." In his commentary he explains that *dharma* here means simply the pursuit of materialistic interests. He explains that this *dharma* is embraced by a *phalākāṅkṣī,* or one desirous of the fruits of his labor, or by a *rājasī,* or a passionate person. *Dharma* in the specific context of the *puruṣarthas* is always temporary and mundane, and so Śrīla Prabhupāda always distinguishes between *dharma* in this context and *dharma* in its other contexts. Religion interpreted as mere "religious faith" is practically the same as *dharma* in the mundane *puruṣarthas* context, and therefore he is careful to distinguish between ordinary religion and genuine *dharma*.

We may also understand *dharma* by examining religion that is considered not *dharma*. Śrīla Prabhupāda describes this kind of irreligion as *kaitava-dharma*, which he translates as "religious activities that are materially motivated." *Śrīmad-Bhāgavatam* further qualifies *kaitava-dharma* as five kinds of irreligion, or *vidharma*. *Vidharma* refers not just to the materialistic "religion" of the *puruṣarthas*, but to a complete misuse or distortion of religion.

Less ambiguous than the translation "religion" is the translation "religious principles" or "the principles of religion." Śrīla Prabhupāda uses this translation of *dharma* more frequently. This slightly expanded translation conveys the sense of religion that is unchanging, that is intrinsic to human existence. However, even this translation of *dharma* does not fully reveal the complexity and depth that *dharma* has in the writings of Śrīla Prabhupāda. Although he uses convenient English terms for the purposes of translation, and although the context in which *dharma* is found does surely contribute to its sense, he does not rely on these simple translations to convey the full meaning that *dharma* has in Vaiṣṇava philosophy. The struggle in translation merely gives us a clue as to *dharma's* profundity. Now let us examine the various ways in which *dharma* functions philosophically in the thought of Śrīla Prabhupāda.

The Ontological Foundation of Dharma

An analysis of *dharma* in terms of its ontological, sociological, and theological dimensions is justified, because the word takes on many prefixes that indicate these levels of meaning. These prefixed meanings also are often implied by the context within which the word *dharma* alone is found. However, we will find that the ontological analysis demonstrates a common denominator in all these meanings of *dharma*, providing an underlying meaning upon which other meanings are built. The ontological, sociological, and theological levels, on which *dharma* functions in intricate ways, are all collapsed into the single word *dharma*. Thus the complexity of the concept can be seen in the various ways in which the word is applied in Vaiṣṇava philosophy.

Śrīla Prabhupāda establishes the ontological foundation of *dharma* first by referring to the word's etymological root.* He states, "*Dharma* refers to that which is constantly existing with the particular object." He illustrates this point with the metaphor of fire: the constituent qualities of fire are heat and light, without which fire could not exist as fire. "The warmth of fire is inseparable from fire; therefore warmth is called the *dharma*, or nature, of fire." Thus the *dharma* of the living being is that which is inseparable from it, that which is his essential nature and eternal quality. It is that which "sustains one's existence." What, then, is the *dharma* of the living being?

As Śrīla Prabhupāda explains, the very *dharma* (or essential characteristic and occupation) of the living being is service. "Service" presupposes action, and the *Bhagavad-gītā* states that it is impossible for the living being to cease from action even for a moment. Commenting on this verse, Śrīla Prabhupāda says that "it is the nature of the soul to be always active." Furthermore, he observes that all actions performed by living beings are ultimately service, and that "every living creature is engaging in the service of something else." So characteristic is the quality of service that it is seen to be the innate tendency of all living beings, an "essential part of living energy." Thus "service" is presented as an irreducible quality of life.

* The verbal root of *dharma* is *dhṛ*, which means "to hold," "to bear," "to support," "to sustain," and so on.

It is "service" itself that is the *sanātana-dharma*, or "eternal" religion, of the living entity. In the *Śrī Caitanya-caritāmṛta*, too, Lord Caitanya states that the *svarūpa*, or constitutional position, of the living being is the rendering of service to God. From this statement, Śrīla Prabhupāda deduces that there is no living being who does not render service, and that at no time does the living being stop rendering service.

> If we analyze this statement of Lord Caitanya's, we can easily see that every living being is constantly engaged in rendering service to another living being... A serves B master, B serves C master, C serves D master, and so on. In this way we can see that no living being is exempt from rendering service to other living beings, and therefore we can safely conclude that service is the constant companion of the living being and that the rendering of service is the eternal religion of the living being.

The living being's *dharma* of service is not just in relation to other living beings, but is related ultimately to God, or the complete whole. *Dharma* as service refers to that metaphysical position of the living beings as very small parts of the complete whole, or God. If the living being does not consciously participate in, with knowledge of, the complete whole, then its life becomes incomplete:

> [L]iving beings are parts and parcels of the complete whole, and if they are severed from the complete whole, the illusory representation of completeness cannot fully satisfy them. The completeness of human life can only be realized when one engages in the service of the complete whole. All services in this world – whether social, political, communal, international, or even interplanetary – will remain incomplete until they are dovetailed with the complete whole. When everything is dovetailed with the complete whole, the attached parts and parcels also become complete in themselves.

The incompleteness experienced by living beings indicates that they strive for completeness, and this is achieved through a "dovetailing" of service with the complete whole. The living entity's full and conscious participation in activities that harmoniously serve the whole is service.

The Sociological Dimensions of Dharma

The Hierarchical Organization of Human Service

The different types of actions that humans perform are dovetailed with the complete whole through the function of *dharma* in the socio-ethical system called *varṇāśrama-dharma.* This system gradually elevates human beings to conscious participation in the complete whole. Here *dharma* encompasses the full range of human duties and actions in the world in relation to the elevation of the soul to perfection.

Dharma, or "occupational duty," as Śrīla Prabhupāda most often translates it in the context of *varṇāśrama,* is the organization of the various types of human service for the ultimate aim of perfecting that service characteristic. The principle is that one attains perfection by performing one's proper work. One accomplishes this first by identifying the particular nature of his own service, or *sva-dharma,* according to his particular psychophysical condition and harmoniously accommodating it into the total scheme of a God-centered society.

Service is qualified according to progressive stages of life and principal categories of work. The four stages of life, or *āśramas,* consist of a student stage, a working stage in married life, a stage of withdrawal from both work and household life, and a last stage of complete renunciation. The *varṇas,* which come into play in the second stage of *āśrama* (the household stage), are four basic classes or categories of practical work: the teaching class, the administrative and martial class, the professional class, and the working class, which serves the first three classes. The *varṇa* and *āśrama* of a particular person are determined by that person's qualities, or *guṇa,* and by the nature of his past and present activities, or karma.

The *varṇāśrama-dharma* is an arrangement of classes of human service according to people's various qualities and activities that directly reflect various degrees or levels of awareness of the complete whole. Śrīla Prabhupāda explains that "a living being is meant for service activities, and his desires are centered on such a service attitude…The perfection of such a service attitude is attained only by transferring the desire of service from matter to spirit…" As our service becomes gradually directed away from matter toward pure spirit and our desires become completely purified, we progress to higher occupational duties. The different occupational duties indicated by the *varṇas* correspond to different stages of our evolving consciousness of the complete whole. For example, the development of consciousness of the public administrator is greater than that of the professional, and the latter's development of consciousness is greater than that of the simple laborer. The teaching class, or *brāhmaṇa* class, have the most developed consciousness, because to teach they have to realize the complete whole, or Brahman.

The *varṇāśrama-dharma* system presupposes the realities of karma and the transmigration of the soul; a person can improve his human status of activities by performing his proper occupational duties in this life, thereby qualifying himself for higher or more advanced activities in the next human birth. "The system of the *sanātana-dharma* institution is so made that the follower is trained for the better next life without any chance that the human life will be spoiled."

Universal Characteristics of Society

It is important to note that in the above quotation *varṇāśrama-dharma* is called the "*sanātana-dharma* institution." This expresses still another important philosophical understanding about *varṇ-*

āśrama. Here Śrīla Prabhupāda indicates the eternal function of the *varṇāśrama* sociological principle, describing the very *dharma* of human society itself:

> No one can stop the system of *varṇa* and *āśrama,* or the castes and divisions. For example, whether or not one accepts the name *brāhmaṇa,* there is a class in society that is known as the intelligent class and that is interested in spiritual understanding and philosophy. Similarly, there is a class of men who are interested in administration and in ruling others. In the Vedic system these martially spirited men are called *kṣatriyas*. Similarly, everywhere there is a class of men who are interested in economic development, business, industry, and making money; they are called *vaiśyas*. And there is another class who are neither intelligent nor martially spirited nor endowed with the capacity for economic development but who simply can serve others. They are called *śūdras,* or the laborer class. This system is *sanātana* – it comes from time immemorial, and it will continue in the same way. There is no power in the world that can stop it.

Because *varṇāśrama-dharma* was created by God it can never be destroyed, although it may be distorted or perverted, as in the present-day caste system.

Varṇāśrama-dharma is carefully distinguished from the present caste system found in India, where a person's *varṇa* and *āśrama* are decided solely by his birth. At present, even if a person born into a family of laborers acquires the qualities of a learned *brāhmaṇa,* still, according to the present caste system, that person must remain a laborer. But Śrīla Prabhupāda states that a person's *varṇāśrama-dharma* must be determined by his present qualities and that such an intelligent person should take up the appropriate *varṇa* despite a familial orientation toward a different *varṇa*. This principle is confirmed in *Śrīmad-Bhāgavatam*.

The Paradoxical Nature of Varṇāśrama-dharma

Although Śrīla Prabhupāda advocates the *varṇāśrama-dharma* system as a means of gradual spiritual advancement, he states that in the present age the perfect practice of *varṇāśrama-dharma* cannot take place:

> The purpose of work is to please Viṣṇu. Unfortunately people have forgotten this. *Varṇāśrama-dharma,* the Vedic system of society, is therefore very important in that it is meant to give human beings a chance to perfect their lives by pleasing Kṛṣṇa. Unfortunately, the *varṇāśrama-dharma* system has been lost in this age... Although we may try to revive the perfect *varṇāśrama* system, it is not possible in this age.

Not only is the *varṇāśrama* system impractical for this age but it is neither entirely nor ultimately necessary: "*Varṇāśrama-dharma* is the systematic institution for advancing in worship of Viṣṇu. However, if one directly engages in the process of devotional service to the Supreme Personality of Godhead, it may not be necessary to undergo the disciplinary system of *varṇāśrama-dharma.*"

We can transcend *varṇāśrama-dharma* by attaining the goal of *varṇāśrama-dharma,* which is the full and direct service to God. However, transcending *varṇāśrama-dharma* does not necessarily entail the renunciation of the social system. We find that even when the goal of *varṇāśrama-dharma* (knowing and pleasing God) is reached, the system is still utilized, although the distinctions between services become unnecessary when all the social orders are completely absorbed in satisfying God:

> Everyone's aim should be to satisfy the Supreme Personality of Godhead by engaging his mind in thinking always of Kṛṣṇa, his words in always offering prayers to the Lord or preaching about the glories of the Lord, and his body in executing the service required to satisfy the Lord... In exe-

> cuting the prescribed duties of life, no one is higher or lower; there are such divisions as "higher" or "lower," but since there is actually a common interest – to satisfy the Supreme Personality of Godhead – there are no distinctions between them.

The devotee of God (or, the Vaiṣṇava) transcends all service distinctions but retains his position in *varṇāśrama-dharma* because he is fully satisfying God in that position. Recognizing his particular psychophysical qualities and limitations, he transcends them by engaging them in service to God, thus fulfilling the spiritual purpose of *varṇāśrama-dharma*. Conversely, one who ignores his nature and qualities becomes unconsciously dominated and limited by them, causing future bondage in the material world.

Another aspect of transcending *varṇāśrama-dharma* is that once a person is completely purified he can take up any *varṇa* for the service of God, whereas ordinarily, while still undergoing purification from material conditioning, a person should perform only his own duty. Paraśurāma and Viśvamitra are given as examples of those who, though originally of one *varṇa*, at times acted in another.

Varṇāśrama-dharma is rejected in the discussion between Lord Caitanya and Rāmānanda Rāya. Here Lord Caitanya asks about the ultimate goal of life. Rāmānanda Rāya suggests that it is the execution of prescribed duties to awaken God consciousness, and he quotes the *Viṣṇu Purāṇa*: "The Supreme Personality of Godhead, Lord Viṣṇu, is worshiped by the proper execution of prescribed duties in the system of *varṇa* and *āśrama*. There is no other way to satisfy the Supreme Personality of Godhead. One must be situated in the institution of the four *varṇas* and *āśramas*."

Commenting on Lord Caitanya's response to Rāmānanda Rāya, Śrīla Prabhupāda states, "The system of *varṇāśrama* is more or less based on moral and ethical principles. There is very little realization of the Transcendent as such, and Lord Śrī Caitanya Mahāprabhu rejected it as superficial and asked Rāmānanda Rāya to go further into the matter." It is only when Rāmananda Rāya suggests the giving up of all occupational duties in order to render service directly to God that Lord Caitanya is satisfied.

Although Lord Caitanya rejected *varṇāśrama* as external, we know from the *Śrī Caitanya-caritāmṛta* that He rigorously upheld the practice of recognizing the *varṇas* and *āśramas* in His own dealings and advocated the maintenance of etiquette between them. This paradox is also found in the *Bhagavad-gītā:* Arjuna is told to take up his position as a warrior and fight in the battle. But at the very climax of Kṛṣṇa's instruction, Arjuna is told to abandon all varieties of *dharma,* or occupational duties, and to come directly to Him as his only shelter. Yet we know from the *Bhagavad-gītā* and the *Mahabharata's* account of the great war at Kurukṣetra that Arjuna *does* in fact take up his occupation as a warrior and fight the battle. Does this mean Arjuna disregards Kṛṣṇa's paramount instruction to take complete shelter of Him? No, not at all. Arjuna's example epitomizes the paradoxical relationship between the perfect stage of surrender to God and to occupational duty, or the *dharma* of *varṇāśrama.* We know from Śrīla Prabhupāda's writings that the perfection of *dharma* as religion is complete and utter surrender to God along with complete engagement in service to Him, and that the whole purpose of *varṇāśrama-dharma* is to raise a person gradually to this perfection. But once a person attains this perfection and has given up everything (including all occupational duties) in surrender to God, only then does he have the opportunity to enter back into various positions of *varṇāśrama* for the sole purpose of pleasing and serving God. The principle is that a person must first reject occupations or *dharmas* for God, and then he must take them up, after he has completely given himself to God, in order to use them perfectly. Śrīla Prabhupāda calls this *daiva-varṇāśrama-dharma.* Thus the *varṇāśrama-dharma* system organizes the full range of human service or activities while a person is still in a materially conditioned state, and it also may organize the various activities performed directly for God. Therefore *varṇāśrama-dharma* is never fully rejected – on the contrary, it is used both for the gradual attainment of spiritual perfection and also for assisting and expressing the direct service of God.

The Theological Dimensions of Dharma

The "Order" of God

We have discussed the ontological dimension of *dharma* as "service," which Śrīla Prabhupāda calls *"sanātana-dharma."* We have also seen in *varṇāśrama-dharma* that the irreducible factor of "service" is qualified according to the natural, universal divisions of life and work, and *dharma* here is "occupational duty." We saw how these qualified states of service, representing different levels of spiritual development and awareness, were organized for the aim of perfecting service, and how, once having perfected service, a person naturally performs an occupational duty to please God. This is called *daiva-varṇāśrama-dharma,* where *dharma* consists of one's "divine service." There is still another sense in which the word *dharma* is used, and this involves its theological dimension.

At a theological level, *dharma* takes on a different sense as *bhāgavata-dharma,* or the *dharma* of God. According to Śrīla Prabhupāda, *bhāgavata-dharma* offers the "simplest definition" of *dharma,* defining it as "the order of the Supreme Being." The meaning of *bhāgavata-dharma* is further revealed by a key statement from *Śrīmad-Bhāgavatam: dharmaṁ tu sākṣād bhagavat-praṇītam.* This says that actual *dharma,* or religion, is directly (*sakṣat*) manifested from God. (And that is the literal meaning of *bhāgavata-dharma.*) Thus *dharma* in *bhāgavata-dharma,* as "order," has the distinct character of *śabda-brahma,* or the revelation of God.

Śrīla Prabhupāda repeatedly emphasizes the definition of *dharma* as "the order of God," demonstrating what religion is and what it is not. He insists that "we cannot manufacture *dharma.*" He reasons that "no one can manufacture state laws; they are given by the government." Similarly, *dharma* cannot be manufactured but must be revealed by God. "In *bhāgavata-dharma* there is no question of 'what you believe' and 'what I believe.' Everyone must believe in the Supreme Lord and carry out His orders." It is on the authority of God's "order," or revelation, that *dharma* is based. This kind of *dharma* can be transmitted only by God's representatives.

Bhāgavata-dharma is not sectarian religion; it is the universal religion, which shows how everything is connected with God. Śrīla Prabhupāda states, "*Bhāgavata-dharma* has no contradictions. Conceptions of 'your religion' and 'my religion' are completely absent from *bhāgavata-dharma*," and therefore one's identity as a "Hindu" or "Christian" or "Buddhist" or whatever is superficial, because these identities do not necessarily mean that one is performing *bhāgavata-dharma*, or fulfilling the order of God. However, Śrīla Prabhupāda accepts the diversity of religions: "Since everyone has a different body and mind, different types of religions are needed." He also explains that different religions exist because of disagreements based on these limited material conceptions and differences. But "the Absolute Truth is one, and when one is situated in the Absolute Truth, there is no disagreement." On the spiritual platform we find no differences or disagreements, simply a "oneness in religion."

The "order of God" is defined more specifically as the order to live according to the instruction of God. In the discussion of *bhāgavata-dharma* as supreme religion, verse 18.66 from the *Bhagavad-gītā* is usually presented, because therein the necessity of "surrender to God" is declared by Kṛṣṇa Himself: *sarva-dharmān parityajya mām ekaṁ śaraṇaṁ vraja* – "Abandon all varieties of religion and just surrender unto Me." Śrīla Prabhupāda points out that the word *ekam,* meaning "one," shows that religion is ultimately one. The very unity of religion is realized in *bhakti,* wherein one finds the full realization and perfection of *dharma.*

The Perfection of Service as Bhakti

Bhāgavata-dharma and *sanātana-dharma* meet in *bhakti. Bhakti* means the living entity's response to the order or message of God by consciously participating in His plan as an eternal servitor:

> Factually we are related to the Supreme Lord in service. The Supreme Lord is the supreme enjoyer, and we living entities are His servitors. We are created for His enjoyment, and if we participate in that eternal enjoyment with the Supreme Personality of Godhead, we become completely happy... It is not possible for the living entity to be happy without rendering transcendental loving service unto the Supreme Lord.

This participation of the living being as an eternal servitor of God is called yoga; it consists of the connection of the living entity to the supreme Deity. This connection, or yoga, is made possible by the revelation of God, or *bhāgavata-dharma,* which Śrīla Prabhupāda says "captures the presence of the Supreme," and the living being's response of surrender and service to God. This connection is called *bhakti-yoga.*

Many Western scholars, and even many Hindus, translate the word *bhakti* most often as "devotion," and sometimes as "love" or "worship," which themselves are not unacceptable but may render the word ambiguously. Too often the Westerner takes these translations and relegates the experience of *bhakti* either to the mere subjective and emotional or to the realm of peculiar phenomena in the history of religions. But Śrīla Prabhupāda's contrasting translation of *bhakti* as "devotional service" is truly significant, because it indicates that *bhakti* is not an isolated emotional experience but rather a genuine cognitive experience in direct response to the supreme reality.

It is important to note that in the translation "devotional service," "devotion" is not the primary element but qualifies the substantive "service." But *bhakti* is not just any service; rather, it is devotional service, service that corresponds to the perfection of service itself, or the highest service: *sa vai puṁsāṁ paro dharmo yato bhaktir adhokṣaje. Bhakti,* therefore, is the supreme occupation (*paro dharmaḥ*) of the living entity because it is service performed directly in relation to God (*adhokṣaje*). In the above verse, *bhakti* is correlated with *dharma* in its most essential and highest way. *Bhakti*, indeed, is therefore the essence of *dharma*.

Conclusion

Thus we have seen that *dharma* finds its highest expression in *bhakti*, devotional service to God. We have also seen that *bhakti* is defined in terms of *dharma* precisely because *bhakti* is the perfection of service – and *dharma* indeed does provide the full philosophical backdrop within which the experience of *bhakti* is properly understood. Through an examination of the ontological, sociological, and theological dimensions of *dharma*, we have been able to see how the concept of *dharma* functions in complex ways, signifying an understanding of reality that is profoundly comprehensive and virtually untranslatable, and therefore unfamiliar to the West. In the end, *dharma* as a concept is meant not merely to provide an exercise in philosophical discourse but to be personally realized, and this is possible through the practice of *bhakti*.

Finding Peace in Kṛṣṇa's Service

A conversation between His Divine Grace
A. C. Bhaktivedanta Swami Prabhupāda and John Lennon

In 1969, Śrīla Prabhupāda and a group of his young disciples lived at Tittenhurst with John Lennon and Yoko Ono. In this conversation Śrīla Prabhupāda honors John's interest in world peace and explains how people can become peaceful by understanding three things.

~

Śrīla Prabhupāda: You are anxious to bring about peace in the world. I've read some of your statements and they show me that you're anxious to do something Actually, every saintly person should be anxious to bring peace to the world. But we must know the process. In *Bhagavad-gītā,* Lord Kṛṣṇa explains how to achieve peace:

bhoktāraṁ yajña-tapasāṁ
sarva-loka-maheśvaram
suhṛdaṁ sarva-bhūtānām
jñātvā māṁ śāntim ṛcchati

People can become peaceful by knowing three things. If people perfectly understand only three things, then they'll become peaceful. What are they? First of all, Lord Kṛṣṇa says that He is the real enjoyer of all the sacrifices, austerities, and penances that people undertake to perfect their lives. For instance, your own musical activities are also a form of austerity. Your songs have become popular because you have undergone some austerities. You have come to perfection, but that required some penances and austerities. Scientific discoveries also require austerities. In fact, anything valuable requires austerity. If one works very devoutly and painstakingly, one becomes successful.

That is called *yajña,* or sacrifice. It is also called *tapasya,* or penance. So Kṛṣṇa says that He is the enjoyer of the results of your *tapasya.* He claims, "The result of your *tapasya* should come to Me. Then you'll be satisfied."

The second thing people should remember is that Kṛṣṇa is the supreme proprietor. People are claiming, "This is my England," "This is my India," "This is my Germany," "This is my China." No! Everything belongs to God, Kṛṣṇa. Not only this planet belongs to Kṛṣṇa, but all other planets in the universe.

Still, we have divided even this planet into so many nations. Originally, this planet was not divided. From the historical accounts in the *Mahābhārata* we understand that the whole planet was once ruled by a single emperor who resided in India in the place called Hastināpura, the site of modern Delhi. Even up to five thousand years ago there was only one king, Mahārāja Parīkṣit. The whole planet was under one flag and was called Bhārata-varṣa. But gradually Bhārata-varṣa has become smaller and smaller and smaller. For instance, very recently, just twenty years ago, the remaining portion of Bhārata-varṣa, now called India, was divided into Pakistan and Hindustan. Actually, India was one, but now it has been reduced by the partition. This dividing is going on.

But actually this whole planet is God's place. It is nobody else's place. How can we claim possession? For example, you have given me this place to stay in. If I stay for one week and then claim, "Oh, this is *my* room," is that a very nice thing? There will immediately be some disagreement, some trouble. Rather, I should recognize the actual fact, namely, that you have kindly spared this room. By your permission I am living here comfortably. And when it is necessary for me to leave, I shall go.

Similarly, we all came here into the kingdom of God empty-handed and we go empty-handed. So how can we claim that this is my property, this is my country, this is my world, this is my planet? Why do we make such claims? Is it not insanity? So Lord Kṛṣṇa says, *sarva-loka-maheśvaram:* "I am the Supreme Lord of every place."

Thirdly, we should always remember that Kṛṣṇa is the real friend of every living entity and that He is sitting as a friend within everyone's heart. He's such a nice friend. In this material world, we make friendships, but they break up. Or my friend lives somewhere, and I live somewhere else. But Kṛṣṇa is such a nice friend that He is living within – within me and within my heart. He is the best friend of all living beings. He's not just the friend of a select few, but He is dwelling even within the heart of the most insignificant creature as Paramātmā, or Supersoul.

So if these three things are understood clearly, then one becomes peaceful. This is the real peace formula.

In *Bhagavad-gītā* the Lord also says, "Whatever action is performed by a great man, common men follow in his footsteps. And whatever standards he sets by exemplary acts, all the world pursues." The idea is that if something is accepted by the leading persons the ordinary persons follow. If the leading persons say it is all right, then others also accept it. So by the grace of God, Kṛṣṇa, you are leaders. Thousands of young people follow you. They like you. And if you give them something actually spiritual, the face of the world will change.

The Kṛṣṇa consciousness movement is not newly manufactured. From the historical point of view, it is at least five thousand years old. The *Bhagavad-gītā,* which is the basis of Kṛṣṇa consciousness, was spoken by Lord Kṛṣṇa five thousand years ago. Of course, *Bhagavad-gītā* is generally regarded as an Indian religious book. But it isn't – it's not simply Indian or Hindu. The *Bhagavad-gītā* is meant for all people of the world, and not even just for human beings but for all other living creatures as well. In chapter fourteen the Lord says, "It should be understood that all species of life, O son of Kuntī, are made possible by birth in this material nature and that I am the seed-giving father."

This indicates that the eternal living entity appears in varieties of temporary, material forms, just like we here now have the forms of ladies, gentlemen, and young men. We all have different forms. This whole world is full of varieties of life, but Kṛṣṇa says, *ahaṁ bīja-pradaḥ pitā:* "I am the father of all of them." *Pitā* means "father." So the Lord claims all living entities as His sons.

Some people may say that Kṛṣṇa is Indian, Kṛṣṇa is Hindu, or Kṛṣṇa is something else. But no – Kṛṣṇa is actually the Supreme Personality of Godhead, the seed-giving father of all living things on this planet. This Kṛṣṇa consciousness movement was started by Kṛṣṇa Himself. Therefore, it isn't sectarian; it's meant for everyone.

And in *Bhagavad-gītā* Kṛṣṇa describes the universal process for worshiping Him: *man-manā bhava mad-bhakto, mad-yājī māṁ namaskuru.* "Engage your mind always in thinking of Me and become My devotee. Offer obeisances to Me and worship Me. Being completely absorbed in Me, surely you will come to Me."

Kṛṣṇa says, You should always think of Me: let your mind always be engaged in Me, Kṛṣṇa. Just become My devotee. If you want to worship, just worship Me. If you want to offer respects, offer them to Me. And if you do this, then without a doubt you'll come to Me. This is a very simple method. Always think of Kṛṣṇa. There is no loss, and the gain is very great.

So if one chants Hare Kṛṣṇa, one undergoes no material loss, but gains spiritually. So why not try it? There is no expenditure. Everything has some price, but the Hare Kṛṣṇa mantra is different. Lord Kṛṣṇa and His followers in disciplic succession do not sell it; rather, they distribute it freely. We simply say to everyone, "Chant Hare Kṛṣṇa. Dance in ecstasy." It is a very nice thing.

So, I have come to your country, England, and especially here to your home to explain this Kṛṣṇa consciousness movement. It is very beneficial. You are intelligent boys. So my request to you is that you try to understand this Kṛṣṇa consciousness philosophy with all your powers of reason and argument. Kṛṣṇadāsa Kavirāja, the author of *Caitanya-caritāmṛta*, says, *śrī-kṛṣṇa-caitanya-dayā katha karaha vicāra, vicāra karile citte pāe camatkāra:* "If you are indeed interested in logic and argument, kindly apply it to the mercy of Śrī Caitanya Mahāprabhu. If you do so you will find it strikingly wonderful." So just apply your powers of judgment to the mercy of Lord Caitanya. If you scrutinize His mercy, you'll find it sublime.

We are not forcing people to accept the Kṛṣṇa consciousness movement. Rather, we are putting it before them for their judgment. Let them judge it. We are not a sectarian religious movement – Kṛṣṇa consciousness is a science. So we ask you to judge it scrutinizingly with all your intellect. And we are sure you will find it sublime. And if you find it sublime, then why not help put it before the world?

Have you read our book *Bhagavad-gītā As It Is*?

John Lennon: I've read bits of *Bhagavad-gītā*. I don't know which version it was. There are so many different translations.

Śrīla Prabhupāda: Yes, there are different translations in which the authors have given their own interpretations of the text. Therefore I have prepared our *Bhagavad-gītā As It Is*. Even Indian authors sometimes misrepresent *Bhagavad-gītā*. For instance, one prominent Indian politician tried to give his own interpretation of the *Bhagavad-gītā*. Say you have a box for a fountain pen. Everyone knows it is a fountain pen box. But someone might say, "No, it is something else. That is my interpretation." Is that very good?

Interpretation is required only when things are not understood clearly. If everybody can understand that this box is a fountain pen box, where is the necessity for interpretation? *Bhagavad-gītā* is clear; it is just like sunlight, and sunlight does not require the aid of a lamp.

dhṛtarāṣṭra uvāca
dharma-kṣetre kuru-kṣetre
samavetā yuyutsavaḥ
māmakāḥ pāṇḍavāś caiva
kim akurvata sañjaya

Dhṛtarāṣṭra uvāca means that King Dhṛtarāṣṭra, the father of Duryodhana, is asking his secretary, Sañjaya, about his sons, who are facing the Pāṇḍavas on the Battlefield of Kurukṣetra. *Māmakāḥ* means "my sons." *Pāṇḍavāḥ* refers to the sons of King Pāṇḍu, the younger brother of Dhṛtarāṣṭra. *Yuyutsavaḥ* means "with fighting spirit." So Dhṛtarāṣṭra is saying, "My sons and the sons of my younger brother Pāṇḍu are assembled on the battlefield, ready to fight each other." The place where the battle will be fought is called Kurukṣetra, which is also *dharma-kṣetra,* a place of pilgrimage. *Kim akurvata.* "Now that they have assembled at Kurukṣetra," asks Dhṛtarāṣṭra, "what will they do?" This place, Kurukṣetra, still exists in India. Have you been to India?

John Lennon: Yes, but not to that place. We went to Hrishikesh.

Śrīla Prabhupāda: Oh, Hrishikesh. Hrishikesh is also a famous place of pilgrimage. Similarly, Kurukṣetra is a place of pilgrimage near Delhi. It has been known as a place of pilgrimage since the Vedic times. In the *Vedas* it is stated, *kuru-kṣetre dharmaṁ yājayet:* "If you want to perform a religious ceremony, you should go to Kurukṣetra." Therefore Kurukṣetra is called *dharma-kṣetra,* a place of pilgrimage.

In other words, Kurukṣetra is an actual historical location. And the Pāṇḍavas and the sons of Dhṛtarāṣṭra are actual historical personalities. Their history is recorded in the *Mahābhārata.* But in spite of these facts, some people interpret *kuru-kṣetra* as "the body," and the Pāṇḍavas as "the senses." These things are going on, but we object. Why should anyone interpret *Bhagavad-gītā* like that when the facts are there, presented so clearly?

Bhagavad-gītā is a very authoritative and popular book, so unscrupulous authors try to put forward their own half-baked philosophies in the guise of commentaries on *Bhagavad-gītā*. Therefore, there are so many false and misleading interpretations of *Bhagavad-gītā* – 664 or so. Everyone thinks he can interpret the *Bhagavad-gītā* in his own way. But why? Why should this be allowed? We say, No, you cannot interpret *Bhagavad-gītā*. Otherwise, what is the authority of *Bhagavad-gītā*? The author of *Bhagavad-gītā* did not leave it to be interpreted by third-class men. The author is Kṛṣṇa, the Supreme Lord. He said everything clearly. Why should an ordinary man interpret His words? That is our objection.

Therefore, we are presenting *Bhagavad-gītā As It Is*. In *Bhagavad-gītā* you'll find very elevated philosophy and theology as well as sociology, politics, and science. Everything is there, and everything is clearly explained by Kṛṣṇa. So this Kṛṣṇa consciousness movement means to present *Bhagavad-gītā* as it is. That's all. We have not manufactured anything.

Be happy and make all others happy. This is Kṛṣṇa consciousness. *Sarve sukhena bhavantu*. That is the Vedic idea: let everyone be happy. Caitanya Mahāprabhu said the same thing. He wanted this Kṛṣṇa consciousness movement to be preached in every village and in every town of the world. It will make people happy. He foretold this. The purpose of any great mission, or of any high ideals, should be to make people happy, because in this material existence there is no happiness. That is a fact. There cannot be any happiness here.

This place is not meant for happiness. In *Bhagavad-gītā* Lord Kṛṣṇa Himself says that this world is *duḥkhālayam aśāśvatam*. *Duḥkhālayam* means it is a place of miseries, and *aśāśvatam* means it is temporary. Everything here is temporary. So you might accept that this material world is a miserable place and say, "All right, it's miserable, but I accept it." But that attitude has no value, because the material nature will not even allow you to stay here and accept the misery. This world is *aśāśvatam*, temporary. You have to leave.

But Kṛṣṇa says there is a way to end this miserable existence: "After attaining Me, the great souls, who are *yogīs* in devotion, never return to this temporary world, which is full of miseries, because they have attained the highest perfection." If somebody comes to Me, says Kṛṣṇa, then he doesn't have to return to the miserable conditions of life in the material world.

So we should understand what Kṛṣṇa is saying here. Nature is so cruel. In America, President Kennedy thought he was the most fortunate man, the happiest man. He was young, he was elected President, he had a nice wife and children, and he was respected all over the world. But within a second [*Śrīla Prabhupāda snaps his fingers*] it was all finished. His position was temporary. Now what is his condition? Where is he? If life is eternal, if the living entity is eternal, then where has he gone? What is he doing? Is he happy or is he distressed? Has he been reborn in America? In China? No one can say.

But it is a fact that as a living entity he's eternal – he's existing. That is the beginning of the *Bhagavad-gītā's* philosophy. *Na hanyate hanyamāne śarīre.* After the destruction of this body, the living entity is not destroyed: he is still there. Just like in your childhood you had a small body. That body is no more, but you still exist. So it is natural that when this body ceases to exist you will continue to exist in another body. It's not very difficult to understand. The soul is eternal and the body is temporary. That's a fact.

Therefore this present life is meant for manufacturing the next body. That is Vedic knowledge. In this life we are creating our next body. For instance, a boy may be studying very nicely in school. In this way he is creating his adult body. As a young man he will enjoy the results of his boyhood education. By education he can get a nice job, a nice house. So in this sense we can say that the young boy at school is creating his next body.

Similarly, we are all creating our next bodies according to our karma. By karma most people will take another material body. But Kṛṣṇa says it is possible to create a spiritual body so that you can come to Him. He says that those who worship Him go to His spiritual planet after death.

The whole Vedic philosophy teaches that if you want to go to a particular planet you must have a suitable body. You cannot go with this body. For instance, people are now trying to go to the moon planet. They are attempting to go with their material bodies but they cannot stay there. But Kṛṣṇa gives the process for going to other planets, and the highest planet is Kṛṣṇa's planet. You can go there. "Those who worship the demigods will take birth among the demigods; those who worship ghosts and spirits will take birth among such beings; those who worship ancestors go to the ancestors; and those who worship Me will live with Me."

One who worships Kṛṣṇa does not come back again to this miserable material condition. Why? He has attained the highest perfection, to go back to Kṛṣṇa. So this is the greatest benediction for human society, to train people to go back to Kṛṣṇa's spiritual planet.

How Work Can Be Worship

A conversation between His Divine Grace
A. C. Bhaktivedanta Swami Prabhupāda and his disciples

A karmī *works for his own sense gratification and a* bhakta *works for Kṛṣṇa's sense gratification. That is the difference between a nondevotee and a devotee.*

~

Devotee: What does Kṛṣṇa mean when He says in the *Bhagavad-gītā* that we should be desireless?

Śrīla Prabhupāda: He means that we should desire only to serve Him. Śrī Caitanya Mahāprabhu said, *na dhanaṁ na janaṁ na sundarīṁ kāvitam vā jagad-īśa kāmaye:* "I don't want wealth. I don't want followers. I don't want beautiful women." Then what does He want? "I want to serve Kṛṣṇa." It is not that He says, "I don't want this, I don't want that. Let Me become zero." No.

Devotee: The nondevotee also says he knows what he wants, but he says, "I can accomplish the same good results without Kṛṣṇa."

Śrīla Prabhupāda: Then he is a fool, because he does not know what "good results" really are. Today he is struggling very hard for one "good result," but tomorrow he'll desire something else, because he must undergo a change of body when he dies. Sometimes he's taking the body of a dog and desiring one "good result," and sometimes he's taking the body of a demigod and desiring another "good result." *Bhramatām upary adhaḥ:* he's wandering up and down the universe, just like – what is that?

Devotee: A ferris wheel.

Śrīla Prabhupāda: Yes. Sometimes he is rising to an elevated position, and then again he must come down and take the body of a dog or hog. This is going on.

brahmāṇḍa bhramite kona bhāgyavān jīva
guru-kṛṣṇa-prasāde pāya bhakti-latā-bīja

"After wandering up and down the universe for many lifetimes, one who is very fortunate comes to devotional life by the mercy of the spiritual master and Kṛṣṇa."

Devotee: Well, the nondevotee will say, "We are also doing good service. You are distributing food, and we are also distributing food. You are opening schools, and we are also opening schools."

Śrīla Prabhupāda: Yes, but we are opening schools that teach Kṛṣṇa consciousness while your schools are teaching illusion. The problem is that the rascals cannot understand the difference between *bhakti* and karma. *Bhakti looks* like karma, but it's not karma. In *bhakti* we also work, but for Kṛṣṇa's sake. That is the difference.

For example, Arjuna fought in the Battle of Kurukṣetra, but because he fought for Kṛṣṇa he is accepted as a great devotee. Kṛṣṇa told him, *bhakto 'si me ṅ priyo 'si me:* "Arjuna, you are My dear devotee." What did Arjuna do? He fought, that's all. But he fought for Kṛṣṇa. That is the secret. He did not change his fighting capacity as a warrior, but he changed his mentality. At first he was thinking, "Why shall I kill my kinsmen? Let me leave the battlefield and go to the forest and become a mendicant." But Kṛṣṇa wanted him to fight, so at last he surrendered and did it as a service for Kṛṣṇa. Not for his own sense gratification, but for Kṛṣṇa's sense gratification.

Devotee: So sense gratification is there even in devotional service?

Śrīla Prabhupāda: Yes. A *karmī* works for his own sense gratification and a *bhakta* works for Kṛṣṇa's sense gratification. That is the difference between a nondevotee and a devotee. Sense gratification is there in either case, but when you work for your personal sense gratification it is karma, and when you work for Kṛṣṇa's sense gratification it is *bhakti*. *Bhakti* and karma look similar, but the quality is different.

Another example is the behavior of the *gopīs*. Kṛṣṇa was a beautiful boy and the *gopīs* were attracted to Him. They wanted Him as their lover, and they went out from their homes in the middle of the night to dance with Him. So it appears that they acted sinfully – but they did not, because the center was Kṛṣṇa. Therefore Caitanya Mahāprabhu recommends, *ramyā kācid upāsanā vraja-vadhū-vargeṇa yā kalpitā:* "There is no better mode of worshiping Kṛṣṇa than that practiced by the *gopīs*."

But the rascals think, "Oh, this is very good. Kṛṣṇa danced in the middle of the night with other men's wives, so let us also gather some girls and dance and we will also enjoy like Kṛṣṇa." This is a gross misunderstanding of Kṛṣṇa's pastimes with the *gopīs*. To prevent this misunderstanding Śrīla Vyāsadeva has devoted nine cantos of the *Bhāgavatam* to describing Kṛṣṇa's position as the Supreme Personality of Godhead. *Then* he gives a description of Kṛṣṇa's behavior with the *gopīs*. But the rascals jump immediately to the Tenth Canto, to Kṛṣṇa's dealings with the *gopīs*. In this way they become *sahajiyās*.

Devotee: Will such persons experience a change of heart since they're somehow or other associating with Kṛṣṇa?

Śrīla Prabhupāda: No. Kaṁsa also associated with Kṛṣṇa – but as an enemy. That is not *bhakti*. *Bhakti* must be *ānukūlyena kṛṣṇānuśīlanam:* favorable devotional service. One should not imitate Kṛṣṇa or try to kill Him. That is also Kṛṣṇa consciousness, but it is not favorable and therefore it is not *bhakti*. Still, the enemies of Kṛṣṇa get salvation, because they have somehow or other thought of Kṛṣṇa. They get impersonal liberation, but they are not allowed to enter into the pastimes of Kṛṣṇa in the spiritual world. That benediction is reserved for those who practice pure loving devotion to Kṛṣṇa.

Taking to Kṛṣṇa Consciousness

His Divine Grace A. C. Bhaktivedanta Swami Prabhupāda

"Always think of Me. Become My devotee. Worship Me, and offer your homage unto Me. The result is that you will come to Me without fail. I promise you this, because you are My very dear friend."

~

In India, all scriptures and great spiritual teachers, including Śaṅkarācārya, an impersonalist, accept Kṛṣṇa as the Supreme Lord. In the beginning of his commentary on the *Bhagavad-gītā*, Śaṅkarācārya says that Nārāyaṇa is transcendental to this manifested and unmanifested creation, and in the same commentary he says that the Supreme Personality of Godhead, Nārāyaṇa, is Kṛṣṇa appearing as the son of Devakī and Vasudeva. Thus in this respect there is little difference of opinion about Kṛṣṇa. Those who are authorities, be they personalists or impersonalists, are in agreement that Kṛṣṇa is the Supreme Lord.

When Kṛṣṇa was present on this planet He proved by His activities and opulence that He is the Supreme Lord. If we are actually anxious to understand who and what the Supreme Lord is, all of the information is given in Vedic literatures. If we utilize whatever we have in our possession to understand God, Kṛṣṇa will prove that He is the Supreme Personality of Godhead. If we but accept this one fact, then all of our education is complete. It is fashionable to research to try to find out who is God, but this is not necessary. God is present, and He Himself says:

mattaḥ parataraṁ nānyat
kiñcid asti dhanañjaya
mayi sarvam idaṁ protaṁ
sūtre maṇi-gaṇā iva

"O conqueror of wealth (Arjuna), there is no truth superior to Me. Everything rests upon Me, as pearls are strung on a thread." (*Gītā* 7.7)

This information is not only given in *Bhagavad-gītā* but in other scriptures as well, and it has been accepted from the very beginning by great teachers like Śaṅkarācārya, Rāmānujācārya, Madhvācārya, Lord Caitanya, and many other stalwart authorities. Even at the present moment those who do not accept Kṛṣṇa as the Supreme Lord are accepting the knowledge given by Kṛṣṇa to Arjuna. So in this way they are accepting Kṛṣṇa indirectly. If one accepts *Bhagavad-gītā* as a great book of knowledge, he is also accepting Kṛṣṇa. There is no doubt that the Supreme Absolute Truth is Kṛṣṇa and that we have our eternal relationship with Him.

Our eternal relationship with God is *sabhājana:* God is great and we are subordinate. He is the predominator and we are the predominated. The duty of the subordinate is to please the predominator. Similarly, if we want to be happy, we must learn how to make Kṛṣṇa happy. This is the process of Kṛṣṇa consciousness.

But how is it to be understood that the Supreme Lord is satisfied by our service and labor? It is actually possible to perfect our service or occupational duty. Everyone has some service to perform according to his designations. He may be an Indian or American, Hindu, Muslim, or Christian, man, woman, *brāhmaṇa, kṣatriya, vaiśya, śūdra,* or whatever – in any case he is meant to do some sort of work, and that work is his occupational duty. Perfection of duty can be tested by seeing whether the Supreme Lord is satisfied by its execution. The Supreme Lord's satisfaction can be tested by the Lord's representative, the spiritual master. Therefore it is important to seek out a real representative of the Supreme Personality of Godhead and work under him. If he is satisfied, then we should know that the Supreme Lord is also satisfied. That is explained by Viśvanātha Cakravartī Ṭhākura:

yasya prasādād bhagavat-prasādo
yasyāprasādān na gatiḥ kuto 'pi
dhyāyaṁ stuvaṁs tasya yaśas tri-sandhyaṁ
vande guroḥ śrī-caraṇāravindam

"By the mercy of the spiritual master one is benedicted by the mercy of Kṛṣṇa. Without the grace of the spiritual master no one can make any advancement. Therefore I should always remember the spiritual master. At least three times a day I should offer my respectful obeisances unto the lotus feet of my spiritual master." (*Śrī Gurvaṣṭakam* 8)

The spiritual master is the representative of the Supreme Lord. How does he become the representative? If one says that such-and-such an object is a pair of spectacles, and if he teaches his disciple in that way, there is no mistake as to the identity of the object. The spiritual master is he who has captured the words of a particular disciplic succession. In the case given, the key word is "spectacles" – that's all. The spiritual master does not have to say anything beyond that. This is the qualification. Kṛṣṇa says, "I am the Supreme," and the spiritual master says, "Kṛṣṇa is the Supreme." It is not that to be a representative of Kṛṣṇa or to be a spiritual master one has to have any extraordinary qualification. He simply has to carry the message from the authority as it is without any personal interpretation. As soon as there is some personal interpretation, the message is lost and the instructions become offensive. A person who interprets the scriptures according to his own whims should be immediately rejected.

Once Lord Caitanya Mahāprabhu said, "You must at least have enough sense to test to find out who is a spiritual master and who is not." For instance, if we want to purchase something we must at least have some idea of what that thing is; otherwise, we will be cheated. If we want to purchase a mango from the market we must at least know what type of food a mango is and what it looks like. Similarly, we must have some preliminary knowledge of the qualifications for a bona fide spiritual master. *Bhagavad-gītā* itself gives some information about the succession of spiritual masters. Lord Śrī Kṛṣṇa says:

imaṁ vivasvate yogaṁ
proktavān aham avyayam
vivasvān manave prāha
manur ikṣvākave 'bravīt

evaṁ paramparā-prāptam
imaṁ rājarṣayo viduḥ
sa kāleneha mahatā
yogo naṣṭaḥ parantapa

sa evāyaṁ mayā te 'dya
yogaḥ proktaḥ purātanaḥ
bhakto 'si me sakhā ceti
rahasyaṁ hy etad uttamam

"I instructed this imperishable science of yoga to the sun god Vivasvān, and Vivasvān instructed it to Manu, the father of mankind, and Manu in turn instructed it to Ikṣvāku. This supreme science was thus received through the chain of disciplic succession, and the saintly kings understood it in that way. But in course of time the succession was broken, and therefore the science as it is appears to be lost. That very ancient science of the relationship with the Supreme is today told by Me to you because you are My devotee as well as My friend; therefore, you can understand the transcendental mystery of this science." (*Gītā* 4.1–3)

That original spiritual disciplic succession was broken, but now we can receive the same message by studying *Bhagavad-gītā*. In *Bhagavad-gītā* Kṛṣṇa speaks to Arjuna just as in a far distant time He spoke to the sun god. If we accept the words of Arjuna and Kṛṣṇa, it may be possible for us to understand *Bhagavad-gītā*, but if we want to interpret it in our own way, the results will be nonsensical. The best way to understand *Bhagavad-gītā* is to accept a bona fide spiritual master. This is not very difficult.

Arjuna says that he accepts all that Kṛṣṇa has said to him because Kṛṣṇa is the Supreme Personality of Godhead:

naṣṭo mohaḥ smṛtir labdhā
tvat prasādān mayācyuta
sthito 'smi gata-sandehaḥ
kariṣye vacanaṁ tava

"Arjuna said, My dear Kṛṣṇa, O infallible one, my illusion is now gone. I have regained my memory by Your mercy, and now I am fixed without any doubt, prepared to act according to Your instructions." (*Gītā* 18.73)

As Arjuna, we should accept Kṛṣṇa as the Supreme Personality of Godhead and do as He says:

yat karoṣi yad aśnāsi
yaj juhoṣi dadāsi yat
yat tapasyasi kaunteya
tat kuruṣva mad-arpaṇam

"O son of Kuntī, all that you do, all that you eat, all that you offer and give away, as well as all austerities that you may perform, should be done as an offering unto Me." (*Gītā* 9.27)

By accepting Kṛṣṇa in this spirit, we can attain complete knowledge. If, however, we do not accept Kṛṣṇa and interpret *Bhagavad-gītā* in our own way, then everything will be spoiled.

If we are sincere, we will get a sincere spiritual master by the grace of Kṛṣṇa. If, however, we want to be cheated, Kṛṣṇa will send us a cheater, and we will be cheated throughout our lives. That is actually going on. For those who do not want to understand Kṛṣṇa as He is but want to understand by dint of their own imperfect vision, Kṛṣṇa, God, remains unknown.

The whole process is to accept Kṛṣṇa and His instructions and therefore to render devotional service unto Him. It is Śrīmatī Rādhārāṇī who is the very embodiment of perfect devotional service. In the *Brahma-saṁhitā* Rādhārāṇī is described as Kṛṣṇa's expansion of His spiritual potency. In this way, She is nondifferent from Kṛṣṇa. The *gopīs,* who tend Rādhā and Kṛṣṇa, are not ordinary women or girls; they are expansions of Kṛṣṇa's pleasure potency. Rādhārāṇī and the *gopīs* should never be accepted as ordinary women; indeed, to understand their position we need the guidance of a spiritual master. If we living entities want to actually associate with Rādhārāṇī, that may be possible, although She is not an ordinary woman. We can become associates of Rādhārāṇī by qualifying ourselves in advanced devotional service.

In devotional service there is no frustration; even if we perform only a small amount it will grow. Devotional service is never lost. As far as material things are concerned, whatever we gain in the world will be lost when the body is finished. But since we are eternal spiritual sparks, our spiritual assets go with us, gradually fructifying. In this way those who have previously cultivated transcendental consciousness come in contact with Kṛṣṇa consciousness through this movement. Interest in Kṛṣṇa consciousness is not commonplace. In *Bhagavad-gītā* it is said that out of many millions and billions of persons, only one is interested in achieving perfection. If we can advertise that simply by reading this book and meditating for fifteen minutes anyone can immediately get power, become successful in business, and pass his examination, many people would be attracted to the book. People are not attracted to Kṛṣṇa consciousness because they prefer to be cheated by *māyā*. They think that the perfection of life is in eating a great supply of food or in sleeping twenty hours or in having a new mate every night or every day. People are interested in these things, but not in the perfection of life.

Every intelligent man should at least experiment with Kṛṣṇa consciousness. He should say, "All right, I have been enjoying this eating and sleeping for so many lives. These things were available for me to enjoy in my bird and animal bodies. Now in this life let me restrict the four principles of animalistic life – eating, sleeping, defending, and mating – and let me devote my time to developing Kṛṣṇa consciousness. In this way my life will be successful."

It is not that we have coined this term "Kṛṣṇa consciousness." Kṛṣṇa consciousness is the oldest phrase in the history of the world:

man-manā bhava mad-bhakto
mad-yājī māṁ namaskuru
mām evaiṣyasi satyaṁ te
pratijāne priyo 'si me

man-manā bhava mad-bhakto
mad-yājī māṁ namaskuru
mām evaiṣyasi yuktvaivam
ātmānaṁ mat-parāyaṇaḥ

"Always think of Me. Become My devotee. Worship Me, and offer your homage unto Me. The result is that you will come to Me without fail. I promise you this, because you are My very dear friend. Engage your mind always in thinking of Me, engage your body in My service, and surrender unto Me. Completely absorbed in Me, surely will you come to Me." (*Gītā* 18.65, 9.34)

The phrase *man-manā bhava mad-bhakto* means "just be always conscious of Me." This then is Kṛṣṇa consciousness. In the *Bhagavad-gītā* Kṛṣṇa is repeatedly saying that we should worship Him, offer obeisances unto Him, and then come to Him. The *Bhagavad-gītā* clearly points to the absolute necessity of Kṛṣṇa consciousness; it is accepted as the essence of the *Upaniṣads*. Even from the historical point of view it has no comparison. It has been calculated on the basis of archeological evidence that Kṛṣṇa spoke the *Bhagavad-gītā* on the Battlefield of Kurukṣetra more than five thousand years ago. So this Kṛṣṇa consciousness movement, even from the historical point of view, is five thousand years old. Its philosophy is the oldest in the history of the world. If we wish to trace it even further back we find that Śrī Kṛṣṇa spoke it earlier to the sun god. Kṛṣṇa is eternal, and consciousness of Kṛṣṇa is also eternal. In this way Kṛṣṇa consciousness should be approached. It should not simply be considered a theory.

When Kṛṣṇa consciousness is covered by any other consciousness, we experience our contaminated conditional life. When the sky is clear, we can see the sun's brilliant effulgence, but when it is covered by clouds we cannot see it. We may be able to perceive the sunlight, but we cannot see the sun disc itself. When the sky is clear it is in its natural condition. Similarly, our consciousness is eternally Kṛṣṇa consciousness because we are part and parcel of Kṛṣṇa eternally. This is asserted in the fifteenth chapter of the *Bhagavad-gītā:*

mamaivāṁśo jīva-loke
jīva-bhūtaḥ sanātanaḥ
manaḥ-ṣaṣṭhānīndriyāṇi
prakṛti-sthāni karṣati

"The living entities in this conditional world are My fragmental parts, and they are eternal. But due to conditioned life, they are struggling very hard with the six senses, which include the mind." (*Gītā* 15.7)

Somehow or other we have come in contact with material nature, and because of the mind and the six senses we are struggling hard to exist. That is Darwin's theory – the struggle for existence, survival of the fittest. However, the actual fact is that our constitutional position is not one of struggle. Struggle is the position of animal life. Human life should be blissful and should have as its goal spiritual advancement. At one time that was India's principle of life, and there was a class of people, the *brāhmaṇas,* who engaged themselves exclusively in spiritual culture. Although brahminical cultural life is enunciated in the scriptures of India, it is not for Indians alone, but for all human beings. The *Vedas* were written for all humankind, but it so happened that when the *Vedas* were written what is now known as the Indian culture was the only one extant. At that time, the whole planet was called Bhāratavarṣa, after Emperor Bharata Mahārāja, the son of Ṛṣabhadeva. Bharata Mahārāja ruled the whole planet, but gradually the planet was divided up. So the *dharma* of Vedic culture should not simply be considered Indian or Hindu in a sectarian sense.

Often the word *dharma* is translated to mean religion, but to conceive of *dharma* as a religion is to misconceive the word. In general usage, the word religion refers to a particular type of faith. The word *dharma* does not. *Dharma* indicates the natural occupation of the living entity. For example, wherever there is fire, there is heat and light, so it may be said that heat and light are the *dharma* of fire. Fire cannot change its *dharma*. In the same way, liquidity is an intrinsic quality of water, and this quality cannot be changed. If it is, it can no longer be considered water. The *dharma* of the individual soul can never be changed, and that *dharma* is the occupational duty of rendering service unto the Supreme Lord. Faiths and religions can be changed. Today I may be a Hindu, but tomorrow I may become a Christian or Muslim. In this way faiths can be changed, but *dharma* is a natural sequence, a natural occupation or connection.

Kṛṣṇa says that as soon as there is a discrepancy in the discharge of the *dharma*s of the living entities, when there is an upsurge of unnatural activities, He descends. One of the principal purposes of His descent is to reestablish religious principles. The best system of religion is that which best trains us to surrender unto the Supreme Lord. This is the basic principle underlying the *Bhagavad-gītā*. We can select our own religion and be Hindu, Muslim, Buddhist, Christian, or whatever as long as we know the real purpose of religion. Indeed, *Śrīmad-Bhāgavatam* does not recommend that we give up our present religion, but it does hint at the purpose of religion. That purpose is love of Godhead, and that religion that teaches us best how to love the Supreme Lord is the best religion.

In this age especially there is a general decay in the consciousness of the masses of people. A few people remember that there is a God, but for the most part people are forgetting Him. Therefore they cannot be happy. People are thinking that God is dead, or that we have no obligation to God, or that there is no God. This sort of thinking will never make for happiness. When civilization is godless or atheistic, as it is today, God or His representative comes to remind people of their relationship with the supreme consciousness.

When Sanātana Gosvāmī inquired from Lord Caitanya, "What am I? Why am I always in a miserable condition? What is the position of all living entities?" Śrī Caitanya Mahāprabhu immediately answered that the real identity is that of servant of God. We should not understand the word *servant* in the sense of materialistic servant. To become a servant of God is a great position. People are always trying to get some government post or some position in a reputed business firm because the service rendered in such positions earns great profits. Although we are very anxious to get good positions in the government service, we do not stop to think of getting a position in God's service. God is the government of all governments.

God's service is *dharma*. This *dharma* may be described differently in different countries according to different cultural and climatic conditions or situations, but in every religious scripture obedience to God is instructed. No scripture says that there is no God or that we as living entities are independent – not the Bible, the Koran, the *Vedas,* or even the Buddhist literatures. Generally, according to Buddhist philosophy, there is no individual soul and no supreme soul, but actually since Lord Buddha is accepted by Vedic literatures as an incarnation of God, by obeying Lord Buddha one is actually following God. In the *Śrīmad-Bhāgavatam* there is a list of incarnations, and Lord Buddha is accepted as one of them. *Śrīmad-Bhāgavatam* was compiled by Vyāsadeva five thousand years ago, and Lord Buddha appeared about 2,600 years ago, so *Śrīmad-Bhāgavatam* actually foretold the event of his incarnation. Lord Buddha preached that there is no God and no soul, that this body is a combination of matter, and that when we dissolve this material combination sensations of misery and happiness will no longer exist. Then Śaṅkarācārya appeared to preach that the external feature of Brahman, the body, is merely an illusion. In all religions, temple worship and acceptance of authority are present. We may accept Kṛṣṇa or Lord Jesus Christ or Jehovah or Lord Buddha or Śaṅkarācārya or Guru Nanak, but in any case acceptance of authority is required.

In the *Bhagavad-gītā* Lord Śrī Kṛṣṇa is accepted as the supreme authority. Sometimes Kṛṣṇa descends personally, and sometimes He descends by His incarnations. Sometimes He descends as sound vibration, and sometimes He descends as a devotee. There are many different categories of *avatāras.* In this present age Kṛṣṇa has descended in His holy name, Hare Kṛṣṇa, Hare Kṛṣṇa, Kṛṣṇa Kṛṣṇa, Hare Hare/Hare Rāma, Hare Rāma, Rāma Rāma, Hare Hare. Lord Caitanya Mahāprabhu also confirmed that in this Age of Kali, Kṛṣṇa has descended in the form of sound vibration. Sound is one of the forms the Lord takes. Therefore it is stated that there is no difference between Kṛṣṇa and His name.

Today people have forgotten their relationship with God, but this incarnation of Kṛṣṇa in the form of His holy names, this chanting of Hare Kṛṣṇa, will deliver all the people of the world from their forgetfulness. Lord Caitanya Mahāprabhu says that if we chant or associate with the chanting of the holy names of Kṛṣṇa, we will reach the highest perfectional stage of life. According to *Śrīmad-Bhāgavatam* there are different processes for different ages, but the principle of each process remains valid in all ages. It is not that the chanting of Hare Kṛṣṇa is effective in this age and not in Satya-yuga. Nor is it that people were not chanting the holy names of Kṛṣṇa in Satya-yuga. In Satya-yuga meditation was the main process, and great *munis* meditated for periods extending upwards of 60,000 years. In this age, however, perfection by that means of meditation is not possible because we are so short-lived. Consequently in this age it is especially recommended that we all sit down together and chant Hare Kṛṣṇa. It is very easy, and everyone can take part in it. There is no necessity of education, nor are any previous qualifications required. In this age people are also very slow and unfortunate, and they are contaminated with bad association. Caitanya Mahāprabhu introduced the chanting of Hare Kṛṣṇa, Hare Kṛṣṇa, Kṛṣṇa Kṛṣṇa, Hare Hare/ Hare Rāma, Hare Rāma, Rāma Rāma, Hare Hare as a great means of propaganda for spreading love of God. It is not that it is recommended only for Kali-yuga. Actually, it is recommended for every age. There have always been many devotees who have chanted and reached perfection in all ages. That is the beauty of this Kṛṣṇa consciousness movement. It is not simply for one age, or for one country, or for one class of people. Hare Kṛṣṇa can be chanted by any man in any social position, in any country, and in any age, for Kṛṣṇa is the Supreme Lord of all people in all social positions, in all countries, in all ages.

Chapter Nine

A Practical Guide to Bhakti-yoga

Introduction

Many people ask what it means to become a devotee of Kṛṣṇa. Some think it requires them to give up their present occupation, change their hairstyle, and live in an *āśrama*. But this is not the answer Kṛṣṇa gives Arjuna in the *Bhagavad-gītā*. Rather, Krsna says, "Arjuna, you should always think of Me in the form of Kṛṣṇa and at the same time carry out your prescribed duty of fighting. With your activities dedicated to Me and your mind and intelligence fixed on Me, you will attain Me without doubt."

Arjuna did not have to leave his duties as a military man to meditate. What he did have to do was fix his mind and intelligence on Kṛṣṇa. As Kṛṣṇa told Arjuna, this is possible by suitable practice and determination. One may practice Kṛṣṇa consciousness while living in an *āśrama* or temple, or one may practice while living at home.

Spiritual life, like material life, is a practical pursuit. The difference between the two is that we perform material activities for temporary gains and spiritual activities for gains that are eternal. Since we need to know what to do and how to do it, to guide us we have scriptures like the *Bhagavad-gītā* as well as bona fide spiritual masters coming in the line of teachers from Kṛṣṇa Himself.

Śrīla Prabhupāda, in his books, explains the timeless practices of devotional service, in this way providing spiritual knowledge to bring us closer to Kṛṣṇa. Kṛṣṇa says in the *Bhagavad-gītā*

(18.55), *bhaktya mam abhijanati:* "I can be known only by devotional service." By studying Śrīla Prabhupāda's instructions we can learn to act in Kṛṣṇa's loving service. And so we can go beyond having merely theoretical knowledge to actually acting in knowledge.

This final section of the book explores three things we can do to introduce the spiritual dimension into our life:

- Build relationships with spiritually minded people
- Embrace a diet that nourishes body, mind, and soul
- Practice mantra meditation

The first piece in this section, a lecture given by Śrīla Prabhupāda in Mumbai, India, speaks of how and where to find a guru. Although a guru is necessary to spiritual development, we also need friends. The second essay therefore discusses the importance of finding friends who share our spiritual aspirations.

Along with spiritual association, embracing a nonviolent diet is essential to clear the mind and heart for higher spiritual understanding. As Nobel Prize–winning author Isaac Bashevis Singer said after becoming a vegetarian at age fifty-eight, "We are all God's creatures – that we pray to God for mercy and justice while we continue to eat the flesh of animals that are slaughtered on our account is not consistent... Various philosophers and religious leaders try to convince their disciples and followers that animals are nothing more than machines without a soul, without feelings. However, anyone who has ever lived with an animal – be it a dog, a bird, or even a mouse – knows that this theory is a brazen lie, invented to justify cruelty."

And so the third and fourth articles in this section: "Falling for Fido," which points out the duplicity inherent in keeping pets but killing other animals, and "Reverence for All Life," where we hear how understanding the nature of the soul fosters nonviolence.

Next comes a talk between Śrīla Prabhupāda and George Harrison, John Lennon, and Yoko Ono about the importance of chanting Hare Kṛṣṇa. In the last essay in the book, Śrīla Prabhupāda explains the meaning of the Hare Kṛṣṇa mantra and the purpose of chanting it.

The Importance of Accepting a Spiritual Master

His Divine Grace A.C. Bhaktivedanta Swami Prabhupāda

Part of creating spiritual relationships is associating with devotees who are advanced in loving God. These devotees often serve as gurus, and an aspiring devotee is encouraged to accept spiritual initiation from such a person. Spiritual masters train and guide disciples in how to revive their active relationship with God, and help disciples during difficult times. In the following lecture given in Mumbai, India, in November 1974, Śrīla Prabhupāda explains who is a guru and why we need one.

~

In *Śrīmad-Bhāgavatam* we read, "The most powerful sage Maitreya was a friend of Vyāsadeva's. Being encouraged and pleased by Vidura's inquiry about transcendental knowledge, Maitreya spoke as follows."

This is the process for getting transcendental knowledge: to approach the proper person, the guru, and submissively hear from him. *Tad viddhi praṇipātena paripraśnena sevayā*. Although the process is very easy, one must know the process and follow it. For example, suppose your typewriter is not working. Then you have to go to the proper person – someone who knows how to fix it. He will immediately tighten a screw or fix something else, and it works. But if you go to a vegetable seller for repairing the machine, that will not be good. He does not know the process. He may know how to sell vegetables, but that does not matter. He does not understand how to repair a typewriter.

Therefore the Vedic injunction is *tad-vijñānārthaṁ sa gurum evābhigacchet*. If you want to learn transcendental knowledge (*tad-vijñāna*), you must approach a guru. Actually, human life is meant for understanding transcendental knowledge, not material knowledge. Material knowledge all pertains to the body. A medical practitioner may have so much knowledge of the mechanical arrangement of the body, but he has no knowledge of the spirit soul. Therefore he cannot help you fulfill the goal of your life.

The body is a machine made by nature (*yantrārūḍhāni māyayā*). For those who are very much attached to this machine the meditative yoga system is recommended. In this system one learns to perform some gymnastics and concentrate the mind so that eventually the mind may be focused on Lord Viṣṇu. The real purpose is to understand Viṣṇu, the Supreme Lord. So the yoga system is more or less a mechanical arrangement. But the *bhakti* system is above this mechanical arrangement. Therefore *bhakti* begins with the search for *tad-vijñāna*, spiritual knowledge.

So if you want to understand spiritual knowledge you have to approach a guru. One meaning of the word guru is "weighty." Therefore the guru is one who is "heavy" with knowledge. And what is that knowledge? That is explained in the *Kaṭhopaniṣad: śrotriyaṁ brahma-niṣṭham. Śrotriyaṁ* means "one who has received knowledge by hearing the *Vedas*, the *śruti*," and *brahma-niṣṭham* indicates one who has realized Brahman, or rather Parabrahman, Bhagavān, the Supreme Personality of Godhead. That is the guru's qualification.

One must hear from those who are in the line of preceptorial succession, or disciplic succession. As Lord Kṛṣṇa says in the *Bhagavad-gītā, evaṁ paramparā-prāptam*. If one wants standard transcendental knowledge, not upstart knowledge, one must receive it from the *paramparā* system, the disciplic succession.

Another meaning of the word *śrotriyam* mentioned above is "one who has heard from a guru in the disciplic succession." And the result of this hearing will be *brahma-niṣṭham,* "He is firmly fixed in the service of the Supreme Personality of Godhead." He has no other business. These are the two main qualifications of a bona fide guru. He does not need to be a very learned scholar with an MA, BA, or PhD. No. He simply needs to have heard from the authority in disciplic succession and be fixed in devotional service. This is our system.

In the verse under discussion we see that Vidura was hearing from Maitreya Ṛṣi and that Maitreya was very much pleased (*viduraṁ prītaḥ*). Unless you satisfy your guru very nicely, you cannot get the right knowledge. That is natural. If you receive your guru properly and give him a very nice place where he can sit comfortably, and if he is pleased with your behavior, then he will speak very frankly and very freely, which will be beneficial for you. This is the case with Vidura and Maitreya: Maitreya Ṛṣi was very much pleased with Vidura, and thus Maitreya imparted instructions to him.

Lord Kṛṣṇa recommends the same procedure in the *Bhagavad-gītā*: *tad viddhi praṇipātena paripraśnena sevayā,* "One must offer obeisances to the guru, inquire from him, and serve him." If you simply go and ask the spiritual master questions in a challenging spirit but do not accept his instructions and do not render service, then you are wasting your time. The word used here is *praṇipātena,* "offering obeisances with no reservation." So reception of transcendental knowledge is based on this *praṇipāta*. That is why Kṛṣṇa says later, *sarva-dharmān parityajya mām ekaṁ śaraṇaṁ vraja:* "Give up everything else and just surrender unto Me." Just as we have to surrender to Kṛṣṇa, we have to surrender to Kṛṣṇa's representative, the spiritual master.

The guru is the external representative of Kṛṣṇa. The internal guru is Kṛṣṇa Himself (*īśvaraḥ sarva-bhūtānāṁ hṛd-deśe 'rjuna tiṣṭhati*). It is not that Kṛṣṇa is only in Goloka Vṛndāvana, the spiritual world. He is everywhere, within every atom and within everyone's heart (*goloka eva nivasaty akhilātma-bhūtaḥ*). The manifestation of Kṛṣṇa in the heart is the Paramātmā, or Supersoul. I am an *ātmā*, an individual soul; you are an *ātmā*. We are both situated locally – you are situated within your body and I am situated within my body. But the Paramātmā is situated everywhere. That is the difference between the *ātmā* and the Paramātmā. Some people think there is no difference between the *ātmā* and the Paramātmā, but there is a difference. They are one in the sense that both of them are cognizant living entities, but they are different in that the Paramātmā is all-pervading and the *ātmā* is localized. Kṛṣṇa confirms this in the *Bhagavad-gītā: kṣetra-jñaṁ cāpi māṁ viddhi sarva-kṣetreṣu bhārata,* "Besides the individual soul in each body I am also present as the Supersoul." The word *kṣetra-jña* means "the knower of the *kṣetra*, or body." So I am the knower or occupier of my body. The body is just like a house, with a tenant and a landlord. The tenant may occupy the house, but the landlord is the proprietor. Similarly, we *ātmās* are simply tenants of our bodies; we are not the proprietors. The proprietor is the Paramātmā. And when the proprietor says, "Get out of this house, get out of this body," you have to leave your body. That is called death. This is Vedic knowledge.

So one who is inquisitive to understand the ultimate goal of life must approach a proper guru. An ordinary man interested in the bodily comforts of life doesn't require a guru. Today, however, a guru is generally taken to mean someone who can give you some bodily remedy. People will approach some so-called saintly person and ask, "Mahātmājī, I am suffering from this disease." "Yes, I have a mantra that will cure you." That sort of guru is accepted – to cure some disease or give some wealth. No. Lord Kṛṣṇa says in the *Bhagavad-gītā,*

tad viddhi praṇipātena
paripraśnena sevayā
upadekṣyanti te jñānaṁ
jñāninas tattva-darśinaḥ

One should approach a guru to learn about *tattva,* the Absolute Truth, not to acquire some material benefit. One should not search out a guru to cure some material disease. For that there is a medical practitioner. Why should you search out a guru for that purpose? A guru is one who knows the Vedic scriptures and who can teach us to understand Kṛṣṇa.

Of course, we cannot understand Kṛṣṇa fully. That is not possible. We have no such capacity, because Kṛṣṇa is so great and we are so limited. Kṛṣṇa is so great that even He does not understand Himself. He does not know why He is so attractive. Therefore, to understand what makes Him so attractive He came as Lord Caitanya, adopting the ecstatic emotions of Śrīmatī Rādhārāṇī. So to understand Kṛṣṇa fully is not possible, but if we try to understand Him as far as our limited capacity allows, that is our perfection. That is why Kṛṣṇa says,

janma karma ca me divyam
evaṁ yo vetti tattvataḥ
tyaktvā dehaṁ punar janma
naiti mām eti so 'rjuna

"One who knows the transcendental nature of My appearance and activities does not, upon leaving the body, take his birth again in this material world, but attains My eternal abode, O Arjuna."

If we think that Kṛṣṇa is a human being like us, then we are *mūḍhas,* fools and rascals. We will be mistaken if we think, "Since my body is made of material elements, Kṛṣṇa's body is also made of material elements." In the *Bhagavad-gītā* Kṛṣṇa says that the material energy belongs to Him: *daivī hy eṣā guṇamayī mama māyā.* This material world is Kṛṣṇa's. We cannot say *mama māyā,* "This material energy is mine." No. We are under the control of the material nature. But Kṛṣṇa is the controller of the material nature: *mayādhyakṣeṇa prakṛtiḥ sūyate sa-carācaram.* That is the difference between Kṛṣṇa and us. Understanding that this material nature is working under the direction of Kṛṣṇa is real knowledge.

It is not possible to understand in detail how things are going on, but we can understand the summary – *janmādy asya yataḥ:* "Everything has emanated from the Supreme Absolute Truth, Kṛṣṇa." That much knowledge is sufficient. Then you can increase your knowledge – how the material nature is working under the direction of Kṛṣṇa, how Kṛṣṇa's energies are interacting, and so on. That is advanced knowledge. But if we simply understand Kṛṣṇa's statement in the *Bhagavad-gītā* – *mayādhyakṣeṇa prakṛtiḥ sūyate sa-carācaram:* "This material energy is working under My direction" – that is perfect knowledge.

The modern scientists think that matter is working independently, that everything has evolved due to chemical evolution. No. Chemical evolution cannot produce life. Life comes from life. As Kṛṣṇa says in the *Bhagavad-gītā, ahaṁ sarvasya prabhavo mattaḥ sarvaṁ pravartate:* "Everything emanates from Me." This is the reply to the scientists. And the *Vedānta-sūtra* confirms, *athāto brahma jijñāsā, janmādy asya yataḥ:* "Now one should inquire into the Supreme Brahman, which is that from whom everything emanates." The Supreme Brahman is Kṛṣṇa.

The whole world is a combination of two things: *jaḍa* and *cetana,* dull matter and living entities. Both come from Kṛṣṇa. As He says in the *Bhagavad-gītā,*

apareyam itas tv anyāṁ
prakṛtiṁ viddhi me parām
jīva-bhūtāṁ mahā-bāho
yayedaṁ dhāryate jagat

"Besides the inferior, material energy, there is My superior, spiritual energy, the living entities who are exploiting the material nature." Why is the spiritual energy superior? Because the living entities are utilizing the material nature. For example, we advanced living entities, human beings, have created the modern civilization by utilizing matter. That is our superiority. In this way we have to acquire *tattva-jñāna,* understanding of the Absolute Truth.

The *Vedānta-sūtra* confirms that human life is meant for understanding the Absolute Truth: *athāto brahma jijñāsā*. And the explanation of the *Vedānta-sūtra* is the *Śrīmad-Bhāgavatam*. The *Vedānta-sūtra* states that the Absolute Truth is *janmādy asya*, that from whom, or from which, everything has emanated. Now, what is the nature of that source? This question is answered in the *Śrīmad-Bhāgavatam: janmādy asya yataḥ anvayād itarataś ca artheṣu abhijñaḥ*. That source is *abhijñaḥ*, cognizant. Now, matter is not cognizant, so that source must be life. Therefore the modern scientific theory that life comes from matter is wrong. Life comes from life. And the *Śrīmad-Bhāgavatam* continues, *tene brahma hṛdā ya ādi-kavaye*. "He imparted Vedic knowledge to Lord Brahmā." So unless one is a living entity, how can he impart knowledge?

The *Bhāgavatam* is the natural explanation of the *Vedānta-sūtra* by the same author, Śrīla Vyāsadeva. In the verse under discussion it is said Vidura was *dvaipāyana-sakha*, a friend of Dvaipāyana. Dvaipāyana means Vyāsadeva. Vyāsadeva compiled the *Vedānta-sūtra* and then explained it in the *Śrīmad-Bhāgavatam* (*artho 'yaṁ brahma-sūtrāṇāṁ*). If we read some artificial commentary on the *Vedānta-sūtra* we'll misunderstand. Generally, the Māyāvādīs [impersonalists] give prominence to the commentary by Śaṅkarācārya, called the *Śārīraka-bhāṣya*. But that commentary is unnatural. The natural commentary is by the author himself, Śrīla Vyāsadeva.

According to our Vedic system, the *ācārya* must understand the *Vedānta-sūtra* and explain it. Then he'll be accepted as an *ācārya*. Therefore both of the main *sampradāyas* [spiritual communities], the Māyāvādī *sampradāya* and the Vaiṣṇava *sampradāya*, have explained the *Vedānta-sūtra*. Otherwise, they would not have been recognized as authoritative. Without understanding the *Vedānta-sūtra* nobody can understand what is Brahman, the Absolute Truth. Similarly, here it is said that Vidura understood transcendental knowledge (*ānvīkṣikyām*) from Maitreya. Who is Maitreya? Dvaipāyana-sakha, the friend of Vyāsadeva. One friend knows the other friend – what his position is, what his knowledge is. So since Maitreya was the friend of Vyāsadeva that means he knows what Vyāsadeva knows.

So we have to approach a spiritual master who is in the disciplic succession of Vyāsadeva. Many people claim, "Oh, we are also following Vyāsadeva." But that following cannot be superficial. One has to actually follow Vyāsadeva. For example, Vyāsadeva accepted Kṛṣṇa as the Supreme Personality of Godhead. This is stated in the *Bhagavad-gītā,* in the section where Arjuna says to Kṛṣṇa, *paraṁ brahma paraṁ dhāma pavitraṁ paramaṁ bhavān:* "O Kṛṣṇa, you are Para-brahman, the Supreme Person." But one may say it was because Arjuna was the friend of Kṛṣṇa that he accepted Him as the Supreme. No. Arjuna gave evidence: "Vyāsadeva also accepts You as the Supreme Lord." Similarly, Vyāsadeva begins the *Śrīmad-Bhāgavatam,* his commentary on the *Vedānta-sūtra,* by saying *oṁ namo bhagavate vāsudevāya:* "I offer my obeisances unto Vāsudeva, Kṛṣṇa, the Supreme Personality of Godhead."

So if we actually are interested in understanding spiritual knowledge, we must approach an *ācārya,* and an *ācārya* is one who follows Vyāsadeva. In the verse under discussion, Maitreya, the friend of Vyāsadeva, is the *ācārya.* He is so exalted that he has been described as Bhagavān. In general, the word *bhagavān* indicates Kṛṣṇa, the Supreme Personality of Godhead (*kṛṣṇas tu bhagavān svayam*). But sometimes other powerful persons, such as Lord Brahmā, Lord Śiva, Nārada, Vyāsadeva, or Maitreya, are also addressed as Bhagavān. Although the actual Bhagavān is Kṛṣṇa, such persons are sometimes called Bhagavān because they have attained as much knowledge of Kṛṣṇa as possible. It is not possible to have cent percent knowledge of Kṛṣṇa. Nobody can do that. Even Brahmā and Śiva cannot do that. But those who follow Kṛṣṇa's instructions fully are also sometimes called Bhagavān. However, that Bhagavān is not an artificial Bhagavān. A real Bhagavān must know what Kṛṣṇa has taught and follow His instructions.

So here it is said, *viduraṁ prīta,* "Vidura pleased Maitreya." Their conversation wasn't simply talking between friends. No.

Vidura was eager to receive transcendental knowledge, and Maitreya was pleased with him. How can one please the spiritual master? That we have mentioned before: *praṇipātena paripraśnena sevayā.* You can please the guru simply by surrendering to him, inquiring from him, and by rendering him service: "Sir, I am your most obedient servant. Please accept me and give me instruction." Arjuna also followed this process. At the beginning of the *Bhagavad-gītā* he said to Kṛṣṇa, *śiṣyas te 'haṁ śādhi māṁ tvāṁ prapannam:* "I am Your disciple and a soul surrendered unto You. Please instruct me." Even though Arjuna was a very intimate friend of Kṛṣṇa, still, while learning the *Bhagavad-gītā* from Him he surrendered to Kṛṣṇa and said, "I am no longer Your friend; I am Your disciple. Now I am under Your full control. Please instruct me."

So this is the process of approaching a guru. You must be very inquisitive and ask questions, but not to challenge the spiritual master. It is said, *jijñāsuḥ śreya uttamam:* You should approach the spiritual master to understand the spiritual science. You shouldn't try to defeat him. One should not say, "I know better than you. Let us talk." No. That is not the proper way to approach a guru. You must find a guru to whom you can surrender (*praṇipātena*). If you cannot surrender to the guru, then don't waste your time and his time. First of all surrender to the bona fide guru. This is the process of understanding transcendental knowledge.

Thank you very much. Hare Kṛṣṇa.

Finding Spiritual Friends

Satsvarūpa Dāsa Goswami

Association is like a crystal that reflects anything put before it. If we spend time with materialists, we'll become materialistic, and if we spend time with spiritually minded people, we'll become spiritually minded ourselves.

~

Just as a person who desires to improve his tennis will seek out tennis experts and enthusiasts, so a person interested in spiritual life will want like-minded friends. But where do we find them? And even if we meet students of self-realization and God consciousness, does it mean we will automatically develop loving friendships with them? The scripture states, "Seek and you will find; knock and the door will be opened to you." And so it is with spiritual friendships.

The surest way to find God conscious companions is to join with the topmost pure devotees, saints, and sages. Although most of them lived many centuries ago, we can be with them now in their writings, their teachings, and through their living followers. Although the pure devotees of a past age are not walking the earth today, we can become kindred spirits with them and benefit in a very personal way in their association.

According to Vedic knowledge, there are two ways to become

intimate with advanced spiritual persons. One way is through their direct association, such as walking beside them, sitting and talking with them, and so on. This is called, in Sanskrit, *vapuḥ*. The effect of a friendship with an advanced devotee is described by Bhaktivinoda Ṭhākura in *Harināma Cintāmaṇi:* "If one stays near a pure devotee of Kṛṣṇa for some time, one can receive the *bhakti* [devotional energy] flowing from his body. If one can bind that energy within one's heart, after one develops strong faith *bhakti* will develop... Thus if one lives close to a devotee of Kṛṣṇa, devotion will soon appear within one's own heart."

When we are not in the presence of spiritual friends but we associate with them by hearing and following their instructions, that is called *vāṇī*. Of the two, the experts state that the *vāṇī* form of relationship is stronger and everlasting, whereas *vapuḥ*, although especially sweet, is subject to time, death, and other forms of human separation. Either in the form of *vapuḥ* or *vāṇī*, spiritual friendships are very influential. As one Vedic teacher said, "Association is very important. It acts just like a crystal stone, which will reflect anything put before it."

The influence we receive through teachings and writings can act negatively or positively. For example, the nineteenth-century German poet Goethe poured out his youthful anguish in a novel, *The Sorrows of Young Werther,* and the tragic result was that several young men committed suicide after reading it. As submissive readers can become degraded or doomed by poisonous writings, so the opposite is true: we can gain the highest goal of life, revival of our blissful, eternal relationship with God, by faithfully associating with pure souls through their biographies or recorded teachings.

But we cannot live only in books. We live in a world of people – family, friends, fellow workers, neighbors. As we traverse the spiritual path, we naturally want companions. For the inner life, we want close friends, not just formal or official relationships with people who are strangers to our soul. Personal association is so important that the Vedic scriptures caution us against living with those who are averse to godly life. In fact, when Lord Caitanya was asked by a follower to define a Vaiṣṇava He replied, "He is one who avoids the association of materialistic people, sense enjoyers, and nondevotees." On another occasion, when Lord Caitanya asked His learned disciple Rāmānanda Rāya what was the most painful experience, Rāmānanda Rāya replied, "Apart from separation from the devotee of Kṛṣṇa, I know of no unbearable unhappiness." And it is stated in the *Bṛhad-bhāgavatamṛta,* "Out of all kinds of desirable things experienced in the life of a living entity, association with the devotees of the Lord is the greatest. When we are separated from a devotee, even for a moment, we cannot enjoy happiness."

We can increase our chances of forming spiritual friendships by visiting a place such as a temple of Kṛṣṇa. But devotees are not found only in temples. Neither do they belong to a particular religious sect, live in a particular part of the world, or belong to a particular sex or age group. They are known by their genuine symptoms, which are described in the scriptures. *Śrīmad-Bhāgavatam* (3.25.21) states:

> The symptoms of a *sādhu* are that he is tolerant, merciful, and friendly to all living entities. He has no enemies, he is peaceful, he abides by the scriptures, and all his characteristics are sublime.

In *The Nectar of Instruction,* written in the sixteenth century, Rūpa Gosvāmī analyzes devotees in three categories and advises us to honor *all* devotees. He describes the neophyte class as those who sometimes chant God's names but don't strictly follow all the rules of spiritual life. Devotees in the intermediate stage strictly follow rules and are fixed in their convictions about devotional service to God. Above all are the pure devotees, who harbor no envy toward any living creature, and who see everyone as a servant of God.

We should see all the devotees as our friends, and yet there is an art for selecting proper persons with careful discrimination. Rūpa Gosvāmī further explains that there are six kinds of loving exchanges among devotee friends:

> Offering gifts in charity, accepting charitable gifts, revealing one's mind in confidence, inquiring confidentially, accepting *prasāda,* and offering *prasāda* are the six symptoms of love shared by one devotee and another.

The art and etiquette of friendships in Kṛṣṇa consciousness can be best learned from genuine devotees.

If one has not developed a good spiritual friendship among the people he works and lives with, then he should pray for this and seek it out. We cannot keep aloof from spiritual friendships and at the same time please the Supreme Personality of Godhead. Lord Kṛṣṇa says, "He who says he is My devotee is not My devotee. But he who is a devotee of My devotee is actually My devotee." Similarly, Narottama dāsa Ṭhākura, a great Vaiṣṇava poet, wrote, "No one has ever become liberated without the association of devotees."

But perhaps my readers are already aware of the importance of spiritual friendships. And perhaps you already have connections with spiritual friends. In that case, let us simply remind each other not to neglect these valuable ties. Let us go to our friends and share the happiness of God-centered love. As described by Lord Kṛṣṇa in the *Bhagavad-gītā* (10.9): "The thoughts of My pure devotees dwell in Me, their lives are fully devoted to My service, and they derive great satisfaction and bliss from always enlightening one another and conversing about Me."

Falling for Fido

Mathureśa Dāsa

A sidewalk slip inspires some thoughts on our schizoid policy toward animals. A look at one of the West's sacred cows.

~

Down the street from the house where I live, a tall hedge borders the sidewalk for twenty yards or so, creating a shady, sheltered stretch of pavement. Special things happen there. On warmer evenings you get occasional curbside parties – a carload of teenagers, voices raised above a blaring radio. And during the day, crews from the electric company, telephone company, or city department of streets sometimes pull their trucks over and take a snooze. But the primary function of the stretch, and the most important one to know about if you're a pedestrian, is to serve as a dumping ground for dog feces. Especially in the early evening, you see dog owners walk their charges down to this piece of sidewalk, turn the other way for a moment or two (scanning the sky for early stars and trying not to think of dinner), then jerk the leash and head home. I'd guess this twenty-yard area services most of the dogs within a four- or five-block radius.

Having to regularly pick my way past the hedge makes me wonder: Why, while they slaughter other animals by the millions every day, are men so devoted to dogs, to the point of patiently standing by while these creatures answer the call of nature? Dogs are faithful, obedient, and easily pleased, I know, so they provide a buffer, or a substitute, for less reliable human companionship. Pigs and cows just aren't as outgoing or affable, and even if they were, you still wouldn't want them jumping into your lap. Perhaps, in addition, dogs aren't as tasty as some other animals. Perhaps they don't fatten as easily. Even if they did, we wouldn't kill them. When I was growing up in Cleveland, I had a beagle named Geronimo who was fat as a barrel. I'd never have butchered Geronimo. He was a member of the family.

However, while we have practical reasons for singling dogs out for special treatment, the *Bhagavad-gītā* teaches us to see all living creatures equally. The *Gītā* says that each living being is an eternal spirit soul, part and parcel of the Supreme Soul, Lord Kṛṣṇa. All living beings, therefore, are members of Kṛṣṇa's family. Seeing equally doesn't mean that we should shake hands with tigers or embrace rattlesnakes, but that we shouldn't give unnecessary trouble to any soul. Even though cows, pigs, and chickens don't make good house pets, they feel pain as much as dogs do. And by Kṛṣṇa's law of karma, whatever pain we give them we have to suffer in turn ourselves.

Each time I am obliged, because of inattention while ambling down the sidewalk, to hose off my shoes, I grow more curious about man's infatuation with canines. One morning last week, after slipping on a particularly large deposit and nearly falling, I resolved to look deeper into this infatuation. Later that day, while shopping at the local Acme supermarket, I visited the dog food section – aisle five, about the middle of the store. Dog food occupied all four shelves on one side of the aisle for almost the entire length of the aisle. (Cat food and kitty litter took up the remaining space.) I recognized Geronimo's old favorites, Ken-L-Ration and Gravy Train, and I counted almost a dozen other brands, both dried and canned. Most brands were adorned with dog portraits, similar in some ways to the kid portraits on cereal boxes a couple of aisles over – both dogs and kids were portrayed as bright-eyed junior members of the family.

Dogs *are* junior members of God's universal family, younger brothers to man, and therefore they are deserving of our care. But twelve brands of specially prepared food? Hugging a tiger is foolish, but so is spending so much for something that ends up on the sidewalk, or on the rug.

The dog food aisle runs the full length of the store, where, set against the back wall, one finds an equally long display: the meat cooler. Chickens, turkeys, pigs, cows, and sheep. Why no portraits here? These are also family members – "children" of the Supreme Lord and man's younger brothers and sisters. Like us, they have heads, necks, legs, hearts, livers, tongues (right there in the cooler, wrapped in cellophane). Like us they enjoy eating, sleeping, mating, and taking care of their young. Like us they know fear and pain. And like us they are eternal, individual spirit souls, mired in by flesh and bone. The only difference is that they have less intelligence and are therefore helpless before our butcher's ax.

This wasn't the first time I had contemplated man's inconsistent policy toward animals, or the first time I'd seen how a supermarket exemplifies that policy. But on this supermarket visit, as I stood by the meat cooler, still vexed by my near fall on the sidewalk, I was militantly curious, asking myself, "How can people live with this and not go nuts?" On the human carnivore's mental landscape, the aisle for the glorification of dog (and the sidewalk for the reception of his excrement) intersects with the aisle for the slaughter of other animals, yet the carnivore admits to no contradiction. Isn't that a denial of the plain facts, of reality? And isn't denial of reality bound to produce some kind of mental strain, or mental illness? Isn't it in fact *indicative* of mental illness?

"Come off it!" says the carnivore. "Those animals are meant to be eaten. They're meant to be killed. They're food animals."

"Meant by whom?" is the reply. "It's obvious that *you* mean to kill and eat them, but where is the evidence of an intention other than yours? 'Intend' indicates there is a person intending, so who, besides you, is that?" Hardened criminals feel fully justified in doing what they do: their victims are *meant* to be victimized. But *I* don't think animals are meant to be killed, and neither do the animals. Nor is the "meant to be" philosophy confirmed by any scriptural authority, although when the carnivores get their bloody hands on scripture, they naturally try to prove otherwise. The Vedic literatures say that flesh food is meant only for dogs and cats. So a man's appetite for a dog's food indicates that he's not only infatuated with dogs, he emulates them. Any dog would be in seventh heaven sniffing around the grocery meat department.

But the meat cooler is not the last word in man's schizoid policy toward his animal brothers. Walking down to the end of the meat section, I came to another cooler, this one running the length of the side wall and packed with milk and milk products. For the first five yards or so, gallon and half-gallon milk containers are stacked three high and four deep, and cream and buttermilk fill the shelves above. Pint and half-pint containers – yogurt, sour cream, cottage cheese, and so on – fill the next section. After that there are butter and twenty kinds of cheese and, across the aisle, a freezer full of ice cream.

Now if the dog gets special treatment because he's sociable, faithful, and eager to defend home and master, then why doesn't the cow, who supplies the ingredient for this wealth of delicious food products, also receive special treatment? Not that we should keep one or two heifers at home and take them for walks around the block, or that our supermarkets should have an aisle of hay and oats. No. All we need do is stop cutting the cow's throat. If you have to eat cow's flesh, or any animal's flesh, be patient. They all die in time.

Westerners deride the apparently irrational respect afforded animals, cows in particular, by followers of India's Vedic literature. "Sacred cow" has come to indicate anything falsely held to be immune from reasonable criticism. It's true the Vedic literature asserts that the cow is sacred – in the sense that she is especially favored by the Supreme Lord Kṛṣṇa and that her care and protection by man lead to the development of higher, nobler qualities in human society. While this assertion is not immune from criticism, to prove it irrational we'd have to stop killing cows and observe for ourselves the effects of such a moratorium.

But sacredness aside for the moment, followers of the Vedic literature also point to the cow's undeniable contributions – to those coolers full of milk, butter, and cheese, those freezers full of ice cream. We've all been enjoying milk and milk products ever since we were weaned. My two-year-old son consumes a quart of cow milk a day. That must be at least as much as he used to suckle. The dog may be our best friend, but the cow is our second mother. How much more a member of the family could she be?

The *Vedas* teach us to give protection not only to the cow but to all living things, including dogs and cats. The Vedic injunction is *māhiṁsyāt sarvā-bhūtāni:* Do not harm any living thing. The *Vedas* even enjoin that as part of all great religious ceremonies, everyone in the community, including animals like cats and dogs, must be generously fed. Worship of God is complete only when all of His family members have been duly satisfied.

But the Vedic literature advises that we give special attention to the cow, because she nourishes us and because she assists us in spiritual advancement. She is useful in every respect. What to speak of milk, even cow dung has its uses – as fertilizer and in making fine incense, for example. That's a lot more than you can say for dog feces.

Reverence for All Life

Girirāja Swami

The word vegetarian, *coined by the founders of the British Vegetarian Society in 1842, comes from the Latin word* vegetus, *meaning "whole, sound, fresh, or lively," as in* Homo vegetus *– a mentally and physically vigorous person. The original meaning of the word implies a balanced philosophical and moral sense of life – a lot more than just a diet of vegetables and fruits. The key to being a vegetarian therefore is more than simply avoiding meat; it is acknowledging the origin of all life.*

~

Late in 1997 I received a phone call from Sri Bhari B. R. Malhotra, a prominent industrialist based in Pune, India, inviting me to speak at a conference on "Reverence for All Life." Considering the Malhotras' relationship with Śrīla Prabhupāda – he had called them "our good friends" – and wanting to present the message of Kṛṣṇa, I accepted.

The list of the conference organizers was impressive. Prominent representatives from various fields and cultures had joined together to promote vegetarianism. The conference was held on the grounds of the most prestigious hotel in Pune. Gathered on stage were distinguished leaders from the fields of religion, politics, science, business, social work, and even the military. Thousands of delegates from around the world sat in the audience.

The program began with a representative from each religion reciting a short prayer of invocation. Then all the participants on stage joined to light a sacred lamp. One after another, the distinguished speakers appealed for compassion, nonviolence, and reverence for all life. Finally my turn came to speak:

"I am very pleased to be with you today and wish to express my gratitude to the organizers, especially my dear friend Sri Bhari Malhotra, his older brother, Sri S. P. Malhotra, and all the other great souls who have helped organize and make this function so successful.

"We are here to appreciate and develop reverence for all life. The *Bhagavad-gītā,* which is a scientific explanation of the Supreme Soul and His relationship with the individual soul, explains that all life emanates from the supreme life, or God, known in Sanskrit as Kṛṣṇa. When we have reverence for God, naturally we have reverence for all life. If we love God, naturally we will love all living entities, who come from Him. Lord Kṛṣṇa states in the *Bhagavad-gītā, mamaivāṁśo jīva-loke jīva-bhūtaḥ sanātanaḥ*: 'All living entities are My fragmental parts and parcels, and they are eternal.'

"The *Bhagavad-gītā* also explains that a learned person sees all living entities equally – *paṇḍitāh sama-darśinaḥ* – because he sees the same soul within the different varieties of bodies. My spiritual master, His Divine Grace A. C. Bhaktivedanta Swami Prabhupāda, used to say, 'We want brotherhood, but what does it mean to be brothers? It means we have the same father.' Only when we recognize God as the supreme father can we have real brotherhood. Knowing God to be the supreme father, we can understand that if we deal with God's other children nicely, God will be pleased. But if we try to exploit and commit violence upon one another, how will the supreme father be pleased? And if God is not pleased, how can we expect peace and prosperity in the world?

"Animals are also children of God, although they have less

developed intelligence. They resemble human children, who also do not have developed intelligence, or developed speech. Nor can they defend themselves. But in a family the strong are meant to protect the weak. For a stronger older brother to torture or massacre a baby is a terrible crime. How upset and angry the father would be! Animals should be treated like our younger brothers or sisters, to be protected, not exploited or slaughtered so we can eat their flesh.

"By Kṛṣṇa consciousness, by realizing that God is the supreme father of all living entities, we can actually achieve brotherhood and unity among all living beings.

"Now, we have heard many wonderful talks today. I felt enlightened by hearing the noble thoughts expressed by the esteemed participants. We have heard about the need for love, for compassion, for reverence for all life. We have heard of the horrors of cruelty and violence inflicted on less fortunate living beings. But we are faced with the practical fact that so many human beings do not love as much as they should. Nor do they have as much compassion or reverence as they should. So how to create the love and other finer sentiments we value? There must be some process.

"The *Gītā* and other scriptures of the world advise us that to develop love for God, which naturally includes love for all living entities, we must adopt a spiritual process. And the best process recommended for the present age is the chanting of the holy names of God. The Vedic scriptures advise:

harer nāma harer nāma
harer nāmaiva kevalam
kalau nāsty eva nāsty eva
nāsty eva gatir anyathā

'One should chant the holy names, chant the holy names, chant the holy names. There is no other means of success in the age of Kali [the present age].' [*Bṛhan-nāradīya Purāṇa* 3.8.126]

"The Koran too advises that one should chant the names of

God. For many years I had the opportunity to go to Pakistan and teach Kṛṣṇa consciousness. I was pleased to meet some very learned Muslim friends of ours. Just as the Hindus have *Viṣṇu-sahasra-nāma*, 'The Thousand Names of Viṣṇu,' the Muslims have 'Ninety-Nine Names of God.' The Koran (7.180) states, 'The most beautiful names belong to God, so call on Him by them.' And learned Muslims understand that they can achieve the perfection of life by chanting the holy name of God at death. I even learned from my Muslim friends how vegetarianism is part of the teachings of the Koran, and I saw a book by a Muslim physician entitled *Vegetarianism and the Koran*.

"Similarly, the Bible enjoins that one should praise the name of the Lord with cymbals and drums. And in the teachings of Buddha, one is advised to chant the holy names of God: 'All who sincerely call upon My name will come to Me after death, and I will take them to paradise.' [Buddhist *Sūtras*, Vow of Amida Buddha, 18]

"So the chanting of the holy names of the Lord is a universal process recommended in all scriptures for the current age, and unless we adopt a practical means for purifying the heart of hatred and anger and violence, our pontification and platitudes will not really bring the desired results. So I appeal to you all. Many of you are important leaders in society. Even if you are not very big leaders, you are leaders in your society, in your community, in your family. Please consider the need to chant the holy names of God to purify the heart of the sinful desire to commit violence on other living entities.

"All over the world we have practical experience of the effects of chanting the names of God. The Vedic literature explains that in this age, the Age of Kali, the Lord Himself, Śrī Kṛṣṇa, appears as Śrī Kṛṣṇa Caitanya. Five hundred years ago Caitanya Mahāprabhu predicted:

pṛthivīte āche yata nagarādi grāma
sarvatra pracāra hoibe mora nāma

'In every town and village of the world, My name will be sung.'

"ISKCON's founder and spiritual master, His Divine Grace A.C. Bhaktivedanta Swami Prabhupāda, was instrumental in fulfilling the desire and prediction of Lord Caitanya. And what has been the consequence of chanting throughout the world? People addicted to all sorts of bad habits have given up their vicious activities and are following regulative principles: no meat, fish, or eggs, no intoxication, no gambling, and no illicit sex. Those who from babyhood were fed meat, without any consideration that meat-eating is wrong, have become vegetarians, or 'Kṛṣṇatarians,' who eat only sanctified food offered to the Lord. The potency of chanting the names of God is so great. And I believe that our aspirations for reverence for all life, for an end to unnecessary violence, can be successful only if people are engaged on a large scale in chanting the holy names of God.

"Thank you very much. Hare Kṛṣṇa."

Sri Bhari Malhotra interjected, "Why don't we all chant!"

I continued: "Actually, these names of God are not sectarian. There is no question of a Hindu God or a Muslim God or a Christian God. There is only one God, who is the supreme father of all of us. And He is not Hindu, Christian, or Muslim, but He is the supreme spirit soul.

"So now we'll chant Hare Kṛṣṇa, and later, if any of you want to lead the chanting of any other name of God, we will also be happy to join in."

I led the audience in chanting the Hare Kṛṣṇa mantra responsively, first two words at a time, then four, then eight, and finally all sixteen words. Eventually almost everyone in the audience – respectable ladies and gentlemen of various faiths – were standing and clapping and singing: Hare Kṛṣṇa, Hare Kṛṣṇa, Kṛṣṇa Kṛṣṇa, Hare Hare/ Hare Rāma, Hare Rāma, Rāma Rāma, Hare Hare.

I thought, "Now the conference is successful. The participants have chanted the holy names of Kṛṣṇa, the origin of all life."

On the Strength of Chanting Hare Kṛṣṇa

A conversation between His Divine Grace
A.C. Bhaktivedanta Swami Prabhupāda,
George Harrison, John Lennon, and Yoko Ono

If a mantra has so much power, why should it be secret? It should be distributed. People are suffering. If a mantra has potency, all people should be able to take advantage of it.

~

Śrīla Prabhupāda: You have very good musical abilities. The Vedic mantras were all transmitted through music. The *Sāma-veda* in particular is full of music.

yaṁ brahma varuṇendra-rudra-marutaḥ
stunvanti divyaiḥ stavaiḥ vedaiḥ
sāṅga-pada-kramopaniṣadair
gāyanti yaṁ samā-gāḥ

"I offer my humble obeisances to the Supreme Lord, whom great demigods like Brahmā, Varuṇa, Indra, Śiva, and the Maruts praise with transcendental prayers. Those who know the *Sāma Veda* sing about Him with different Vedic hymns."

Sāma-veda means the followers of the *Sāma Veda*. *Gāyanti* means that they are always engaged in music. Through musical vibrations they are approaching the Supreme. *Gāyanti* means singing. So Vedic mantras are meant to be sung. *Bhagavad-gītā* and *Śrīmad-Bhāgavatam* can be sung very nicely. This is the proper way of chanting Vedic mantras. Simply by hearing the vibration, people will receive benefit, even if they do not understand the meaning. [*Śrīla Prabhupāda then chants some mantras from* Śrīmad-Bhāgavatam.]

Simply by transcendental sound vibration everything can be achieved. What kind of philosophy are you following? May I ask?

John Lennon: Following?

Yoko Ono: We don't follow anything. We are just living.

George Harrison: We've done meditation. Or I do my meditation – mantra meditation.

Śrīla Prabhupāda: Hare Kṛṣṇa is also mantra.

John Lennon: Ours is not a song, though.

George Harrison: No, no. It's chanting.

John Lennon: We heard it from Maharishi. A mantra each.

Śrīla Prabhupāda: His mantras are not public.

George Harrison: Not out loud … no.

John Lennon: No – it's a secret.

Śrīla Prabhupāda: There's a story about Rāmānujācārya, a great Kṛṣṇa conscious spiritual master. His spiritual master gave him a mantra and said, "My dear boy, you chant this mantra silently. Nobody else can hear it. It is very secret." Rāmānujācārya asked his guru, "What is the effect of this mantra?" The guru said, "By chanting this mantra in meditation you'll get liberation."

So Rāmānujācārya immediately went out to a big public meeting and said, "Everyone chant this mantra. You'll all be liberated." [*Laughter.*] Then he came back to his spiritual master, who was very angry. His guru said, "I told you that you should chant silently!" Rāmānujācārya answered, "Yes, I have committed an offense. So whatever punishment you like you can give me. But because you told me that this mantra will give liberation, I have given it to the public. Let everyone be liberated, and let me go to hell – I am prepared. But if by chanting this mantra everyone can be liberated, let it be publicly distributed."

His spiritual master then embraced him, saying, "You are greater than me."

You see? If a mantra has so much power, why should it be secret? It should be distributed. People are suffering. So Caitanya Mahāprabhu said to chant this Hare Kṛṣṇa mantra loudly. Anyone who hears it, even the birds and beasts, will become liberated.

Yoko Ono: If Hare Kṛṣṇa is such a strong, powerful mantra, is there any reason to chant anything else? For instance, you talked about songs and different mantras. Is there any point in the chanting of another song or mantra?

Śrīla Prabhupāda: There are other mantras, but the Hare Kṛṣṇa mantra is especially recommended for this age. But other Vedic mantras are also chanted. As I told you, the sages would sit with musical instruments, like the *tambura,* and chant them. For instance, Nārada Muni is always chanting mantras and playing his stringed instrument, the *vīṇā.* So chanting out loud with musical instruments is not a new thing. It has been done since time immemorial. But the chanting of the Hare Kṛṣṇa mantra is especially recommended for this age. This is stated in many Vedic literatures, such as the *Brahmāṇḍa Purāṇa,* the *Kalisantaraṇa Upaniṣad,* the *Agni Purāṇa,* and so forth.

And apart from the statements of the Vedic literature, Lord Kṛṣṇa Himself, in the form of Lord Caitanya, preached that everyone should chant the Hare Kṛṣṇa mantra. And many people followed Him. When a scientist discovers something, it becomes public property; people may take advantage of it. Similarly, if a mantra has potency, all people should be able to take advantage of it. Why should it remain secret? Why should it be for only a particular person?

John Lennon: If all mantras are just the name of God, then whether it's a secret mantra or an open mantra it's all the name of God. So it doesn't really make much difference, does it, which one you sing?

Śrīla Prabhupāda: It *does* make a difference. For instance, in a drug shop they sell all types of medicines for curing different diseases. But still you have to get a doctor's prescription in order to get a particular type of medicine. Otherwise, the druggist won't supply you. You might go to the drug shop and say, "I'm diseased. Please give me any medicine you have." But the druggist will ask you, "Where is your prescription?"

Similarly, in this Age of Kali the Hare Kṛṣṇa mantra is prescribed in the scriptures. And the great teacher Caitanya Mahāprabhu, whom we consider to be an incarnation of God, also prescribed it. Therefore, our principle is that everyone should follow the prescription of the great authorities. *Mahājano yena gataḥ sa panthāḥ.* We should follow in the footsteps of the great authorities. That is our business. The *Mahābhārata* states,

tarko 'pratiṣṭhaḥ śrutayo vibhinnā
nāsāv ṛṣir yasya mataṁ na bhinnam
dharmasya tattvaṁ nihitaṁ guhāyāṁ
mahājano yena gataḥ sa panthāḥ

This Vedic mantra says that if you simply try to argue and approach the Absolute Truth, it is very difficult. By argument and reason it is very difficult, because our arguments and reason are limited. And our senses are imperfect. There are many confusing varieties of scriptures, and every philosopher has a different opinion, and unless a philosopher defeats other philosophers he cannot become recognized as a big philosopher. One theory replaces another, and therefore philosophical speculation will not help us arrive at the Absolute Truth. The Absolute Truth is very secret. So how can one achieve such a secret thing? You simply follow the great personalities who have already achieved success.

So our Kṛṣṇa consciousness philosophical method is to follow the great personalities, such as Lord Kṛṣṇa, Lord Caitanya, and the great spiritual masters in disciplic succession. Take shelter of bona fide authorities and follow them – that is recommended in the *Vedas*. That will take you to the ultimate goal.

In *Bhagavad-gītā* Lord Kṛṣṇa also recommends this process.

The Lord says, "I instructed this imperishable science of yoga to the sun god, Vivasvān, and Vivasvān instructed it to Manu, the father of mankind, and Manu in turn instructed it to Ikṣvāku." Kṛṣṇa is saying, My dear Arjuna, don't think that this science of Kṛṣṇa consciousness is something new. No. It is eternal, and I first spoke it to the sun god, Vivasvān, and Vivasvān spoke it to his son Manu, and Manu also transferred this knowledge to his son, King Ikṣvāku.

The Lord further explains,

evaṁ paramparā-prāptam
imaṁ rājarṣayo viduḥ
sa kāleneha mahatā
yogo naṣṭah parantapa

"This supreme science was thus received through the chain of disciplic succession, and the saintly kings understood it in that way. But in course of time, the succession was broken, and therefore the science as it is appears to be lost."

Evaṁ paramparā-prāptam: In this way, by disciplic succession, the knowledge is coming down. *Sa kāleneha mahatā yogo naṣṭah parantapa:* But in the course of time the succession was broken. Therefore Kṛṣṇa says, "I am speaking it to you again."

So a mantra should be received from the disciplic succession. The Vedic injunction is *sampradāya-vihinā ye mantrās te nisphala mataḥ*. If your mantra does not come through the disciplic succession, it will not be effective. *Mantrās te nisphala. Nisphalaḥ* means that it will not produce the desired result. So the mantra must be received through the proper channel or it will not act. A mantra cannot be manufactured. It must come from the original Supreme Absolute, coming down through the channel of disciplic succession. It has to be received in that way, and only then will it act.

According to our Kṛṣṇa consciousness philosophy, the mantra is coming down through four channels of disciplic succession: one through Lord Śiva, one through the goddess Lakṣmī, one through

Lord Brahmā, and one through the four Kumāras. The same thing comes down through different channels. These are called the four *sampradāyas*, or disciplic successions.

So one has to take his mantra from one of these four *sampradāyas;* then only is that mantra active. If we receive the mantra in that way, it will be effective. And if one does not receive his mantra through one of these *sampradāya* channels, then it will not act; it will not give fruit.

Yoko Ono: If the mantra itself has such power, does it matter where you receive it, where you take it?

Śrīla Prabhupāda: Yes, it does matter. For instance, milk is nutritious. That's a fact; everyone knows. But if milk is touched by the lips of a serpent, it is no longer nutritious. It becomes poisonous.

Yoko Ono: Well, milk is material.

Śrīla Prabhupāda: Yes, it is material. But since you are trying to understand spiritual topics through your material senses, we have to give material examples.

Yoko Ono: Well, no, I don't think you have to give me the material sense. I mean, the mantra is not material. It should be something spiritual; therefore, I don't think anybody should be able to spoil it. I wonder if anybody can actually spoil something that isn't material.

Śrīla Prabhupāda: But if you don't receive the mantra through the proper channel, it may not really be spiritual.

John Lennon: How would you know, anyway? How are you able to tell? I mean, for any of your disciples or us or anybody else who goes to any spiritual master – how are we to tell if he's for real or not?

Śrīla Prabhupāda: You shouldn't go to just *any* spiritual master.

John Lennon: Yes, we should go to a true master. But how are we to tell one from the other?

Śrīla Prabhupāda: It is not that you can go to just any spiritual master. He must be a member of a recognized *sampradāya*, a particular line of disciplic succession.

John Lennon: But what if one of these masters who's not in the line says exactly the same thing as one who is? What if he says his mantra is coming from the *Vedas* and he seems to speak with as much authority as you? He could probably be right. It's confusing – like having too many fruits on a plate.

Śrīla Prabhupāda: If the mantra is actually coming through a bona fide disciplic succession, then it will have potency.

John Lennon: But the Hare Kṛṣṇa mantra is the best one?

Śrīla Prabhupāda: Yes.

Yoko Ono: Well, if Hare Kṛṣṇa is the best one, why should we bother to say anything else other than Hare Kṛṣṇa?

Śrīla Prabhupāda: It's true, you don't have to bother with anything else. We say that the Hare Kṛṣṇa mantra is sufficient for one's perfection, for liberation.

George Harrison: Isn't it like flowers? Somebody may prefer roses and somebody else may like carnations better. Isn't it really a matter for the individual devotee to decide? One person may find that Hare Kṛṣṇa is more beneficial to his spiritual progress, and yet another person may find that some other mantra may be more beneficial for himself. Isn't it just a matter of taste, like choosing a flower? They're all flowers, but some people may like one better than another.

Śrīla Prabhupāda: But still there is a distinction. A fragrant rose is considered better than a flower without any scent.

Yoko Ono: In that case, I can't –

Śrīla Prabhupāda: Let's try to understand this flower example.

Yoko Ono: Okay.

Śrīla Prabhupāda: You may be attracted by one flower and I may be attracted by another flower. But among the flowers a distinction can be made. There are many flowers that have no fragrance and many that have fragrance.

Yoko Ono: Is that flower that has fragrance better?

Śrīla Prabhupāda: Yes. Therefore your attraction for a particular flower is not the solution to the question of which is actually better. In the same way, personal attraction is not the solution to choosing the best spiritual process. In *Bhagavad-gītā* Lord Kṛṣṇa says, "As one surrenders unto Me, I reward him accordingly." Kṛṣṇa is the Supreme Absolute. If someone wants to enjoy a particular relationship with Him, Kṛṣṇa presents Himself in that way. It's just like the flower example. You may want a yellow flower, and that flower may not have any fragrance. That flower is there; it's for you, that's all. But if someone wants a rose, Kṛṣṇa gives him a rose. You both get the flower of your choice, but when you make a comparative study of which is better, the rose will be considered better.

So Kṛṣṇa reveals Himself in different ways to different types of seekers. Realization of Kṛṣṇa, the Absolute Truth, is of three varieties: Brahman, Paramātmā, and Bhagavān. Brahman, Paramātmā, and Bhagavān are simply three different features of the Absolute Truth. The *jñānīs,* or empiric philosophers, reach the impersonal Brahman. The *yogīs* focus on the Supersoul, Paramātmā. And the devotees aim at Bhagavān, or Kṛṣṇa, the Supreme Personality of Godhead. But Kṛṣṇa and the Supersoul and the impersonal Brahman are not different. They are all like the light, which is opposed to darkness. But even in light there are varieties.

In the *Vedas,* the three features of the Absolute Truth are explained by the example of sunlight, sun globe, and sun god. In the sunshine there is light, and in the sun globe there is also light. Within the sun globe dwells the predominating deity of the sun planet, and he must also be full of light. Otherwise, where does all the sun's light come from? Brahman God's impersonal aspect is compared to the sun's rays, the Supersoul is like the sun globe, and Kṛṣṇa is like the personality of the sun god. But taken together they are all the sun.

Nevertheless, distinctions remain. For instance, just because the sunshine comes through the window into your room you cannot say that the sun itself has come. That would be a mistake. The sun is many millions of miles away. In a sense, the sun is present in your room, but it is a question of degree. So the degrees of spiritual realization in Brahman, Paramātmā, and Bhagavān realization are different.

Yoko Ono: But you said that if the milk is touched by the lips of a serpent it will become poisonous. A lot of churches probably had good teachings in the beginning, but over time their messages have deteriorated. Now how can a person decide if the message of Brahman that you're talking about will always remain in its pure state? How can you be sure it won't be poisoned by serpents?
Śrīla Prabhupāda: That's an individual matter. You have to become a serious student.
Yoko Ono: Well, what do you mean by "serious student"? I mean, we're born serious or born – you know – unserious.
Śrīla Prabhupāda: Being a serious student means that you try to understand the distinction between Brahman, Paramātmā, and Bhagavān.
Yoko Ono: But does it depend on knowledge? I mean, the final judgment you make?
Śrīla Prabhupāda: Everything depends on knowledge. Without knowledge how can we make progress? To be a serious student means to acquire knowledge.
Yoko Ono: But it's not always the knowledgeable ones who –
Śrīla Prabhupāda: Yes; no one can know the Absolute Truth completely. That is because our knowledge is very imperfect. But still, as far as our knowledge allows, we should try to understand the Absolute Truth. The *Vedas* say, *avan mānasa gocara.* The Absolute is so great and unlimited that it is not possible for us to know Him completely; our senses do not allow it. But we should try as far as possible. And it is possible, because, after all, we are part and parcel of the Absolute. Therefore, all of the qualities of the Absolute are there in us, but in minute quantity. But that minute quantity of the Absolute within us is very great when compared to material knowledge.

Material knowledge is practically no knowledge whatsoever. It is covered knowledge. But when one is liberated, and attains liberated knowledge, his knowledge is very much greater than the greatest material knowledge. So, as far as possible, we should try to understand Brahman, Paramātmā, and Bhagavān. The

Śrīmad-Bhāgavatam states. "Learned transcendentalists who know the Absolute Truth call this nondual substance Brahman, Paramātmā, or Bhagavān." Now again, what is the distinction among these three degrees of knowledge? Actually, knowledge of Brahman, knowledge of Paramātmā, and knowledge of Bhagavān are knowledge of the same thing.

There is another example in this connection. Imagine you are looking at a hill from a distant place. First of all you see a hazy form on the horizon like a cloud. Then if you proceed closer you'll see it as something green. And if you actually walk on the hill, you'll see so many varieties of life – animals, men, trees, and so forth. But from the distance you just see it vaguely like a cloud.

So although the Absolute Truth is always the same, it appears different from different angles of vision. From the Brahman point of view, it appears like a hill seen as a cloud. When viewed as Paramātmā, the Absolute can be compared to the vision of the hill as something green. And when the Absolute is realized as the Supreme Person, Bhagavān, it is just like seeing the hill from up close. You see everything in complete detail.

Therefore, although the person who sees Brahman, the person who sees Paramātmā, and the person who sees Kṛṣṇa are all focusing on the same thing, their realization is different according to their respective positions.

These things are very nicely explained in the *Bhagavad-gītā,* wherein Lord Kṛṣṇa says, "I am the source of all spiritual and material worlds. Everything emanates from Me. The wise who know this perfectly engage in My devotional service and worship Me with all their hearts." Kṛṣṇa says, I am the source of everything – Brahman, Paramātmā, everything. Elsewhere in *Bhagavad-gītā* it is clearly stated that Kṛṣṇa is the source of Brahman: *brahmaṇo hi pratiṣṭhāham.*

So knowledge of Brahman and Paramātmā are included within knowledge of Kṛṣṇa. If one has knowledge of Kṛṣṇa, he automatically has knowledge of Paramātmā and Brahman. Such a person automatically achieves the result of the yogic principle of meditation, namely, realization of the Supersoul, Paramātmā. And he also achieves the result of empirical philosophical speculation, namely, realization of Brahman. Beyond that, he is situated personally in the service of the Supreme Lord, Kṛṣṇa.

So if you make a comparative study, you'll find that knowledge of Kṛṣṇa includes all other knowledge. The *Vedas* confirm this, *yasmin vijñāte sarvam evaṁ vijñātam bhavati:* "If you understand the Supreme, then all knowledge becomes automatically revealed." And in *Bhagavad-gītā* it is stated, "Knowing this we have nothing more to know." So, first of all we have to seriously study the Vedic knowledge. Therefore, I am asking you to become serious students. By understanding Kṛṣṇa, you will understand everything.

The Meaning of the Hare Kṛṣṇa Mantra

His Divine Grace A. C. Bhaktivedanta Swami Prabhupāda

Kṛṣṇa consciousness is not an artificial imposition on the mind. This consciousness is the original energy of the living entity. When we hear the transcendental vibration, this consciousness is revived.

~

This transcendental vibration of Hare Kṛṣṇa, Hare Kṛṣṇa, Kṛṣṇa Kṛṣṇa, Hare Hare/ Hare Rāma, Hare Rāma, Rāma Rāma, Hare Hare is the sublime method for reviving our Kṛṣṇa consciousness. As living spiritual souls we are all originally Kṛṣṇa conscious entities, but due to our association with matter since time immemorial, our consciousness is now polluted by the material atmosphere. In this polluted concept of life, we are all trying to exploit the resources of material nature, but actually we are becoming more and more entangled in our complexities. This illusion is called *māyā,* or hard struggle for existence over the stringent laws of material nature. This illusory struggle against the material nature can at once be stopped by revival of our Kṛṣṇa consciousness.

Kṛṣṇa consciousness is not an artificial imposition on the mind. This consciousness is the original energy of the living entity.

When we hear the transcendental vibration, this consciousness is revived. And the process is recommended by authorities for this age. By practical experience also, we can perceive that by chanting this *mahā-mantra,* or the Great Chanting for Deliverance, one can at once feel transcendental ecstasy from the spiritual stratum. When one is factually on the plane of spiritual understanding, surpassing the stages of sense, mind, and intelligence, one is situated on the transcendental plane. This chanting of Hare Kṛṣṇa, Hare Kṛṣṇa, Kṛṣṇa Kṛṣṇa, Hare Hare/Hare Rāma, Hare Rāma, Rāma Rāma, Hare Hare is directly enacted from the spiritual platform, surpassing all lower states of consciousness – namely, sensual, mental, and intellectual. There is no need of understanding the language of the mantra, nor is there any need of mental speculation nor any intellectual adjustment for chanting this *mahā-mantra*. It springs automatically from the spiritual platform, and as such, anyone can take part in this transcendental sound vibration, without any previous qualification, and dance in ecstasy.

We have seen it practically. Even a child can take part in the chanting, or even a dog can take part in it. The chanting should be heard, however, from the lips of a pure devotee of the Lord, so that immediate effect can be achieved. As far as possible, chanting from the lips of a nondevotee should be avoided, as much as milk touched by the lips of a serpent causes poisonous effect.

The word *harā* is a form of addressing the energy of the Lord. Both *kṛṣṇa* and *rāma* are forms of addressing directly the Lord, and they mean "the highest pleasure, eternal." *Harā* is the supreme pleasure potency of the Lord. This potency, when addressed as *hare,* helps us in reaching the Supreme Lord.

The material energy, called as *māyā,* is also one of the multipotencies of the Lord, as much as we are also the marginal potency of the Lord. The living entities are described as superior energy to matter. When the superior energy is in contact with the inferior energy, it becomes an incompatible situation. But when the supreme marginal potency is in contact with the spiritual potency, *Harā,* it becomes the happy, normal condition of the living entity.

The three words, namely *harā, kṛṣṇa,* and *rāma,* are transcendental seeds of the *mahā-mantra,* and the chanting is a spiritual call for the Lord and His internal energy, Harā, for giving protection to the conditioned soul. The chanting is exactly like a genuine cry by the child for the mother. Mother Harā helps in achieving the grace of the supreme father, Hari, or Kṛṣṇa, and the Lord reveals Himself to such a sincere devotee.

No other means, therefore, of spiritual realization is as effective in this age as chanting the *mahā-mantra,* Hare Kṛṣṇa, Hare Kṛṣṇa, Kṛṣṇa Kṛṣṇa, Hare Hare/ Hare Rāma, Hare Rāma, Rāma Rāma, Hare Hare.

Appendixes

The Authors

His Divine Grace A. C. Bhaktivedanta Swami Prabhupāda appeared in this world in 1896 in Calcutta, India. He first met his spiritual master, Śrīla Bhaktisiddhānta Sarasvatī Gosvāmī, in Calcutta in 1922. Bhaktisiddhānta Sarasvatī, a prominent religious scholar and the founder of sixty-four Gauḍīya Maṭhas (Vedic institutes), liked this educated young man and convinced him to dedicate his life to teaching Vedic knowledge. Śrīla Prabhupāda became his student and, in 1933, his formally initiated disciple.

At their first meeting, in 1922, Śrīla Bhaktisiddhānta Sarasvatī requested Śrīla Prabhupāda to broadcast Vedic knowledge in English. In the years that followed, Śrīla Prabhupāda wrote a commentary on the *Bhagavad-gītā,* assisted the Gauḍīya Maṭha in its work and, in 1944, started *Back to Godhead,* an English fortnightly magazine. Singlehandedly, Śrīla Prabhupāda edited it, typed the manuscripts, checked the galley proofs, and even distributed the individual copies. The magazine is now being continued by his disciples.

In 1950 Śrīla Prabhupāda retired from married life, adopting the *vānaprastha* (retired) order to devote more time to his studies and writing. He traveled to the holy city of Vṛndāvana, where he lived in humble circumstances in the historic temple of Rādhā-Dāmodara. There he engaged for several years in deep study and writing. He accepted the renounced order of life (*sannyāsa*) in 1959. At Rādhā-Dāmodara, Śrīla Prabhupāda began work on his life's masterpiece: a multivolume commentated translation of the eighteen-thousand-verse *Śrīmad-Bhāgavatam* (*Bhāgavata Purāṇa*). He also wrote *Easy Journey to Other Planets.*

After publishing three volumes of the *Bhāgavatam,* Śrīla Prabhupāda came to the United States, in September 1965, to fulfill the mission of his spiritual master. Subsequently, His Divine Grace wrote more than fifty volumes of authoritative commentated translations and summary studies of the philosophical and religious classics of India.

When he first arrived by freighter in New York City, Śrīla Prabhupāda was practically penniless. Only after almost a year of great difficulty did he establish the International Society for Krishna Consciousness, in July of 1966. Before he passed away on November 14, 1977, he had guided the Society and seen it grow to a worldwide confederation of more than one hundred *āśramas,* schools, temples, institutes, and farm communities.

In 1972 His Divine Grace introduced the Vedic system of primary and secondary education in the West by founding the *gurukula* school in Dallas, Texas. Since then his disciples have established similar schools throughout the United States and the rest of the world.

Śrīla Prabhupāda also inspired the construction of several large international cultural centers in India. At Śrīdhāma Māyāpur, in West Bengal, devotees are building a spiritual city centered on a magnificent temple – an ambitious project for which construction will extend over many years to come. In Vṛndāvana are the Krishna-Balaram Temple and International Guesthouse, *gurukula* school, and Śrīla Prabhupāda Memorial and Museum. There are also major temples and cultural centers in Mumbai, New Delhi, Ahmedabad, Siliguri, and Ujjain. Other centers are planned in many important locations on the Indian subcontinent.

Śrīla Prabhupāda's most significant contribution, however, is his books. Highly respected by scholars for their authority, depth, and clarity, they are used as textbooks in numerous college courses. His writings have been translated into over fifty languages. The Bhaktivedanta Book Trust, established in 1972 to publish the works of His Divine Grace, has thus become the world's largest publisher of books in the field of Indian religion and philosophy.

In just twelve years, despite his advanced age, Śrīla Prabhupāda circled the globe fourteen times on lecture tours that took him to six continents. In spite of such a vigorous schedule, Śrīla Prabhupāda continued to write prolifically. His writings constitute a veritable library of Vedic philosophy, religion, literature, and culture.

Bhaktisvarūpa Dāmodara Swami (Dr. Thoudam Singh, PhD, 1937–2006) was an extraordinary combination of scientist, spiritualist, active promoter of world peace, interfaith leader, educator, poet, singer, and cultural ambassador. He is known for his work to create an interface between science and religion for a deeper understanding of life and the universe. He received his PhD in Physical Organic Chemistry from the University of California, Irvine, in 1974, and went on to contribute a number of papers in the field of fast proton transfer kinetics in model biological systems using stopped-flow technique and NMR spectroscopy. He also worked on gas phase reaction mechanisms using Ion Cyclotron Resonance (ICR) spectroscopy. Between 1970 and 1971 he studied Vaiṣṇava Vedānta under Śrīla Prabhupāda, accepting initiation from him in 1971, and in 1974 was appointed Director of the Bhaktivedanta Institute, which promotes the study of science and Vedānta. He organized three International conferences on science and religion: the First and Second World Congress for the Synthesis of Science and Religion (1986 and 1997) and the First International Conference on the Study of Consciousness within Science (1990). All three were attended by a galaxy of prominent scientists and religious leaders, including several Nobel Laureates. He organized the Second International Congress on Life and its Origin: Exploration from Science and Various Spiritual and Religious Traditions in Rome in 2004.

Bhaktisvarūpa Dāmodara Swami authored or edited several books, including *What is Matter and What is Life?* (1977), *Theobiology* (1979), *Synthesis of Science and Religion: Critical Essays and Dialogues* (1987), *Thoughts on Synthesis of Science and Religion* (2001), and *Seven Nobel Laureates on Science and Spirituality* (2004). He was editor-in-chief of the Bhaktivedanta Institute's journal *Savijnanam: Scientific Exploration for a Spiritual Paradigm* and a founding member of the United Religions Initiative (URI). He was also president of its Manipur Cooperation Circle and instrumental in starting its Kuala Lumpur Cooperation Circle.

He started a network of schools in Northeastern India where students receive education centered on spiritual values. He was founder and director of the Ranganiketan Manipuri Cultural Arts Troupe, which performs worldwide.

Girirāja Swami (Glenn Teton) was attending Brandeis University in Boston when he met Srīla Prabhupāda in March of 1969. After graduating from Brandeis *cum laude,* he accepted formal initiation from Śrīla Prabhupāda. He was then given the opportunity to travel to India with Śrīla Prabhupāda and to oversee the development of Hare Krishna Land in Juhu, Mumbai, a thriving temple community and center of Vaiṣṇava culture and education.

Girirāja Swami has been instrumental in the development of the Bhaktivedanta Ashram at Govardhana and more recently of Kirtan Ashram (a home for renounced women), the Bhaktivedanta Hospice, and the Vrindavan Institute of Palliative Care, all in Vṛndāvana, India.

Since 1982 Girirāja Swami has toured extensively throughout India and a number of other countries, often teaching at the Vaishnava Institute for Higher Education in Vṛndāvana. More recently he has been giving presentations on various aspects of *bhakti-yoga* at the retreats and workshops run by Bhagavat Life.

Now based in Southern California, he is the author of *Watering the Seed* (Mountain King Books, 2000), is a frequent contributor to *Back to Godhead* magazine, and is working on several other publications, including books about his search for a spiritual master and his early days in the Boston temple, his travels with Śrīla Prabhupāda in India from 1970 to 1972, and the story of Śrīla Prabhupāda's monumental efforts in Mumbai.

Graham M. Schweig, PhD is a scholar of Comparative Religion who focuses on the religions of India. He is a specialist in love mysticism, concentrating on religions of the heart. Schweig did his graduate studies at Harvard University and the University of Chicago, and received his doctorate in Comparative Religion from Harvard. Schweig has taught at Duke University and the University of North Carolina, and was Visiting Associate Professor of Sanskrit at the University of Virginia. He is currently Associate Professor of Philosophy and Religious Studies and Director of the Indic Studies Program at Christopher Newport University, on the Virginia Peninsula.

Schweig is a long-time practitioner of meditational and devotional yoga under the guidance of traditional teachers since 1967. In the early 1970s he was initiated by Srila Prabhupāda, from whom he received the Sanskrit name Garuḍa Dāsa. He is an internationally known teacher of *bhakti* and yoga and offers workshops at major yoga centers and conferences as well as public lectures at the Smithsonian Institute in Washington, DC.

Schweig's ultimate interest is to find religious truths within Indic traditions that contribute powerful symbols which can speak beyond their religious boundaries, moving religion toward world peace. He has contributed numerous pieces to encyclopedia volumes, journals, and books. In 2005 his book *Dance of Divine Love: India's Classic Sacred Love Story,* was published by Princeton University Press, and in 2007 *Bhagavad Gita: The Beloved Lord's Secret Love Song* was published by HarperOne, a division of Harper Collins. He has several more books coming out with Princeton University, HarperOne, and Columbia University Presses.

Hridayānanda Dāsa Goswami (Dr. Howard J. Resnick, PhD) was initiated by Śrīla Prabhupāda in 1970 and accepted vows of renunciation in 1972. After Śrīla Prabhupāda's departure from the world in 1977, Hridayānanda Dāsa Goswami was the first Westerner in history to successfully translate and comment on the canonical *Bhāgavata Purāṇa* from within the tradition.

Hridayānanda Dāsa Goswami received his PhD in Sanskrit and Indian Studies from Harvard University in 1996. As a visiting scholar at UCLA, he has taught the history, philosophies, and religions of India at the Graduate Theological Union in Berkeley and, most recently, at the University of Florida in Gainesville. He has also published articles with such institutions as Harvard, Columbia, and the University of California. Having lectured at leading universities throughout the United States, Europe, India, and South America, Hridayānanda Dāsa Goswami is a much sought after speaker by colleges, universities, divinity schools, civic groups, and religious organizations of all kinds.

He has recently completed his first novel, in which a contemporary story frames an ancient tale. His current project is to present the great epic narrative of South Asia, the *Mahābhārata*, as a three-part historical novel.

Jayādvaita Swami – editor, publisher, and teacher – is a disciple of Śrīla Prabhupāda, initiated in 1968 at the age of nineteen. He served as an editor or assistant editor for nearly all the books of Śrīla Prabhupāda published during Śrīla Prabhupāda's lifetime. Along with these services, he has lectured extensively at colleges and universities, especially in the United States. In 1978 he accepted the renounced order, *sannyāsa*, and spent several years traveling, part of that time with a party of pilgrims on a journey by foot through various states in India, stopping in a different town or village every night.

In 1987 he co-founded the Vrindavan Institute for Higher Education. Since 1988 he has served as a director of Śrīla Prabhupāda's publishing house, the Bhaktivedanta Book Trust. From

1991 through most of 1998 he served as editor-in-chief of *Back to Godhead* magazine, for which he had been an assistant editor for several years. Recently he served as editor of a three-volume translation and commentary for *Śri Bṛhad-bhāgavatāmṛta,* a sixteenth-century Sanskrit philosophical and devotional work by Śrīla Sanātana Gosvāmī, and *Śrī Kṛṣṇa Līlā Stava,* by the same author. Apart from his services in publishing, he travels widely, teaching about the philosophy and culture of Kṛṣṇa consciousness.

Kalakaṇṭha Dāsa (Carl Woodham), a disciple of Śrīla Prabhupāda, has been practicing and teaching Krishna consciousness since 1972. He has managed and developed Kṛṣṇa conscious temples and communities in several major cities and raised three children with his wife, Jitāmitra Dāsī. Along with developing a successful business to support his family, he also served his local community as a town councilman and a court mediator. His writings include *The Song Divine, Pastimes of the Supreme Person, A God Who Dances,* numerous management manuals, and articles for *Back to Godhead* magazine.

Mathureśa Dāsa was initiated by Śrīla Prabhupāda in 1971 and has written on and off for *Back to Godhead* magazine since 1978. He lives in Gainesville, Florida.

Navīna Śyāma Dāsa (Navin Jani) grew up attending ISKCON temples, first in Cleveland, Ohio, and later in Laguna Beach, California. He is an honors graduate of Stanford University who went on to earn a Master's degree in Urban Planning from the University of Florida and a Bhakti Shastri degree from the Mayapur Institute of Higher Education. He has a passion for the Vedic arts and sciences, particularly Vastu Veda, for which he offers consulting services through his website, VastuShyam.com.

Navīna Śyāma currently lives in Alachua, Florida, where he and his wife, Krishna Priyā Dāsī, serve at the Bhaktivedanta Academy, a Hare Kṛṣṇa Montessori school for children of all backgrounds, ages 3 to 12.

Ravīndra Svarūpa Dāsa (William H. Deadwyler, III, PhD) was initiated by Śrīla Prabhupāda in 1971. He holds MA and PhD degrees in Religion from Temple University, Philadelphia, and a BA in Philosophy from the University of Pennsylvania. He is a contributing editor of *Back to Godhead* magazine. Among his articles and publications are *Charismatic Gurus and Managing Directors: Leadership Issues Arising in Retrofitting a Medieval Tradition for the Modern World, Cleaning House and Cleaning Hearts: Reform and Renewal in ISKCON, The Religions of Others in ISKCON's Eyes,* and a book, *Encounter with the Lord of the Universe: Collected Essays 1978–1983.*

Satsvarūpa Dāsa Goswami was a pioneer in the early days of ISKCON and is a senior disciple of Śrīla Prabhupāda. He managed ISKCON Press, which grew into the Bhaktivedanta Book Trust. He was also editor-in-chief of *Back to Godhead* magazine until 1991.

Satsvarūpa Dāsa Goswami is the author of Śrīla Prabhupāda's authorized biography, the *Śrīla Prabhupāda-līlāmṛta,* and has established himself as a prolific Vaiṣṇava writer and poet, having published numerous articles and over one hundred books, including memoirs, poetry, essays, novels, and studies based on Vaiṣṇava scripture. His writings have been translated into over forty languages. In recent years he has also created hundreds of paintings, drawings, and sculptures that attempt to capture and express his perspective on the culture of Kṛṣṇa consciousness in the West. His work was favorably reviewed by the *Washington Times.*

Satsvarūpa Dāsa Goswami now lives in Delaware, where he continues to write and, when his health permits, to lecture on Kṛṣṇa conscious philosophy.

Satyarāja Dāsa (Steven J. Rosen) is editor-in-chief of the *Journal of Vaishnava Studies,* a biannual publication exploring Eastern thought. He is also associate editor of *Back to Godhead* magazine and the author of over twenty books on Indian philosophy and Vaiṣṇava culture. His recent titles include *Essential Hinduism* (Praeger, 2006), *Krishna's Song: A New Look at the Bhagavad Gita*

(Greenwood, 2007), and *The Yoga of Kirtan: Conversations on the Sacred Art of Chanting* (FOLK Books, 2008). He is an initiated disciple of Śrīla Prabhupada.

Viśākhā Devī Dāsī (Jean Papert Griesser) received an Associate of Applied Science degree with honors from Rochester Institute of Technology and shortly afterwards published her first book, *Photomacrography: Art and Techniques*. In 1970 she traveled to India, where she met Śrīla Prabhupāda, accepting initiation from him in Vṛndāvana in 1971. As a photographer, she traveled with and photographed Śrīla Prabhupāda and his students in India, Europe, and the United States. As a writer, she wrote numerous articles for *Back to Godhead* magazine and two books, *Our Most Dear Friend*, a *Bhagavad-gītā* for children, and *Bhagavad-gita: A Photographic Essay*, a fully illustrated summary study of *Bhagavad-gītā*. Viśākhā also assists her husband, Yadubara Dāsa, in making documentary films on Śrīla Prabhupāda and on the philosophy and culture of Kṛṣṇa consciousness. They live with their children at Śaraṇāgati Village, a rural community in British Columbia, Canada, where Viśākhā is writing another book, *Happiness, Harmony, and the Bhagavad-gītā: Lessons from a Life-changing Move to the Wilderness.*

Glossary

ācārya – one who teaches by example.
Age of Kali – *See:* Kali-yuga.
ananta – lit., "without end"; eternal.
ārati – a ceremony in which one greets and worships the Supreme Personality of Godhead in the Deity form.
Arjuna – one of the five Pāṇḍava brothers; Lord Kṛṣṇa spoke the *Bhagavad-gītā* to him.
artha – wealth; economic development.
āsana – seat; a sitting posture in yoga practice.
āśrama – one of the four spiritual orders of life – *brahmacārī* (student life), *gṛhastha* (married life), *vānaprastha* (retired life), and *sannyāsa* (renounced order); the place where spiritual practices are executed.
aṣṭāṅga-yoga – a mystic yoga system propounded by Patañjali in his *Yoga-sūtras* and consisting of eight parts progressing from moral practices to deep meditation on God.
ātmā – the self (refers sometimes to the body, sometimes to the soul, and sometimes to the senses).
avatāra – lit., "one who descends."

Bhagavad-gītā – lit., "Song of God"; a seven-hundred-verse record of a conversation between Lord Kṛṣṇa and His disciple, Arjuna, from the *Bhīṣma Parva* of the *Mahābhārata* of Vedavyāsa.

Bhagavān – an epithet of the Supreme Personality of Godhead, Kṛṣṇa, meaning "He who possesses in full the opulences of wealth, beauty, strength, knowledge, fame, and renunciation."

bhāgavata – anything related to Bhagavān, the Supreme Lord, especially His devotee and the scripture *Śrīmad-Bhāgavatam*.

bhakta – a devotee of the Lord; one who performs devotional service (*bhakti*).

bhakti (bhakti-yoga) – the practice of offering devotional service to the Supreme Lord.

bhakti-rasa – the spiritual tastes derived from performing devotional service.

Bhaktivinoda Ṭhākura – (1838–1915) the great-grandfather of the present-day Kṛṣṇa consciousness movement and grand-spiritual master of His Divine Grace A. C. Bhaktivedanta Swami Prabhupāda.

Bharata (Mahārāja) – an ancient king of India and great devotee of Kṛṣṇa from whom the Pāṇḍavas descended.

Bhārata-varṣa – a name for the earth (now for India), derived from King Bharata, an ancient king.

Brahmā – the first created living being and secondary creator of the material universe.

brahmacārī – a celibate student under the care of a guru. One in the first order of spiritual life (*See: varṇāśrama-dharma*).

Brahman – (1) the infinitesimal spiritual individual soul; (2) the impersonal, all-pervasive aspect of the Supreme; (3) the Supreme Personality of Godhead; (4) the *mahat-tattva*, or total material substance.

brāhmaṇa – a member of the intellectual or priestly class; a person wise in Vedic knowledge, fixed in goodness, and knowledgeable about Brahman, the Absolute Truth; one of the four occupations in the *varṇāśrama* system.

Brahma-saṁhitā – an ancient Sanskrit scripture recording the prayers Brahmā offered to Govinda (Kṛṣṇa), recovered from a temple in South India by Śrī Caitanya Mahāprabhu.

Buddha – an incarnation of Kṛṣṇa, he lived during the 5th century

BC. He descended to bewilder atheists and to dissuade them from performing unnecessary animal sacrifices.

Caitanya Mahāprabhu – (1486–1534) Lord Kṛṣṇa in the aspect of His own devotee. He appeared in Navadvīpa, West Bengal, and inaugurated the congregational chanting of Kṛṣṇa's holy names (*saṅkīrtana*) to teach pure love of God.

daiva – divine.

dharma – religious principles; the natural occupation or essential quality of a thing; that eternal occupational duty of a living entity that is inseparable from the soul itself.

dhīra – someone capable of remaining undisturbed by the vagaries of the material world; sobriety.

Dhṛtarāṣṭra – father of the Kauravas and uncle of the Pāṇḍavas.

dhyāna-yogī – one who practices meditation.

Durgā – wife of Lord Śiva and the goddess presiding over material nature.

Duryodhana – the first-born and chief of the one hundred sons of Dhṛtarāṣṭra and chief rival of the Pāṇḍavas.

Dvāpara-yuga – the third age of the cycle of four *yugas*.

Goloka – the highest spiritual planet in the kingdom of God; Lord Kṛṣṇa's personal abode.

gopīs – the cowherd girls of Vṛndāvana; Kṛṣṇa's most surrendered and confidential devotees.

Goswami – lit., "master of the senses." Generally indicates one in the renounced order.

Govinda – epithet of the Supreme Lord Kṛṣṇa meaning "One who gives pleasure to the land, cows, and senses."

gṛhastha – a householder living according to the Vedic social system; one who practices spiritual life while maintaining his family in Kṛṣṇa consciousness; the second order of Vedic spiritual life.

guru – lit., "heavy" [with knowledge]; a spiritual master.

Hare Kṛṣṇa mantra – a sixteen-word prayer composed of the names Hare, Kṛṣṇa, and Rāma: Hare Kṛṣṇa, Hare Kṛṣṇa, Kṛṣṇa Kṛṣṇa, Hare Hare/ Hare Rāma, Hare Rāma, Rāma Rāma, Hare Hare.
Hari – an epithet of Kṛṣṇa meaning "He who removes all obstacles from the path of spiritual progress."

Īśopaniṣad – one of the 108 principal Vedic scriptures known as the *Upaniṣads*.

japa – the soft recitation of Kṛṣṇa's holy names in private meditation, with the aid of prayer beads.
jīva – the living entity, who is an eternal soul, individual but part of the Supreme Lord.
jñāna – knowledge.
jñāna-yogī – one who approaches the Supreme by cultivating knowledge; one who practices yoga through the predominantly intellectual process of trying to discriminate between matter and spirit.

kaitava-dharma – cheating religion.
kaivalya – the impersonal liberation of merging into the Brahman effulgence emanating from the Lord.
Kali-yuga – the present age, the fourth and last in the cycle of *yugas*, known as the "Age of Quarrel and Hypocrisy."
kāma – lust; the desire to gratify one's senses.
karma – lit., "action"; action pertaining to the development of the material body; any material action that will incur a subsequent reaction; the material reaction one incurs due to material activities.
karma-kāṇḍa – the division of the *Vedas* dealing with how to perform fruitive work and sacrifice for the fulfillment of desires.
karma-mīmāṁsā – one of the six main Vedic philosophies, it

states that the subtle laws of nature reward or punish one according to how one acts, without reference to an independent God.

karma-yoga – action in devotional service; the path of God realization attained by dedicating the fruits of one's work to God.

karmī – a materialist.

kīrtana – the chanting of God's names.

Kṛṣṇa – the Supreme Personality of Godhead and source of all expansions of God.

kṣatriya – third of the four orders in the *varṇāśrama* system. A warrior, administrator, or member of some other occupation that rules and protects others according to the system of four social and four spiritual orders.

kṣetra – lit., "field"; the "field of activities" for the conditioned soul, specifically the material body.

kṣetra-jñā – one who is conscious of the body.

Kuntī – the mother of the Pāṇḍavas and Lord Kṛṣṇa's aunt. She is also known as Pṛthā.

Kurukṣetra – a holy place about ninety miles north of New Delhi where the *Mahābhārata* war was fought and where Kṛṣṇa spoke the *Bhagavad-gītā.*

Lakṣmī – the goddess of fortune and eternal consort of Lord Nārāyaṇa.

Mahābhārata – An important and famous historical scripture which narrates the history of the Kuru dynasty and the Kurukṣetra war. The *Bhagavad-gītā* is contained in the *Mahābhārata.*

mahā-mantra – the "great chant" for deliverance: Hare Kṛṣṇa, Hare Kṛṣṇa, Kṛṣṇa Kṛṣṇa, Hare Hare/ Hare Rāma, Hare Rāma, Rāma Rāma, Hare Hare.

Mahārāja – a title for a king, ruler, or renunciant (*sannyāsī*).

mantra – lit., *man* – mind, *tra* – to deliver; a pure sound vibration that is used in meditation to deliver the mind from material inclination and illusion. A transcendental sound or Vedic hymn, prayer, or chant.

Martyaloka – lit., "the world of death"; Earth.

māyā – lit., "that which is not"; illusion, unreality, deception, forgetfulness.

Māyāvāda – the impersonal philosophy first propounded by Śaṅkarācārya, which proposes the unqualified oneness of God and the living entities (who are both conceived of as being ultimately formless) and the nonreality of manifest nature; the philosophy that everything is one and that the Absolute Truth is not a person. A proponent of Māyāvāda philosophy is called a Māyāvādī.

mokṣa – liberation from material bondage.

mūḍha – a fool or rascal; an asslike person.

mukti – liberation of a conditioned soul from material consciousness.

Nanda Mahārāja – Kṛṣṇa's father in Vṛndāvana.

Nārada Muni – a pure devotee of Kṛṣṇa and a son of Brahmā. Nārada travels throughout the universe in his eternal body, glorifying devotional service and teaching the science of *bhakti*.

Nārāyaṇa – the majestic, four-armed expansion of Kṛṣṇa.

Narottama dāsa Ṭhākura – a renowned Vaiṣṇava spiritual master in disciplic succession from Śrī Caitanya Mahāprabhu. He is famous for his many devotional songs.

Padma Purāṇa – one of the eighteen *Purāṇas,* or Vedic historical scriptures. It consists of a conversation between Śiva and his wife, Pārvatī.

Pāṇḍavas – the five pious *kṣatriya* brothers Yudhiṣṭhira, Bhīma, Arjuna, Nakula, and Sahadeva. They were intimate friends of Lord Kṛṣṇa's and inherited the leadership of the world on their victory over the Kurus in the Battle of Kurukṣetra.

Paramātmā – the Supersoul; the localized aspect of the Supreme Lord who resides in the heart of each embodied living entity and pervades all of material nature.

Patañjali – propounder of the *aṣṭāṅga-yoga* system and author of the *Yoga-sūtras*.

Prahlāda (Mahārāja) – a great devotee of Lord Kṛṣṇa who was persecuted by his atheistic father, Hiraṇyakaśipu, but was protected by the Lord and ultimately saved by Him.

prakṛti – lit., "that which is predominated"; material nature, the energy of the Supreme; the female principle enjoyed by the male *puruṣa*.

pramāṇa – evidence; a proof. The term refers to sources of knowledge that are held to be valid.

prāṇāyāma – the system of breath control used in *aṣṭāṅga-yoga* practice and one of the system's eight limbs.

prasāda – lit., "mercy"; food prepared for Kṛṣṇa's pleasure and offered to Him with devotion.

pratyakṣa – direct sense perception and the first of the five stages of Vedic knowledge-gathering, considered a subordinate, not self-evident, proof of knowledge.

prema – pure love of God.

Purāṇas – lit., "ancient"; the eighteen major and eighteen minor Vedic literatures compiled about five thousand years ago in India by Vyāsadeva.

rajo-guṇa – the mode of passion.

Rāmānujācārya – the great eleventh-century Vaiṣṇava spiritual master of the Śrī *sampradāya*.

rasa – the eternal relationship between the Lord and a living entity; the sweet taste of a relationship, especially between Kṛṣṇa and a soul.

samādhi – total absorption of the mind and senses in the Supreme Godhead and His service.

sampradāya – lit., "community"; a disciplic succession of spiritual masters and their followers.

sanātana-dharma – lit., "the eternal activity of the soul"; the eternal religion of the living being – to serve the Supreme Lord.

Śaṅkarācārya – the incarnation of Śiva who appeared in South India at the end of the 7th century AD to re-establish Vedic authority at a time when India was under the sway of Buddhism, whose tenets denied the authority of the *Vedas*. He established Māyāvāda (impersonalistic) philosophy.

sannyāsī – one in the renounced order and the fourth stage of Vedic spiritual life according to the *varṇāśrama* system.

śāstra – any revealed scripture; Vedic literature.

sat-cid-ānanda (vigraha) – God's form of eternity, knowledge, and bliss.

sattva-guṇa – the material mode of goodness.

Satya-yuga – the first of the four cyclic *yugas* in the progression of universal time.

Śiva – the superintendent of the mode of ignorance (*tamo-guṇa*) and the being responsible for destroying the universe at the time of annihilation.

Śrīmad-Bhāgavatam – the foremost of the eighteen *Purāṇas*. It was written by Vyāsadeva as his commentary on the *Vedānta-sūtra*. Also known as the *Bhāgavata Purāṇa*.

śruti – lit., "that which is heard"; the core Vedic literature, including the four *Vedas* (*Ṛg*, *Sāma*, *Yajur*, and *Atharva*) and the *Upaniṣads*.

śūdra – a laborer; a member of the fourth social order in the *varṇāśrama* system.

Swami – lit., "master"; a title given to a renunciant or guru.

tamo-guṇa – the material mode of ignorance.

tapasya – austerity; voluntary acceptance of material trouble to help one make progress in spiritual life.

tattva – truth.

Tretā-yuga – the second in the cycle of four ages.

Upaniṣads – 108 Sanskrit treatises that embody the philosophy of the *Vedas*. The term *upaniṣad* literally means "that which is learned by sitting close to the teacher."

Vaikuṇṭha – lit., "the place of no anxiety"; the eternal planets of the spiritual world and abode of Lord Nārāyaṇa.

Vaiṣṇava – a devotee of the Supreme Lord Viṣṇu, or Kṛṣṇa.

vaiśya – member of the mercantile or agricultural class, according to the *varṇāśrama* system of four social orders and four spiritual orders.

vānaprastha – retired life; the third order of life according to the *varṇāśrama* social system.

varṇa – one of the four Vedic occupational divisions, distinguished by the quality of work and a person's situation according to the modes of nature (*guṇas*).

varṇāśrama-dharma – the Vedic social system of four social and four spiritual orders. The four occupations are *brāhmaṇa* (intellectuals and priests), *kṣatriya* (warriors and administrators), *vaiśya* (mercantile and agriculturalists), and *śūdra* (laborers). The four spiritual orders are *brahmacārī* (celibate students), *gṛhastha* (householders) *vānaprastha* (retired), and *sannyāsa* (renunciants).

Vedānta-sūtra (Vedānta) – Vyāsadeva's conclusive summary of Vedic philosophical knowledge, written in brief codes.

vīṇā – a stringed musical instrument similar to a sitar.

Vyāsadeva – the literary incarnation of God and the greatest philosopher of ancient times. Compiler of the original Vedic literature, including the eighteen *Purāṇas, Vedānta-sūtra,* the *Mahābhārata,* and the *Upaniṣads.*

yajña – a Vedic sacrifice.

yoga – lit., "yoke"; a spiritual discipline meant for linking one's consciousness with the Supreme Lord, Kṛṣṇa.

Guide to Sanskrit Pronunciation

The system of transliteration used in this book conforms to a system that scholars have accepted to indicate the pronunciation of each sound in the Sanskrit language.

The short vowel **a** is pronounced like the **u** in b**u**t, long **ā** like the **a** in f**a**r. Short **i** is pronounced as **i** in p**i**n, long **ī** as in p**i**que, short **u** as in p**u**ll, and long **ū** as in r**u**le. The vowel **ṛ** is pronounced like **ri** in **ri**m, **e** like the **ey** in th**ey**, **o** like the **o** in g**o**, **ai** like the **ai** in **ai**sle, and **au** like the **ow** in h**ow**. The *anusvara* (**ṁ**) is pronounced like the **n** in the French word *bo***n**, and *visarga* (**ḥ**) is pronounced as a final **h** sound. At the end of a couplet, **aḥ** is pronounced **aha**, and **iḥ** is pronounced **ihi**.

The guttural consonants – **k, kh, g, gh,** and **ṅ** – are pronounced from the throat in much the same manner as in English. **K** is pronounced as in **k**ite, **kh** as in Ec**kh**art, **g** as in **g**ive, **gh** as in di**g-h**ard and **ṅ** as in si**ng**.

The palatal consonants – **c, ch, j, jh,** and **ñ** – are pronounced with the tongue touching the firm ridge behind the teeth. **C** is pronounced as in **ch**air, **ch** as in staun**ch-h**eart, **j** as in **j**oy, **jh** as in he**dgeh**og, and **ñ** as in ca**n**yon.

The cerebral consonants – **ṭ, ṭh, ḍ, ḍh,** and **ṇ** – are pronounced with the tip of the tongue turned up and drawn back against the dome of the palate. **Ṭ** is pronounced as in **t**ub, **ṭh** as in ligh**t-h**eart, **ḍ** as in **d**ove, **ḍh** as in re**d-h**ot, and **ṇ** as in **n**ut.

The dental consonants – **t, th, d, dh,** and **n** – are pronounced in the same manner as the cerebrals, but with the forepart of the tongue against the teeth.

The labial consonants – **p, ph, b, bh,** and **m** – are pronounced with the lips. **P** is pronounced as in **p**ine, **ph** as in u**ph**ill, **b** as in **b**ird, **bh** as in ru**b-h**ard, and **m** as in **m**other.

The semivowels – **y, r, l,** and **v** – are pronounced as in **y**es, **r**un, **l**ight, and **v**ine respectively. The sibilants – **ś, ṣ,** and **s** – are pronounced, respectively, as in the German word *sprechen* and the English words **sh**ine and **s**un. The letter **h** is pronounced as in **h**ome.

London Temple

Situated in London's West End, amidst the commotion of the modern city, the Radha-Krishna Temple is an oasis of spiritual culture. From Monday to Saturday at 1 PM and 6 PM, we hold open classes on the philosophy of Krishna consciousness. On Sundays, our famous Hare Krishna love feast entertains and inspires many guests with spiritual music, philosophy, and sumptuous vegetarian food.

To experience a revitalising taste of Krishna consciousness, you are more than welcome to come and pay us a visit. Our temple is located at 10 Soho Street, two minutes' walk from Tottenham Court Road tube station. The attached Govinda's restaurant is open Monday through Saturday from 12 PM to 9 PM.

For further information regarding our programmes visit www.iskcon-london.org. Or phone us on 020 7437 3662. Our e-mail is london@pamho.net

Bhaktivedanta Manor

Set in 70 acres of countryside, Bhaktivedanta Manor, a farm and spiritual community of around fifty residents, is open to all visitors. There is a full curriculum of classes and workshops, with courses in subjects from Vedic medicine (Ayurveda) and mantra meditation to vegetarian cooking; we'll even give you hands-on training in ploughing with a team of oxen! And if you're looking to deepen your spiritual experience, you can also come on a retreat, joining in the life of the community for a weekend or more. Special introductory talks on the philosophy of *Bhagavad-gītā* are included.

The Manor is only 13 miles from London, just a short distance from junction 5 of the M1, and close to tube and rail stations.

Please write or phone for further information: Bhaktivedanta Manor, Hillfield Lane, Aldenham, Watford, Herts, WD25 8EZ; Tel: 01923 851000; E-mail: bhaktivedanta.manor@pamho.net; Web: www.krishnatemple.com

Swansea Temple (Wales)

Come and experience Krishna consciousness at our Swansea temple. You will find a haven of spiritual culture and sumptuous vegetarian cuisine just two minutes' walk from the city centre. Our acclaimed Govinda's restaurant and gift shop is open Monday to Thursday from 12 PM–3 PM; Friday and Saturday from 12 PM–6 PM. Every Sunday we hold the famous Hare Krishna love feast from 2 PM to 5 PM.

We also have an introductory programme consisting of chanting, philosophy, and a vegetarian meal every Tuesday evening between 7 PM and 8.30 PM. Entrance £3.

For more information contact: The Hare Krishna Temple, 8 Craddock St, Swansea SA1 3EN; Tel: 01792 468469; E-mail: info.iskconwales.org.uk; Web: www.iskconwales.org.uk

Karuna Bhavan (ISKCON Scotland)

Situated 25 miles south of Glasgow off the M74 motorway, the small community sits neatly on the hill overlooking the old Scottish village of Lesmahagow, and the atmosphere is tranquil, set in peaceful countryside. If you would like to visit the temple please telephone us first so that we can make proper arrangements to receive you nicely.

For further information regarding visits, programmes, festivals, etc., please telephone 01555 894790 and ask for Prabhupada Prana. Fax 01555 894526. E-mail: karunabhavan@aol.com